WHERE THE WILD THINGS WERE

# POSTMILLENNIAL POP
General Editors: Karen Tongson and Henry Jenkins

*Puro Arte: Filipinos on the Stages of Empire*
Lucy Mae San Pablo Burns

*Media Franchising: Creative License and Collaboration in the Culture Industries*
Derek Johnson

*Your Ad Here: The Cool Sell of Guerrilla Marketing*
Michael Serazio

*Looking for Leroy: Illegible Black Masculinities*
Mark Anthony Neal

*From Bombay to Bollywood: The Making of a Global Media Industry*
Aswin Punathambekar

*A Race So Different: Performance and Law in Asian America*
Joshua Takano Chambers-Letson

*Surveillance Cinema*
Catherine Zimmer

*Modernity's Ear: Listening to Race and Gender in World Music*
Roshanak Kheshti

*The New Mutants: Superheroes and the Radical Imagination of American Comics*
Ramzi Fawaz

*Restricted Access: Media, Disability, and the Politics of Participation*
Elizabeth Ellcessor

*The Sonic Color Line: Race and the Cultural Politics of Listening*
Jennifer Lynn Stoever

*Diversión: Play and Popular Culture in Cuban America*
Albert Sergio Laguna

*Open TV: Innovation beyond Hollywood and the Rise of Web Television*
Aymar Jean Christian

*Antisocial Media: Anxious Labor in the Digital Economy*
Greg Goldberg

*More Than Meets the Eye: Special Effects and the Fantastic Transmedia Franchise*
Bob Rehak

*Spreadable Media: Creating Value and Meaning in a Networked Culture*
Henry Jenkins, Sam Ford, and Joshua Green

*Playing to the Crowd: Musicians, Audiences, and the Intimate Work of Connection*
Nancy K. Baym

*Old Futures: Speculative Fiction and Queer Possibility*
Alexis Lothian

*Anti-Fandom: Dislike and Hate in the Digital Age*
Edited by Melissa A. Click

*Social Media Entertainment: The New Industry at the Intersection of Hollywood and Silicon Valley*
Stuart Cunningham and David Craig

*Video Games Have Always Been Queer*
Bo Ruberg

*The Power of Sports: Media and Spectacle in American Culture*
Michael Serazio

*The Race Card: From Gaming Technologies to Model Minorities*
Tara Fickle

*Open World Empire: Race, Erotics, and the Global Rise of Video Games*
Christopher B. Patterson

*The Content of Our Caricature: African American Comic Art and Political Belonging*
Rebecca Wanzo

*Stories of the Self: Life Writing after the Book*
Anna Poletti

*The Dark Fantastic: Race and the Imagination from Harry Potter to the Hunger Games*
Ebony Elizabeth Thomas

*Hip Hop Heresies: Queer Aesthetics in New York City*
Shanté Paradigm Smalls

*Digital Masquerade: Feminist Rights and Queer Media in China*
Jia Tan

*The Revolution Will Be Hilarious: Comedy for Social Change and Civic Power*
Caty Borum

*The Privilege of Play: A History of Hobby Games, Race, and Geek Culture*
Aaron Trammell

*Unbelonging: Inauthentic Sounds in Mexican and Latinx Aesthetics*
Iván A. Ramos

*Sonic Sovereignty: Hip Hop, Indigeneity, and Shifting Popular Music Mainstreams*
Liz Przybylski

*Style: A Queer Cosmology*
Taylor Black

*Normporn: Queer Viewers and the TV That Soothes Us*
Karen Tongson

*Where the Wild Things Were: Boyhood and Permissive Parenting in Postwar America*
Henry Jenkins

# Where the Wild Things Were

*Boyhood and Permissive Parenting
in Postwar America*

Henry Jenkins

NEW YORK UNIVERSITY PRESS
New York

NEW YORK UNIVERSITY PRESS
New York
www.nyupress.org

© 2025 by New York University
All rights reserved

Library of Congress Cataloging-in-Publication Data

Names: Jenkins, Henry, 1958- author.
Title: Where the wild things were : boyhood and permissive parenting in postwar America / Henry Jenkins.
Description: New York : New York University Press, [2024] | Series: Postmillennial pop | Includes bibliographical references and index.
Identifiers: LCCN 2024012973 (print) | LCCN 2024012974 (ebook) | ISBN 9781479831869 (hardback) | ISBN 9781479831890 (paperback) | ISBN 9781479831883 (ebook) | ISBN 9781479831876 (ebook other)
Subjects: LCSH: Parent and child—United States. | Parenting—United States. | Boys—United States.
Classification: LCC HQ755.85 .J45 2024 (print) | LCC HQ755.85 (ebook) | DDC 306.8740973—dc23/eng/20241121
LC record available at https://lccn.loc.gov/2024012973
LC ebook record available at https://lccn.loc.gov/2024012974

This book is printed on acid-free paper, and its binding materials are chosen for strength and durability. We strive to use environmentally responsible suppliers and materials to the greatest extent possible in publishing our books.

Manufactured in the United States of America

10 9 8 7 6 5 4 3 2 1

Also available as an ebook

CONTENTS

Introduction: "We Want Children to Be Polite and They Are Rude": Permissiveness Defined — 1

PART I: THE EMERGENCE OF PERMISSIVE CULTURE

1. "Making a New Pattern": How Permissiveness Took Shape — 23
2. The Understanding Angel: The Child Study Movement and Empathetic Engagement — 47
3. "No Matter How Small": The Democratic Imagination of Dr. Seuss — 74
4. "Sometimes My Kids Seem like a Bunch of Kangaroos": Desire, Transgression, and Permissiveness — 100

PART II: LIVING IN PERMISSIVE CULTURE

5. Dennis the Menace, "the All-American Handful" — 131
6. Gerald McBoing-Boing and the Island of the Misfit Boys — 161
7. "I Like You Just the Way You Are": Understanding Fred Rogers — 185
8. Permissiveness and the Black Child — 207

PART III: THE SPACES OF THE PERMISSIVE IMAGINATION

9. Between Backyards and the Great Outdoors — 233
10. *Jonny Quest*, *Maya*, and the Promise of "World Brotherhood" — 253

11. "Danger, Will Robinson": Accommodating the Boy Scientist
   in *Lost in Space*     280

   Coda     303

   *Acknowledgments*     319

   *Notes*     323

   *Index*     353

   *About the Author*     368

   *Color insert follows page 184*

# Introduction

*"We Want Children to Be Polite and They Are Rude":*
*Permissiveness Defined*

"No parent wakes up in the morning planning to make his child's life miserable." Thus begins Haim G. Ginott's 1965 guide *Between Parent and Child*.[1] Born in Tel Aviv in 1927, Ginott's varied career included elementary school teacher, resident psychologist for NBC's *Today Show*, and professor of child psychology at New York University. His book spent more than a year on the *New York Times* bestseller list, reflecting an expanding market for advice literature addressing parents, given the success of Benjamin Spock's *Baby and Child Care* (first published in 1946 and growing in popularity across the 1950s and early 1960s). Ginott's book adopts an explicitly "permissive" approach, understanding what an earlier generation might have seen as misbehavior as reflecting a failure to communicate: "No one deliberately tries to make his child fearful, shy, inconsiderate, or obnoxious.... We want children to be polite and they are rude; we want them to be neat and they are messy; we want them to be confident and they are insecure; we want them to be happy and they are not."[2]

To overcome these challenges, parents should express their expectations and address children's needs: "He wants us to understand him. He wants us to understand what's going on inside himself at that particular moment. Furthermore, he wants to be understood without having to disclose fully what he is experiencing. It is a game in which he reveals only a little of what he feels, needing to have us guess the rest."[3] Ginott instructs parents how to play this guessing game, moving between broad principles and practical applications. "How do we know what he feels? We look at him and listen to him, and we also draw on our emotional experience."[4] Let's label these practices as empathetic introspection. Such understanding must shape parents' everyday approach: "Our inner motto is: let me understand. Let me show that I understand. Let me show in words that do not automatically criticize or condemn."[5]

*The Fabulous Fifties*, a 1960 CBS television special, featured shifts in child-rearing practices among the trends that defined the previous decade. A comedy segment parodied the efforts of the modern parent—in this case, the father—to apply permissive practices in disciplining a boy who has separately asked both parents for money to purchase the same school supplies. The father (Shelley Berman) is thrown off guard by the unpredictable and sometimes irrational choices his son ("Flip" Mark) is making: the boy uses his father's democratic impulses—such as telling the boy to sit where he wants—to defer the disciplining— as he shifts from chair to chair throughout the conversation. The boy's dialogue includes non sequiturs the father does not know how to interpret, and the boy does not know how to explain. And the boy rationalizes his choices by deploying familiar permissive concepts, such as talking about the expressive potential of the modeling clay he purchased with the excess money. In the end, the father seeks to punish him by demanding that he stay in his room but is defeated even here, storming off after the boy negotiates exceptions to this rule. Here, the comedy stems from the widely recognized gap between permissive ideals and their application.

Broad ideas about child psychology, empathy, and democracy are essential to permissiveness: a discursive formation, a cluster of interlocking ideas and practices, a structure of feeling that took shape across the twentieth century and reached its greatest influence in the 1950s and 1960s. Here is how Ginott describes his approach: "Permissiveness is an attitude of accepting the childishness of children. It means accepting that 'boys will be boys,' that a clean shirt on a normal child will not stay clean for long, that running rather than walking is the child's normal means of locomotion, that a tree is for climbing and a mirror is for making faces."[6] Reading this passage, one might be tempted to say that permissiveness is a theory of childhood that explains children's emotional and social development, seeing certain "wild and untamed" attributes as part of children's nature. For Ginott, "childishness" would have referred to acting like a child, which for writers of this period would have included images of rambunctiousness and messiness but also curiosity, fairness, and imagination.

The "new" permissive approach was signaled in the first few decades of the twentieth century by the shift from feeding on schedule (a practice disciplining the child's body, reining in their emotions, and restraining their actions within an adult-centered world) toward feeding on demand (where the parents were expected to interpret the child's various cries, feeding them when hungry, comforting them when hurt, and providing them company when lonely). From there, parents turned toward child psychology, investigating youngsters' emotional and fantasy lives. Permissiveness is defined in terms of what it permits. Ginott explains, "Strong feelings do not vanish by being banished; they do diminish in intensity and lose their sharp edges when the listener accepts them with sympathy and understanding."[7]

If permissiveness freed children from constraints, it imposed new expectations on parents regarding how they should behave in response to children's outbursts. Advocates of more permissive approaches offered parents insights on how they should interpret and enable children's emotional expression, even as they prepared their children for a world that was unlikely to tolerate behaviors it saw as brattish: "A parent who listens with attentiveness conveys to the child that his ideas are valued and that he is respected. Such respect gives the child a sense of self-worth. The feeling of personal worth enables the child to deal more effectively with the world."[8] Ginott justifies this approach as a recognition of children's rights: "The essence of permissiveness is the acceptance of children as persons who have a constitutional right to have all kinds of feelings and wishes. The freedom to wish is absolute and unrestricted; all feelings and fantasies, all thoughts and wishes, all dreams and desires, regardless of content, are accepted, respected, and permitted expression through appropriate symbolic means."[9] Ginott's phrase "the freedom to wish" captures the ways children were connected to a larger vision of a more democratic culture.

For critics, the term "permissiveness" conjured images of a world without limits, a world where parents are at the mercy of tyrannical tykes. But Ginott and the other childcare experts saw setting "limits" without intensifying conflicts as essential: "Destructive behavior is not permitted; when it occurs, the parents must intervene and redirect it into verbal outlets and other symbolic channels. . . . In short, permissiveness is the acceptance of imaginary and symbolic behavior.

Over-permissiveness is the allowing of undesirable acts. Permissiveness brings confidence and an increasing capacity to express feelings and thoughts. Over-permissiveness brings anxiety and increasing demands for privileges that cannot be granted."[10]

Having abandoned the more discipline-centered approaches of their own upbringing, parents struggled with doubts about how far they should let their children go:

> Civilization has cast parents in the role of "killjoys" who must say no to many of the small children's greatest pleasures, no sucking of the thumb, no touching of the penis, no picking of the nose, no playing with feces and no making of noise. . . . Some restrictions are inevitable if the child is to become a social being. However, parents should not overplay their role of policemen for civilization, lest they invite avoidance, resentment, and hostility.[11]

Here, adult impulses—such as a repulsion at certain bodily functions—need to be suppressed for children to grow without inhibition, repression, or trauma. Permissiveness situates children's natural response to the world within a nexus of adult power, where what one adult might tolerate another seeks to shut down. And ironically, no matter how it might seek to dislodge parental authority over children's bodies, the concept assumes that adults are the ones who might grant permission.

## Becoming Permissive

*Where the Wild Things Were* focuses on the discursive effort required to adjust to this new model of parent–child relations. Such efforts were conducted through advice literature for parents and through children's fictions, stories across all media that represented and were addressed to the world of the American child.

*We*—the postwar generation—were the "wild things" in the permissive imagination; our subjective experiences of the world were the focus of adult speculation. Critics accused us of acting like "wild animals" because no effort had been made to "tame" our impulses, while advocates spoke of our "unbridled" energy. By the late 1960s, when many of the initial baby-boom children were college-age, they were said to be "wild in the streets." In *Wild Things*, Jack Halberstam writes about Max, the protagonist of Maurice Sendak's children's book *Where the Wild Things Are*, as embodying "the wild not simply as a space beyond the home but also as a challenge to an assumed order of things." I want to second Halberstam's conception of wildness as "a chaotic force of nature, the outside of categorization, unrestrained forms of embodiment, the refusal to submit to social regulation, loss of control, the unpredictable,"[12] for the child in the permissive imagination is all these things. The child embodied a natural freedom (in the Rousseauian sense) to operate on the outer limits of the civilized order, a potential to escape adult limitations, and a new world order that the writers who used such metaphors wanted to achieve. In both advice literature and children's fictions, the child is often depicted as a "wild animal" or a "wild Indian," suggesting a space outside the civilized domain. As Robin Bernstein argues, the presumption of childhood innocence that justified such wildness in white children was rarely if ever accorded Black children or for that matter, Native children, making permissiveness a form of white privilege.[13]

Keep in mind that adults were willing accomplices to our wildness, making efforts to accommodate our messes and noise. Consider, for example, a 1964 commercial announcing the launch of Transogram's Trik-Trak, a racing-car toy that allowed children to set up the track as the battery-powered car was in motion. As the announcer explains, the toy allows your car to "go anywhere, room to room, all over the house." And if the point was not clear enough, there is a diagram showing the car traveling across all the rooms including the parents' den and bedroom. A boy shouts "Trik-Trak," and his father puts aside his paper and lifts his legs so the car can run under his feet, smiling and saying "Terrific." It's hard to imagine any working father being so cheerful about the car disrupting his evening paper in this way, but the fantasy was potent, not just for the child but also for the adult.

As I enter my sixties, I reflect on this period with nostalgia: the works discussed here shaped the kind of man I would become. In some cases, I returned to the same copies, kept in storage all these years. Some passages of this book are explicitly autobiographical, most are implicitly so. But this book is more than a trip down memory lane. By reengaging with my parents' generation, I have discovered

Figure I.1: Henry's suburban boyhood was informed by an infrastructure of permissive ideas, embodied by the *Parents* magazine on the coffee table.

things I had missed about these texts before. Consider this image (figure I.1) taken from one of my parents' slides: I always focused on myself, sitting across the room, wearing a striped shirt. I was surprised, then, to notice the pile of *Parents* magazines on the coffee table in the foreground. The choices my parents made were guided by the best practices in child development and in the service of a larger civic responsibility. Though invisible to the children whose lives it helped to shape, this advice literature was omnipresent.

Many advice-book writers saw themselves as promoting a more scientifically grounded approach to parenting. Some of what they saw as science has been thoroughly debunked—for example, the theory that the child recapitulates the history of the "human race'" or their involvement in eugenics. Other aspects—such as Freudian psychology or Mead's early fieldwork—have been disputed by more recent accounts. But the importance of these writers' moral philosophy concerning the relations between children and adults does not rest on claims of scientific validity alone, and these debates do not undercut permissiveness's historical importance in shaping the American family (and through it, the American society) during a period running roughly from 1946 (the publication of Spock's book) to 1968 (the beginnings of a strong conservative backlash).

When advice-literature writers referred to the American child as "he," they were adopting normative practice of the period: "he" stands in for both masculine and feminine cases. Benjamin Spock was early to note the gendered politics around pronouns, writing in his 1957 edition: "I want to apologize to the mothers and fathers who have a girl and who are frustrated by having the child called 'him' all through this book. It's clumsy to say **him or her** every time, and I need **her** to refer to the mother."[14] In the Victorian era, the ideal child was often a girl; Alice, Dorothy, Wendy, Anne of Green Gables, Rebecca of Sunnybrook Farms, and many more come to mind, who frequently broke free from constraining norms, spoke their mind, ventured beyond the domestic sphere, and engaged in "unladylike" behavior. Another wave of stories in the 1930s and 1940s, but increasingly fringe by the 1950s, depicted young girls—whether outspoken orphans (such as Annie or the characters played by Shirley Temple) or spunky pranksters (such as Little Lulu, Little Audrey, or the Harvey girls).[15]

The ideal child of the permissive era was a boy—almost always white, suburban, straight, middle-class, Christian (mostly Protestant), and above all, American. These were all-American boys, often depicted in red-and-white-striped shirts, blue jeans, and Keds, with disheveled hair, smudged cheeks, and dreamy eyes. Even Charlie Brown had a stripe on his shirt, albeit a jagged, anxious one. These boys turned their parents' bedrooms upside down or talked back to kings in the pages of Dr. Seuss's best-selling books. They were rescued by Lassie or led astray by Flipper. These boys are curious, adventuresome, messy, noisy, rough-and-tumble, muddy even. They explore the world, questioning everyone and everything. They sometimes disobeyed and often escaped adult supervision; they were natural leaders and embraced a democratic style of living. This focus on boys assumed that while girls would and often did read books about boys, boys tended to actively avoid books about girls, and it was boys, the perception went, who most needed help in learning to read.[16]

Beyond that, the traits associated with boyhood aligned with the ways America viewed itself as a nation coming out of the Second World

War—bold, fearless, outgoing, wild, open for action, eager to explore the world, and curious about the future. Yet, they were also the traits that led the country into colonialist and military excursions; the "Boys will be boys" ethos has been used ever since to justify the worst excesses of toxic patriarchy.

There are certainly adventurous girls in the children's literature of the period—from Harriet the Spy to Pippi Longstocking or even Scout in *To Kill a Mockingbird*—but they were far fewer, less central to the conversation, and in the case of Pippi, foreign in origin. For this reason, among others, my book focuses on boy-centered narratives and thus reads the advice literature for what it tells us about masculinity. These are also the children's fictions most important for me as a boy raised by gender-normative parents. Throughout, I will be asking what it means that the child in the permissive imagination is so often male just as I ask why it matters that these boys are overwhelmingly white. Throughout, I use "child" when referring to the advice literature's constructions and "boy" when referring to children's fictions, but do not forget that much of what is written about "the child" assumes that the child is male.

This is necessarily a partial account of the permissive imagination—far from exhaustive even regarding the subject matter it does consider. Many, perhaps most, readers of a certain age will find one or another favorite missing. More than once, I have been asked about the relative absence of *Leave It to Beaver*. I can offer several possible explanations for why I lean toward Dennis Mitchell and away from Beaver Cleaver, who follows many of the same genre formulas. Part of what interests me about Dennis is that he appears across media—comic strips, comic books, and television—while Beaver appears almost exclusively on television (and a short-lived comic book). Hank Ketcham has a definite authorial voice and strong views, especially about gender and race, which allow us to examine a more conservative yet still permissive stance. Jay North as an actor also appears in *Maya*, which I also wanted to discuss. But ultimately, it is a matter of personal preference. Dennis lives in my personal mythology. I watched *Beaver*—everyone my age did—but never fully embraced him.

How did this cluster of ideas and practices I am labeling the "permissive imagination" take shape? Rather than a rigid periodization, I am drawing on a more dynamic model of cultural change developed by Raymond Williams. Williams stresses "the dynamic interrelations, at every point in the process of historically varied and variable elements." New ideas do not erase old ones but build upon them. Aspects of cultural traditions are always being pushed aside to make room for the new or carried forward to temper its impact. Williams proposed that dominant (the most widely adopted meanings and practices), emergent ("new meanings and values, new practices, new relationships"), residual ("formed in the past but . . . still active in the cultural process"), and even archaic ("wholly recognized as an element of the past") may coexist, mutually informing the "structure of feeling" common to a particular period.[17] Thinking of permissiveness as a structure of feeling suggests its aesthetic, social, and emotional dimensions as it is embodied in everyday practices (such as the way adults might kneel on the floor to speak eye-to-eye to children), elements of style (Fred Rogers's direct address and slow pace, the whimsy of Dr. Seuss or Maurice Sendak, the ways photographers such as Ruth Orkin and Helen Leavitt center children's expressive practices), and so much more.

"Permissiveness," always a relative term, was often defined against John Watson the behaviorist, a dominant voice of the prewar period.[18] But the behaviorist model did not go unchallenged in its own time. The roots of permissiveness as an emergent perspective go back to the Progressive Era (1890–1920), when Dorothy Canfield Fisher helped to popularize a version of the Montessori method through her fiction (*The Home-Maker*) and her advice writing. Fisher was well ahead of her time but she was not alone. Fisher collaborated with Sidonie Matsner Gruenberg in rallying a group of complementary thinkers who articulated a method of Child Study and translated these insights into advice for parents. Josette Frank and Anna W. M. Wolf are representatives of the expansion of the Child Study discourse in the 1930s and 1940s.

Dorothy Baruch, an educator and child advocate, was the primary voice for a more democratic approach to family life. Baruch, like Fisher, presented her insights in child-rearing guides but also helped to shape fictional representations—in her case, the Sally, Dick, and Jane books that introduced my generation to reading. Having embraced feeding on demand, writers extended this approach to factor in children's other bodily—even erotic—desires as things that needed to be accepted and accommodated. With this came a larger reassessment of "discipline," seeking to understand and address the root causes of children's behavior. Under this paradigm, children had core rights that needed to be respected. The hope was that the next generation would be more comfortable with their bodies and their identities, more democratic in their impulses, more exploratory in their learning, and more connected with the world around them than the previous generation saw itself to be. Dorothy Baruch describes the ideal outcome:

> We hope they will become adults who are able to get along without fights and wars, who will want to settle disputes by more civilized means, but who will stand up for themselves and for what they believe to be right.... The ideal is the personality which will maintain itself against opposition as it feels the necessity and which will not perpetually be yielding, giving in submissively to any and every influence that comes near.[19]

With the publication of Spock's *Baby and Child Care*, permissiveness became the dominant paradigm for parenting and remained so until the late 1960s, when it faced increased challenge from feminists because of its normalization of gender roles and from conservative critics because of the suspicion that tolerance of disruptive behaviors had paved the way for the counterculture. This approach was also informed by a multitude of women—themselves mothers, often women's rights advocates—whose contributions have been largely neglected. Ginott's *Between Parent and Child* concludes with a short list of "books you may find enjoyable and useful," which includes works by Baruch, Wolf, and Selma Fraiberg.[20]

In *The Permissive Society*, Alan Petigny argues that America during the Truman and Eisenhower years was less conservative, complacent, and contained than popular memory might suggest: "During the latter half of the 1940s, and continuing throughout the 1950s, the popular ingestion of modern psychology, coupled with changes in child-rearing and religious practices, constituted an unprecedented challenge to traditional moral constraints."[21] Many of the experts and creatives discussed here held progressive (and sometimes radical) beliefs and saw themselves as helping to reshape American society for a postwar era by reimagining the American family (which they saw as more fluid and more open to experimentation) and reshaping the American child (whom they saw as coming into the world free of the fears and prejudices that had led to the failure of their own generation to overcome racism or embrace global citizenship).

By the late 1960s, conservative backlash toward Spock and his contemporaries would lead to the formation of a "dare to discipline" approach that saw itself as putting adults back in control over children's lives. This model remains a potent reactionary force today, while permissiveness has retained a residual status. Many contemporary culture-war struggles reflect the clash between these two models, as I will explore more fully in the book's coda.

## What Fred Rogers Can Teach Us about Permissiveness

Given this focus on the intersection between adult advice literature and children's fictions, let's consider Fred Rogers, host of *Mister Rogers' Neighborhood* (1968–2001). The 2018 release of Morgan Neville's documentary, *Won't You Be Neighbor?*, solidified an expanding interest in Rogers's life, philosophy, and legacy. As director Neville explains, "in a much more cynical age that we live in today, to be confronted by such emotional sincerity is overwhelming and ultimately, I think, kind of cathartic . . . [as we watch Rogers explain] to these unformed people what it means to be a person and a neighbor and a citizen. And how we should think of other people and how we should think of ourselves."[22] Rogers modeled a more accepting social system through his interactions with his human guests and through the make-believe world of King Friday and Daniel Tiger. Rogers spoke to *all* children—girls as well as boys—but this has not prevented many recent accounts from foregrounding his impact on boys and men. I discuss Rogers more fully later, but consider one example of how permissive discourse was expressed through his program:

> Sometimes people are good
> And they do just what they should.
> But the very same people who are good sometimes
> Are the very same people who are bad sometimes.
> It's funny, but it's true.
> It's the same, isn't it for me and you. . . .

> Sometimes people get wet.
> And their parents get upset.
> But the very same people who get wet sometimes
> Are the very same people who are dry sometimes.

Here, we see permissive ideas about shifting concern from children's personalities ("bad children") to specific behavior that needed correction, about trying to understand why children sometimes act out and becoming more tolerant of actions like jumping into mud puddles.

Neville's documentary was followed by a substantial biography, Maxwell King's *The Good Neighbor*;[23] a dramatic film, Marielle Heller's *A Beautiful Day in the Neighborhood*; and an acclaimed podcast, Carvell Wallace's *Finding Fred*. Rogers was a remarkable man, but these works view him as exceptional and some of the recent works—*Beautiful Day* in particular—function as modern saints' tales, where Rogers performs miracles like healing wounded relationships between men and their fathers. Rogers's status as an adult who cares about children connects him to many other permissive thinkers who used empathetic introspection to better understand what children were feeling and why they acted the way they did. Rogers was strongly linked to permissiveness as a student of Margaret McFarland (whose work was primarily in the practice of observing children and advising mothers, leaving precious few written traces of her thinking) and as a participant in the Arsenal Family and Children's Center in Pittsburgh (alongside Benjamin Spock, Erik Erikson, and T. Berry Brazelton). *Won't You Be My Neighbor* never examines this group's strong influence on the expressive mechanisms (music, performance, art) through which Rogers helped children develop a deeper understanding of their emotional lives. For example, consider how Ginott characterizes music: "The main purpose of music education is to provide an effective outlet for feelings. A child's life is full of restrictions, regulations and frustrations. . . . Music is one of the best avenues of release; it gives sound to fury, shape to joy, and relief to tension."[24] Rogers embodies a similar philosophy when he teaches his child viewers to take a pen or paintbrush to draw what a piece of music makes them feel, and he himself models such a practice by making broad strokes with complete abandon. Rogers was an exemplary figure rather than an exceptional one, one of the last and most persistent voices in a conversation that stretched across the twentieth century.

It is worth considering why *Won't You Be My Neighbor?* spoke so powerfully to Americans in the context of Donald Trump's presidency. First and most immediately, the documentary tapped a desire to return to the world of our own childhood, now imagined as a simpler and less troubled time. Nostalgia often constitutes a form of the utopian imagination, projected backward rather than forward in time.[25] Svetlana Boym distinguishes between restorative nostalgia (which, like Trump's "Make America Great Again," seeks to turn back the clock toward a more conservative past) and reflexive nostalgia (which taps inspiration from the past to continue to struggle to build a better world in the future). Insofar as my book is read as nostalgic, I hope it is read as a form of reflexive nostalgia, seeking to reexamine the past, warts and all, to inspire new thinking about how the family could become, in our time as it was imagined in the past, a force for progressive change in American society. Second, Rogers models an alternative form of adult masculinity—one defined around gentleness, patience, playfulness, creativity, and above all, empathy—all qualities that contrast sharply with the toxic masculinity, the rage, and the bullying that characterize the current moment. And third, the concept of the "neighbor" represents a particular form of the civic imagination, a way of thinking about "community" that ensures everyone's basic needs (especially belonging and acceptance) are met.[26] Fred Rogers was an ordained Presbyterian minister and saw television as an extension of his moral project. Neville discusses Rogers's impact: "He was talking about how we build a neighborhood, and these fundamental questions of how we live together in society, and how we should treat each other, a kind of reminder of the basic human values we all share and we all ascribe to when we decide to live together in a community."[27] *Won't You Be My Neighbor?* suggests how Rogers might react to the current moment (though Trump's name is never mentioned). Conservative critics had criticized Rogers's vision of a world where everyone is "special," a perspective dismissed through the term "snowflake." And the film's final moment of silence, as the various participants think about people who made a difference in their lives, constitutes a call for civic renewal.

## "Just a Spoonful of Sugar . . .": Walt Disney's *Mary Poppins* (1964)

To understand how children's fiction might be read in relation to the discourses offered by advice literature, consider the case of Walt Disney's *Mary Poppins* (1964). Disney's movie pits permissive ideas against more discipline-centered approaches, offering a model for a thoroughly modern upbringing. The Disney film establishes two criteria by which a new nanny might be selected, the first consisting of "requirements" from Mr. Banks, and the other a contract of sorts as the Bankses' children describe how they might curb their misconduct if they receive fair treatment.[28] To understand the contrast between the two approaches, we might consider a chart Rudolf Dreikurs offered in *Children: The Challenge* (1964) the same year Disney's *Mary Poppins* was released.

| | |
|---|---|
| Autocratic society | Democratic society |
| Authority figure | Knowledgeable leader |
| Power | Influence |
| Pressure | Stimulation |
| Demanding | Winning cooperation |
| Punishment | Logical consequences |
| Reward | Encouragement |
| Imposition | Permit—Self-determination |
| Domination | Guidance |
| Children are to be seen & not heard | Listen! Respect the child |
| You do it because I said to | We do it because it is necessary. |

Dreikurs situates many permissive traits on the "democratic society" side of the ledger.[29]

Mr. Banks describes his ideal candidate:

> Required. Nanny. Firm, Respectable, No nonsense.
> A British nanny must be a gen'ral!
> The future empire lies within her hands
> And so the person that we need to mold the breed
> Is a nanny who can give commands!
> A British bank is run with precision;
> A British home requires nothing less!

> Tradition, discipline, and rules must be the tools,
> Without them, disorder, chaos, moral disintegration;
> In short you have a ghastly mess!

Here, the key notions—"precision," "firmness," "discipline," "rules," on the one hand, and disorder and moral disintegration on the other—come directly from the discipline-centered advice of behaviorism. Ada Hart Arlitt's 1930 book *The Child from One to Six* warned that the child "will not know that there are laws that govern the universe unless he knows that there are laws that govern the home."[30] The home was to be regulated not by "mother love" but by the "kitchen time-piece." Children should be fed and put to bed on a fixed schedule. Elsewhere in the film, Mr. Banks sings, "It's 6:03, and the heirs to my dominion are scrubbed and tubbed and adequately fed."

The prewar discourse drew analogies to industrial (or, in Banks's case, commercial) processes. This same language runs through the writings of John Watson, the man often credited with defining the prewar paradigm, or what Dreikurs labels "autocratic society." Mr. Banks summarizes his desire to prepare children for the competitive environment: "The children must be molded, shaped, and taught / That life's a looming battle to be faced and fought." The best methods for achieving these goals required the father and those (such as the nanny) under his "command" to maintain authority over the young.

As with Watson, patriarchal power was linked to a distrust of maternal sentimentality, or what Banks refers to as "slipshod, sugary, female thinking." Banks seeks a polite distance from his children: "I'll pat them on the head and send them off to bed." Here is Watson's advice on such matters:

> There is a sensible way of treating children. Treat them as though they were young adults. . . . Let your behavior always be objective and kindly firm. Never hug and kiss them, never let them sit in your lap. If you must, kiss them once on the forehead when they say good night. Shake hands with them in the morning. Give them a pat on the head if they have made an extraordinarily good job of a difficult task.[31]

The ideal child was engineered to be easy to manage at home and disciplined for adult jobs.

Watson wanted "impartial" children with few emotional attachments and limited erotic interests. Following his advice, middle-class mothers moved from breastfeeding toward bottle-feeding, seeing a carefully calculated formula as offering better nutrition, while showing little interest in the loss of the affective bond between mother and child. By feeding the child on a regular schedule, putting it to bed and picking it up according to the clock, toilet training it at the appropriate age, parents would instill good habits.

Doing so required that parental authority be absolute and unwavering, that discipline be systematic and strict. Arlitt's *The Child from One to Six* advocated that parents should "cut down the number of times that one speaks to the child. Speak only when necessary, then expect to be obeyed."[32] The signs of adult authority were to be overt and unmistakable; the separation between the child's sphere and the parents' rigidly enforced. The danger of "spoiling the child" was ever present and often irreversible. Mother's love was "an instrument which may inflict a never healing wound, a wound which may make infancy unhappy, adolescence a nightmare, an instrument which may wreck your adult son or daughter's vocational future and their chances for marital happiness."[33]

The children's advertisement represents a different ideal:

> If you want this choice position
> Have a cheery disposition
> Rosy cheeks, no warts!
> Play games, all sorts
> You must be kind, you must be witty
> Very sweet and fairly pretty
> Take us on outings, give us treats
> Sing songs, bring sweets.
> Never be cross or cruel.
> Never give us castor oil or gruel
> Love us as a son and daughter.
> And never smell of barley water.

If Banks wants a nanny who will give commands, the children want one with a "cheery disposition." She should engage with them through jokes, songs, outings, and games. She must win their cooperation. And the children agree not to misbehave if the nanny respects their needs (suggesting that they have sufficient rights and power to negotiate with adults):

> If you won't scold and dominate us
> We will never give you a cause to hate us.
> We won't hide your spectacles
> So you can't see
> Put toads in your bed
> Or pepper in your tea.

Their previous nanny described the Banks children as "little beasts" needing a "ruddy zookeeper" (i.e., "wild things"). The children argue that the nanny's discipline provoked them to act out, a perspective shared by many permissive experts. Mr. Banks rejects such claims, tearing up the children's advertisement. But when Mary Poppins arrives, she holds the children's advert, taped together again.

Poppins's more permissive approach is summed up by the lyrics of "A Spoonful of Sugar," which encourages the Banks children to put away their toys. A disorderly nursery was one of Watson's pet peeves: "Children with toys all over the floor do not have time at the end of the day to clear them all up carefully. . . . You buy a toy box but the toys are dumped in by the armful and thrown about the room at random the next day until the child comes upon the one he wants."[34] Mary Poppins approaches the problem in her own way:

> In ev'ry job that must be done
> There is an element of fun.
> You find the fun and SNAP!
> The job's a game
> And ev'ry task you undertake
> Becomes a piece of cake.
> A lark! A spree!
> It's very clear to see. . . .
> Spoonful of sugar helps the medicine go down.

Mary Poppins, issuing no commands, redirects the children's attention, using pleasure ("a spoonful of sugar") to motivate them. Cleaning the room becomes a game rather than a chore.

Disney's *Mary Poppins* is structured around the project of helping the father develop a more constructive relationship with his children. Mr. Banks's name defines him through his job. Despite Banks's efforts to teach them the virtues of capitalist empire building, Michael refuses to hand over his tuppence as a deposit, wanting to make a compassionate gift to the Bird Woman outside Saint Paul's Cathedral. When the children's disruptions result in a run on the bank, the father is fired. By this point, he has also found his home overrun by soot-covered chimney sweeps. And, in the aftermath, he has a conversation with Bert (who also uses reverse psychology) about the importance of spending more time with his children: "When your little tykes are crying, you haven't time to dry their tears and see those grateful little faces smiling up at you.... You've got to grind, grind, grind at that grindstone though childhood slips like sand through a sieve. And all too soon, they've up and grown, and then, they've flown and it's too late for you to give."

Dick Van Dyke plays Bert as an adult who remains imaginative, playful, and jocular; who finds creative expression through his work; who understands the emotional life of children; and who still maintains the ability to speak to the adult world. Mr. Banks retains his dignity but, at the bank, the father internalizes Bert's anarchic spirit: laughing, telling jokes. The moment is ironic given that Banks confronts Van Dyke as the ancient bank president, a fossilized capitalist patriarch.

Everyone is convinced that Mr. Banks might try to kill himself without the job that has defined his life. Instead, he encourages everyone to fly a kite. And Mary Poppins flies off into the sunset.

## The Scope and Structure of the Book

The next section considers "The Emergence of Permissive Culture." Chapter 1 introduces two figures who inform this book—Margaret Mead and Benjamin Spock—intervening at a key transition in the American family, helping baby-boom children and their parents adjust to changing social norms. Chapter 2 argues that an emergent perspective on parenting was shaped by the Child Study Association of America and maps the movement's focus on empathetic introspection as seen in *The Home-Maker* (1924), *The Littlest Angel* (1945), and *The Boy with Green Hair* (1948). Chapter 3 considers Dr. Seuss, the postwar era's most popular children's writer, discussing his movement from wartime work as a propagandist into his peacetime work as a creator of children's fictions. Chapter 4 discusses the shifting understanding of children's desires, especially erotic desires, exploring how works as diverse as *Where the Wild Things Are* (1963), *Little Fugitive* (1953), *The Twilight Zone*'s "It's a Good Life" (1961), and *Alfred Hitchcock Presents*' "Bang! You're Dead" (1961) suggest a reworking of cultural responses to transgressive behaviors.

The section on "Living in a Permissive Culture" discusses the period when permissiveness was dominant. Chapter 5 considers Dennis the Menace—introduced as a comic strip in 1951 and brought to television in 1959—as a cross-media success that embodies the permissive paradigm. Chapter 6 explores *Gerald McBoing-Boing* (1950), *Harold and the Purple Crayon* (1955), *It's the Great Pumpkin, Charlie Brown* (1966), and other fictions concerning how the culture might accommodate or assimilate the exceptional, creative, and nonconforming boy. Chapter 7 explores how Fred Rogers drew insights from child-study research at the Arsenal Family and Children's Center, deploying songs and puppets to help children to express their emotions. Chapter 8 asks whether permissiveness was a primarily or exclusively white ideal, how permissiveness addressed racial difference, and how it was adopted and adapted by the Black community, discussing, among other things, *Fat Albert and the Cosby Kids* (1972) and *Sesame Street* (1969) as children's programming intentionally addressing children of color.

The next section, "The Spaces of the Permissive Imagination," explores how children's fictions expand the range of environments children can access—in their imagination if not in reality. Chapter 9 uses stories about nature and outdoor life—*Flipper* (1964) and *My Side of the Mountain* (1959)—to consider how these writers balance freedom of movement and domesticity. Chapter 10 taps discourse about "universal brotherhood" and "global citizenship" by considering two narratives—*Jonny Quest* (1964) and *Maya* (1967)—depicting friendship between a white, American boy and a brown, Indian boy. Chapter 11 discusses how science fiction—in this case, *Lost in Space* (1965)—interested boys in the sciences.

The coda returns to our two key figures—Spock and Mead—who sat down together in late 1971 for a conversation with *Redbook* magazine, an exchange that reflects the different ways they navigated the politics of the counterculture and feminism. From there, I trace the aftermath of those debates, mapping the emergence of both feminist and conservative alternatives to permissiveness, and their influence on contemporary culture wars.

PART I

The Emergence of Permissive Culture

1

"Making a New Pattern"

*How Permissiveness Took Shape*

*Where the Wild Things Were* offers an account of an American culture in transition as the authors in question reimagined the family to meet the needs of the postwar era. The primary architects of this new permissive paradigm were Benjamin Spock and Margaret Mead, but they were not writing in isolation. In this chapter, I outline the context within which the permissive paradigm took shape—starting with the demographic changes that led to the so-called baby boom, then considering how Spock and Mead reshaped how baby-boom parents understood their roles. I will sift the evidence we have—often from advice books themselves—suggesting that those parents only partially embraced these new models, actively questioning the changes they were being asked to make. What made permissive culture so generative was precisely the need to address those uncertainties with either advice or fictional models. Finally, I consider how the rise of permissiveness related to the shifting racial politics of the 1950s and 1960s. Permissiveness resulted in an erasure of racial difference, at least initially. In stepping away from racial stereotypes, 1950s and 1960s children's fictions also stepped away from representing people of color, complicit in segregation regardless of their liberal self-perceptions.

My Life and Welcome to It

I begin this account in my own backyard. In 1965, the so-called baby-boom generation constituted a quarter of the American population—altogether, 72.5 million American children under the age of ten.[1] I was one of them. I was born in 1958 at the dawn of what was then perceived as a new era, variously described as the space age, the age of television, the global age, the civil rights era, or the permissive era. My parents raised me with Dr.

Spock in one hand and Dr. Seuss in the other. Spock was the best-selling author for adults in the 1960s, Seuss, the best-selling author for children. Ann Hulbert has suggested important parallels between the two good doctors: "A child born in the middle of the baby boom might be forgiven for getting Dr. Spock and Dr. Seuss mixed up . . . Dr. Spock joined Dr. Seuss in making room for fantasy—often frightening—in the psyches of the young and of their parents. . . . Yet they also insisted that everybody come to terms with reality—and more than that, develop a sense of mastery and of social morality."[2] *Where the Wild Things Were* documents the postwar explosion of discourse about childhood and parenting: a growing field of advice literature for parents and an expanding body of fictions for children.

My mother's father was upper-middle-class: at various points in her lifetime, he owned his own barbershop, ran the local draft board, and worked as a deputy sheriff. My father's father had been raised on a South Georgia farm, left home to serve during World War I, and found little to keep him down on the farm once he had seen Paris. He moved to Atlanta, developed a trade (sheet metal work), and pursued it for the rest of his working life. My mother and father had been childhood sweethearts who got married, in their late teens, not long after the end of the Second World War. By the mid-1950s, one out of every two first-time brides in the United States were in their teens.[3] My father served as a fireman in the peacetime navy. He attended Georgia Tech on the GI Bill, studying architecture and starting his own construction company; my mother attended secretarial school and helped keep the books. By 1960, in more than ten million households, both husband and wife worked—an increase of 333 percent since 1940.[4] Fueled by postwar expansions of the consumer economy, by 1960 more than 65 percent of American families had achieved what the Census Bureau defined as a middle-class standard of living, as compared with 30 percent in 1929.[5] Seventy-five percent of American families owned their own car, and 90 percent owned a television.[6] By the late 1950s, my parents owned their own home, their own car, a television set, and even leased land on a North Georgia lake, where they had built their own cabin (which, as it happens, is where I first conceived of this book). They were enjoying the good life.

My grandparents had lived in the midtown "streetcar" suburbs in the 1920s and 1930s. By the time I was born, the Jenkins family had moved into a new suburb farther out from the urban core. Not long after, my father's parents moved into a house less than a mile away, but my mother's family remained in their midtown homestead. This was during a huge wave of suburbanization, during which some 13.5 million new homes were built, 11 million in new residential communities.[7] By 1960, more than a quarter of all American families lived in the suburbs, with the rest divided evenly between rural and urban communities.[8] Our house had sprawling front and back yards with dogwood trees and azalea bushes. We hosted Easter-egg hunts for the neighborhood kids. We had a swing set, a slide, a sandbox, and a tree house. When we got older, we could ride our bikes on safe subdivision streets and play in empty lots with other children. And we had a dog—a mutt with collie blood—who reminded us of Lassie. Not everyone was enjoying this good life, but this is what a "normal childhood" looked like in the popular imagination.

In 1957, there were 4.3 million babies born, setting a record for the highest number of births ever recorded in American history.[9] I was born a year later. Many factors shaped the dramatic population growth known as the baby boom. First, a generation of women postponed having children during the Depression and war years and were giving birth later in life. Second, postwar women married younger and also had their children younger. Nearly one-third of American women had their first baby before they reached their twentieth birthday. My mother and father were exceptions: they were almost thirty when they had me, though more typically they had my brother four years later. Third, postwar parents had more children than the previous generation; the number of families with at least two children jumped 46 percent.[10]

My family, like 70 percent of all American families of the period, was Protestant.[11] Both my grandparents and my father were Baptist deacons. My mother ran the Vacation Bible School.

I was one of 5,643 white babies born in Dekalb County, Georgia, that year, compared with 762 "nonwhite" children.[12] Both Black and white babies were born in Piedmont Hospital, where I was delivered, but it would be many more years before our paths would cross again. I lived in a segregated neighborhood, attended a segregated church, and went to a segregated school. This effect was achieved through redlining: banks would not loan money to Black families who wanted to move into mostly or all-white communities; de facto segregation was the norm. The first time I saw a Black child was when my mother drove our maid home. Much as Jennifer Ritterhouse describes in her book *Growing Up Jim Crow*, my encounters with Black children were infrequent and informal, not structured through schools or churches, and certainly not embedded in shared living conditions.[13] The imaginary world I occupied as a child was also redlined: few Blacks or other minorities appeared in the fictions I consumed. Whiteness was the default across all media. Many Black children consumed these stories. Audience members at my talks have mentioned the experience of growing up in a world where Buckwheat in *Little Rascals* was the only Black face they saw on television and wondering about the lack of discipline at Dennis Mitchell's house. They knew these fictions were not for or about them.

I was a middle-class, suburban, Protestant, white boy whose parents also fit the statistical norms for their generation. I was a scrawny little guy with honey-colored hair, hazel eyes, and glasses; this mix of traits led me to identify closely with the various representations of American boyhood found in popular media. And this may account for why, in my sixties, I find myself reconstructing the iconography and discourse of this moment.

Consider another photograph my parents took of me (figure 1.1). My favorite plush and plastic toys arrayed around me, I am grinning mischievously, the king of my own domain. This image suggests the richness of the material culture produced for children and hints at the way these toys bridged between the domestic space of my upbringing and the imaginative space of the fictions I consumed. So many of these toys are based on characters from popular media at a time when the move from generic stuffed animals to media tie-in products was at a turning point.[14]

My Southern Baptist parents were permissive in some senses—they facilitated a very active fantasy life, encouraged me to express my feelings through art, and placed few restrictions on the media I consumed—but I remained very aware of their authority. My parents were cobbling together a piecemeal approach from a range of different sources, including their fundamentalist interpretation of the Bible. Above all, they had Benjamin Spock's ever-present *Baby and Child Care* (the early-1950s date on their edition suggests that it might have been passed down to them

Figure 1.1: The vivid imaginative lives of postwar children were sustained by the material culture of the era, as suggested by Henry's army of plush characters, many from popular media.

from one of my three uncles, all of whom had children well before they did). By 1952 US sales of his book had reached four million, and it would sell another million copies per year for the rest of the decade. A 1961 survey, commissioned by its publisher, found that almost two-thirds of new mothers had read Spock and four out of five of those consulted it twice a month or more.[15]

Representation of 1950s suburban America stressed the social rewards of community living.[16] But many families, mine among them, had moved to neighborhoods where they knew no one. Turning inward to focus on their own children, my parents maintained few adult friends. In their case, they had close access to my grandparents, but many were moving across the country and sought advice from books on the best ways to raise their children. Spock's book had greeted an entire generation of new parents: "Trust yourself. You know more than you think you do. Bringing up your baby won't be a complicated job if you take it easy, trust your instincts, and follow the directions your doctor gives you."[17] Much has been written about the contradiction between "trust yourself" and "follow the directions." Behind the scenes, Spock himself was struggling with how insights from child psychology (and psychoanalysis) might relate to pediatrics:

> In 1938 I had been in practice for five years—and had one child of my own—when Doubleday asked me to write a parent's guide on the physical and psychological sides of child-rearing. I said quite sincerely that I didn't know enough. I was still trying to reconcile Freudian concepts with what mothers were telling me about their babies, about breastfeeding, weaning and toilet training. There was no doubt in my mind that Freud and the babies were both right, but it took years for me to find the way to reconcile them. . . . Top-level professors of pediatrics in many medical schools had a fundamental, unconscious uneasiness about dealing with feelings. Their temperamental make-up and their natural interest in impersonal aspects of disease—disturbances in body chemistry, unusual immune reactions, invading bacteria and viruses—make them skeptical about emotional disorders and about doctors who focus on them.[18]

Despite such misgivings, Spock found the confidence to write his book; in return, many American parents had enough confidence in Spock to raise their children according to his methods. Daniel Thomas Cook describes how mothers embraced parenting as a "moral project," seeking to address the contradictions of their own lives through tending to children's emotional needs: "Childhood arises as a dynamic perplexity that never quite resolves itself but that, as an ongoing problematic, enables—indeed, demands—assertions about human nature."[19] Seeking to resolve this "dynamic perplexity," this generation of adults—parents, educators, and scholars—turned to science, in particular, psychology, to anchor truths about the nature of childhood.

Benjamin Spock issued new editions of his best-selling book every few years to reflect his own evolving understanding of the needs of children. In his 1974 book, *Raising Children in a Difficult Time*, Spock labels himself as "anti-permissive":

> I've always believed and written: that parents should stick by their ethical convictions, and feel no hesitation in showing them to their children; that they should ask their children for cooperation and respect; that children

who are held up to high ideals and considerate behavior are not only a lot of pleasure to live with, but they are happier themselves. To put it frankly, I'm as much irritated as anyone by children who are chronically rude, unhelpful, and always demanding more for themselves. How did I ever get the reputation among some people of being an advocate of excessive permissiveness? . . . The accusation was accepted mainly by people who never read *Baby and Child Care*.

The key word may be "excessive": Spock *was* permissive in the sense we are using the term, but these writers almost always set up a straw man (or woman) who pushed these ideas too far, creating brats rather than good little children. Spock understood himself as providing counterbalance to the state of American parenting, pushing back in the late 1940s against a model he felt too focused on disciplining the child and pushing back in the 1960s at a point when he felt permissiveness had been carried too far. Spock's efforts to recalibrate his advice are suggested by a note in the 1957 edition:

> If you are an old reader of the book you will see a lot has been changed, especially about discipline, spoiling, and the parent's part. When I was writing the first edition, between 1943 and 1946, the attitude of a majority of people toward infant feeding, toilet training, and general child management was still fairly strict and inflexible. However, the need for greater understanding of children and for flexibility in their care had been made clear by educators, psychoanalysts and pediatricians, and I was trying to encourage this. Since then, a great change in attitude has occurred and nowadays there seems to be more chance of a conscientious parent getting into trouble with permissiveness than with strictness. So, I have tried to give a more balanced view.[20]

Spock may have protested too much, emphasizing the moderate and even conservative aspects of his advice, while ignoring the many ways that it *did* represent a radical break with established wisdom. He was consciously counterbalancing other writers and thus smoothing over what might otherwise have been a rougher paradigm shift.

These comments also suggest the ways permissiveness was always defined in comparison with the idea of more rigid parental control.

Instead, Spock advocated displacing authoritarian parenting with "authoritative leadership": "The principles are the same that apply in the parent's management of his own children or in the officer's control over his men or in the executive's relationships with his subordinates. . . . Good leadership, I think, always has to combine the element of confidence in one's right to lead, a genuine liking for those being led, and definite ideas of what to expect from them."[21] Spock saw his readers as servicemen (and women) returning to civilian life and transitioning into corporate jobs. He had first started drafting his book during the war as a column for *PM* magazine and adjusted it to speak to postwar life. Like most child-rearing experts before him, his norms emerged from his observations of middle-class families, even if he universalized them to speak about childhood more generally.

## Margaret Mead Reimagines the Postwar American Family

On August 10, 1956, *CBS Radio Workshop* opened with the sound of a baby crying, suggesting that crying is a natural response in babies and the "only thing that changes is what we do about it."[22] Written by Johanna Johnston, identified in the broadcast as "a mother," "Only Johnny Knows" dramatizes the shifts in parenting advice through the ages, mostly summed up around this question of how indulgent adults should be of children's demands. "What do I do? What does he want?" asks the frazzled mother, only to be met by a range of advice: "Pick him up! Let him lie! Feed him! Coddle him!" The "modern" perspective is personified through a series of quotations from Dr. Spock: "You can't spoil your baby by feeding him when he is hungry, comforting him when he is miserable. Enjoy and love your baby. He doesn't have to be sternly trained. . . . A mother will be alright if she is flexible and adjusts to the baby's needs. Study a child. He knows when he is hungry and needs cuddling." The episode is framed as a debate between a "modern mother" uncertain about her options and a male observer frustrated over the lack of constraint parents exercised over contemporary children. The episode suggests how aware postwar Americans were about the negotiation of a new family life. Along the way, the episode acknowledges some core ambivalences—recognizing that applying these "modern" principles represents "hard work," especially for mothers; that these new models reflect commercial values ("Our country lives by full production, and the only way to keep up with the tide is by constant consumption. Johnny is a brand new market"); that the family is governed by entertainment values ("Johnny thinks he has to be entertained all of the time! Fun! Fun! Fun!"); and that the modern family's goal is to ensure that their child's life will "be happy" with the hope that the "happy satisfied child" knows how to manage its own desires.

"What Johnny Knows" is in many ways an unauthorized dramatization of Martha Wolfenstein's groundbreaking essay "Fun Morality," published two years before. Wolfenstein helped to popularize psychoanalysis in America, particularly regarding the emotional lives of children.[23] The prewar paradigm, she argues, saw the relations between parents and children primarily in terms of discipline and authority; the postwar model saw parent–child relations increasingly in terms of pleasure and play. The prewar paradigm stressed the importance of forming necessary habits for productive life; the postwar paradigm sought to limit inhibitions upon basic impulses and desires. Wolfenstein traces the changing advice offered to parents by the Children's Bureau of the United States Department of Labor. The "fun morality," Wolfenstein argues, was partially a response to the expansion of the consumer marketplace and the prospect of suburban affluence: "Instead of feeling guilty for having too much fun, one is inclined to feel ashamed if one does not have enough. Boundaries formerly maintained between play and work break down."[24] The transition from a wartime economy based on heightened production and rationing to a booming peacetime economy depended on the expansion of consumption, creating jobs around production for domestic use.

"Fun Morality" first appeared in the book Wolfenstein and Margaret Mead coedited in 1955, *Childhood in Contemporary Cultures*. The book was a project of the Columbia University Research Seminar on Contemporary Cultures that Margaret Mead ran with Ruth Benedict. For Mead and Wolfenstein, reliance on advice literature said much about the dynamic nature of contemporary American culture:

> In traditional cultures, where the same pattern is repeated from generation to generation, the elders are authorities in these matters. But in a changing culture, the elders lose their infallibility. American parents, for instance, do not expect to bring up their children in the way they

were brought up, any more than they would want to live in the house in which they were raised or to drive around in the family car of their childhood. They hope to bring up their children better than they were brought up themselves. For guidance in this undertaking, they turn to the contemporary expert, the pediatrician or family doctor, and to the writings of doctors, psychologists, teachers, and the increasing number of specialists in parent education.[25]

As books became cheaper and thus more disposable with the postwar rise of paperback publishing, parent guides and children's books could be gifted at baby showers, allowing more rapid and far-reaching shifts in the popular understanding of child psychology. The baby boom was similarly beneficial to the publishers of children's books, such as Little Golden Books, who reported that their sales increased to over four times the prewar level.[26] Advice books provide "an ideal of what the child should become; recommended means of achieving this ideal; and cautionary stories of what may happen from taking the wrong course, the negative counterpart of the ideal, the picture of what it is feared the child might become."[27]

By the late 1940s, Mead had shifted her attention from Samoa and her other international field sites toward understanding the American family. As Mead explains, "The anthropologist's one special area of competence is the ability to think about a whole society and everything in it.... We cannot know the details of each facet of our complex culture, but we can keep our eyes on the way the different facets are related one to another."[28] She was incredibly prolific across the next few decades—not only writing a regular column for *Redbook*, where she offered her insights on many contemporary trends, but also writing extensively for *Parents*, *TV Guide*, and other popular periodicals. She wrote a book on raising creative children for the US Children's Bureau and collaborated with photographer Ken Heyman on *Family*, a best-selling photo book looking comparatively at families around the world. In a July 1963 *Redbook* article, she explained her commitment to being a public intellectual:

> I do this because I believe that in a democracy it is essential for the layman to understand the gist of the work being done in our highly compartmentalized academic disciplines. This is particularly so in the social

sciences, where it is essential that public understanding keeps in step with the increased understanding of the social scientist. I believe that almost any idea can be stated simply enough so that it is intelligible to laymen and that if one cannot state a matter clearly enough so that even an intelligent 12-year-old can understand it, one should remain within the cloistered walls of the university and laboratory until one gets a better grasp of one's subject matter.... I have made it a practice to try to alter the climate of opinion so that new ideas may bud and flower.[29]

*Redbook* is central to this study, but since it stopped print publication in 2019, it may be less familiar to readers now. Starting in 1903, *Redbook* was a traditional women's magazine, but in the 1960s and early 1970s, editors such as Robert Stein and Sy Chassler ensured that it was also a magazine where leading thinkers shared their ideas with popular audiences. At the time Mead, Benjamin Spock, and others were regular contributors, the magazine's circulation was roughly three million each month. For many scholars interested in her anthropological career, Mead's writing for parents gets little notice, often viewed as a digression from more scholarly pursuits, rather than at the heart of her postwar project as her own experiences as a mother drew her focus in this direction.

The Margaret Mead Papers at the Library of Congress contain several pages of Mead's field notes (dated July 30, 1940) recording the health of her daughter Mary Catherine Bateson, who had been born on December 8, 1939:

> One lower tooth, arrived without the teething being noticeable, and gum swollen for another accompanied by a good deal of rubbing her gums with hard objects and on hard objects.
>
> Bowels: 3 movements a day and very even in consistency.
>
> Sleep: about half the nights she has been wakeful, waking up about every hour crying and waking with a wail in the morning. Other half of the time, but not a regular every other night alternation, sleeps 11 hours and wakes in a good humor....
>
> The only things I don't like are this growing flabbiness and the pimples which worry her a little and are very unsightly, so worry her nurse. I plan to start final weaning in the middle of August, and have her completely weaned by the middle of September.[30]

Her pediatrician, Benjamin Spock, makes detailed suggestions but concludes, "To this doctor she sounds as if she was doing wonderfully. Have a good time. Sincerely Ben."

Mary Catherine Bateson later wrote a memoir of her childhood, *With a Daughter's Eye*: "She [Mead] would record the hours at which I demanded feeding and then, by analyzing those times, construct a schedule from the order imminent in my own body's rhythms which would make the process predictable enough so she could schedule her classes and meetings and know when she should be home to feed me."[31] She suggests that these notes "do not really belong to me, are not private records," but rather part of her mother's research.[32] The willingness to talk in concrete and material language about breast milk and poop was part of the permissive paradigm's breakthrough, reflecting a Freudian conception of sexuality and a new commitment to raising children who would be less inhibited about their bodies. Bateson makes an interesting, if unlikely, claim that she was "the first breast-fed and 'self demand' baby he [Spock] had encountered." Spock's book cites anthropological insights in his own effort to justify these choices so he may have learned such practices from Mead, but there are other plausible alternative sources suggesting he could have encountered this concept of feeding on demand earlier. Regardless, Bateson writes: "Spock was blessedly relaxed about letting my mother do as she wanted, abandoning the fixed schedules that were regarded as essential to health, but he seems to have been only partially aware of the innovation taking place in front of his eyes."[33]

Mead and others in her circle (Martha Wolfenstein, Edith Cobb, Rhoda Métraux, David Reisman, and Ken Heyman among them) helped to map key debates in the permissive era—about the structure of the family, the nature of suburban communities, children's creativity and their need for access to outdoor space, how to prepare children to live in a more diverse society, young people's perceptions of science, and so much more. *Childhood in Contemporary Cultures* represented a culmination of this research and will be referred to often here. Such circles were communities of people working together toward common interests, exchanging ideas, influencing each other's work, and they often functioned as conduits between the worlds of scholarship and cultural production, places where artists and storytellers might be informed by larger discourses about childhood and parenting.

American family life, Mead argued, had been shaped by several decades of disruption. First, there had been the immigrants who came to America in the late nineteenth and early twentieth centuries; their children had rejected old-world traditions to become more American. There were also the dislocations felt by families, like my own, that had moved to the city from the country, shifting from agriculture-based to industrial lifestyles. Then there was the generation that had postponed starting a family during the Depression and the war. Consequently, baby-boom parents had few memories of what the typical American family had looked like before. Mead wrote in November 1945: "This leaves two courses open to them, either to fashion a pattern out of partial remembrance . . . or to make a new pattern for themselves altogether."[34] What will happen, Mead asks, "if the young people of this generation realize that the world is theirs for the making, that because of the break between peace and war, they can—if they wish—reject the whole model?"[35] Developing this new model will require intentionality. Otherwise, she fears:

> It is this younger group who will be most lost, most groping, most likely to take short cuts and easy solutions, most likely to become a "lost generation." The only way in which this can be prevented is to help these young people think it through, give them a chance to discuss the whole problem, to realize why they are at sea, to talk over the kind of life their elder brothers and sisters have been living, to label those aspects of it which don't belong in *their* lives now. . . . There is no older generation who can give these models to them. The most we can do is to help them find them themselves.[36]

Mead calls upon "the symbol-makers, the writers, the artists, the radio broadcasters and the filmmakers" to be "enlisted" into producing new narratives—the shared designs out of which the postwar family would be constructed.[37] Mead had enormous sympathy for the mothers who, due to suburbanization and the restructuring of the American family, had less access to help from their own mothers than previous generations had. Mead wrote poignantly of "the isolated, exposed position of two very young parents attempting to rear several children all by themselves with no one to advise and comfort, no one to take over in emergencies, no one to rely on in the small day-by-day details of living."[38]

Throughout *Where the Wild Things Were*, I will situate some of the era's most popular children's fictions in relation to the debates around child development and psychology that preoccupied my parents' generation, seeing the first as implicitly—and, in some cases, explicitly—addressing the concerns of the latter. At times, there was direct contact between child-rearing advocates and children's media-makers: they shared the same publications; they worked in the same organizations; and, sometimes, the storytellers actively responded to pedagogical insights. But keep in mind the various agents who process such works between their site of creation and their site of reception. Margaret Mead makes a similar point in her 1955 book *Childhood in Contemporary Cultures*, where she describes "Modern Children's Stories," a project to create a children's book to reflect insights from the Child Study movement:

> It became increasingly clear that, after all, five-year-old children don't buy books and that the children's needs or preferences had to be mediated by layers of other people—mothers, fathers, grandmothers, aunts, librarians, publishers, bookstore buyers, experts—all of whom had a full quota of fears and hope and a much more substantial quota of firmly entrenched values and prejudices than the children for whom the story had been designed.... The cultural process by which artists and writers, sensitive to changing values, prefigure those values in their work and the guardians of public taste and morals accept and reject what they produce proved to be too complex and sensitive for such self-conscious activity.[39]

This is what Jacqueline Rose described as the "impossibility" of children's fiction.[40] Such works tell us far more about adults, their values, their aspirations, their emotional needs, than about children's actual experiences.[41] In many cases, the authors were veterans settling down and raising their children according to Spock and thus absorbing these ideas as any other adult in their culture would. Just as child-rearing advice negotiated the transition from prewar to postwar paradigms, the creators of children's fiction similarly negotiated around the assumptions of gatekeepers, and the biases and tastes of parents and grandparents. Consequently, residual elements were at play in even the most progressive children's texts—some nostalgic tug toward earlier versions of parenting. At the same time, these works made it through all of those filters and into many American households, showing some "fit" with the values with which parents were raising their children. *Childhood in Contemporary Cultures* explains: "Songs and stories, pictures, dances, and theatrical shows are among the gifts which a child may receive from his culture."[42] These works are ways the culture transmits its values, telling children how adults view them, how they are meant to behave, what risks and opportunities the world offers them, and how they should feel about their circumstances. These "gifts" in many cases are literal—things adults offer children as treats or rewards for being good. Often, adults consume such stories along with their children—reading them aloud, sometimes acting them out.

## Parenting in Transition

Following Mead and Wolfenstein's example, my research depends on a series of juxtapositions between advice literature that articulates underlying theories and children's fictions that often dramatize the challenges of raising independently minded children. These juxtapositions are meant to be suggestive, showing parallels across works aimed at children and adults. This juxtaposition does not imply direct causality since it would be hard to establish that the writers, artists, and media-makers were directly influenced by these specific experts. Rather, both genres participate in larger conversations among the parents of the baby-boom generation.

Reformulating family life was a gradual transition rather than the dramatic change often implied by Wolfenstein's prewar and postwar distinction. Certainly, major events—the Depression, the war, the space race, and others—had consequences for family life, promoting new concepts, questioning established wisdom, and shifting the metaphors through which parenting was discussed. For example, the Depression made questions of how children managed money more urgent, while the war forced consideration of violent play on the one hand and patriotism and democracy on the other. That said, the ideas that shaped my generation were a composite of thinking about childhood assembled across several decades. On my family bookshelves, there were some books handed down from other family members as they entered childbearing years, while other books repackaged and republished essays that had been written over a decade earlier, meaning that few parents were totally up-to-date on the latest trends.

For a more fluid perspective on the permissive paradigm, consider Katherine M. Wolf's 1953 book *The Controversial Problem of Discipline*. Her account suggests that some permissive ideas were embraced at least by the elite classes during the prewar period:

> Before the nineteen twenties, few parents and educators questioned the thesis that the developing being has to be taught to conform with the requirements of society, and that such teaching has to be reinforced by what we know as punishment and reward.... Then came a revolution, initiated by psychiatrists, psychologists and educators.... Misinterpreting, or perhaps only half understanding, the real meaning of progressive education, many parents, doctors and educators felt an increasing sense of guilt if they imposed their demands on children.[43]

Wolf captures the whiplash some parents felt as one set of norms displaced another. She describes her own discomfort with some potential outcomes of a more permissive approach:

> Aggression was permitted since it was thought to represent the free acting-out of the child's personality.... In many homes the furniture was soiled and broken, the books torn to pieces.... Parents revolted, feeling that they had some right to share their homes with their children. Their revolt never reached the printed page, however, because they felt guilty about their protest and usually expressed it in vehement scolding or in spanking for minor misdemeanors rather than in theoretical statements.[44]

As Wolf notes, parents were all over the map: "If we are asked to talk about the discipline problem, we are bewildered, first because we cannot judge in advance the attitude of the audience we face; it may be still, or already, 'disciplinarian'; already, or still 'progressive.'"[45]

This book draws inspiration from Norbert Elias's *The History of Manners* (1982), which uses etiquette books from the Middle Ages to map shifting "thresholds of shame" around the body. Elias traces prescriptions regarding nudity and bodily function, cleanliness and especially table manners—many of the same issues that are addressed in the child-rearing guides. Elias did not read these manners books as reflecting actual practices, which, in any case, are difficult if not impossible to reconstruct centuries later. Rather, he saw these authors as seeking to shape behavior and anticipate shifts in norms before they occur. By looking comparatively, he observes how humans internalize certain standards: where an actual prohibition needs to be expressed, it suggests the possibility, even the likelihood, that this norm may be violated.

Postwar advice literature never modeled a household that was permissive in any absolute sense. Rather, there were shifting zones of permission, with parents negotiating between their own expectations and community standards. Mead and Wolfenstein (1954) note that postwar parents "provide opportunities for freedom, carelessness and spontaneity and for control and neatness in the same house, with differential rules for the living-room, playroom, bathroom, front and back hall."[46] Every boomer knew there were certain things you couldn't do in front of company, even if they were otherwise normal in the family. And, because parents were trying to raise their children differently, there were often contradictions between their learned, conscious choices and their unguarded reactions. As Spock wrote in 1962: "One of the commonest and most frustrating aspects of human nature is that what our parents did to us in childhood that made us cross we have a way of doing to our own children in turn—even though we disapprove of it."[47]

All of these contradictions and inconsistencies reflected the transitional status of new ideas, being dispersed and absorbed at different rates and understood to different degrees by different parents. Spock described in 1962 how these shifts resulted in conflicts:

> Now we ought to stop and admit that there have been violent changes in child-care teaching in the past twenty years. It requires extraordinary flexibility on the part of a grandmother to be able to accept them, to be able to stifle her anxiety about them. The grandmother was probably taught, when she was raising her children, that to feed a baby off schedule caused indigestion, diarrhea, and spoiling, that regularity of the bowels was a cornerstone of health and that early rigorous toilet training would foster this. But now the grandmother is suddenly expected to believe that

flexibility in feeding schedule is not only permissible but desirable . . . that toilet training should not be imposed against the child's will. It's hard to make these changes sound drastic to a young mother of today who is so familiar with them. To be able to sympathize with the alarm of a grandmother she would have to imagine some fantastic new advice such as to feed her newborn baby fried pork or to bathe him in cold water![48]

Spock stresses that parents are going to be awkward and tense if they break too much with their own comfort zones, so much of his advice is flexible enough to be applied with varying degrees of license, depending on the family.

Read closely, these parenting guides hint at the gaps between the advice as written and the ways it might have been applied. Spock describes parents who he felt pushed permissiveness too far:

> Such parents often quote theories about the importance of self-expression and individuality, the unwholesome effects of repression. When such cases get completely out of hand and are referred to a child-guidance clinic, it often turns out that the parents were so properly brought up that they never dared act, speak or even think aggressively. When they come to have a child of their own, they unconsciously enjoy letting him express the impoliteness, selfishness and aggressiveness which they had to suppress so completely in themselves. This blinds them to the fact that the behavior is offensive to others and disturbing to the child.[49]

All of this allows us to observe the process of cultural negotiation Raymond Williams described as the culture works through new ways of seeing the world, absorbing what it can, rejecting what doesn't fit.

## "You've Got to Be Carefully Taught": The Whiteness of Permissive Culture

These transitions in ideas about childcare can be traced back to the origins of the Child Study movement in the early twentieth century; how its legacy informs the permissive imagination is the central focus of chapter 2. Here, I consider one particular outgrowth of the Progressive Era—the ways that the permissive imagination was founded on certain assumptions surrounding whiteness that imperfectly fit the realities of Black America. The initial focus of Child Study was on reforming the conditions that impacted the lives of low-income, immigrant, and minority children, especially those living in urban environments. Increasingly, the focus shifted toward the raising of "normal" children, in other words, white, middle-class children. Normality was also defined through the norms of child development shaped by observational work. Since the early 1930s, Yale University's Arnold Gesell had been a leading voice promoting scientifically grounded child management; he was to childhood what Masters and Johnson were to human sexuality. Returning to a tradition of surveys begun by his teacher, G. Stanley Hall, Gesell interviewed thousands of American parents, recording each stage of their children's development and publishing encyclopedic works mapping children's biological and cognitive development. Working with Francis Ilg, Gesell made this data more readily available to postwar parents, hoping to lower stress by helping them to understand their child's individualized development in comparison with others in their cohort. Martha Weinman Lear, a critic of permissive parenting, wryly notes that many parents used such norms as competitive benchmarks.[50] Black children were underrepresented in this research, which tended to foreground white, middle-class practices and perspectives. We might see this conflation of "normal" with whiteness as perhaps the original sin of the Child Study movement.[51]

Advice writers had little to say directly about Black childhoods, sometimes expressing discomfort about knowing how to speak to the realities of Black lives. But they did sometimes address concerns about whether white children were being taught to hate people of different races and ethnicities.[52] A book responding to parents' questions about family life in wartime confronted this query:

> Until recent events forced us into a horrible dilemma, my husband and I believed and taught our children that hate and war were the most destructive forces on earth. We taught them also to respect and believe in the reasonableness of human beings of all races and nationalities. Now there is an orgy of hate let loose. I believe my older children can keep their balance, but I dread the effect on the little ones. Must even the babies hate?[53]

While some animosity toward the enemy was a consequence of the war, the Child Study Association of America advised: "The best thing we can do is to help our children to be fair to others of enemy alien descent with whom they come in contact and who are certainly not responsible for this war. If they really love justice they will not tolerate ostracizing the classmate whose parents come from Germany, or ridiculing Japanese children in their community, or stealing fruit from the corner grocer whose name and accent are Italian."[54] As the war ended, the focus expanded to include not simply people of other nations but also people of diverse races living in the United States. The novelist Pearl S. Buck (1952) explained: "It is the duty of every parent and teacher to see that in our own community the children are made aware of the problem of race and to pass on, not prejudices, but freedom of choice for the new generation to deal with what in their time may be a choice that will result either in world harmony or the greatest and most horrible war the human race has yet seen."[55]

These wartime writers saw helping their own children to deal fairly with people of other races as part of their patriotic duty. As Buck reminds her readers, "Do not forget that Nazism had as twin doctrines the false ideas that one race is superior to another and that the male is superior to the female. Both of these notions are at the root of tyranny in society."[56] And both, Buck felt, need to be resolved to prevent future race wars.

In *Glass House of Prejudice* (1946), Dorothy W. Baruch challenged readers to confront their own prejudices to better prepare their children to live in a more diverse society. Baruch was the founder and director of the Gramercy Cooperative Nursery School. In the late 1920s, she directed the parent-education department at the National Council of Jewish Women. For much of her career, Baruch ran a private practice treating children with psychological issues. Between 1939 and 1953, she published eight books on child psychology, education, and family life. Baruch translated the wartime struggle against fascism into a model of democratic parenting.

*In Glass House of Prejudice,* Baruch notes that fascists encouraged American isolationism through tapping racial prejudices, dividing the population against itself and diminishing concerns for the plight of European Jews: "Why, as the hate messages flew across America, were they lifted in such eager hands? Unless they were in some fashion welcome, would they have been so closely embraced?"⁵⁷ She asks: "Did we expect to rescue the people of other countries from intolerance and persecution and to disregard what is happening to millions in our own country? Why have we allowed the break between Americans of different races to widen so that whole masses of people have come to feel that they are unwanted and they do not essentially belong?"⁵⁸

Such attitudes, she concluded, had been taught, and so a concerted effort might ensure that the new generation were taught to embrace the richness of American culture. Racism took root as children worked through their anger and frustrations over ways they had been unfairly treated, directing rage outward against those different from themselves, rather than inward, toward family members who often sparked those feelings. As the 1949 musical *South Pacific* recounted:

> It's not born in you.
> It happens after you are born.
> You've got to be carefully taught to hate and fear....
> You've got to be taught to be afraid of people
> whose eyes are oddly made
> and people whose skin is a different shade.

Consider how the song sees racism as a set of "learned" cultural prejudices mapped onto biological differences.⁵⁹ Following this same logic, Baruch concludes, "If children could grow up learning to handle their hostile emotions and having guidance in doing so all along the way, the vicious circle of hatred could be diminished even in one generation."⁶⁰

Baruch shares the story of a classroom of ten-year-olds that "suddenly went wild" when the teacher left the room, chanting that one little boy, Jerry, was a "dirty jew." Confronting the class, the teacher suggests that the children seemed to be feeling "very, very mean" and needed to find a way to share those feelings:

> They decided they wanted to draw about it. Before they started, the teacher assured them that they could make their pictures show mean feelings coming out in any way they liked. Some drew pictures of cannons shooting men to pieces. Others drew pictures of people setting fire to houses. One boy drew a man and a woman and a baby with nooses

around their necks.... When they were through with the drawings, the children crowded into small groups, looking at the different pictures. The teacher smiled to herself when she noticed two of the boys who had been among Jerry's worst persecutors. Their arms were now around his shoulders. They were intimately pursuing the friendship that they had denied before.[61]

Baruch's account expresses the support, at least among progressive educators, for the project of promoting "racial harmony," a phrase blurring racial and ethnic distinctions in its application.

Children's book writers in the immediate postwar era similarly sought a more accepting society. Consider, for example, *In Henry's Backyard*.[62] Columbia University anthropologists Ruth Benedict (Mead's mentor) and Gene Weltfish had written a pamphlet, *The Races of Mankind* (1943), to help debunk myths that had been spread by fascists overseas and racists at home.[63] In 1945, United Productions of America (UPA) produced an animated short based on the pamphlet, and in 1948 a children's book based on the original text and illustrated with pictures from the film was released. Henry, the story's protagonist, dreams that "the whole world became so small that it fit nicely into his own backyard and all sorts of odd people had become his neighbors." Henry needs to overcome his fears as he confronts such cultural and racial differences: "Then suddenly he felt... an ugly sort of tug... that stopped him. It was his Green Devil, who lived inside him. It had slithered... out... of him. And it whispered, 'don't speak to these people, Henry! You won't like them. They're DIFFERENT!'"[64] The book helps Henry—and the reader—overcome their prejudices: "We're not born haters.... We've only got one world and we're all in it."[65]

Such direct representations of racism, or for that matter, racial difference would become less and less common the deeper we move into the 1950s. Postwar storytellers generally avoided the negative racial stereotypes found all too commonly in the 1930s and 1940s. But they frequently responded by constructing an all-white world or by moving into the realm of allegory. In a nuanced, multilayered analysis, Philip Nel argues that children's book authors had minds like sponges, which absorbed, sometimes unconsciously, influences from all directions. He argues that *The Cat in the Hat*, for example, might be described as "mixed race" because its origins lay in both white and Black culture (including Black-faced minstrelsy), that as a consequence it may be hard to see some of the stereotypical representations upon which it was built, and it may generate contradictory or ambivalent feelings about race as we contemplate the presence of this trickster character in a white household.⁶⁶

It was easier to avoid representing minoritized children than to construct alternative framings. Consider, for example, the case of P. D. Eastman, one of the animators who worked on *The Races of Man*. Eastman had served in the US Signal Corps during the war, working on the Private Snafu training films under Theodor Geisel, better known today as Dr. Seuss. Eastman also collaborated with Geisel as a scriptwriter and storyboard artist on *Gerald McBoing-Boing*. And in the early 1960s, Geisel invited Eastman to contribute to his Beginner Books series. Eastman is today best known for his picture books, *Go Dog Go* (1961) and *Are You My Mother?* (1960).⁶⁷

At the risk of overreading a simple fable, *Are You My Mother?* depicts a baby bird's first encounter with difference, not the racial difference *In Henry's Backyard* depicted, but rather the differences between species. As the baby bird is about to hatch, its mother departs in search of food, leaving the infant to confront the world on his own. The newborn asks each new creature he encounters whether they are its mother. Across the book, the baby bird again and again discovers places where he does not belong: "The kitten was not his mother. The hen was not his mother. The dog was not his mother. . . ." In the end, a giant steam shovel—the SNORT!—returns him to the loving care of his own mother. The book is a reassuring story suggesting that everyone has a loving mother and that children do not necessarily notice the differences that matter to adults. But it is also a story where birds of a feather flock together. I do not mean to suggest that *Are You My Mother?* is a racist work. If anything, it tries to be "color-blind" by removing the story from the human realm altogether, but in the context of a society struggling with segregation, it stresses hominess, comfort, and familiarity. In shifting from cultural categories such as race to biological categories such as those distinguishing animal species, Eastman made such distinctions seem more natural and logical.

For most of the period, children's fictions were segregated just as decisively as children's lives were, the majority of the child-rearing advice books assumed a white middle-class reader, and the majority of children's films and programs had an all-white cast. Fewer Black parents were raising their children according to Dr. Spock. They could not afford the risks—misbehaving Black boys might have lethal encounters with cops. Permissiveness constituted a form of white privilege, no matter how much these authors might have wished otherwise. Their normalization of whiteness, their silence about racism, made children's fictions complicit in America's inequalities.

# 2

## The Understanding Angel

*The Child Study Movement and Empathetic Engagement*

Martha Wolfenstein perceived a dramatic shift in attitude toward children before and after the Second World War. Many accounts, then and now, contrast the behaviorism of John Watson and the humanism of Benjamin Spock. Rick Caulfield states it bluntly: "Until the publication of Spock's book, parenting experts, such as John B. Watson, advocated strict adherence to rigid schedules in rearing infants and children."[1] The contrasting perspectives of Watson and Spock are often explained in terms of a growing discomfort with more authoritarian structures and a desire for a more child-centered approach. Those accounts are not totally wrong; something qualitatively different was happening. As we saw in my analysis of *Mary Poppins*, the distinction between prewar and postwar models is a useful heuristic for mapping differences in attitudes and approaches across time. But this transition was messier and more prolonged than suggested.

Focusing exclusively on male researchers has the effect of erasing women who may have been more influential in shaping these ideas than most prior accounts have suggested. In *Childhood in Changing Cultures*, Margaret Mead noted the significant number of women engaged in Child Study:

> Women's traditional preoccupation with young children made the study of children a natural choice, and there is also reason to believe that the study of children may be easier—in the present generation of research workers—for women than for men. Although we are now entering a new era in which fathers take a great deal of care of young children, the present working generation grew up in a period when childcare was women's work. For men who are studying infants and young children, if they are not comfortable in a temporary identification with a woman's role, the

> alternative route to understanding is remembering their own childhood feelings and experiences. Women investigators need not take this arduous route but, instead, can identify easily with the remembered roles of mother, grandmother, nurse, and primary teacher, as they spend hours working with, or thinking about, young children.[2]

Mead acknowledges that the field of Child Study had been driven by women. Yet, those women have been written out of more recent accounts, not simply because of patriarchal norms that devalue women's contributions more generally, but also because acknowledging them would get in the way, ironically, of a feminist narrative that sees the liberation of women from male experts as central to second-wave feminism. This response is understandable given what Shari L. Thurer says about how Spock shifted popular understanding of infants and children:

> Mother's job was to respond to the baby's emotional needs (in effect to read the baby's mind), gratify its wants, tolerate its regressions, stimulate its cognitive development, and above all, to feel personally fulfilled in carrying this out.... Now that the infant dictated its demands, the mother's routine was determined by those requirements.... Rather than pursue her own ends in life, she was to maneuver, pretend, and manipulate so that her child would become "well-adjusted."[3]

Spock and the other childcare writers were held responsible for women's domestic containment at a moment when feminists were insisting on their right to work outside the home and calling for better childcare options as part of the support system they needed. Missing from this account is the reality that many in the Child Study movement were themselves women's rights advocates, whose work anticipated key elements in Spock's thinking. This chapter will focus on several generations of such women—chief among them Dorothy Canfield Fisher, Sidonie Matsner Gruenberg, Josette Frank, and Anna W. M. Wolf. Each drew on their own experiences as mothers and their close observation of children to question the established wisdom about parenting and in the process, lay the foundation for the permissive paradigm. These women traveled in the same circles, appeared in the same publications, coedited books and otherwise influenced each other's work, so while concerns and terminology shifted over the decades, there was also a strong throughline across their writings. Underpinning these ideas was the sense that children's interests and the rights of women were closely aligned. The Child Study movement would translate research breakthroughs, such as those made by Gesell and his associates, into a larger philosophical system, an analytic method, and an affective structure. Historian Kathleen W. Jones reports:

> These forward-looking scientists and practitioners declared that human activity was driven by universal needs, that childhood was marked by incremental stages of development, with personality patterns formed in youth and displayed throughout life, and that motives or explanations for behavior lay hidden beneath the surface manifestations of decision making.... Where child developmentalists saw the child as a series of norms to be investigated through academic research, child guiders saw the child as a problem to be solved through psychological intervention.[4]

This chapter will consider the Child Study movement as an important predecessor of the permissive paradigm, one that encouraged parents toward empathetic engagement with their children and thus promoted the concept of a child-centered household. We will start with the works (both fiction and nonfiction) of Dorothy Canfield Fisher, who was an important figure in introducing Montessori methods to Americans and a founding figure in the Child Study movement. I will map the movement, its parent-education efforts, its ideas about children's emotional life, and its approach to media consumption. Then, I will apply these concepts to two works of the immediate postwar period—Charles Tazewell's book *The Littlest Angel*, published in 1946, and Joseph Losey's feature film *The Boy with Green Hair*, released in 1948, both signaling the shifts that immediately followed the Second World War. Both structure their drama around adult attempts to better understand and address the problems of boys who somehow are estranged from their social environment. In other words, they dramatize the practices associated with Child Study but apply them to fantastical circumstances—a nonconforming angel and a boy whose hair changes color.

## Dorothy Canfield Fisher's *The Home-Maker* (1924)

Stephen, the youngest son in Dorothy Canfield Fisher's novel *The Home-Maker* (1924), was described as "a sober-faced little boy in clean gingham rompers, with a dingy Teddy-bear in his arms," a boy known for his refusal to obey adults.[5] The first thing we learn about Stephen is that his Teddy helped to quell his outbursts: "Days when he had been punished and then shut, screaming furiously, into the bedroom to 'cry it out,' he had gone about blindly feeling for Teddy through his tears, and, exhausted by his shrieking and kicking and anger, had often fallen asleep on the floor, Teddy in his arms, exercising that mystic power of consolation."[6]

*The Home-Maker* is often discussed in terms of its adult narrative: a woman works, and her husband stays home after an accident leaves him crippled; they both discover that they are happier outside traditional gender roles. The wife, Eva, advances rapidly through the ranks at the local department store, while her stay-home husband, Lester, forges new insights into child development. The novel ends with the threat that his improving health might force the couple back into gender conformity. Yet, in an October 1924 interview, Fisher stated that her novel was less interested in women's rights than in children's rights.[7] The book contrasts the mother's approach of letting children "cry it out" and the father's efforts to address their emotional needs.

Born in 1879 in Lawrence, Kansas, Fisher was a key figure in educational reform, best known for helping to popularize the works of Maria Montessori in the United States.[8] Fisher's writings were an extension of her lifetime serving on the state school board of Vermont and working on behalf of blind WWI veterans, adult education, and prison reform, among other causes. We can draw direct links between her advice books—specifically, *A Montessori Mother* (1912) and *Mothers and Children* (1914)—and her fictional account of a "normal" family in crisis. *The Home-maker*, like the nonfiction works, targeted adult readers, mostly women.

In Fisher's novel, Eva understands her parenting primarily in terms of tending to physical health, hygiene, and nutrition, while remaining so focused on the housework that she has no time for her children's emotional needs:

> What was her life? A hateful round of housework, which, hurry as she might, was never done.... No rest from the constant friction over the children's carelessness and forgetfulness and childishness. How she hated childishness!... Sometimes, in black moments like this, it seemed to her that she had such *strange* children, not like other people's, easy to understand and manage, strong, normal children.... What could you do for a child who *wanted* to be bad, and told you so in a loud scream?[9]

Eva doesn't understand what causes her son's outbursts and she cannot grasp why he resists her plans to wash his "germ-ridden" Teddy. The mother hides the bear without the boy's permission. Stephen reaches out to his father but gets interrupted by the mother's scolding. So, for the first few chapters, Stephen has no allies in what his father imagines to have been his "fierce struggles against forces stronger than he."[10] Fisher describes Stephen's horror when another mother shows Eve the bear she has washed, "that hideous, pitiable, tragic wreck ... the dreadful remains" she held by "one limp, lumpy arm."[11] Eva sees toys as distractions while she performs her housework. For the boy, the bear lives in his imagination.

When his dad asks him about Teddy, Stephen is overwhelmed that his father took the time to hear the boy's perspective, and Lester

> was horrified to see Stephen reduced so low. He was more horrified at the position in which he found himself, absolute arbiter over another human being, a being which had no recourse, no appeal from his decisions.... [He was] shamed to the core by Stephen's helpless dependence on his whim, a dependence of which Stephen was so tragically aware, all his stern bulwarks of anger and resistance broken down by the extremity of his fear—fear for what he loved![12]

The father's reassuring response that nothing would happen to the bear without the boy's permission represents the turning point in their relationship.

In *Mothers and Children* (1914), Fisher mounts a critique of "autocratic" parenting, the effort to "master" the child rather than helping children "master" their emotions. Fisher advocates that children and adults respect each other's needs. She promoted providing children with their own space—a "rough-and-tumble sanctuary" where "the mother's tendency towards adult neatness and order" will be suspended to allow them freedom to make their own choices: "It can be made clear to them that they have no more right to invade the living-room with a troop of playmates and to start a game of tag there, innocent as is that amusement, than their elders have to go into the children's sanctum to try to read or sleep off a headache."[13]

Similarly, in *A Montessori Mother*, Fisher (1912) argues that just as the idea that women might be entitled to "personal liberty" was "once" viewed by men as "dynamite under the foundations of society," then "you can imagine how startling and thrilling is the first glimpse of its application to children."[14] In 1907, the Italian physician and educator Maria Montessori had opened her first Casa dei Bambini, a school for working-class children, designed to reflect her progressive views on education. By the time Fisher visited Montessori to see the Casa in action and shared her observations with American mothers, word of Montessori's remarkable successes had spread. The first US Montessori school opened in Tarrytown, New York, in 1911, with the financial support of Alexander Graham Bell. Fisher saw Montessori schools as modeling an educational practice suited to a democratic society and translated those same principles into advice for how to run the ideal home. Parents, she said, should grant children "as full a measure of liberty as possible, exercising our utmost ingenuity to make the family life an enlightened democracy."[15] Montessori's schools depended on children's "natural instincts" to ensure good behavior, creating no "unnecessary rules." Returning to parallels between the struggles for women's rights and her early advocacy of children's rights, she warns that her female readers should not treat their children as men treat them, "with patronizing, enfeebling protection" but rather allow children room to make—and learn from—mistakes.[16] Montessori felt that an "anthropological analysis" of the child should precede any formal education: "Children must be free to develop in the best way possible according to the potentiality of their life."[17]

Across *The Home-Maker*, the father seeks innovative solutions to common conflicts, with insights emerging from watching how his children behaved with minimal adult regulation: "We have executive sessions, the children and I, to figure out our ways and means to cope with life and not get beaten by small details."[18] Lester's "executive sessions" anticipate later ideas such as family councils. One such solution involved putting old newspapers on the floor, allowing children to make messes, which can be cleaned up without fuss and bother. Lester abandons demands for tidiness, not allowing the neighborhood to police his choices about how to manage his children. Fisher, similarly, urges mothers to reject unreasonable domestic expectations if meeting them comes at the expense of nurturing children's emotional needs: "The children can go with holes in their stockings, and with uncombed hair; the house can be unswept, the beds unmade. . . . Any of the dreadful things we usually think of as 'impossible' are infinitely better for the children's moral health . . . than a mother constantly scolding . . . or repressing unjustly the innocent activities of her children."[19]

By contrast, the father and his daughter, Helen, figure out the best way to crack an egg, making a mess but laughing the whole time. In the process, the father learns about the daughter's desire for self-expression and pride in her developing womanhood. Lowering such standards frees the father to apply his mind to identifying the social and emotional causes of the children's problems and developing pragmatic solutions: "Now for months he had the opportunity for continuous observation, he perceived that there was nothing so darkly inexplicable, after all, nothing that resisted a patient, resourceful attempt to follow up those loose ends and straighten out some of the knots. Even in the tragic tangle of Stephen's strange little nature, Lester felt he had begun to find his way."[20] The father approaches each child differently, protecting Stephen's Teddy, speaking with Helen about her creative writing, and giving the other son, Henry, a puppy.

In *Mothers and Children*, Fisher (1914) notes how rarely the tools of child analysis were applied in parenting practices: "Do we parents, as a rule, make any definite efforts to see what sort of children we have before we begin to try to influence them? . . . Do we face honestly the facts of the case, which are that we are presented with a brand-new human being, different from every other human being who has ever lived, and that our job is to somehow guess at the treatment that is best for him?"[21]

Instead of studying the particular child, Fisher argues, most parents imagine the perfect child and discipline away any trait not resembling that ideal.

Lester concludes that no nanny would be able to give the children the focused attention of a loving parent: "He thought of how he used his close hourly contact with them as a means of looking into their hearts and minds; how he used the work-in-common with them as a scientist conducts an experiment station to accumulate data . . . so that his decisions might be just and farsighted as well as loving."[22] Fisher argues that the more discipline-centered approaches had not succeeded in making children "run like clockwork" for the simple reason that "they are not clocks, but human beings."[23] Parents should remind themselves that "children are not little fierce wild animals to be tamed and subjected as tigers and hyenas are kept in subjection" and that they face "the same inherited bad tendencies, passions and desires which cloud our own lives."[24]

Applying techniques of child analysis, Fisher pays attention to the nuances of how her child characters behave. This attention to their inner lives manifests during an extended sequence describing Stephen's exhausting efforts to master an eggbeater. In *A Montessori Mother*, she writes that the kitchen is for the small child "a veritable treasure-house of Montessori apparatus," if children were only freed to engage with them as they wanted;[25] she speaks of "the creative rapture to be evolved from a lump of dough or a fumbling attempt to fathom the mysterious inwardness of a Dover eggbeater."[26] In *The Home-Maker*, Fisher traces the external signs of the boy's shifting emotional responses—from quiet reflection to red-faced indignation—as he works through the problem. And she shares the father's reflections as he observes the boy: "Would Stephen conquer, or would he give up? Was there real stuff behind that grim stubbornness which had given them such tragic trouble? . . . Stephen was to the egg-beater, to all of life, as he himself would be, put suddenly in charge of a complicated modern locomotive."[27] Stephen persists, he succeeds, and the father and son celebrate his victory, before the exhausted boy crawls off to cry, happily, and falls asleep, clutching his bear.

Fisher's ideas about childhood represent an emergent perspective, especially when her focus on freeing the child from unnecessary constraint is read against more discipline-centered paradigms. She anticipates many elements of the Child Study approach: the focus on the child's inner life, the need to accommodate noise and mess, the connections between play and learning. Fisher insisted that not every woman was emotionally suited to motherhood; she advocated that the primary responsibilities for childcare should fall on the parent with the greatest aptitude—in this case, the father. Fisher also showed sympathy for the women who felt trapped, unable to fulfill their own ambitions: "Let a woman, while she is still young, search her heart to know what would have been her keenest interest if she had not become a mother; and then let her hold fast to that interest through all the busy rush of rearing a family, let her hold fast to it in the face of other demands.... Let her keep her little flame alive."[28] Her ideas would be expanded by several subsequent generations of women in the Child Study movement.

## The Child Study Movement and Parents' Education

The Society for the Study of Child Nature was formed in 1888 by five upper-class mothers, who wanted to better understand children from "mental, moral, and physical" perspectives. They credited ethical philosopher Felix Adler, who had been a mentor of Sidonie Matsner Gruenberg, the organization's longtime president, for inspiring the initial gathering. The group originally hoped to sponsor a kindergarten but saw a more urgent need to inform others about their discoveries, creating resources that might guide parents. The organization changed its name first to the Federation for Child Study in 1908 and then to the Child Study Association of America in 1924.

The Federation for Child Study's vision was summarized in their 1913 statement of purpose:

> All normal parents are possessed by an intense desire to establish sympathetic relations with their children; to win and hold their respect and confidence and to become, in the most intimate sense, their companions.... The failure of most parents to approach the ideal relation which they desire to have with their children is due to the fact that they do not keep in touch with their children's environment and thus fail to understand the influences affecting their nature and their inner lives.[29]

Kathleen W. Jones discusses a shift of attention in the first years of the twentieth century away from the "troublesome child," understood as immigrant and working-class, embodying "the ailments of a rapidly changing society—generational stress, urban living, industrial poverty, ethnic diversity and multicultural standards of behavior."[30] With child labor laws having been passed successfully, the group now focused on "normal children," that is, the children of the white middle classes, children who responded to norms of child development. The psychiatrist Douglas Thom, one of the many experts whose research informed the movement, explained in 1927, "Most children are normal. Few if any are perfect."[31] Parents of the educated classes were being taught to anticipate emotional and psychological touchstones in their children's development so they might internalize best practices. Jones describes "a psychological paradigm that individualized and democratized (or disassociated from a class identity) the troublesome child, that turned common childhood behaviors into symptoms of psychiatric diagnoses, and that established the child's emotional vulnerability as the primary source of problems."[32]

The Child Study Association bridged between laboratory research on child development and mothers as observers of their own children. Historian Alice Boardman Smuts reports that in 1918, there were only three psychologists and two psychiatrists in America who identified themselves as full-time scholars of children. By 1930, there were more than six hundred exploring these topics.[33] Writing about the legacy of G. Stanley Hall, who had also tapped mothers as research collaborators, historian Julia Grant writes: "Hall's belief that women would have a part to play in the emerging science of child psychology was immensely appealing to these middle-class mothers, who saw themselves uniquely suited to understand children's psyches."[34]

The Child Study Association launched a movement of mothers' clubs where women could come together and share problems and insights, reading and discussing child-development texts. The association advocated for parental education, often through their strong connections with the Parent Teacher Association and later, *Parents*. They explained their goals in a 1922 book, *Outlines of Child Study*: "We must make deliberate and systematic effort to replace impulse with purpose in all our dealings with children. . . . The Federation has undertaken to separate usable knowledge from mere opinion."[35] Through parents' education, key insights were more widespread at least among middle-class and upper-middle-class parents. A 1926 guidebook summarized the value of such sessions: "Mothers—and increasingly, fathers—bring to the Child Study group a variety of problems ... from seemingly trivial daily irritations to serious behavior difficulties. Each problem must be approached with due consideration of all of its impending circumstances and yet there are general and fundamental principles which will help ... not only in meeting the immediate situation, but in becoming progressively able to understand—even to forestall—problems in the future."[36]

A topic might be initiated by a participant or arise in response to prompts designed to encourage parents to exchange their perspectives around a shared concern. For example, one 1928 guide asks: "Is it helpful or harmful to have strong, lively imaginations? Have parents anything to do with the imagination of their children? ... Does imagination help us to understand other people better?"[37] As parents share perspectives, the group leader responds with child-psychology insights. And the parents list actions that promote the social benefits and deflect the problems they associate with children's play. For example, parents might help children to distinguish between pretend and reality or praise children for their creative output. Learning to become a better parent is thus linked to developing a deeper understanding of the child's emotional needs, redirecting children toward constructive behavior.

The association's focus on children's inner lives distinguishes it from the behaviorists, such as Watson, who treated children's brains as black boxes that could not be directly accessed. Children, Watson felt, could only be understood through their surface behaviors, and could only be impacted by rewards and punishments. By contrast, the Child Study movement, according to Alice Boardman Smuts, sought to "look beyond children's troublesome behavior for hidden desires, emotional conflicts, cultural deprivation, or other circumstances that might have been responsible."[38] Their approach emphasized empathetic reflection on *why* children misbehave and symbolic expression as a means of catharsis. Empathy is not sympathy, which might have been what guided earlier reform efforts, such as those directed against child labor. Empathy requires one to sense other people's emotions, to read them as like one's own, and thus to be able to imagine what someone might be thinking about a situation and why. The result was a form of advice literature grounded in storytelling and modeling a process of analysis that might lead parents to identify and respond to children's emotional needs. The goal was to encourage parents to stay in touch not only with the material conditions impacting the child but also with their fantasy and emotional lives.

The Child Study Association materials start from the premise that "boys and girls are independent, individual personalities, worthy of the respect of adults."[39] They continue: "It is natural for parents to feel that the children whom they brought into the world belong to them, but too many fathers and mothers handle their children as they do their material possessions, and expect their boys and girls to be entirely subject to their ministrations, wishes and decisions."[40] The group's stress on the rights of autonomous, expressive children links this movement to the rights of women.

## Making Sense of Children's Social and Emotional Lives

In the rest of the chapter, I will turn my attention to the writings of several key women who published advice books for parents in the 1930s and 1940s. Fisher partnered with Gruenfeld on the publication of *Our Children: A Handbook for Parents* in 1932, an anthology of insights from key figures in the movement, which would be republished and revised several times over the following decades. Because of their focus on the cultural and social context, they were among the first to discuss children's literary and media consumption habits, identifying stories that allow children the emotional outlets they require.

Gruenberg had been trained in child psychology at Felix Adler's Ethical Culture School in New York City, then known as the Workingman's School. Collaborating with her husband, Benjamin Gruenberg, she published books on progressive parenting. Her 1912 book *Your Child Today and Tomorrow* translated insights from the Child Study movement into advice parents could apply at home, including early advocacy for giving children an allowance so they could make meaningful choices that impacted their own lives. She was the director of the Child Study Association from 1924 to 1950, also teaching parents' education at Columbia Teachers College and New York University. Gruenberg sought to restructure society to ensure that women enjoyed meaningful lives:

> While she loves her children as much as mothers in the past loved theirs, a mother today is almost bound to feel a certain resentment at being a shut-in. To make this resentment worse, her children and her husband are sure to sense her dissatisfactions and to be unfavorably affected by them.... Wouldn't we do better to help such a young mother return to her professional work, rather than to mark as somewhat peculiar the occasional woman who tries to do so?[41]

Gruenberg called for mothers to develop "sympathetic insight . . . quick observation . . . and sound sense," suggesting that many of the "heartbreaks, misunderstandings, and estrangements between parents and child" could be avoided if parents had a deeper knowledge of "the nature of the child's mind."[42] Mothers were to "bear constantly in mind that the child is not merely a miniature man or woman, but that each stage of his development represents a distinct combination of instincts, impulses and capacities."[43]

How many mothers, she asks, can "direct those instincts without thwarting them?" For example, she responds to adult concerns about boys' tendencies to form neighborhood gangs by suggesting why this form of social organization might offer the boy a sense of belonging, a shared purpose, and "sympathy and understanding such as he can find nowhere else."[44] Only by respecting how gangs serve boys' developmental needs can adults address other concerns: "How can we save, and strengthen the fine qualities which this spontaneous association with other boys produces without encouraging the lawlessness and the destructiveness and the secretiveness of the gang? . . . Then, when this is perfectly clear to us, we will take the next step, which will be to use all of the resources of the homes and of the community to change the antisocial gang into a *club*."[45] The unstructured gang can lead toward antisocial behavior, whereas clubs such as the Boy Scouts offer space for adult guidance. Too much adult control, too much overt talk about morality and the club "degenerates into a preachy, Sunday-School class."[46]

Anna M. W. Wolf, another movement leader, encouraged mothers to "consider the child's life . . . with a view to discovering the causes of his dissatisfaction. . . . An intelligent and experienced mother who has the ability to identify herself with her child and to feel as he is feeling often becomes expert at ferreting these things out."[47] The effective mother seizes every opportunity to uncover hidden motives shaping her child's behavior, asking "what the child is feeling about his parents, about the other people in his world, and about himself." A good mother delays punishment until she understands: "Angry feelings, destructive tendencies . . . cannot be altered by curbing their external expression alone. They must be treated at the source if there is to be a fundamental change."

The core model here is affective (concerned with what a good home feels like), interpretive (concerned with what actions mean to each family member) and expressive (recognizing that the child is learning to read the mother just as the mother is learning to read the child): "Children always learn best from persons whose good will they trust and whom they are therefore willing to work with, instead of against. . . . Children are quick to sense meaning in a tone of voice, in a facial expression, or in our over-eagerness to get them out of the way or hustle them off to bed."[48] Good parenting did not simply regulate the child's actions:

> What children need more than anything else is a home where parents like children and enjoy them. This means far more than just liking to play with them. It means taking time to study a child's interests. It means helping him develop step by step, whether in skills with hands and body, making friends with others his own age, or delving into the world of books and ideas. It means listening to a child and trying to understand his language. It means giving close attention to changes, knowing how and when the child's growth is best served by helping him, and when he's better off if left alone.[49]

Celebrating the growing child's unlimited curiosity, Wolf ponders, "How can we preserve for him all this fine energy, this inquiring spirit, this insatiable will to explore and to pursue his own ends, and yet at the same time tame and civilize him so that he can meet the demands of living?"[50]

One pamphlet from the Child Study Association summed up this philosophy: "Children's behavior is not random and haphazard as it appears on the surface, but really purposeful [and] . . . children act in accordance with their deep inner drives and feelings. . . . Children should feel that their parents, and teachers too, are on their side, willing and interested to get at the source of the difficulty."[51] Parents should shape the child's choices through friendly persuasion: "There should be as few forbidden things as possible; and instead of trying to think up ways of preventing a child from doing what he wants we can try teaching him skills that protect him and encourage him to go ahead for all his worth."[52]

## Children and Media Consumption

Gruenberg writes about children's active imaginations: "As soon as a child knows a large number of objects and persons and names he will begin to rearrange his bits of knowledge into . . . a little world of his own."[53] This emphasis on children's environments made the Child Study advocates early critics of the roles media played in children's lives, especially as radio and later, television entered the home. As early as 1933, the Child Study Association formed subcommittees tasked with making recommendations about the most constructive ways to integrate radio programs into children's lives, rejecting censorship as impractical and undesirable. The association soon extended this advice to film, children's books, comics, and television.

The Child Study writers often sound like contemporary cultural-studies scholars in their emphasis on children's agency to select and ascribe personal significance to resources from the surrounding culture. As one Child Study advocate, Josette Frank, explained, "What we put into their lives is far more important than what we take out."[54] Frank was the organization's key spokesperson for media-related advice. A former secretary for Teddy Roosevelt, Frank, as a young woman, had fought for child labor laws before joining the Child Study movement in 1923 and turning her attention to children's reading in 1936: "We can best guide our children's reading if we let our children's reading guide us. Instead of trying to mold them into preconceived patterns of 'what the well-read child should read,' let us rather encourage them to find their way to real experiences of their own in the vast world of books."[55]

From the start, Frank not only sought to guide parents toward what she saw as the most constructive responses to children's reading and media choices, but also to reshape what resources were available. She edited collections for children, such as *Poems to Read to the Very Young*, and oversaw a project to translate classic literary works, from *Alice in Wonderland* to *Robinson Crusoe*, into more child-friendly language. And at the peak of the 1950s moral panic over comic books, she assumed the role of adviser to National Comics, the company that is today known as DC Comics, where she reviewed scripts, advocated for alternative practices, but also defended the medium to parents' groups, earning the scorn of reformers like Frederic Wertham.

Children's choices were not random but reflected a search for stories that compensated for things missing in their lives: "Children have their own private reasons for liking what they like. We do not always know what these reasons are, but we do have to give their feelings room, unless we have evidence that their choices are actually harmful."[56] In a collective 1947 statement, the Child Study Association advised: "Perhaps they need this escape from their well-ordered lives and our incessant demands. Children have always found this kind of relief in imaginary exploits, as the folk and fairy tales of many lands testify. Perhaps you don't recognize the pattern in this modern dress, but it's very much the same."[57]

With children's media consumption, the starting point needs to be observation and sympathetic analysis to identify why children are making such choices: "If an eight-year-old is truly frightened by a children's program (not just pretending), it seems likely that she feels anxious and fearful about something more deeply personal. The radio story may set it off, but the anxiety probably goes deeper. . . . She may need help with something more important than her choice of radio programs."[58] Contrasting with other research on children's media consumption (for example, the Paine Fund research on our "media-made children"), the emphasis is not on media influence but rather the issues children are working through:

> When a child seems to spend most of his time watching television, parents will do well to take stock of what else is happening in his life. What other satisfactions does he have? What activities does he enjoy at home, at school or in the neighborhood? Is he interested in what others in his family are doing? Is he happy at school? Does he have friends? It isn't enough to insist that he "read a book" or "play" or "go out for some fresh air." What book? Play what and with whom? And what is there to invite him out of doors?[59]

The goal should be not to get rid of "bad" media but to create a better balance with other potential activities: "Parents can't hope to censor all of the reading, listening, and play of their children—nor should they—but they can offer their children help in finding more wholesome forms of amusement. If the books and play equipment and activities encouraged by parents really meet their children's needs, ordinarily the less desirable interests will not gain too strong a hold."[60]

Parents might watch and discuss favorite programs with their children—showing interest in the things that matter to them: "They need to feel free to talk over their movie-made ideas and questions with parents who are neither shocked nor bored by their interest, and who understand their confusion."[61] The Child Studies movement did not see violent play as necessarily a worry if it occurs within an otherwise healthy context: "Children have always played out their impressions of the world around them. Such play gives boys a chance to identify with fathers, older brothers and other heroes of fact and fiction. It also gives them a chance to work off aggressive feelings without actually hurting anybody."[62]

The Child Study movement's insights provide three ways that might help us to understand children's fictions. First, given the focus on character building, Child Study literature helps us to read fictions as tools for understanding the emotional dynamics of children's lives. Second, the Child Study movement provides a distinctive narrative structure as we watch sympathetic adults (like the father in *The Home-Maker*) reshape the world to accommodate children's needs. And third, the Child Study movement saw media consumption as informing children's development, allowing for pleasure and release, play and imagination. In the next sections, I apply these analytic tools to *The Littlest Angel* (1945) and *The Boy with Green Hair* (1948), as we trace the gradual shift from wartime concerns to those of the postwar era.

## *The Littlest Angel* (1945)

The protagonist of Charles Tazewell's children's book and radio drama *The Littlest Angel* is no angel, or at least this boy has no clue how to behave like adults expect angels to behave. Tazewell describes the boy's failures in endearing terms, even if we understand how much his conduct disappoints those charged with putting him on the righteous path. The first thing we learn is that he left home without a handkerchief and now stands "snuffing" before the "kindly Gatekeeper," making "a most unangelic sound." When the Littlest Angel joined the heavenly chorus, "he inevitably sang off-key . . . spoiling its ethereal effect." As Tazewell describes him, "His halo was permanently tarnished where he held onto it with one hot, little chubby hand when he ran, and he was always running. Furthermore, even when he stood very still, it never behaved as a halo should. It was always slipping down over his right eye."

Tazewell maintains sympathy both for the boy who does his best to please the adults and for the adults who anticipate order and decorum. In *The Parents' Manual: A Guide to the Emotional Development of Young Children* (1943), Anna M. W. Wolf celebrates boyhood's untamed exuberance as needing protection from adult constraints:

> He will ask questions by the hour, will climb, run, punch, and kick. It will be hard to make him sit at a desk with books, or keep himself neat, or pay attention to the demands of time, or submit to the social amenities. How can we preserve for him all this fine energy, this inquiring spirit, this insatiable will to explore and to pursue his own ends, and yet at the same time tame and civilize him so that he can meet the demands of living?[63]

Both Wolf and Tazewell direct our sympathy toward boys through a succession of active verbs; he is defined by what he does. He cannot sit still, yet he also cannot arrive anywhere on time. The Child Study tradition would ask "why" he behaves in this ungodly manner, explaining his inability to perform the tasks (such as appropriately using his wings or holding onto his halo) as reflecting his immature physical development or unresolved psychological issues. Since awkwardness and disruption are natural attributes of boyhood, society must not only accommodate but celebrate them.

Several of Tazewell's other stories—*The Littlest Snowman*, which was read every year during the holiday season on *Captain Kangaroo*; *The Small One*, which was the basis for a 1978 animated Walt Disney short; and *The Lullaby of Christmas*, which had been a highly successful radio drama and record—follow a similar pattern. Tazewell was best known as a radio dramatist. He wrote *Littlest Angel* as a radio script but it remained unproduced until he rewrote it as a children's book. The book inspired several media productions including a 1950 children's record featuring Loretta Young and a 1969 television dramatization featuring Johnny Whitaker, Edmund Gwynne, and Cab Calloway.

Child Study writers often promoted a more holistic conception of discipline that moved beyond punishment and toward guidance. In Tazewell's book, the boy is called before the aptly named Understanding Angel, fearing that he is about to be "disciplined." True to his name, the Understanding Angel seeks to identify and rectify the problem's roots:

> Suddenly almost before he knew it, he was standing close to the Understanding Angel and was explaining how very difficult it was for a boy who suddenly finds himself transformed into an angel. . . . There wasn't anything for a small angel to do. And he was very homesick. Oh, not that paradise wasn't beautiful! But Earth was beautiful too! Wasn't it created by God himself? Why, there were trees to climb, and brooks to fish, and caves to play at pirate chief, the swimming hole, and sun, and rain, and dark and dawn, and thick brown dust, so soft and warm beneath your feet![64]

The Understanding Angel listens as the boy shares what's driving his misbehavior. Wolf told her readers: "Successful parents are those who can remember what it was like to be a child. They put themselves in their child's place and feel as he is feeling."[65] And having experienced such empathy, the boy shares his longing for a box he kept under his bed. The Understanding Angel promises that the boy will have his box as soon as possible,[66] and having made this promise, he uses every resource to keep it. Learning to trust the adult world, the boy more fully meets its expectations: "Everyone wondered at the great change in the Littlest Angel, for among all the cherubs in God's kingdom, he was the most happy. His conduct was above the slightest reproach. His appearance was all that the most fastidious could wish for."[67] The box contains the boy's "treasures," the earthly delights the boy collected through the years. Butterfly wings, bird's eggs, rounded stones, a leather strap that belonged to his dog, all carry memories of good times he enjoyed. For example, Tazewell recounts that "two white stones [had been] found on a muddy riverbank, where he and his friends had played like small, brown beavers." Both the animal imagery and the focus on mud pervade permissive descriptions of boys' lives.

Later, the young angel must decide what to gift the newborn Christ and again confronts the limits of his own abilities, unable to write a poem or compose music that would compare favorably with the creations of mature angels. But the boy recognizes Jesus as another boy, who might value the same things he values, and so places his box of treasures among the other gifts. When God opens his present, the boy "wept hot, bitter tears" of shame, but God proclaims, "Of all the gifts of all the angels, I find that this small box pleases me most. Its contents are of the earth and of men. . . . These are the things my son, too, will know and love and cherish and then, regretfully, will leave behind him when his task is done." God, like the Understanding Angel, does what the Child Study movement leaders advocated—understanding and appreciating the child's gift on its own terms. And in the process, the story helps the child reader forge a connection between divine and everyday experiences.

Earlier Christian philosophies saw sensual pleasure as dangerous, pulling the child toward temptation and sin. Such puritanical views went hand in hand with advocacy for strong physical discipline designed to beat out the devil. But the writers of the 1930s and 1940s saw the senses as a bridge between earthly and divine knowledge. Tazewell imagines that Jesus might appreciate the boy's treasure box, and in other books children come to God through an appreciation of His earthly handiwork. Such books incorporate permissive themes into religious education. Consider Olive W. Burt's 1942 poem "God Gave Me Eyes," which formed the basis for a popular children's picture book, illustrated by Ellen Segner. Burt shows how the senses bring children closer to God: "God gave me eyes that I might see the wonder of a blossoming tree, my dolly's face, my storybook, and how the various creatures look."[68] Verse by verse, the poem explores the other senses before returning, at last, to the figure of a Creator: "I thank you God, for making me so that I hear and feel and see; and since these dear gifts come from you, I'll use them in the ways you want me to." Segner's illustrations depict a young girl and her brother as they share sensual experiences. In one drawing, the boy celebrates taste by licking chocolate from a mixing bowl, and in the process, smearing it around his mouth—another variant on the trope of

And good things Mother cooks for me.

Figure 2.1: Ellen Segner and Olive W. Burt's 1941 book *God Gave Me Eyes* depicts children's sensuality as a pathway to understanding the divine.

the child who is so invested in what he is doing as to be indifferent to his appearance (figure 2.1). Cleanliness may be next to godliness, but boys are always a little devilish.

Jane Werner Watson, longtime senior editor for the Little Golden Books series, similarly tapped sensuality to communicate her conception of "God's love," a theme most fully explored through *My Little Golden Book About God* (1952). Here, she encourages children to explore the natural world—from the distant stars to their own backyards—in search of signs of a Creator: "Bend down to touch the smallest flower. Watch the busy ant tugging at his load. See the flashes of jewels on the insect's back. This tiny world your two hands can span, like the oceans and the mountains and far-off stars, God planned."[69] Illustrator Eloise Wilken depicts wide-eyed children peering into bird's nests, looking into the skies, and hugging their parents.

The Understanding Angel and God (the ideal dad) both take the time to understand the misfit boy and appreciate his value. The book represents certain tendencies of boys—such as the desire to muck about in mud—as natural, universal, even divine. And here, sensuality and curiosity are given a specifically Christian inflection—as a way children can appreciate God's creations. *The Littlest Angel*, for all its spiritual undertones, is surprisingly coy about death, about how a young boy went to heaven in the first place. In the next section, we will consider a text more directly addressing children's questions about war.

### *The Boy with Green Hair* (1948)

When war strikes, Anna W. M. Wolf writes in the opening passages of *Our Children Face War* (1942): "Our impulse is to hide them away and keep them safe—absolutely safe. There must be a way, we think, as we brace ourselves, to keep the horror from coming anywhere near them."[70] But she concludes that the signs of war will creep into children's lives in countless ways. The parent's role is to monitor their responses, comforting them and preparing them for any challenges the war imposes. Perhaps the most important Child Study writer about wartime problems, Wolf advised parents:

> The best thing they can do for their children is to help them day by day not to forget, but to understand, and to find a place for themselves, too, in America at war. . . . Boys know airplane models and gun models in detail and pore over charts and diagrams of military tactics. . . . When encouraged by their parents or organized and instructed at school, they sell war savings stamps as eagerly as tickets for a church benefit, or ring doorbells on the hunt for old rubber with all the cheerful competitiveness of the young American out to put *his* team, his school, his town, well over the top.[71]

Released three years after the Second World War ended, Joseph Losey's *The Boy with Green Hair* is preoccupied with the ways the past war (and the threat of a future war) impact a boy's life. Though the war is over, the characters are still working through its consequences for their lives. The film includes a sequence of Peter (the protagonist) and Gramps (his foster father) returning from collecting used clothing to send to war orphans. They are greeted at the gates by a smiling teacher and the other children. The classroom walls are bestowed with posters urging them to give generously to "overseas children" whose lives have been disrupted by the conflict. Shortly, another child suggests to Peter that one of the poster children "looks like you." At first, we are not sure what is meant—some ethnic connection, perhaps—before the child completes his thought and tells Peter that he is a war orphan. This is a truth the adults had been shielding from him, but the teacher has apparently shared it with the other children in an effort to encourage kindness. Peter demands the truth. Sending the other children away, his foster father and teacher acknowledge that he should have been told the facts long ago. Peter bravely asserts that he already knew but as soon as the adults leave, he angrily rips the poster.

Later, when Gramps tries to heal the rift, Peter glares, fingering the propeller on a model airplane, remaining sullenly silent. If Wolf saw playing with model planes as symptomatic of how normal children process wartime realities, the Child Study Association's *Children in Wartime* addresses parents who worry about war toys: "Boys have always played games that gave release to their war-like feelings. . . . Up to a certain point this is perfectly normal—a real safety-valve."[72] Losey shows how war enters children's lives even when adults think they are insulating them. One scene focuses on the boy's face as, in a grocery store, he overhears an adult conversation debating how America should respond to the possibility of yet another war. As Peter collects groceries from the lower shelf, the adults turn their backs to the camera, and we hear their off-screen voices. While the adults are unaware of his presence, the audience is encouraged to study actor Dean Stockwell's reactions as tension slowly builds.

The secret of the parents' death hovers over the narrative—most explicitly in the form of a letter Peter hands off to a succession of foster parents, none of whom provide the boy with the security and love he needs. When he arrives at Gramps's house, we observe the armor he projects toward adults. He insists on carrying his own suitcase up the stairs, he asks which rooms he can enter and what things he should not touch, he demands to know how long he will be staying, and finally, he purposefully smashes something to see how his new foster father will react. Only when Gramps patiently suffers each challenge does the boy announce, "I think I will stay—until Mother and Father get back." Gramps earns his trust through magic tricks, jokes, songs, and a bit of the Irish blarney. We watch the teacher go through a similar process to help Peter feel at home in her schoolroom. So, given the betrayal he feels from both when the truth of the parents' deaths emerges, viewers know how hard it will be for that trust to be rebuilt. Wolf would have advised adults against withholding such truths:

> The child is likely, by a hundred different tokens, to know what has happened. He cannot go on forever believing, in the absence of all the normal signs, that his father is "away at a sanitarium"; he is deceived only for a short time by the fictitious messages that have no familiar ring. . . . Above all, he senses his mother's displeasure at his questions; he notes all the changes in her, and these things soon stir his anxiety. . . . It has been shown again and again that in trying to conceal the truth, we succeed only in denying the child the solace of wholesome grief, the restorative power of sharing it with someone he loves, the necessary outlet of tears and mourning.[73]

The father's letter, to be read on Peter's sixteenth birthday, contains the withheld truth. Enraged by the adult silences, Peter rips the letter, not knowing or wanting to know what it contains. Even when the truth starts to emerge, Peter is told only that the parents have died as heroes: "They could have gotten out but they stayed behind and died trying to save other boys and girls like yourself." From this, Peter draws his own conclusions: "They didn't care about me. They just cared about saving other children." Only in the final moments does Gramps read aloud the father's letter and address the boy's concerns, having thought, wrongly, that the boy would only really understand when he was older: "We left you, Peter, because we had to. We had a job to do. Try to understand that it was for our great love for you and for all the world's children."

The boy awakens one morning to discover that his hair has turned green, and we watch how people react to his difference. Peter is initially perplexed, assuming that some green soap rubbed off on him, and then, bemused, makes faces in the mirror and restyles his hair for comic effect. A neighbor girl expresses admiration initially, though later she shares her mother's fears that green hair may be contagious. Gramps talks a good game about green hair being special, but then presses a baseball cap firmly over the boy's head as they enter the streets. The teacher tries to normalize the situation, taking a matter-of-fact poll of hair color, finding that an equal number of the children have red and green hair.[74] Earlier representations of the barber, the grocer, the doctor, and the milkman as friendly neighbors give way to more fearful reactions, as the adult world closes ranks against the boy. A gang chases Peter on their bikes, waving scissors and threatening to cut his hair. The leader of the pack, a blond bespectacled boy, panics when he loses his glasses but when Peter helps to find them, the boy cries out, directing rage born from vulnerability against the boy with the green hair.

Throughout, the film offers a nightmarish image of how postwar American society was directing suspicion against those who were different. While the boy in the glasses compares Peter's hair to his own experience of being treated as a sissy, the film opens a range of other possible analogies—from antisemitism to anticommunism. The film's director, Joseph Losey, had been part of the Federal Theater Project, where he helped to develop the genre of the Living Newspaper, highly topical stage productions that commented on the current state of the world. He had joined the Communist Party in 1946 (two years before the film's release) and would be blacklisted by the House Un-American Activities Committee just one year later, escaping to Europe where he continued to produce films outside the Hollywood system. These characters may not openly address the era's belief that "better dead than red" but they do act upon the idea that it is better to be mean than green.

Peter has not chosen to have his hair turn green, but he becomes increasingly militant against the pressure to cut or dye his hair so that he can be like everybody else. And the hair color soon takes on political significance when Peter has a vision of war orphans asking him to use the attention he is drawing to tell the world that they must prevent another war: "If enough people believe you, there never will be another war and there never will be any more war orphans." The naivete of this message has been criticized. Yet, the idea that Peter and the other children might have political agency reflects the era's hopes for a more democratic (and globally connected) society. But these hopes are quickly dashed, as kindly Gramps conforms to his neighbors' pressure: "The last thing I want to do is to hurt you but people have been talking.... Such strange fancies have been cluttering up your heart lately. I want you to be happy and carefree like the other boys your age." As the barber shaves Peter's head, the adults cluster around him and the children watch through the window, eager to see the disorder resolved. Following the forced haircut, the adults stand in silence, some satisfied, others watching with guilt and shame, as Peter flees in tears.

The film was framed by an exchange between Peter (a bald runaway) and a psychologist who claims to be an "expert on boys," and who gets Peter to open up by sharing hamburgers and a malt. From the start, Peter sees little reason to tell his story because no one will believe him, and by the film's conclusion, the psychologist remains skeptical. But the psychiatrist, along with the doctor, teacher, and foster father, ultimately embraces his antiwar message. And Peter's activism is endorsed by the dead father's letter: "Remember us as having died with millions of other people for something fine and worthwhile. It will have been fine; it will have been worthwhile if those who have not died do not forget. If they forget, remind them. Remind them, Peter." There are truths within these fantastical sequences—especially the ways that the community imposes conformity—whether or not we accept that the boy's hair turned green overnight.

We can draw a direct line from the father in Dorothy Canfield Fisher's *The Home-Maker* to the Understanding Angel and Gramps in these two postwar children's fables. They model a particular notion of parenting as the pursuit of insights into children's minds, a process advanced by the Child Study Association. The process of asking probing questions to decipher the context for children's disruptive behavior creates its own narrative trajectory as a caring adult, often a father figure, seeks to understand and accommodate children's unexpressed needs. As we will see in chapter 6, this plot structure became widespread in the postwar era, one of the primary means by which the media reassured children and their parents that the world would celebrate rather than regulate children's expression. *The Boy with Green Hair* signals the transition from the concerns of the war years to those of the postwar era—from the need to unify around a cause to the pressure to conform to the unreasonable demands of more fearful neighbors. In the next chapter, we will discuss another transitional work—*The 5,000 Fingers of Dr. T.* (1953)—to better understand notions of democratic parenting and how Dr. Seuss fit into the permissive-era home and classroom.

## 3

## "No Matter How Small"

*The Democratic Imagination of Dr. Seuss*

Children's Reading and Children's Thinking are the rock bottom base upon which the future of this country will rise. Or not rise. In these days of tension and confusion, writers are beginning to realize that Books for Children have a greater potential for good, or evil, than any other form of literature on earth. They realize that the new generations *must* grow up to be more intelligent than *ours*.
—Dr. Seuss, "Brat Books on the March"[1]

We do not want our children to let protest against domination pile up inside until it has reached proportions beyond all reason. Nor do we want them to be so dependent that they grow willing to follow no matter what kind of ruler. . . . We want our children to resist unfairness and injustice, even in the laws of their land. *We* want them to cherish and stand up for their own rights and the rights of their fellow men. We want them to reject the rule of all Hitlers.
—Dorothy W. Baruch, *Parents Can Be People*[2]

When Horton the elephant, in Dr. Seuss's *Horton Hears a Who!* (1954), listens to "a very faint yelp" of a microscopic civilization living on a dust speck and tries to rally his neighbors to protect the endangered Who village, he gets caught between two different communities. On the one hand, there is the conformist world of the Wickershams who crush individualistic tendencies. On the other, there is the civic-minded community of Whoville, "a town that is friendly and clean." As a crisis threatens their survival, the Whos rally: "This is your town's darkest hour! The time for all Whos who have blood that is red to come to the aid of their country!"

Horton's situation encapsulates the dilemmas many liberals faced, torn between the conflicting values of community and individualism, frightened by mob rule and, yet, dedicated to democracy. *Horton* expresses a nostalgia for the Whoville-like America of the war years when political differences were forgotten in the name of a common cause. Many liberals and radicals had joined forces to confront the threat of fascism overseas and to defend the New Deal at home. As part of the "Popular Front," a particular formulation of progressive politics during the war, they had sought to contain their differences and broaden their support, employing "democracy" as a code word for social transformation (including the resolution of economic inequalities) and "fascism" as a general term for concentrated power (including the entrenched authority of union-busting corporations). Many on the left shared a common vision of what the ideal postwar society would look like. Internal tensions (especially centering on Stalinism) shook this alliance's stability. As the war ended, anticommunist hysteria led many "fellow travelers" to repudiate their earlier ideological partnerships; others protested the collapse of individual liberties and the Wickersham-like conformity. In an important reassessment of the book, Katie Ishizuka and Ramón Stephens suggest that Horton's story should be read as an example of "white saviorism," since it is only through Horton's intervention that the voices of the Whos can be amplified to the world.[3] They see the book as a perpetuation of negative stereotypes about the Japanese that Seuss had helped to craft during his own wartime work. As such, we can see Seuss, like many other Popular Front writers, as torn between democratic and antidemocratic perspectives, some of them consciously embraced and some of them unconsciously absorbed from the culture around him.

The sympathetic portrayal of Horton (a liberal out of sync with his community) contrasts sharply with the description of Jo-Jo as a "very small, very small shirker" (someone who places personal interests ahead of the larger cause). Jo-Jo endangers his community by withholding his small voice. Only when Jo-Jo "the Smallest of All" contributes do the Wickershams and the other animals commit themselves to the Whos' preservation. *Horton* is not only a plea for the rights of the "small," but also an acknowledgment that even the "small" have obligations to the general welfare.

Seuss dedicated *Horton* to Mitsugi Nakamura, a Kyoto educator he had met during a fact-finding mission to Japan that involved researching the American occupation's impact on educational and child-rearing practices. Seuss's *And to Think That I Saw It on Mulberry Street* (1937) and *The 500 Hats of Bartholomew Cubbins* (1938) had been adopted for postwar "reeducation" in both Japan and Korea. Seuss knew *Horton* would be used to train not only American children, but children in emerging democracies about the relationship between the individual and the community. He was impressed by his discovery that Japanese children, educated according to American principles, were embracing Western cultural values.[4] Asked to draw pictures of their future, Japanese schoolchildren depicted themselves in helping professions, healing the sick, educating the ignorant, and rebuilding their society; Seuss felt the previous generation would have seen their futures as warriors. Young girls imagined business careers closed to their mothers. In confronting postwar Japan, Seuss saw both the prospect of legitimate friendship across cultural differences and the dangers of a culture that only a few years before was hopelessly militaristic and imperialistic. His participation in the reeducation of Japan cannot simply be reduced to cultural imperialism without regard to his idealistic goals. Yet, it never can be separated from the mechanisms by which those goals were imposed upon another country. Seuss despised the "indoctrination" practices he associated with the wartime German and Japanese educational systems. Overt attempts to moralize violated youngsters' trust. The child, for Seuss, was born already possessing, as a birthright, the virtues of a democratic citizen—a sense of fairness, a hunger to belong and participate within the community. The challenge was to protect children from adults' antidemocratic influences, especially from the crushing impact of authoritarian institutions. The children's writer served democracy not by becoming its propagandist (a role Seuss had played during the war) but by teaching children to trust their own responses to an unjust world.

*Horton*'s insistence that "a person's a person, no matter how small" summarizes this paradigm. According to other writers, such as Dorothy Baruch, the ideals of democracy were to be embedded into the micropractices of everyday life. These ideals about democratic parenting reflected the empathy with children's emotional lives that had emerged before the war from the Child Study movement, but their rhetoric reflected the politics of the war and immediate postwar period. Henry Goddard argued in 1948 that the child "comes into the world with a clean slate, needing only to be guided right to grow into an adult with the highest ideals to which man has attained."[5] Childhood was imagined as a utopian space through which America might reinvent itself. Children's fiction, in this context, became a vehicle for teaching both children and adults this new mode of democratic thinking. As Mauree Applegate explained a few years later: "If the democratic process is to improve or even continue, the skills of living together must be taught children with their pablum."[6] In *Learning from the Left*, Julia Mickenberg writes: "The books . . . point toward solutions that affirm the possibility of reshaping American society and institutions to embody the nation's democratic promise; that is, they show individuals and communities actively working against injustice and toward enlightenment."[7]

By 1954, when he wrote *Horton*, Seuss had spent most of his professional life writing for humor magazines with a primarily adult readership and translating what he had learned into the tools of persuasion—first, working in advertising, then, doing editorial cartoons for the Popular Front newspaper *PM*, and, finally, scripting propaganda and training films for Frank Capra's Signal Corps unit. The postwar period saw a gradual narrowing of his attention onto children's writing. Seuss's transition from wartime propaganda to postwar children's fables parallels the emergence of this discourse of "democratic" parenting. Whereas he once sought to change the hearts and minds of adults, he now placed his hope in raising a generation with different opportunities. Works like *Horton*, the Bartholomew Cubbins books, *Yertle the Turtle*, and *The 5,000 Fingers of Dr. T* reflect the writer's attempt to map the power relations between children and adults. These books shaped Seuss's understanding of his social mission and prepared the way for his later commercial successes. Seuss provides our point of entry for understanding how ideas about democratic parenting shaped the permissive imagination. At the same time, Seuss's use of nonsense and fantasy in books like *The Cat in the Hat* set him apart from pedagogical authorities who embraced realistic representations of "here and now." The permissive paradigm created a domestic context in which Seuss's nonsense made sense.

## Dr. Seuss as Propagandist (1940–1947)

Dr. Seuss is the pen name of Theodor Geisel. Seuss in the 1930s was largely associated with writings for adults via humor magazines and advertising, though he had experimented with writing for children—most notably in *And to Think That I Saw It on Mulberry Street* (1938). In 1940, Seuss became an editorial cartoonist for the newly created tabloid *PM*, an important organ of the Popular Front movement. The Popular Front, as referred to earlier, was an informal coalition of progressive and radical thinkers and artists who put aside their differences to fight for shared interests during the Depression and war years; many of those accused of communist sympathies after the war had forged such affiliations in support of a more democratic culture. *PM*'s publisher, Ralph Ingersoll, had quit his lucrative job as *Time* publisher to create what he claimed would be a new kind of newspaper. *PM* operated without advertising to be free of obligations to special interests and provided regular sections devoted to labor, civil rights, and women's issues. Ingersoll's political philosophy was stated directly and succinctly in *PM*'s 1940 prospectus: "We are against people who push other people around, in this country or abroad. We propose to crusade for those who seek constructively to improve the way men live together."[8] Larry Ceplair and Steven Englund identify four dominant strands in Popular Front ideology: (a) opposition to the rise of fascism in Europe and Asia; (b) support for "defenders of democracy and the victims of fascist aggression"; (c) resistance to "domestic fascism" and isolationism; and (d) criticism of big business's role in busting unions and opposing New Deal reforms.[9] *PM* embraced all four strands. Max Lerner wrote years later that "the common ground we had was Adolf Hitler and Franklin Roosevelt, one the serpent to be slain, the other the hero to slay him."[10]

Historian Michael Denning cautions against seeing the Popular Front as a cohesive political strategy.[11] Rather, Denning argues, the Popular Front represented a "structure of feeling," a way of understanding contemporary social experience, shaping the political and cultural activities of many artists and intellectuals who would not have viewed themselves as radicals. Seuss's participation within a succession of groups Denning associates with the Popular Front (*PM*, the Capra unit, UPA, Stanley Kramer's production group, etc.) suggests some "affiliation" with its cultural politics, even if we cannot label his beliefs.

Many of Seuss's cartoons lampooned isolationists and fascists, the "America first-isms of Charles Lindbergh and Senators Wheeler and Nye—and the rotten rot that the Fascist priest, Father Coughlin, was spewing out on radio."[12] Increasingly, Seuss focused on the forces dividing Americans. In one cartoon, Seuss depicts the American nation as an enormous boat; everyone is rowing together except for one man who fires his slingshot at another crew member: "I don't like the color of that guy's tie" (February 25, 1942). His campaign against defeatism and divisiveness led him to embrace other aspects of the *PM* ideology, including opposition to the anticommunist Dies Committee, segregationism, antisemitism, union busting, and corporate greed. More troubling was a series of cartoons that supported the Japanese incarceration camps. Like Ingersoll, he was "against people who push other people around." Seuss later told an interviewer, "When I joined up I told them I didn't care for a lot of their economic policies and a lot of their political policies."[13]

When America entered the war, Seuss enlisted, assigned to the film unit Frank Capra established in the Signal Corps to explain to the American people "why we fight." Like Seuss, many key participants in the Capra unit worked in children's literature. Eric Knight, the British-born "local color" novelist best known for *Lassie Come Home*, helped to determine the overall shape of the Why We Fight series. W. Munro Leaf, who had written the children's story *The Story of Ferdinand*, and P. D. Eastman, the author of *Are You My Mother?* both collaborated with Seuss on the Private Snafu animated shorts. These children's writers provided the simple, straightforward prose and evocative art needed for Capra's films. And these same writers and animators were core architects of postwar children's culture. Seuss, for example, would later collaborate with Chuck Jones, an animator on the Snafu shorts, on the television version of *How the Grinch Stole Christmas*.[14]

Like other Popular Front participants, Seuss hoped that the men who wore the uniform would return home changed by working side by side with those from other nations or races. A disillusioned Seuss warned in a December 7, 1944, memo: "Much of what we have gained is, at the moment of victory, threatened.... Racial tension within our Army threatens to grow.... Many soldiers who have seen Europe are eager to turn their backs upon it.... Disillusionment, cynicism, distrust, bitterness, are already souring the milk of human kindness; maggots are already eating the fruits of victory."[15] After the war, Seuss worried that their address to the enlisted men had been too childish: "We tend to talk down to the soldier when we should be talking *with* the soldier. His world is mud and we tend to talk to him from our world of clean sheets."[16] Seuss felt the Capra unit had confronted impossible challenges, trying to instill democratic thought in adults whose prejudices had already been determined by their upbringing.

Throughout his wartime work, Seuss had expressed repeated outrage at people who mislead or manipulate the "small." In one of his *PM* cartoons, an America First mom reads to her children the story of Adolf the Wolf: "And the wolf chewed up the children and spit out their bones—but those *were foreign children* and it really didn't matter" (October 1, 1942). Another cartoon depicts Hitler and Mussolini unconvincingly disguising themselves as Santa Clauses, arriving with empty bags and with "Benito Claus" declaring, "This year I'm afraid my kiddies suspect who I really am!" (1942). Horrified by fascist indoctrination of children's minds and exploitation of their bodies, Seuss's script for *Your Job in Germany* warns that the most "dangerous" Germans the Americans would encounter were those who had been children when the Nazis rose to power: "They were brought up on straight propaganda, products of the worst educational crime in the entire history of the world."[17] *Design for Death*, another Seuss-scripted film, closes with a call for a more "democratic" postwar culture, identifying "the problem of educating our kids—*all our* kids—to be smarter than we've been." The children born into the postwar world offer "another chance" for peace, social equality, and democratic participation. This formulation is bound up with American nationalism, seeing "indoctrination" as the fostering of foreign ideologies and "education" as fostering American thinking. As Seuss entered the postwar era, he turned his attention to the challenges of addressing children.

## The Utah Lectures (1947): Seuss and the Postwar Era

In July 1947, Seuss gave a series of lectures and writing workshops at the University of Utah. His unpublished notes offer insights into his thoughts about children's literature as he entered the postwar era. Seuss's main lecture identified the need to reject banal and sugarcoated children's books in favor of works possessing the "vigor" of popular culture, striving for a middle ground between the high and the low. Seuss urged would-be children's writers to examine the popularity of comics, seeking a hybrid form that combined entertainment and uplift: "Over *here*, we put our readers to sleep. Over *there*, they wake 'em up with action.... Over *here*, we bore them with grandpa's dull reminiscences of the past. Over *there*, they offer them glimpses of the future."[18] Stressing the centrality of pleasure in motivating young readers, he warned against being "torchbearers" more interested in message than story: "The Japanese indoctrinated their kids with Shinto legends. Dictators, Hitler, Mussolini, indoctrinated kids' minds politically. (A job the U.S. Army is trying to undo now.)"[19] At the same time, he feared comics had no core values. The ideal children's book made reading "fun" *and* meaningful.

Distancing himself from wartime politics, Seuss's embrace of "democracy" still contained criticisms of the existing order, recognizing America's failures to fulfill its own ideals. In his Utah lectures, Seuss introduced race, stressing the "unhappy life" minorities experience in an America "which preaches equality but doesn't always practice it."[20] He challenged would-be writers to avoid racist stereotypes and urged a greater commitment to equality and justice. Ethnic and racial humor, including Black, Irish, and Jewish stereotypes, had been Seuss's stock-in-trade in the early 1930s. There, Seuss introduced exotica in the form of imaginary peoples and creatures, while his nonsense words were inspired by Yiddish, German, or Slavic languages. Like his war buddy Eastman, Seuss struggled to depict a more inclusive society while avoiding overt representations of racial difference. Old concerns about implicit and explicit racism across his work resurfaced in the debates that surrounded the announcement in 2021 that his estate was withdrawing some of his children's books, including *Mulberry Street*, from circulation. Ishizuka and Stephens have traced the persistence of various exotic and racist representations of foreignness (including Arabs in turbans, Africans in grass skirts, or "a Chinaman who eats with sticks") across his works, from the editorial cartoons to the postwar children's books.[21] As Philip Nel wrote in the *Washington Post*:

> Dr. Seuss does both racist and anti-racist work, often at the same period in his career. The 1940s cartoons are both racist against the Japanese and support civil rights for African Americans; the 1950s children's books include the racist caricature of *If I Ran the Zoo*, but also the anti-discrimination messages of *Horton Hears a Who!* and . . . *The Sneetches*. Dr. Seuss is recycling racist caricature at the same time he's striving to oppose racist ways of thinking.[22]

Seuss (1947) told his Utah audience that his stories "rise out of a child's psychology, rise out of a child's basic needs. If you go contrary to those needs, you're headed for trouble. If you write with these needs in mind, you'll have a chance of having children accept you."[23] Seuss suggested that *Horton Hatches the Egg* responded to a child's need to belong, to be accepted by others, to have a secure place within society. He urged potential writers to take children's frustrations seriously: "Children are thwarted people. Their idea of tragedy is when someone says you *can't* do that."[24] His best children's stories addressed children's anger toward parental rules and in doing so, respected children's innate sense of justice. More generally, Seuss's whimsical stories fulfilled children's needs for spontaneity: "They want *fun*. They want *play*. They want *nonsense*."[25]

Seuss's list of children's needs closely parallels the "emotional foods" Dorothy Baruch (1949) felt children required for their "emotional nourishment": affection, belonging, achievement, recognition, and understanding. Baruch, one of the most important wartime authorities on children, merged psychological insights with a core commitment to progressive reform. Seuss and Baruch both sought to protect children's imagination and sensuality from adult belittling. Baruch wrote: "There is a propulsion in every human being to fulfill himself in the deepest, richest and soundest way that he can. If only he is not beaten back too unmercifully. If only he is not too defeated. If only he is not hurt so much and made so angry that his real potentialities cannot get through."[26] Baruch was among a group of writers who spoke about "democratic" family lives; understanding their framework can contextualize Seuss's commitment to children's literature as a means of social change.

## Democracy Begins at Home

Anna W. M. Wolf ends *Our Children Face War* (1942) with what she anticipates will be the war's legacy:

> We shall work heart and soul for some sort of plan for world federation in partnership with all other nations regardless of race or color, who favor progress towards a democratic way of life.... We shall work heart and soul for the kind of society where for all men there is "freedom from want"—what Vice-President Wallace meant when he said that we are fighting "for the right of every child to a quart of milk a day." If it turns out that this means the comfortable classes surrendering some of their comforts, let us be ready permanently to surrender them.[27]

Wolf wanted children to see their parents as people who "feel deeply on matters of the state, of moral and spiritual truth, and ... translate these feelings into their acts as citizens."[28]

Much like Wolf, Baruch responded to the war's potential disruptions of American family life involving the father's absence, children's aggressive play, government restrictions, and hostility toward citizens of German and Japanese ancestry. Wartime children, she felt, needed security, unconditional acceptance, and self-respect; children needed a space to express their frustration over restrictions without censure or penalty: "Home and school will need to incorporate democratic principles into daily ongoing work so that children come to know them intimately and well.... To our children, democracy must not be something you-speak-of-but-do-not-live-by. It must assume reality."[29] Yet, Baruch feared that many parents suffered from authoritarian tendencies: "If he lives in a home.... where a dictator holds sway, he will be unlikely to form sound concepts concerning the democratic way of life."[30] Baruch described how one family reimagined the power relations between father and son:

> Each person now had a right to talk about the injustices he felt. Each person had a right to say his say in order to create conditions which would

be more compatible with the welfare of the group as a whole. . . . A new strength flourished. The strength of closeness, of confidence, of faith born of knowing that whatever was honestly felt and expressed would be acceptable; that each person had a right to free expression. Leadership replaced domination.[31]

Democratic participation required balancing autonomy with the need to respect norms.

These writers saw children as progressive forces bringing about a more peaceful world and a more just society. *Your Child Meets the World Outside* (1941) acknowledged that its goal was not simply to help "fit children to an existing world," but to give them "the tools with which to understand it" and "an ability to change it, to shape it toward their own ends."[32] Baruch (1944) warns, "If a child bows down in submission, if he is forever the good little boy, . . . he will be the last to raise a voice against any Fuehrer person who rises on the scene. He will continue to need just such a person to tell him how to steer and what to do."[33] The child was not to be so bound by social convention that "he cannot take his part in helping to change society—to weed out its ills and put it into better shape."[34]

"Democracy is something you do, not something you talk about," wrote University of Chicago political philosopher George B. de Huszar in his 1945 book *Practical Applications of Democracy*. "It is more than a form of government, or an attitude or opinion. It is participation."[35] Huszar, whose ideas were promoted by the Child Study Association, outlined how democratic practices, embraced as everyday collective decision-making, can intensify "the warm, personal, satisfying human relationships that develop when men join together in groups." For Huszar, the key was what he called the "problem-centered group," with the Parent Teacher Association cited as a prime example of a space where adults made decisions on behalf of collective interests. *Practical Application of Democracy* also argues that students should be involved in the decisions that most directly impact their lives: "It is a fatal mistake to believe that democratic education consists in merely teaching children some facts about our government and making them recite the Declaration of Independence."[36] Like Baruch, he worries that "authoritarian structure in education develops either children who are inhibited and obedient or children who evolve aggressive traits through being excessively frustrated."[37] Progressive critics condemned public schools as too regimented, controlling students rather than allowing them to learn at their individual pace.[38]

As *Our Children in the Atomic Age* (1948) explained: "Eventually we must have men who were born and bred since 1945: men who will be unhampered by the old disproved traditions. That means we must start with the children and give them better care, better bringing-up and better schooling."[39] With the threat of nuclear war hanging over their heads, educators and parents sought to eradicate the divisiveness, the racism, and the narrow-minded nationalism that had led to the last war. Prewar methods were rejected as having been "authoritarian," "dictatorial," "brainwashing," and "mind control," all metaphors carrying resonance in the Cold War era, whether applied to Nazi Germany, Imperial Japan, the Soviet Union, or later still, China and North Korea. Every aspect of family life was now weighed according to its potential effect on the child's democratic thinking. In *Shall Children, Too, Be Free?* (1949), Howard Lane urged parents to repudiate "the old Germanic-type family and school in which the master was clearly recognized and passively obeyed.... We Americans particularly admired the obedience, respectfulness, discipline of the children of Germany and Japan!"[40] *Our Children in the Atomic Age* warned that "strict discipline is the kind called for in armies, where men are trained to kill," not for American homes and schools where children are being prepared for citizenship.[41] These writers could never make the problem of adult power disappear altogether; they acknowledged that children needed adults and that adults determined the environment in which children were to be raised, but children also needed a civic voice.

## Kings, Turtles, and Other Tyrants

Seuss's postwar children's books display a commitment to the small and the weak (often in the form of the child) against the tyrannies of the big and the powerful (often in the form of adults). In the opening passages of *The 500 Hats of Bartholomew Cubbins* (1938), Seuss draws a sharp contrast between the perspective of the king with his "mighty view" peering down and that of his subjects as they look up at the castle:

"It was a mighty view, but it made Bartholomew Cubbins feel mighty small." Seuss consistently chooses the lower vantage point. Casting a peasant as a protagonist reflects Seuss's knowledge of the folktale traditions out of which modern children's fictions emerged.[42] Seuss takes pleasure in ridiculing the pretentious king, the pomposity of his court, the arbitrariness of his rules, and his bratty son—all foils for the disruptions caused by Cubbins's uncontrollable proliferation of hats. When the king orders Cubbins to remove his hat, another appears, and then another, "*Flupp.*" The king's efforts to control and discipline the child are absurdly misdirected, since the boy has no say over the hats' magical reproduction: "The King can do nothing dreadful to punish me, because I really haven't done anything wrong." Seuss also indicates the limits of adult knowledge: "But neither Bartholomew Cubbins, nor King Derwin himself, nor anyone else in the Kingdom of Didd could ever explain how the strange thing had happened." This magical disruption allows the boy to turn the kingdom upside down and then, set it right again.

*The 500 Hats* provided the template for several of Seuss's subsequent stories. In *The King's Stilts*, Lord Droon is a heartless puritan, outraged that his king ends his hard workdays by "having a bit of fun" with stilts. Droon hides the stilts, reducing the king to an apathetic stupor. Only the page boy, Eric, can outsmart Droon and restore the monarch's missing stilts, allowing him to save the kingdom from an approaching flood. Here, Seuss introduces two representations of adult authority—the repressive Lord Droon and the good-natured King Birtram. The king and his page boy bond through play. In the end, the ruler bestows upon Eric a pair of stilts, his reward for unmasking Droon's treachery: "From then on, every day at five, they always raced on stilts together. And when they played, they really PLAYED. And when they worked, they really worked." As Robert L. Griswold has documented, permissive writers reconceptualized fatherhood, shifting attention from fathers' traditional functions as breadwinner and disciplinarian toward a new role as playmate.[43] Experts argued that coming home from work and playing with their sons rejuvenated world-weary fathers, while exposing growing boys to the masculine realm. Play was understood as an escape from social control, as a space of the free imagination. At the same time, this revaluing of play paved the way for the leisure- and consumption-oriented culture demanded by the postwar economy. Once again, we can think about Wolfenstein's "Fun Morality."

In *Bartholomew and the Oobleck*, the megalomaniac King Didd brings destruction upon his kingdom, seeking not only to master his subjects but also to rule the weather. Bored with snow, rain, fog, and sunshine, the ill-tempered king demands his court magicians make something *new* come down from the sky. A sticky green substance called "Oobleck" falls in blobs and gums up the whole city. The commonsensical Bartholomew warns about Oobleck's dangers, but the adults do nothing until it is too late. Bartholomew disciplines the king: "You may be a mighty king. But you're sitting in Oobleck up to your chin. And so is everyone else in your land. And if you won't even say you're sorry, you're no sort of a king at all!"

Dorothy Baruch urged parents to admit their mistakes, question their own authority, and be more accepting when children protested their control. In the democratic family, parental rule was neither absolute nor infallible. Writing in 1949 (the same year as *The Oobleck*), Baruch counseled, "When our children begin to protest that which they see as oppression in our dealings with them, we need to stop and think. We need to take stock."[44] Adults' dictatorial behavior, Baruch argued, was often rooted in their own childhood, when they had felt belittled by their parents: "We, who were once small and helpless, may still need ascendancy to make us feel adequate to cope with life's demands."[45] Adults who bullied children were passing these traits on to the next generation.

Richard Sargent's "Anger Transference," produced for the cover of the March 20, 1954, *Saturday Evening Post*, captures the ways these writers understood the relationship between adult power and childhood trauma (figure 3.1). Across four images the boss scolds the father, the father scolds the mother, the mother scolds the son, and the son scolds his pet. Baruch would have added that the boss's humiliation of the father is itself a by-product of his own humiliations and frustrations as a child. Sargent's visual style today evokes the far more familiar images Norman Rockwell produced, given that Rockwell and Sargent used to compete for cover space at the *Post*.

Seuss captured many of these same themes but in a fundamentally different visual style. He continued to use his stories to confront the

Figure 3.1: Richard Sargent's "Anger Transference" (1954) depicts a cycle where bullying by adults passes down from parent to child.

issues facing American society long after his immediate impressions of the war started to fade. In one Seuss poem, "The Ruckus" (July 1954), the titular creature wants to "make a noise that the whole world will hear," but discovers that he has nothing to say.[46] Yertle the Turtle wants to be "ruler of all that I see," stacking up his subjects so that he can see more and more. In the end, his rule is challenged by the bottom-most turtle, Mack: "I don't like to complain, but down here below, we are feeling great pain. I know, up on top you are seeing great sights, but down at the bottom we, too, should have rights." Mack sends Yertle tumbling face down into the mud: "All the turtles are free as turtles and, maybe, all creatures should be."[47] In Seuss's world, children, the small, those at the bottom are depicted as clear-headed, expressing their dissatisfactions over unreasonable demands. Seuss was continuing Ingersoll's fight against "people who push other people around."

## The 5,000 Fingers of Dr. T. (1952)

The live-action feature *The 5,000 Fingers of Doctor T.*, for which Seuss wrote the script and did many early production designs, represents the fullest elaboration of his conception of children as "thwarted people," struggling to find their own voice in a world dominated by authoritarian adults. Seuss's notes and original drafts for the script offer evidence that he was consciously mapping contemporary insights about child-rearing over images associated with the war, much as writers like Baruch were using wartime metaphors to explain why parents should avoid "dictatorial" choices. *The 5,000 Fingers* deals with the plight of Bartholomew Collins (Tommy Rettig), who finds learning to play the piano a fate worse than death. His instructor, Dr. Terwilliker (Hans Conried), insists that "practice makes perfect." The bulk of the film consists of Bartholomew's dream, in which he and the other boys overthrow Terwilliker and his plans for world domination. As Seuss explained to producer Stanley Kramer: "The kid, psychologically, is in a box. The dream mechanism takes these elements that are thwarting him and blows them up to gigantic proportions."[48]

If this description foregrounds issues of child psychology, central to the finished film, earlier drafts make frequent references to the struggle against fascism. In Bart's waking reality, Dr. T. is "not especially frightening," a "tight-lipped and methodical looking old gentleman ... no more vicious and harmful than Victor Moore."[49] Once we enter Bart's dream, however, Seuss increasingly characterizes Dr. T. as the reincarnation of der Führer. His kingdom is "plastered with posters, showing Dr. Terwilliker in a Hitler-like dictator's pose." His soldiers wear medals that "resemble an iron cross ... engraved with a likeness of Dr. Terwilliker in the center." Bart's mother has a "gauleiter-like allegiance" to Terwilliker that blinds her to her son's agonies. When he is challenged, Dr. T. "flies into a Hitlerian rage."

Many traces of this Hitler analogy remain in the final film. The sets are hyperbolic versions of monumental architecture; the grand

Figure 3.2: *The 5,000 Fingers of Dr. T* (1952) recycles fascist imagery to critique authoritarian styles of pedagogy and parenting.

procession borrows from Leni Riefenstahl's *Triumph of the Will* (1935), with Hitler's blue-helmeted henchmen goose-stepping and holding aloft giant versions of his "Happy Fingers" logo (see figure 3.2). Terwilliker's elaborate conductor's uniform, one reviewer noted, was "a combination of a circus band drum major, Carmen Miranda, and Hermann Goering."[50] Hans Conried's long thin body and his floppy black hair closely resemble Seuss's *PM* caricatures of Hitler (minus the mustache). Conried had narrated *Design for Death*, performing the voices of the fascist leaders. That said, Conried's campy performance often transcends any rigid parallels between Dr. T. and der Führer. The character actor, a longtime veteran of radio comedy, rolls his villainous lines with relish, offering the hapless plumber Zlabadowski a toast with his "best vintage" of pickle juice before ordering him to be disintegrated slowly—"atom by atom—at dawn!" Across several musical numbers, T. seems more like a child at play, enjoying "glorious weather for zipping and zooming," demanding that his men "dress me up" in more and more extravagant duds, including such effeminate clothing as "pink brocaded bodices," "peek-a-boo blouses," and "chiffon Mother Hubbards." Dr. T. fits alongside Yertle the Turtle and young "Adolphkins" within the long tradition of infantile and impulsive tyrants in Seuss's work.

The film's more disturbing images drew on popular memories of concentration camps. Arriving by yellow school buses rather than railway cars, the unfortunate boys are herded through gates, where their comic books, balls, slingshots, and pet frogs are confiscated. Then they are marched to their "lock-me-tights" in the dungeon. There, Dr. T. dreams up tortures for all those who refuse to play his beloved keyboard. The captive musicians have sullen eyes and sunken cheeks and are lean and gaunt in their prison uniforms. Baruch (1942) drew strong analogies between standard classroom practices and the ways children (and soldiers) were treated by the Third Reich: "They have sat at desks, lined up like automata—or like the marching children one sees in fascist countries. They have all performed identically under orders, like the youngest of the youth bands in Germany. They have marched evenly lined up, without uniform or guns, but in no less regimented fashion."[51]

Constructing the sympathetic plumber, Zlabadowski, Seuss drew other wartime associations. In the first-draft script, Zlabadowski is linked with Eastern Europe. "Shaking his head sadly in deep Slavic gloom," Zlabadowski is "a big shaggy . . . [but] kindly Molotov with the cosmic unhappiness of Albert Einstein." As the script progresses, Zlabadowski abandons such associations except for the rather distinctive name, becoming a more all-American type, a reluctant patriot who must first shed his isolationism before he can be enlisted as Bart's ally in the struggle to stop Terwillikerism: "Z's conflict: Desire to help people. Desire to keep out of trouble. An old soldier trying to be a pacifist. He's tired of war. It's futile."[52] In the early drafts, Zlabadowski knows Terwilliker's evil plans but doesn't want to get involved. In the finished film, Zlabadowski represents the ideal permissive father. Initially, he is distracted by his work, dismissing Bart's warnings as wild-eyed fantasies.[53] Ultimately, he becomes a warmhearted playmate (engaging the boy in a pretend fishing trip) and a wise counselor (constructing a sound-stopping device from the contents of the boy's pockets). Angered by Zlabadowski's initial indifference, Bart challenges his adult privileges and sings a song that might have been the anthem for permissive child-rearing: "Just because we're kids, because we're sorta small, because we're closer to the ground, and you are bigger pound by pound, you have no right, you have no right to push and shove us little kids around." Zlabadowski regains his idealism (echoing Ingersoll): "I don't like anybody who pushes anybody around."

In the film's opening scene, Bart offhandedly remarks upon the death of his father, presumably during the war. Zlabadowski and Terwilliker are cast as good and bad surrogate fathers, respectively. In Bart's nightmare, his piano-crazed mother is hypnotized into accepting Terwilliker's hand, a deal to be consummated immediately following the great concert. Not unlike Lord Droon in *The King's Stilts*, Terwilliker represents the prewar patriarch who demands obedience. Bart hopes that the more permissive Zlabadowski will become his father, an arrangement consummated by their blood oath. Zlabadowski understands the needs of boys; he represents the manly virtues of fishing and baseball against Dr. Terwilliker's effeminate high culture (his piano playing, his foppish dress, his fine cigars), defending America against Terwilliker's Germany.

In the end, the task of finding the right father and overcoming the bad patriarch falls squarely on Bart's shoulders. He alone will face Terwilliker, using his "*very* atomic" sound-catching device to disrupt the concert and liberate the children. The closing moments, where rebellious children hurl their music sheets in the air, shouting in defiance, stomping on and punching the piano keys, represents one of the most vivid images of resistance in all of American cinema. By this point, Bart's struggle against Terwilliker has absorbed tremendous ideological weight, a struggle of the freedom-fighting all-American boy against an old-school tyrant, of those who are "closer to the ground" against those who "beat little kids about," of permissive parenting against more authoritarian alternatives.

In the final analysis, Seuss's children's books were as political as any of his war-related work. They helped American parents to imagine how domestic life could be restructured along more democratic lines. They participated in a larger movement to help children overcome the prejudices and the divisiveness that had "poisoned" America's war effort. Seuss offered fantasies where powerful rulers are foolish and destined to end face down in the mud. His stories depicted worlds where children challenge kings and force them to apologize to their subjects, or where kids lead a schoolhouse revolt against an unreasonable teacher.

## From "Here and Now" to "Fun That Is Fun"

Seuss's fantastical worlds fly in the face of the dominant aesthetic for children's reading matter—at least as it had been advanced by librarians, educators, and advice writers over the prior few decades. In 1939, Baruch had proposed: "Many teachers today are aware that children best express themselves in words when their words can germinate and grow out of the soil of experience. Therefore, they encourage talking about things done, about things made, about trips they have taken, about new babies at home, about anything which children wish to recall out of their living."[54]

In making this case, Baruch specifically cites Lucy Sprague Mitchell, who was the first female faculty member at the University of California–Berkeley before helping to establish the Bureau of Educational Experiments, sometimes known as 69 Bank Street. In a profile of their teacher, Mary Phillips and Margaret Wise Brown (best known as the author of *Goodnight Moon*) described 69 Bank Street as "a sort of cooperative town hall for experimental educators . . . where experienced teachers, research workers, writers, anyone concerned with children, may come and benefit from the latest work of child specialists."[55] Through her work with the City and Country Schools, where she observed the day-to-day interactions between teachers and young children, Mitchell developed and modeled a distinctive approach to storytelling, grounded in children's everyday realities: "Her great discovery about children was that they are, above all, explorers, from the time they are babies soberly or playfully handling everything in reach; that in their preschool days, at least, the here-and-now world they can take in directly is big enough, varied enough, to call forth all their young powers of sense and imagination."

In her influential *Here and Now Story Book*, Mitchell (1921) values "anything which a child gives his spontaneous attention, anything which he questions as he moves around the world," starting with the people in the child's own neighborhood.[56] As Baruch (1939), following Mitchell, recounts, "on the way to the nursery they see many things. A postman is collecting letters from a mailbox, a policeman is regulating traffic, a street-car goes by, and the conductor gets out to shift a switch, and wonder of wonders, a fire-engine manned with firemen is just driving out of its station."[57] Mitchell rejected stories that drew too much on fantasy, worrying about "nonsense which is confused with reality" and thus damages children's ability to process their own experiences.[58] Educators encouraged children to construct their own stories and to record and transmit the results, with much of Mitchell's writing centered on her analysis of form and content in stories from children at different ages.

Baruch served on the committee that produced the 1946–47 edition of the Scott–Foresman Sally, Dick, and Jane textbook series for the first-grade classroom. Here, the observational values of the *Here and Now* stories are expressed through the repeated use of the words "look" and "see"—actions children were meant to perform as they engaged with these illustrated primers. Eleanor Campbell, their original illustrator, grounded her art in everyday realism, working with real children as models and updating their outfits based on clothing in the Sears Roebuck and Montgomery Ward catalogs. When the earliest of the Sally, Dick, and Jane books were first published in 1930, reading authority William S. Gray supplemented the text-heavy look of traditional readers with a greater reliance on visual comprehension. He encouraged whole-word recognition (a particular theory of reading that is often set in opposition to sounding out the word through phonetics), and he wanted illustrations to carry the weight of telling the story. Educators asked children to decipher the pictures through a question-and-response process, identifying motives and contexts not conveyed by words alone. This focus on visual literacy became increasingly pronounced over the years, much as media-literacy discourses became more widespread in response to radio during the war and the introduction of television.

Though the *Here and Now Story Book* had stressed urban environments, the world of the Dick and Jane readers was distinctly suburban. Sally, Dick, and Jane live in a multibedroom house with a sprawling backyard, surrounded by the latest toys and fashions; they have a stay-at-home mom and a dad who returns from his job at the end of the day; and they engage with a wide array of other caring adults—teachers, policemen, postmen, milkmen, grocers. Black children would not appear until the mid-1960s, and by that point the book's worldview was widely considered old-fashioned. As a 1951 teacher's edition explained:

> Not all homes are happy or filled with warmth and understanding of children. There are noisy, crowded homes, surrounded by dirt and squalor.... There are homes where the standards of order and cleanliness come first and children second. There are broken homes and unhappy homes where the child feels no sense of belonging.... When such deprived children lose themselves in stories about Dick, Jane and Sally, and live for a time with these happy storybook characters, they experience

the same release from their problems that the adult does when he loses himself in a good book or a movie.[59]

Writing for *Life* in 1954, novelist John Hersey, fresh off a stint as chairman of the Citizens School Study Council of Fairfield, Connecticut, blamed the Dick and Jane readers for diminishing children's imaginations: "Is not revulsion against namby-pamby school readers perhaps a reason why they like lurid comic books so much?"[60] Echoing Seuss's own Utah lectures, Hersey contrasted the "insipid illustrations depicting the slicked-up lives of other children" that he found "uniform, bland, idealized and literal" with the "wonderfully imaginative works" of the best artists and writers for children. In particular, he cited Dr. Seuss, alongside Walt Disney and John Tenniel, for producing works that appealed to children's creativity. William Spaulding, the head of Houghton Mifflin's education division, read Hersey's essay and contacted Seuss to see if he might confront the challenge. One result was *The Cat in the Hat*, a book Seuss wrote using the three-hundred-word vocabulary educators saw as age-appropriate for first graders. Seuss claimed that "cat" and "hat" were the first two words he could find that rhymed.

Margaret Mead was another critic of the realist approach, complaining that classic fairy tales had been displaced by "here-and-now people—postmen, ferryboat captains, farmers, engine drivers; and boys and girls who visited the zoo, rode on trains, spent a day at the seashore, learned what the conductor really did and where milk really came from, how to make friends with a new kitten, what a day in school was like."[61] In this 1962 essay, Mead protested that children were "bored to death" by these "dismally unimaginative" and "denatured, dull" stories, a state she contrasted with the excitement children felt reading fairy tales, classic myths, and books such as *Stuart Little*, *Mary Poppins*, or *The Hobbit*: "There is no body of traditional wonder to teach small children about the difference between dreams and nightmare and reality."[62] In this debate between "here and now" realism and wonder tales, we see the clash between two aesthetics, both with legitimate links to permissive parenting: one celebrated children's observations and the other, their imaginations.[63]

In his first children's book, *And To Think That I Saw It on Mulberry Street* (1938), Seuss had pitted the child, Marco, who let his imagination run wild, against his father who wanted his son to report with accuracy on his own neighborhood: "Keep your eyelids up and see what you can see." But paying close attention on his way to school and back, "I've looked, and I've looked and I've kept careful track" but he found "nothing to tell." Step-by-step, Seuss watched Marco remodel and refine his story, transforming a simple horse into a zebra and then, expanding on the idea until a whole menagerie of creatures were parading through the streets, "a story that no one can beat." But the closer Marco gets to home, the more he finds himself recanting: "He [the father] frowned at me sternly from there in his seat, 'was there nothing to look at. . . . No people to greet? Did nothing excite you or make your heart beat?' 'Nothing,' I said, growing red as a beet, 'But a plain horse and wagon on Mulberry Street.'" Here, Seuss's ending is ambivalent, as the child is forced to accept the "here and now" world to please his father.

And these flights of fancy made Seuss's fictions something rather different from the Dick and Jane books. Surely, it is no coincidence that the girl in *Cat in the Hat* is named Sally (the same as the youngest sibling in the school primers) or that the children are shown bored out of their minds looking out the window on a day when "the sun did not shine. It was too wet to play. . . . Too wet to go out and too cold to play ball," so all they could do was "Sit! Sit! Sit! Sit! And we did not like it, not one little bit."[64] We might compare Seuss's cartoonish image of the backs of the two children looking sadly out the window (figure 3.3a) with a similar image from the school texts as children are entertaining themselves quietly while it rains, seemingly content with their fate (figure 3.3b).[65] In the earlier textbooks, children were asked to "look and see" the world at their doorstep, but in Seuss's story, the playful children are insisting on being seen and heard: "Look (figure 3.3b) at me! Look at me! Look at me NOW!" These words suggest a familiar cry for attention heard often on the playground. In Seuss's story, the trickster, Cat in the Hat, bursts onto the scene, bringing the children "lots of good fun if you wish." Introducing "games" involving ever-broader transgressions of everyday rules, the Cat and his companions, Thing One and Thing Two, smash into their parents' bedroom, rummaging through their closet, and using the mother's dresses as a kite tail they romp about "with big bumps, jumps, and kicks."

One would never find any such reckless play in the Dick and Jane books. In their nostalgic account, Carole Kismaric and Marvin Heiferman write, "Full of energy like most little kids, Dick and Jane and Sally seldom sit still. They spend most of their time out of the house, out of doors, swimming, juggling, kite-flying, racing and throwing balls. In their backyard or on the front sidewalk, they run and jump and swing and slide."[66] As they do, they sometimes have accidents, but they rarely break the rules. In Scott Foresman's world, everything is put into order by the good little boys and girls, modeling what educators saw as normative behavior. In Seuss's story, Sally and her brother are depicted as sometimes pleased, sometimes shocked by the Cat's disruptions. They are not bad kids, but they contain just enough naughtiness to enjoy seeing what the Cat is going to do next. And the children allow these transgressions to continue until the mother's return, despite the warnings of the fish, who speaks on behalf of the orderly and the mundane: "You should not be here when our mother is not." Seuss's images and wordplay are seductive, making the child complicit in this pursuit of "fun that is fun" even if it means sometimes making a mess. And, in the end, the parent reading the book is meant to endorse the idea that children might want to keep secrets from the adults: "Should we tell her the things that went on there that day? Should we tell her about it? Now, what SHOULD we do? Well . . . What would YOU do if your mother asked YOU?" Seuss sets up a distinction between what children "should" do and what *you* "would" do. The two are not the same and the child reader was meant to appreciate the freedom represented by the latter.

Seuss's fanciful stories suggest that there are no limits to the realm of the imagination, which extends, as one of his books suggests, "on beyond Zebra." We might see this implicit appeal to the rights of children to have a secret life as a further domestication of the stories Seuss wrote both before and after the war about bright young boys who challenged adult authorities and even tore their textbooks apart (at least in the closing scenes of *5,000 Fingers*). Once again, Seuss demonstrated that adults had no right to push and shove little kids around.

Whether looking at his shorter fables and fairy tales (such as the Cubbins books, *Yertle the Turtle*, and *Horton Hears a Who!*) or his feature

Sally said, "See my boat.
I want my little boat.
I want my little boat in here."

Jane said, "Dick can get it.
Dick is big.
Dick can go and get it."

"Not now," said Dick.
"I can not get it now."

Figure 3.3a: Illustrations from a Sally, Dick, and Jane school primer (left) and Seuss's *The Cat in the Hat* (right) show how children entertain themselves on a rainy afternoon.

film *5,000 Fingers of Dr. T.*, Seuss often depicts adult authorities as pompous and controlling while seeing the young men who challenge them as freedom fighters. Seuss's focus on nonsense can be read as a defense of children's imaginations against educators who still embraced the aesthetic concerns of the Here and Now movement. That Seuss's wild-eyed books gained parental approval in the 1960s tells us something about how Haim Ginott's "freedom to wish" was being embraced

Figure 3.3b: (*Continued*)

in the home. In the next chapter, we will discuss other images of disruptive, monstrous, transgressive children—the "wild things" that give this book its title. These stories imply a new evaluation of children's desires and pleasures that reflected Spock's popularization of Freudian concepts regarding children's sexual development.

# 4

## "Sometimes My Kids Seem like a Bunch of Kangaroos"

*Desire, Transgression, and Permissiveness*

In a commercial from the late 1950s, three children—two girls and a boy—are bouncing up and down atop the kitchen floor. The mother, hands on hips, watches with dismay: "Good grief! Pogo sticks! Sometimes my kids seem like a bunch of kangaroos!" And at that moment, a dissolve shows bouncing marsupials. "My floors are all scratched up. What a mess!" the mom fumes, before shrugging, "What can you do? I can't change my family." The announcer interjects, "Yes, but you can change your floor wax," before doing an extended spiel for Beacon Quick Gloss, "made especially for heavy family traffic." This advertisement seems emblematic of its moment—not simply in its normative white suburban imagery, but also in accommodating children's messes rather than disciplining their behavior.

The mother's bemused dismissal that she might "change" her family would have seemed alien to previous generations. John Watson saw parents as blacksmiths shaping children's minds into "instruments" appropriate for the modern world: "The fabricator of metal takes his heated mass, places it upon the anvil and begins to shape it according to patterns of his own. . . . So inevitably do we begin at birth to shape the emotional life of our children."[1] Watson's *Psychological Care of Infant and Child* sought to make this process more "scientific" by bringing emotional life under "control." The child was being shaped to work in the industrial world:

> A child who never cries unless actually stuck by a pin . . .—who loses himself in work and play—who quickly learns to overcome the small difficulties in his environment without running to mother, father, nurse or other adult—who soon builds up a wealth of habits that tide him over dark and rainy days—who puts on such habits of politeness and neatness

and cleanliness that adults are willing to be around him at least part of the day; a child who is willing to be around adults without fighting incessantly for notice—who eats what is set before him and "asks no questions"...— who sleeps and rests when put to bed for sleep and rest—who puts away 2 year old habits when the third year has to be faced...—and who finally enters manhood bulwarked with stable work and emotional habits that no adversity can quite overwhelm him.[2]

For Watson, the ideal child was engineered to be managed at home and in the future workplace. This approach is antisentimental, antisensual, and antiseptic. By feeding the child on a regular schedule, putting it to bed and picking it up according to the clock, toilet training it at the appropriate age, parents would instill regularity. Developing good habits required that authority be absolute and unwavering, that discipline be systematic and strict.

Spock and the other postwar authorities, on the other hand, saw children's groping fingers as evidence of a desire to explore their surroundings. Constraint of erotic impulses, far from necessary, was potentially harmful to the child's development. *Parents* magazine warned in 1961, "Much of the actual socializing process is a throttling of the child's spontaneity and a stifling of his creativity," a deformation of mental development that, in a Cold War–appropriate analogy, it likened to "brainwashing."[3] Much like the mother in the Quick Gloss advertisement, parents were to accommodate children's healthy impulses: "The tiny child wants to touch, feel, and taste everything which he can reach. This is his way of learning. Yet, so often mother follows him around turning aside his interest and his curiosity with 'Don't touch that,' 'Don't put that in your mouth.'"[4] Two classic permissive themes intersect: first, a core faith in the body as driven toward pleasure and knowledge, and second, the fear of thwarting that natural growth through adult restrictions.

Across the twentieth century, the threat of childhood diseases gave way to a new focus on psychological health and social development. And then, a model based on discipline and habit was replaced by one based on empathy and acceptance of children's desires and emotions. Spock (1945) explains: "Every baby needs to be smiled at, talked to, played with, fondled—gently and lovingly—just as much as he needs vitamins and calories, and the baby who doesn't get any loving will grow up cold and unresponsive."[5] New research saw psychological harms resulting from sensory deprivation. Margaret A. Ribble's *The Rights of Infants* (1943) stressed the "vital importance" of parents respecting and even encouraging children's sensuousness: "Nature seems to have a purpose in this earliest biological endowment of pleasure, for it gives the child a sense of the goodness of his physical self. . . . Erotic feeling is diffuse in a baby, but it is not misplaced and does not imply something evil which must be weeded out."

The child's body told it when it needed to eat, when it needed to rest, and when it was ready to go potty. Spock cites a study by Dr. Clara Davis that demonstrated that children left to choose their own foods would gravitate toward a well-balanced diet. He appeals to a belief that children, like other animal species, have "some instinctual knowledge of what is good for [them]."[6] Spock rejected the Watsonian notion that good habits can be instilled:

> His bowels . . . will move according to their own healthy pattern, which may or may not be regular. . . . He will develop his own pattern of sleep, according to his own needs. . . . The desire to get along with other people happily and considerately develops within him as part of the unfolding of his nature, provided he grows up with loving, self-respecting parents. . . . You can't drill these into a child from the outside in a hundred years.[7]

Aline B. Auerbach (1951), writing for the Child Study Association, describes the baby's first sensual encounters: "Everything within sight is exciting and interesting as soon as a child finds he can move around—by crawling, sliding, edging sideways or walking—under his own steam. Nothing is safe. Ashtrays, cigarettes, dishes, your favorite book with a bright cover, your sewing box—these are new worlds to explore, first to touch and feel and then to put in his mouth, which is another way of finding out what things are like."[8] Such explorations were to be rendered safe and sanitary: "Set aside a special drawer, or shelf or cardboard box of things he can explore and play with as he will. He will gradually learn from you the difference between what he can play with—and what he can't."[9] Where this is not possible, the child should be taught to sublimate aggressive, destructive, or autoerotic feelings into some more acceptable outlet: "The year-old baby is so eager to find out about the whole world that he isn't particular where he begins or where he stops."[10]

The moral and emotional shifts that allowed the average American to indulge in new comforts were reshaping how they thought about their children's lives. These ideas, Wolfenstein's "fun morality," supported a more consumer-oriented lifestyle. There was an explosion of new products, such as toys or sweetened breakfast cereals, designed to pamper children, but there were also marketing efforts to create brand loyalty in consumers still in the nursery.[11]

Prewar metaphors depicting children as animals and savages might convey an anxiety about control and discipline, the threat that children's misconduct posed, and the importance of the civilizing process. These metaphors assumed different connotations as parents, child-rearing experts, and creators of children's fictions celebrated children as "wild things." Bring on the kangaroos! At the same time, anxiety about a loss of adult control persisted as a counterdiscourse, constituted around the monstrous child allowed too much license becoming a tyrant whose will cannot be challenged if one wants to preserve domestic tranquility.

I will start with a focus on Benjamin Spock and the ways he absorbed ideas from psychoanalysis, anthropology, and other disciplines to inform his advice to parents, resulting in a shifting understanding of children and their pleasure. I will then explore three case studies: Maurice Sendak's *Where the Wild Things Are* (1963); *Little Fugitive* (1953) and more generally the works of Morris Engel and Ruth Orkin; and memorable 1961 episodes of *The Twilight Zone* ("It's a Good Life") and *Alfred Hitchcock Presents* ("Bang! You're Dead"), both featuring Bill Mumy.

## Unpacking Benjamin Spock

However "modern" Spock's advice seemed, its roots can be traced back to early twentieth-century sources—especially Sigmund Freud's writings about child sexuality, Margaret Mead's anthropological explorations of sexual development in other cultural contexts, and G. Stanley Hall's theories of recapitulation. One of Benjamin Spock's primary accomplishments was to introduce Freudian concepts as "common sense." Martha Weinman Lear (1961) was critical of Spock's influence but did acknowledge this accomplishment: "He has simply mastered the trick, as few others have, of serving up Freudian concepts camouflaged in such palatable form that they slide like soda pop down the most distrustful gullet."[12] Permissive parents, aware of the neurosis caused by repression, sought to ensure children's smooth passage through successive stages of sexual development so they could avoid unnatural fixations. Spock was reverse engineering Freud, who had conducted casework on adult pathologies to understand their root causes in childhood trauma. Spock normalized Freud's stages of sexual development as something every child was expected to complete on their path to adulthood, not unlike Gesell and Ilg's stages of cognitive and physical development. Consider, for example, this passage from Dorothy Baruch (1952) tracing the child's movement from the oral to the genital stages:

> Watch a baby. See how he likes to be petted and stroked, how he likes to suck; the pleasure it gives him. . . . As he grows he becomes interested in bowel movements and finds body-pleasure in elimination. You can read it in the self-satisfied expression on his face if you watch in an unprejudiced way when he is quite small. As he develops in his thinking, he makes up fantasies about these things, which are so intimate to him, so near at hand and so close. This is natural. . . . They wonder not only about their own bodies but about the bodies of others and are more or less concerned with similarities and differences between the sexes and between grown-ups and themselves. All children are interested in hollows and protuberances and connect these up in conscious or unconscious fantasies with maleness and femaleness. . . . These things are a normal part of growing up. They are not signs of problems but of normal development.[13]

Advocates of the permissive paradigm translated concepts that had seemed perverse to previous generations into practical and reassuring advice, explaining how to cope with the oedipal phase and its attending traumas. Sexual openness was something parents owed their children, so the task was to overcome their own inhibitions.

This ideal of the sensuous child also reflected the popularization of anthropological discoveries about alternative constructions of sexuality. Margaret Mead's work on the Samoans in the 1920s and 1930s offered America an image of a less sexually repressed society[14] Mead's descriptions of a culture that dealt matter-of-factly with casual nudity, masturbation, and sex play (both heterosexual and homosexual) titillated middle America, challenging it to rethink its taboos. Something of the relations between Mead and Spock is suggested in an October 1959 exchange captured in the Mead papers where Spock asks Mead:

> Can you, from the top of your head, give me one, two or three references on the behavior of children in the age period between 6 and 12 years in several parts of the world. I am curious particularly about the occurrence, absence, variability of such phenomena as we call evidence of latency: relative suppression of sex play, superficial revulsion toward girls on the part of boys, stand-offishness toward parents (primarily between boys and mothers), irritating behavior directed at parents, interest in standards and rules, spontaneous club formation, growing preference for ritualistic games in place of realistic imitation of parents, compulsive habits (such as our children's stepping over cracks), prevalence of tics. It would be nice to know whether there are any suggestions of correlation between latency manifestations and intensity of prohibitions at all age levels against sexuality and aggressiveness.[15]

By this point they were both key public intellectuals, whom parents sought to better understand their children's development. This tidbit represents a potential intersection between the anthropological literature from which Mead drew and the more psychological literature that informed Spock's writings. Less than a week later, Mead responded, "This is the year when everyone is thinking about latency" and listed a range of scholarly projects on latency in "primitive children" before referencing her own paper that was "not quite far enough along for this to be useful to you."[16] Shifting gears, she noted, "Someday we'll have to analyze all the results of your being Cathy's pediatrician. I have a feeling the reverberations are profound." But if such a conversation took place, she left no breadcrumbs for future historians.

Spock often uses the defamiliarizing potential of anthropological observation to contest puritanism. He refers to "lands where childhood masturbation is not disapproved of by anyone" as a contrast to American society where "many people consider genital play in childhood wrong, and almost everybody objects to seeing it in public."[17]

Spock romanticizes the closer relation between man and nature within the more "primitive" stages of human evolution:

> It will help you to realize how natural a flexible schedule is if you stop and think of a mother, far away in an "uncivilized" land, who has never heard of a schedule, or a pediatrician, or a cow. Her baby starts to cry with hunger. This attracts her attention and makes her feel like putting him to breast. He nurses until he is satisfied, then falls asleep. . . . The rhythm of the baby's digestive system is what sets the schedule. The mother follows her instinct without any hesitation.[18]

Spock saw the child as knowing its needs better than its parents and saw what he calls "uncivilized" culture as having a more comfortable relationship to the body.

Spock describes children as recapitulating the evolutionary process, starting as a single-cell organism, working through lower animal forms within the womb, and then slowly learning to walk, talk, and assimilate into the culture: "He's following the whole history of the human race."[19] Spock's ideas about recapitulation had their precedent, half a century earlier, in the work of G. Stanley Hall. Hall imagined that human beings needed to repeat the stages of evolution (through embryonic development and through their social development after birth), becoming young animals and then young savages as they progressed through the stages toward modern civilization.[20] Hall's account takes as given his era's scientific racism, seeing whiteness as the highest cultural achievement. He felt that children younger than eight still needed to express and expel their "animal emotions" before schooling would make them fully human. Children's play with mud, for example, demonstrated that children were "infused" with faint memories of "the species' primordial amphibious origins," reflecting the moment "when our seaborn ancestors first made good their footing on the beach."[21] Similarly, Hall spoke of a "Big Injun stage" that terminated at age eleven, during which the child's tendencies toward tribalism and a testing of adult boundaries mimicked the skills required of more nomadic peoples. Hall's Big Injun stage was institutionalized through the YMCA's Indian Guides program where adult "chiefs" led their boys, organized around tribes, through native-American-themed activities with their accomplishments rewarded with feathers for their headdresses.

Kathryn Hitte's Little Golden Book *I'm an Indian Today* (1961) plays with Hall's concept of the Big Injun stage, depicting a day in the life of John, who decides: "Today, today, I'm an Indian. A wild, wild Indian of the Old Wild West. I'll track in the woods and I'll ride like the wind. I'll kill all the buffalos and I'll sneak up on the settlers! That's what you do when you're a wild, wild Indian of the Old Wild West."[22] The book punctures the boy's fantasies both through illustrations showing his rubber-tipped arrows striking a Teddy Bear when he claims to be killing buffalo and with a depiction of him astride a doghouse when he says he is riding like the wind. Hitte shows him constantly tempted by modern affordances. A wild Indian does not ride a neighbor's bike, chase after fire engines, crave peanut-butter-and-jelly sandwiches, or cry when he skins his knee. By the end, John decides that he may "play" Indian in the future, but he will not "be" an Indian, a distinction that bemuses and confuses his mother (figure 4.1) However much the permissive imagination embraced the "Indian" as an emblem for the "wildness" of white children, actual Native American children were faring much worse whether as students in impoverished reservation schools or separated from their parents.[23] In some ways the celebration of their "wildness" only justified the need to "civilize" Indian children, even as it freed white people to act out.

Mead was skeptical about claims that Western children needed to work through more "primitive" stages: "Each society has its own way of bringing up the children and letting them learn through play, how to be adults in their own society. And these games don't recapitulate the history of the race, but instead fit into the particular society."[24] Mead saw recapitulation as romantic nonsense: "Children aren't little savages; they start from scratch, remembering nothing of tipi and earth lodge, of snow hut or tree dwelling, ready, instead, from the moment of birth to learn to live in this world of 1948."[25]

These metaphors of children as animals, monsters, or savages ("Injuns") persisted as a way that adults understood childish conduct, but permissive writers had greater sympathy than previous (and subsequent)

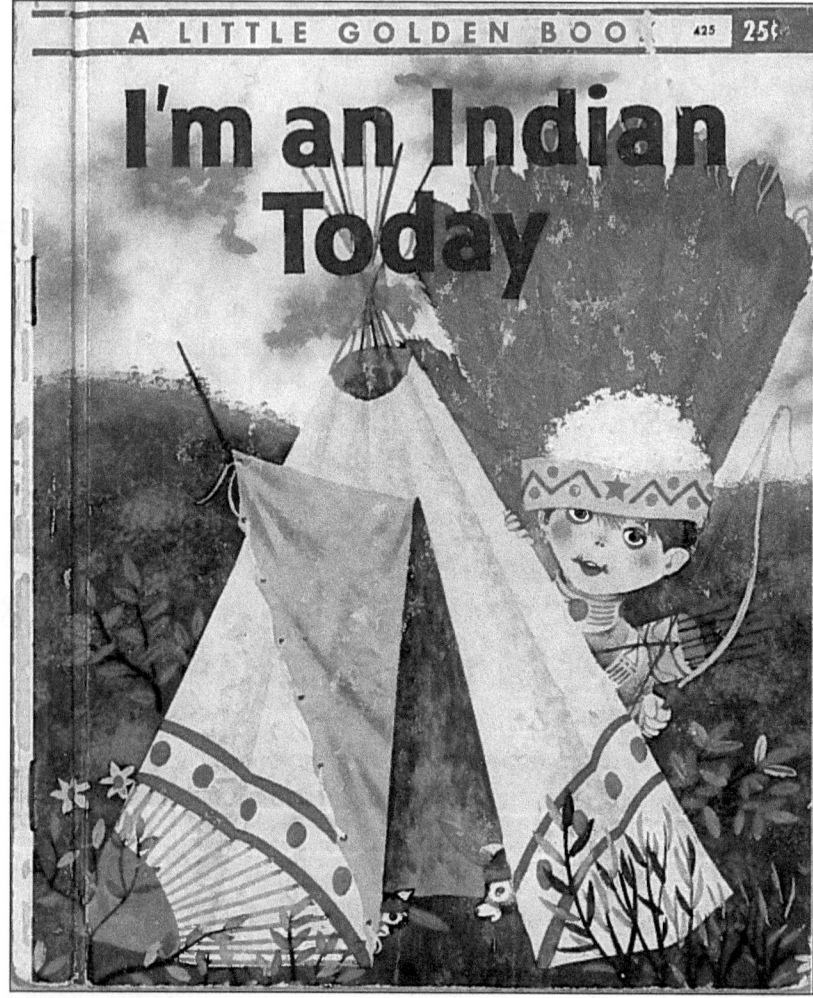

Figure 4.1: The cover of Kathryn Hitte's *I'm an Indian Today* (1961) embodies ideas of recapitulation through its use of "wild Indian" images.

generations for these lapses into primitivism. One *Parents* magazine article, published in 1950, used recapitulation theory to explain disturbing dreams: "Generally, animals, wild beasts and nature in the raw play predominant parts in their dreams. . . . Some believe that it is the child's unconscious memory of life in the jungle, of man's struggle with primitive beasts which is relived in these dreams. In his sleep the child recreates a state which existed for his forefathers; he fights their battles, shares their adventures. As he grows up he sheds these memories and loses them completely along with other primitive traits."[26] The persistence of these ideas suggests how our cultural constructs about childhood are naturalized, as we come to accept that children are not yet integrated into our culture.[27] Thinking of young Americans as acting like kangaroos or Indians allowed adult projections to stick to the child (as in Mead's examples of adult males picturing children as savages as a means of imagining themselves free from nine-to-five jobs). In the rest of the chapter, I consider three different ways images of "wildness" operated within children's fictions.

## Ruth Krauss and Maurice Sendak

Maurice Sendak credited children's book author Ruth Krauss and her husband, author-illustrator Crockett Johnson, with influencing his children's books and inspiring *Where the Wild Things Are*. Sendak had illustrated several of Krauss's books, including A *Hole Is to Dig* (1952) and *A Very Special House* (1953), and they remained close friends, sometimes spending weekends together. Sendak told one interviewer, "[Ruth] turned me into the monster I became, free to express what she knew about . . . the blood lusty child—themes that had not been entertained in the publishing world. In Europe, yes, but not here . . . Max [the protagonist of Sendak's *Where the Wild Things Are*] was like our child."[28] Krauss and Johnson modeled an approach to children's literature about the spontaneous child. Their biographer Philip Nel describes the special efforts Krauss took to depict how children saw the world:

Ruth Krauss conveyed her respect by bringing real children's voices into her work and in so doing changed the ways authors wrote for children. . . . Because she treated them as her equals, children adopted Krauss as one of them, confiding in her, telling her stories, or just playing while she watched. . . . Juxtaposed with Sendak's illustrations of scruffy, uninhibited children, [Krauss] helped pave the way for books that respect children's tough, pragmatic thinking, and unorthodox use of language.[29]

Krauss's attention to children's speech patterns communicated to her readers that someone out there heard them and knew how they felt. She studied anthropology under Ruth Benedict and Margaret Mead, which might account for her ethnographic attention to children's expression.

Krauss's *A Very Special House* (1953) offered a place children could visit whenever they opened her book, "a house for me ME." Sendak's illustrations (figure 4.2) depict children drawing on its walls, bouncing on its furniture, running through the halls, knocking over chairs: "We're sprinkling cracker crumbs under all the cushions . . . and I'm hoping and I'm skipping and I'm jumping and I'm bumping . . . and Everybody's yelling for more More MORE." The boys' mayhem is joined by a menagerie of imaginary playmates, some plausible—"a turtle and a rabbit. And a little dead mouse—I take it everywhere"—and others increasingly improbable: "some monkeys and some skunkeys and a very old lion which is eating all the stuffings from the chairs chairs chairs." Krauss adds to the chaos with her own erratic capitalization, shifts between first and third person, repetition, and the use of noises rather than words. In the "very special house" anything and everything was permitted, especially the expression of feelings, noisemaking, and playing games without rules.

Dorothy Baruch (1949) warned more than a decade earlier: "The thoughts and feelings of childhood are deep and dark. If they creep out inadvertently and we meet them with the shock of believing them abnormal, we do one kind of thing to a child. If we meet them with embracing sympathy born of having already encountered and seen them as natural, we do another."[30] Stories where children encounter or become monsters offer a useful way for adults to acknowledge that everyone has antisocial feelings. Baruch argues that if they are not given a constructive channel, they will burst out in more distressing ways.[31] It was legitimate to set limits on when, how, and where children express such feelings. If, however, parents refuse to listen and learn from children's anger and aggression, they leave their offspring drowning in feelings of inadequacy. Children needed to express themselves by drawing pictures, sharing stories, singing songs, performing their conflicts, or they felt as if they would burst.

Baruch (1949) described one school that set aside a special room for angry children:

Figure 4.2: Ruth Krauss and Maurice Sendak's *A Very Special House* (1953) imagines a utopian realm where children have license to do whatever they want.

> Here was a playroom with a sturdy table and a chair and a linoleum floor and painted walls that could be washed down. The children did many things here which they could do nowhere else. They smeared the walls with clay. They spilled paint indiscriminately over the floor. They used words that would make grandma's hair rise up. . . . The teacher permitted and accepted most of their actions. She put limitations, however, on some. She never allowed a child to hit or kick or otherwise carry out any physical act against her. Nor would she allow any destructiveness which was undesirable or costly. A child could not, for example, take a knife and carve up the table nor could he throw a toy at the window and break it. But otherwise, he could do things which he could not be permitted to do in the regular nursery school rooms downstairs.[32]

Baruch might be describing Krauss's "special house" for untamed behavior.

Max, in *Where the Wild Things Are*, spent his day dressed in a wolf costume, making "mischief of one kind and another." Across the first two pages (figure 4.3), we see him balancing on a stack of books to nail a clothesline to his bedroom wall, using his blanket as a tent, and chasing the family dog, brandishing a fork. After such chaotic conduct, his mother calls him a "wild thing," he growls, and she sends him to bed without supper. Max, in short, behaves in a beastly fashion.

Speaking with Bill Moyers in 2004, Sendak summarized:

> We're not so far away from the gorillas and the apes, those beautiful creatures. . . . And then, we're supposed to be civilized. . . . We're supposed to do all these things which trouble us deeply because it's so against what we naturally would want to do. And if I've done anything, I've had kids express themselves as they are, impolitely, lovingly . . . they don't mean any harm. They just don't know what the right way is.[33]

The spontaneous child reverts back to acting like a wolf or a kangaroo because this child has feelings that need release. Much has been made of Max's anger toward his mother, hardly model behavior, but precisely the kinds of impulses some child-rearing experts advocated parents tolerate. Max's mother does what many permissive parents would have

Figure 4.3: Max in Maurice Sendak's *Where the Wild Things Are* (1963) acts beastly until he finds himself exiled to a land of monsters.

done—send him to his room, where he can do as he pleases but will not be taking out his temper on others. He soon collapses from exhaustion, dreaming of a magical journey to an island inhabited by monsters who behave as frightfully as he has: "They roared their terrible roars and gnashed their terrible teeth and rolled their terrible eyes and showed their terrible claws." Assuming the parental role, Max tells the monsters to "be still." Max becomes the "king of all wild things" and leads the beasts in a "wild rumpus." He sends the monsters to bed without their suppers. Baruch suggested that children be given dolls to replay and work through their more intense emotions. Max does the same with his monsters, discovering how hard it may be to rule. And as he sails back to his own bedroom, the monsters repeat, though this time with different resonance, what he had yelled at his mother: "Please don't go—we'll eat you up—we love you so!" No longer a "wild thing," Max is now in control.

Jack Halberstam offers an extended and nuanced reading, which I can indicate here only through excerpt:

> In... *Where the Wild Things Are*, the bestial is a realm beyond the family but accessible by the child alone.... Max, the small boy who sails for days to reach the wild things, feels himself to be free in the world of adults who do not seek to rule him and feels powerful in the space where instead he occupies the place of the sovereign. But ultimately Max finds that being king is not preferable to being ruled.[34]

Halberstam cites an *Oxford English Dictionary* definition of "wild" especially appropriate in understanding Max's story and the permissive imagination more generally: "Not under, or not submitting to, control or restraint; taking, or disposed to take, one's own way; uncontrolled.... Acting or moving freely without restraint; going at one's own will; unconfined, unrestricted."[35] This definition explains why these "wild things" were ideally linked to America's self-image in the Cold War era, coupling wildness with freedom.

Kenneth Kidd ascribes Sendak's views on the nature of children's emotions and their play both to his engagement with child psychologists (one of Sendak's first books, *Kenny's Window*, was adopted directly from Dorothy Baruch's writings) and his direct observation out the window of his Brooklyn apartment ("I became absorbed in the lives of the children across the street").[36] Golan Y. Moskowitz also ascribes Sendak's ongoing fascination with the wildness of children to his own experiences growing up in an immigrant Jewish family and the constant pressure to assimilate: "The grotesque, horned monsters of his *Where the Wild Things Are* would creatively conflate the explosiveness of early childhood emotion with the unkempt wildness of the greenhorn stereotype.... Like his immigrant parents and relatives, the Wild Things were both dangerous and familiar members of his tribe."[37]

While Sendak's book acknowledges that sometimes Max wants to be bad, there is no suggestion that the protagonist in the more obscure *Christopher John's Fuzzy Blanket* (1959) is meant to be anything other than a good little boy.[38] Its author Dorothy Haas edited more than fifty picture books for toddlers during her years working for Whitman, later World Book Childcraft, and Rand McNally. Artist Florence Sarah

Figure 4.4: The protagonist in Dorothy Haas's *Christopher John's Fuzzy Blanket* (1959) imagines himself as a range of animals through his play.

Winship drew Christopher as a bright-eyed, curly-haired boy with freckles and a broad smile in a loving household with a big backyard. His favorite toy is his big red blanket, which he uses in imaginative ways: "He gets his fuzzy blanket out and pretends he's a one-boy zoo! He's a growly bear, a tall giraffe, or a funny old kangaroo. . . . He likes to sort of wrap it around and pretend he's an Indian boy. Or make an Indian tent out of it, where he plays with his Indian toy" (figure 4.4). Again, we see the persistence of native and animal imagery—even kangaroos! When adults are pictured, they smile with approval. Christopher enjoys unlimited access to the family space—engaging in loud and imaginative play in his own room, but also across the kitchen and living room as he uses his all-purpose blanket to construct his "very special house." Benjamin Spock would have understood the many ways Christopher deploys his blanket: "The most important general truth about toys is that children love to use them creatively. They aren't satisfied for long merely to obey directions and to use them as the inventor and the manufacturer intended. They want to follow their own personal interests, express their own feelings, create their own dramatic situations, and make their own inventions."[39] Christopher confronts a moment of crisis when he can't find his blanket. His mother has run it through the laundry, not unlike the mother in the floor wax commercial, using cleaning products to accommodate her child's play. In the closing picture, a comforted Christopher hugs his now pristine blanket, still hanging on the clothesline, crushing it to his chest. We can contrast this moment with Stephen's anger in *The Home-Maker* that his mother had kidnapped his Teddy Bear without his permission. Here, both the child's misconduct and the mother's responses are read benignly. If Sendack, Krauss, and Haas offer access to children's imaginative lives, the next case study offers a more realistic representation of a boy's movements through the world, although again we see the boy defined in terms of his desire to escape adult control.

### Morris Engel and Ruth Orkin's *Little Fugitive* (1953)

In her essay "The Image of the Child in Contemporary Films," Wolfenstein argues that children's fictions "represent memories and dreams of adults about their own lost childhood, as well as feelings about those mysterious beings, their own children."[40] Adopting a comparative perspective, she considers recent films from Italy, France, Britain, and the United States, exploring the "moral demands" children make on adults. For her American examples, she chose a Hollywood Western, *Shane* (1953); a now largely forgotten B movie, *When I Grow Up* (1951); and *Little Fugitive* (1953), a film made outside the Hollywood system. She maps the search for a heroic father figure. Yet, we might also read each film as addressing children's transgressions of adult expectations. For example, in *Shane*, there's a curious scene just before the main gun battle where the young boy acts out his tension, stabbing the beams around the farmhouse, getting on his mother's nerves. Neither the film nor Wolfenstein explains this uncharacteristic behavior—elsewhere the boy is calm and good-natured—yet a permissive parent might have read these actions as his way of bringing violence under his symbolic control, working through his own relationship to the gun violence that defines adult manhood. This moment suggests the surplus emotion surrounding his assimilation into masculine norms as he crosses a taboo—stabbing and damaging the walls—that even Baruch felt should not be violated.

Wolfenstein's choice of *Little Fugitive* is a curious one. Now regarded as a missing link between Italian neorealism and the French new wave, the film was cited by François Truffaut as a major influence on *The 400*

*Blows*. Comparing *Little Fugitive* to an Italian neorealist work like *Bicycle Thieves* is a bit misleading since the tone of the two films could not be more different—the economic desperation of postwar Rome versus the buoyancy of postwar New York. But *Little Fugitive* was shot on location, using mostly nonprofessional actors, supplementing the script with improvisations designed to take advantage of naturally occurring events. Joey taking shelter from an unexpected rainstorm directly parallels a more famous sequence from *Bicycle Thieves* where a father and son wait out a downpour. The unfettered camera movements—for example, filming while riding a parachute drop—inspired a scene from *400 Blows* where Antoine Doinel clowns inside a spinning carnival ride.

*Little Fugitive* was the work of husband-and-wife-team Morris Engel (who directed) and Ruth Orkin (who edited). Born in Brooklyn, Engel studied photography at the Photo League under Bernice Abbott and later was mentored by Paul Strand. Engel published photographs in *PM*. During the war he served in Combat Photo Unit #8, where he helped record the US landing at Normandy. After the war he taught classes through the Photo League, experimenting with some core themes—children playing in the street and crowds at Coney Island—that informed *Little Fugitive*. California-born Ruth Orkin followed a similar trajectory on the opposite coast: teaching herself how to use a camera, joining the Women's Army Auxiliary in hopes of learning how to make films, and becoming a photojournalist in the postwar era. Her first published (and best-known) photograph was *VE Day, Times Square*, but she also produced a series of images of children playing cards that Edward Steichen selected for *The Family of Man* (1955).[41] Both photographers showed a recurring interest in children's street play. Orkin's 1947 *Jimmy the Storyteller* (figure 4.5) delights in Jimmy's broad gestures and facial expressions. As with Ruth Krauss, Orkin wants to capture the stories children tell. And Engel wants to observe how boys move through the world, an ideal subject for a movie camera with greater mobility than ever before.

*Little Fugitive* was the first of three Engel and Orkin films, each approaching childhood from different vantage points. *Lovers and Lollipops* (1956) was the story of a little girl, also lacking a father, coping with her mother's courtship by a new suitor, and *Weddings and Babies* (1960) depicts a commercial photographer unwilling to marry and raise a family.

Figure 4.5: Ruth Orkin's *Jimmy the Storyteller* (1947) explores the expressiveness of a young boy's dramatic play.

Engel partnered with an old friend, *PM*'s education editor Ray Abrashkin, to write a sparse script (said to have only two thousand spoken words) about a young boy who runs away from home and spends two days alone at Coney Island.[42] The result is an incredibly intimate depiction of growing up in 1950s Brooklyn. What strikes me watching the film in 2023 is how free the boys—seven-year-old Joey Norton and his older brother, twelve-year-old Lennie—are from adult supervision.

Their single mother travels to nurse their ailing grandmother, leaving the twelve-year-old in charge of young Joey. A prank convinces Joey that he has shot and killed his brother. The youngster runs away, stealing the money his mother left for their food and taking the subway by himself to Coney Island, where he survives for two days, sleeping on the beach and gathering bottles to sell for deposit. After Joey has been missing all night, Lennie sets out in a half-hearted search but also as an act of rebellion since his mother had refused to allow him to celebrate his birthday at Coney Island with his friends. The boys finally reunite, race home, and arrive just moments before the mother's return, saying nothing of their adventures.

When Joey goes to the beach, only one attentive man—the "cowboy" who gives children pony rides—notices that Joey is unsupervised. In Wolfenstein's analysis, this man represents a father figure, a Western ideal for a boy fascinated with horses. Boys, she suggests, depend on movie heroes to compensate for a diminished male presence: "The child's capacity for hero worship lacks an object. A stranger must come from afar, the child must journey away from home, or visions of a remote past must be conjured up to provide the missing hero."[43] Fatherless Joey is drawn to this man who possesses "the skills and accoutrements of longed-for masculinity, with his aura of the Far West and his knowledge of horses."[44] Yet, the relationship between Joey and the "cowboy" occupies only a few scenes within a film where the boy does as he pleases. Engel's camera stalks the boy, often from the child's own vantage point, fascinated as he interacts with shadows underneath the boardwalk or takes a swing with a baseball bat almost as long as he is tall. The filmmakers are far more attentive to the child than any adult in his life.

That said, Wolfenstein is right to note the cowboy iconography. In one memorable sequence, Joey poses for a carnival photograph—his boyish head atop a cardboard painting of a cowboy (figure 4.6). There is a similar cutout of a superhero figure left abandoned in the corner, no longer the heroic ideal for American boys in a year when there were more than ninety Western series on American television. The cowboy has a guitar, suggesting the singing-cowboy tradition often associated with child viewers as old Roy Rogers and Gene Autry movies had been sold for television. Joey is wearing a holster belt and two cap guns. When

Figure 4.6: Joey, the protagonist of *Little Fugitive* (1953), confronts the option of the superhero and the cowboy as ideal adult role models.

he finally returns home, he flips on a Western, firing his pistols at the television. Josette Frank (1959) saw no great harm in watching television Westerns but urged parents to use them to inspire more physical activity and imaginative play: "It may not be easy to compete with rootin' tootin' Westerns or interplanetary rocket trips but *playing* cowboys or spacemen can be as much fun as watching them. This kind of play can let off steam, and can also, with some adult guidance, lead to other kinds of active fun."[45]

Joey's brother Lennie models normative activity for a slightly older boy, hanging out with the "gang," reading comics, playing streetball, and even clowning with firearms without any oversight. Engel captures the boy and his pals sprawled on the ground, reading and exchanging horror comics. One boy shows Lennie a gruesome picture, suggesting that he probably wished he could do something to his kid brother: "Joey ain't got that much blood." Another is inspired by a different crime comic: "I know how you could get rid of Joey. You bury him under the sidewalk and cement it up again. They'd never find the body." Lennie responds matter-of-factly, "We'd have to kill him first," to which his friend whines, "Why." Another suggests they stab him with an icicle and let the murder weapon melt. All this chatter functions as a prelude to the abovementioned mean-spirited trick that convinces Joey that he has shot and killed his brother. The entire episode could have come directly from Fredric Wertham's *Seduction of the Innocent*, the cornerstone of his crusade against crime and horror comics. Wertham saw comics as modeling antisocial behavior: "If one were to set out to teach children how to steal, rob, lie, cheat, assault, and break into candy stores, no more insistent method could be devised. It is of course easy and natural to translate these crimes into a minor key: . . . beating and threatening younger children rather than superman heroics."[46] If Joey's engagement with cowboys gives him a vehicle for "hero worship" and a route toward compensatory models of masculinity, Lennie and his friends' engagement with unwholesome comics brings out their worst.[47] Even here, Engel cannot bring himself to depict Lennie as a delinquent, since ultimately he does find his brother and bring him back home.

By comparison, Peggy, the seven-year-old girl in Engel and Orkin's second film *Lovers and Lollipops*, is tethered to her mother. Though she often rebels by running off, she only goes a few feet and even these moments are greeted with panic, and often with a reprimand. As a middle-class girl compared to the working-class boys, Peggy has more toys, most of which—like the Slinky or the mechanical monkey—are designed for indoor play. Of course, the girl longs for more freedom of movement. She brings her doll carriage to the beach and tries to drag it across the sand. Larry's inability to keep up with the girl in crowded spaces becomes a recurring problem in his budding relationship with her mother. Most memorably, he loses Peggy in a parking lot, where, dressed as a cowgirl, she crawls under and around the tires of various cars, pretending to shoot at him. The cowgirl identity offers her freedom to transgress gender roles and escape adult control.

The Engel and Orkin films offer a nuanced portrait of how children acted in the 1950s: boys may mimic Westerns or crime comics, may resent their siblings or rescue them from harm; young girls may be sweet one moment and spoiled the next, may tag along with adults or race away from them in a crowded parking lot. The filmmakers have sympathy for their young characters, adopting a visual style that follows their lives. At the same time, the films express a certain ambivalence toward coming of age in an era of mass media. Here, the children are not animals, monsters, or savages. They are generally good but outside of the watchful eyes of adults, they follow their own laws.

## From "Wild Thing" to Monstrous Child

Even advocates for a more child-centered approach had ambivalences about what might happen if permissiveness was pushed too far. For example, Katherine M. Wolf (1953) expressed such concerns in *The Controversial Problem of Discipline*: "As one watches children hitting each other or breaking their toys in a playground, at school or in their nursery at home, one is frequently struck with how miserable these little heroes look. Even when no irreparable damage has been done, and even when no punishment is likely to follow, one may see a two-year-old who has just won a victory over his playmate, burst into tears or withdraw into a corner."[48]

Wolf's account of aggression and destruction, embarrassment and remorse, captures concerns about freedom becoming license.

The comic strip *Goofus and Gallant*, published for several decades in *Highlights for Children*, represented a junior version of Jekyll and Hyde: Gallant offered an idealized representation of the "good boy," while rude Goofus consistently made bad choices. The characters were created by child psychologist Garry Cleveland Myers and drawn by Anni Matsick. Myers founded *Highlights* in 1946 as a magazine publishing morally conscious and psychologically appropriate entertainment for elementary school children after a career that included publishing guides for parents and teachers, writing a regular column, and hosting a radio show designed to help parents find effective ways of shaping their children's behavior. Myers believed that his strip might model the right and wrong ways of dealing with a given situation. So, for example, Goofus opens other people's packages, doesn't remove his cap when inside, and jacks the television volume to drown out guests, all seen as brattish and boorish behavior. Goofus acts on his impulses without constraint while Gallant accepts and follows adult dictates.[49]

The character Eddie Haskell in *Leave It to Beaver* possesses a similar duality—smarmy with adults, a bully and a prankster when only other children are around. He is especially hard on Beaver, whom he calls "squirt." Haskell's stance can be summed up as "If you can make the other guy feel like a goon first, then you don't feel so much like a goon." While Goofus and Gallant separates the good from the bad, *Beaver* suggests that the two can be combined, often in unstable ways, within the same personality.

The child actor Bill Mumy (Will Robinson in *Lost in Space*), then six years old, appeared in two highly iconic television episodes in 1961, shot just weeks apart: "It's a Good Life," a *Twilight Zone* episode adapted by Rod Serling from a Jerome Bixby short story, and "Bang! You're Dead," one of the few episodes of *Alfred Hitchcock Presents* that Hitchcock himself directed. Mumy's gap-toothed smile, freckled face, and shock of red hair embody the "all-American" boy, while the stories suggest the consequences of giving boys too much freedom (figure 4.7).

In "It's a Good Life," Rod Serling summarizes the core problem: "This is the monster. His name is Anthony Fremont. He's six years old, with a cute little-boy face and blue, guileless eyes. But when those eyes look at you, you'd better start thinking happy thoughts, because the mind behind them is absolutely in charge." Young Anthony rules rural Peaksville, deploying his telekinetic power as a constant threat over the neighborhood. The adults pander to his every whim. They constantly reassure him that he is a good boy and that everything he does is for the best. Otherwise, he might send them to "the cornfield" where they will never be seen or heard from again. Adult desires (to listen to Perry Como records, to drink brandy, or just to enjoy adult conversation) are constantly deferred. The episode's centerpiece is a joyless birthday party whose guest of honor is transformed into a hideous jack-in-the-box. Such constant pandering has turned Anthony from a good-natured boy into a "monster."

In *The Child Worshippers*, Martha Weinman Lear (1961)—a sharp and often witty critic of the permissive mindset—warned that America had become a "child-controlled society":

Figure 4.7: Bill Mumy embodies the monstrous child in "It's a Good Life" (top) and "Bang! You're Dead!" (bottom).

Whole communities are geared largely to their needs. They dominate adult conversations—especially in their absence. . . . Children determine, more often than not, where the family will live. They determine what kind of home it will rent or buy; how it will spend its leisure hours; whom it will befriend; when and where it will vacation; what car it will drive; what foods it will eat; and how it will spend its income upon the myriad educational, social, and cultural activities deemed essential to the burgeoning psyche. And their parents are hounded by ghosts of Freud, harassed by bevies of experts, painfully eager to do the right thing by their offspring, to understand him, to relate to him in Meaningful Ways, to win his love, ward off his traumas, and give him every known advantage.[50]

Lear, however, does not see the child as directing the show (as young Anthony does on *The Twilight Zone*). Rather, she stresses how parenting had become competitive, a means of amassing status.

In *Culture Against Man* (1963), Jules Henry warned that the gender dynamics of the American family reflected this new reality: the mother and father were competing for their children's affections. Interviewing elementary school children, Henry found that the youngsters judged their parents based on what they "let" them do and on a constant tug between gifts and punishments: "Fathers are no longer aloof, controlling figures, and both parents seek gratification from the children at the level of deep feeling; meanwhile, since permissiveness has come to loom large in the child's appreciation of either parent, they now can compete for the child more openly and on a more equal footing than in the past."[51] In "It's a Good Life," adults who lose their temper, who try to discipline the child, or who refuse to respond to his constant demands do not last long. Not only the parents, but all adults compete for Anthony's favor. Much like Wolfenstein, Henry links this impulse-based worldview back to a postwar consumer economy. Looking at classrooms that allow children to act out their emotions, he asks, "How can a teacher . . . release children's emotions without unleashing chaos? How can she permit the discharge of impulse and yet teach subject matter? How can she permit such noise and not lose the message?"[52] Many permissive writers would have resolved these tensions either by trusting children's natural impulses (as Spock does) or by insisting on the value of cathartic release (as Baruch does). But Henry wonders what happens to adult life when adults bow to children's darker impulses.

We might contrast Anthony, the all-powerful white boy, in "It's a Good Life" with Henry, the black boy at the center of another *Twilight Zone* episode, "The Big Tall Wish." Henry's magical wishes alter local particulars—getting his mother an extra fifteen dollars at the end of the month to pay the bills or helping a boxer win a match—but they cannot transcend the fundamental realities of being Black in 1950s America. The world-weary boxer and the boy's mother discuss the challenges: "Little boys with their heads full up with dreams.... When do they suddenly find out that there ain't any magic, when does somebody push their face down on the sidewalk and say to them, 'Hey, little boy, it's concrete, that's what the world is made of, concrete.' When do they find out that you can wish your life away." By the episode's conclusion, Henry has lost his faith in the power of magic, much as the adults have.

*Alfred Hitchcock Presents* adopted a different perspective. In "Bang! You're Dead," Jackie Chester is constantly under foot. Rather than pandering to his whims, Jackie's parents pay no attention, allowing him to wander the neighborhood. The status quo is disrupted by the boy's uncle, who returns to the United States from an extended stay in Africa. Here, we see another example of the alternative father figure Wolfenstein identified: the boy seems indifferent to his own father (a businessman) while the uncle is a larger-than-life adventurer. Africa is constantly described as a space of danger and violence. The uncle confesses to Jackie's parents that he has barely escaped with his life as the situation in an unnamed African country became too inflamed for white men to conduct business there. The uncle has brought back a tribal mask the parents find "frightful," all the more so when the uncle acknowledges that he picked it up following a "bloodbath." At another point, the uncle compares the situation there with his boyhood cowboys-and-Indians fantasies, suggesting that the gun has become something he carries everywhere for protection. Hitchcock evokes white fears of a Black world no longer under their control.

In the background, there's a different discussion of the relationship between whiteness and Blackness: the mother is hosting a dinner party and is increasingly frustrated by how late her maid is. As the mother grumbles, we learn how far the maid lives from the white side of town and how slow the buses are. Once the maid arrives, we see the boy commanding her attention as she prepares dinner. Cleo is played with quiet dignity by Juanita Moore, who only a few years before had received an Academy Award nomination as another maid in Douglas Sirk's *Imitation of Life*. Moore conveys a world-weariness, putting up with this "wild" white boy to support her own children. Here, Hitchcock offers a rare Black perspective on permissive households. Cleo never scolds Jackie but she has no time for his nonsense.

No sooner does the boy get the uncle alone than he demands to know what gifts the man brought. The uncle leaves the boy to unpack his suitcase, promising a gift (a feathered headdress) and a bedtime story. Jackie finds a handgun and bullets that he mistakes for a toy six-shooter and runs to show the older boys who have earlier refused to let him join their gunplay. Hitchcock lets the audience know that the boy is wandering the neighborhood with a loaded gun and then follows his random interactions. From the opening scenes of boys firing cap guns, violent play—especially that associated with the Western—has been normalized as something boys do. Many adults Jackie encounters know the proper scripts for interacting with young "outlaws": the postman jokes about Billy the Kid; a grocery clerk suggests outlaws get ornery when they are hungry and feeds him a free sample. But they pay no attention to what he has in his hand. When the gun goes off, barely missing the maid, the boy races tearfully into his mother's arms. Along the way we get other glimpses into the child-centered culture: a woman is looking for cardboard boxes for a Cub Scout project; a henpecked father begs Jackie to let his daughter ride the mechanical pony because the girl is difficult if she doesn't get her way.

Jackie is no "monster," not like Anthony Fremont. His innocence is assumed. There is something banal about the bloodthirsty play and disturbing about how adults look past what the boy is doing. Hitchcock intended "Bang! You're Dead" to wake up his viewers not simply to the risks of having guns but also of creating a world where gunfights and tribal bloodshed are appropriate children's entertainment.

Across the past three chapters, I have laid the foundations for our understanding of permissive thinking—an emergent perspective in the 1920s and 1930s that gained greater visibility during the war and became the dominant paradigm with the publication of Spock's bestselling book. First, I discussed the Progressive Era roots of the Child Study movement, which encouraged mothers and fathers to develop an empathetic understanding of children's motivations. Parents, teachers, and others were asked to play the role of "Understanding Angels" drawing insights from the latest developments in child psychology. Second, I considered works written about democratic family life during the Second World War. Here, parents were warned against becoming domestic dictators who crushed their children's spirits. Here, we see the emergence of a discourse about children's rights and a questioning of adults who "push and shove us little kids around."

In this chapter, I have described how adults rethought concerns about children's desires, pleasures, and impulses, responding to the popularization of Freudian concepts, especially through Spock's writings. The home was made to accommodate conduct—especially emotional outbursts—that were previously unacceptable. Forms of misbehavior, frequently understood in benign terms, run through the children's fictions discussed here, often expressed through analogies to animals, savages, and monsters. I do not mean to suggest a situation of "anything goes" in the American suburban households of the 1950s and 1960s, but there was great uncertainty about how and where to set limits, a theme explored to comic effect by *Dennis the Menace* as I will discuss in the next chapter.

The permissive paradigm was less revolutionary than sometimes claimed, a patchwork of ideas, some dating back to the dawn of the twentieth century, some emerging during the war or in the postwar period. This continuity with earlier advice literature allowed Spock's insights to seem like "common sense" to parents. Permissiveness served the needs of an increasingly consumerist society, justifying the purchase of toys, candy, cereal, even floor wax in the name of accommodating children's desires, but it did more than this. Permissiveness allowed adults to rethink their domestic lives as helping to construct a more democratic society, and through the representation of the child as a "wild thing," to imagine the possibilities for their own escape from constrained roles.

PART II

Living in Permissive Culture

# 5

# Dennis the Menace, "the All-American Handful"

In his autobiography *The Merchant of Dennis the Menace*, cartoonist Hank Ketcham describes the origins of the fictional tyke he variously described as a "household hurricane," a "teachers' threat," or "the all-American handful." Working in his study on a drawing for the *Saturday Evening Post*, Ketcham heard frustrated "mother noises": "The little darling was supposed to be taking a nap. Instead, he had spent the better part of one hour quietly dismantling his room—bed, mattress, springs, dresser, drapes, and curtain rod. When the accidental load he carried in his underpants was added to his collection of plastic toys, cookie crumbs, and a leftover peanut butter sandwich, it formed an unusual mix."[1] His wife exclaimed, "Your son is a MENACE!," starting Ketcham on the path that led in a matter of weeks to his long-running newspaper comic strip. This story—true or apocryphal—illustrates how Ketcham (like other cartoonists of his generation) authenticated his representation of American boyhood through his own experiences as a father. It reflects Ketcham's tendency to accumulate details of destruction into singular moments of adult–child conflict, which often served as the focal point for his single-panel comics. *Dennis the Menace* became a syndicated newspaper strip in March 1951, five years after the publication of Spock's *Baby and Child Care*. By 1953, Dennis appeared daily in three hundred newspapers and in his own comic book.[2] A CBS sitcom aired from 1959 to 1963.

Bad-boy stories had been a dominant genre in the late nineteenth and early twentieth centuries, playing vital roles in the development of both early film and early comic strips. And they had remained a minor genre for much of the twentieth century, with the occasional comic breaking into real marketplace success. Child-centered comic strips were proliferating again in the 1950s and early 1960s. Charles Schulz's *Peanuts* launched in 1951, one year before Dennis's debut The husband-and-wife team Stan and Jan Berenstain drew cartoons about parents and children for the *Post*, *Collier's*, *Ladies' Home Journal*, *Good Housekeeping*, and *McCall's*, before creating the popular Berenstain Bears books, starting with *The Big Honey Hunt* in 1962.[3] A relative latecomer, Bill Keane introduced *The Family Circus* in 1960. Each developed distinctive ways of representing childhood worlds: Schulz shows Charlie Brown almost totally removed from grown-ups. Stan and Jan Berenstein's full-page drawings, modeled on Bruegel's *Children's Games*, depicted myriads of hyperactive children at the movies, the art museum, the zoo, or the department store. Keane might devote an entire Sunday strip to mapping Jeffy's zigzag movements as his attention was diverted from one task to another. Ketcham's daily strip emerged from the magazine gag-cartoon tradition, often capturing a telling moment in the ongoing conflict between Dennis and the adult world. Keane concisely captures extreme reactions—shock, surprise, horror, anger, or bemusement. Ketcham's attention to domestic detail situated actions and reactions in a suburban home. Readers fluctuate between sympathy for the boy's good intentions and adult perceptions that Dennis is a "little monster."

In the midst of debates about permissiveness, Dennis, "the all-American handful," was, alongside *Peanuts'* Charlie Brown, perhaps America's best-known child. Ketcham remarked in 1953 that Dennis was "typical of almost every American boy in this particular age bracket." Far from unique, "there are literally millions of 'menaces,' the boys making their own surprising and spontaneous reactions to a sometimes hostile and incomprehensible grownup world."[4] While Ketcham saw Dennis as representing all American boys, he was a particular articulation of the permissive imagination, using the genre tradition of bad-boy comedy to express male anxieties about domestic containment and the challenges of fatherhood.

Ketcham had been an animator first under Walter Lantz (Woody Woodpecker) and later, Walt Disney. During the war, he was a navy officer overseeing the production of military training films with these same studios and developed a comic strip, *Half Hitch*, for the post's newspaper. He began his family shortly after returning from service: his son, Dennis, born in 1947. Early on, he developed gag cartoons for the *Saturday Evening Post*. Ketcham in 1990 characterized himself as a "conservative straight-arrow" and often "out of step in light of today's permissiveness": "There is a behavior I expect, certain codes of dress and etiquette I demand, and areas of language and respect I insist upon. . . . There is no room for fads in these basic matters. The fundamentals must never vary if we plan to peacefully share space with others."[5] This negotiation between his own conservative orientation and an often more permissive readership allowed him to calibrate his strip to the dominant "structure of feeling" as this generation of young veterans figured out how they wanted to raise their children. Each could be astonished by how much chaos children make and yet appreciative of children's spirit and energy. Here's how Ketcham characterized his protagonist: "Physically, he is sturdy, active, agile, tireless, and hard-to-catch. Mentally he is lively, inquisitive, imaginative, and of an experimental turn of mind, which frequently leads him into situations he can't always control. Add an unruly shock of hair, freckles, a smudge on his nose, dirt on his pants and traces of paint and chocolate on his hands, and you have Dennis, the All American Handful."[6]

I will situate Dennis in relation to a longer tradition of bad-boy humor in comics and literature, and having done so, consider in what ways Dennis is "bad," how his misbehavior fits within the norms of the permissive household, and how his parents address the problems he causes. I will consider how this conception of boyhood maps gender norms and how Dennis's escape from domesticity allowed adult males some freedom dreams of their own. I will also discuss why it matters that Dennis is white and how his story might make visible some of the racial conflicts associated with white flight. Finally, I will consider how Dennis's lack of constraint was read as reflecting American national character. Across the next few chapters, I will be surveying some representations of what it was like to live in a permissive culture. Chapter 6 considers ugly ducklings and misfits, exploring how tensions between individualism and conformity are resolved; chapter 7 discusses how Fred Rogers helped children learn how to deal with their emotions; and chapter 8 looks at what permissiveness meant for Black families.

## The Bad-Boy Tradition

Leslie Fiedler, writing in 1960, discussed "the Good Bad Boy," whose badness is "a necessary spice to his goodness," his mischievousness a mark of his masculinity. The Good Bad Boy, for Fiedler, represented

America's self-perception as "crude and unruly . . . [but possessing] an instinctive sense of what is right."[7] *Dennis the Menace* straddles the line between Fiedler's Good Bad Boys and Jules Henry's domestic tyrant.[8] In one 1953 daily, Dennis says his evening prayers: "Make me a good boy but not so good I don't have no fun!"[9]

In early panels, Dennis was sometimes demonic. He teaches a neighborhood kid how to make a weapon by filling a sock with sand.[10] The first Dennis panel shows the boy jeering at a cop: "You didn't catch us. We ran out of gas," as his father sweats behind the steering wheel.[11] Over the first few months, Dennis was shown making a list of people he wanted to bite,[12] cutting up the garden hose,[13] targeting a doctor with a slingshot,[14] beating up a neighbor boy,[15] setting a water-bucket trap for his father,[16] giving his dad a hotfoot,[17] scissoring books,[18] drawing on the wall,[19] and dropping a frog down a girl's dress.[20] As Ketcham developed a firmer sense of the character, he set limits: "He is not a Katzenjammer kid. He is a totally well-meaning, totally honest little boy. Everything he does is out of curiosity or just because he is being helpful—in short, all the things that are normal in a young animal."[21] Ketcham refers here to an archetypical comic strip, *The Katzenjammer Kids*, in which two brothers mercilessly committed acts of malice against their immigrant father. The strip would have been widely known by the previous generation and Ketcham is acknowledging here that he took inspiration from the bad-boy tradition of the early 20th century. Dennis was a human tornado racing around the house, smashing lamps, leaving roller skates under feet, or robbing the cookie jar, but his worst mishaps emerged from his attempts to help adults, especially his mother and the Wilsons who live next door. He squirms in the barber's chair, he hides from the doctor and the dentist, he puts goldfish in the bathtub, but these are not pranks directed against adults, just a developing child's efforts to figure out how the world works.

By the time Dennis came to television in 1959, the neighborhood had mellowed toward him. Jay North played Dennis as such a clean-cut, good-spirited, and polite boy that the other characters found it difficult to dislike him. Joseph Kearns's George Wilson is at times a cranky killjoy, spending his days trying to order his stamp collection, fussy over his trampled flowerbeds. He also displays affection for the boy, helping Dennis build a soapbox derby car. Following Kearns's death, John (Gale

Gordon), George's brother, adopts an even more benign view. Himself more active and outgoing, John considers Dennis a friend.

Ketcham initially saw the comic strip as appealing to adults, particularly parents, in their twenties and thirties. The earlier bad-boy stories had also appealed to adult males, offering a nostalgic return to their own mischievous boyhoods. Here, they were being asked to identify with the frustrated fathers of the baby-boom generation. Quickly, Ketcham discovered that the strip had tremendous appeal to children, who imitated Dennis's antics "much as they would play cowboys and Indians."[22] Here, the "menace" became a role model and Ketcham faced greater pressure to tame his behavior, negotiating with the reform and social respectability that had ended the early twentieth-century wave of bad-boy stories. Some of this ambiguity between horror and humor is suggested by a 1957 panel where the boy protests, "You would have laughed if some kid had done that on television!"[23] The television series was pitched to this same double audience of menaced adults and "happy half-pints." Series writer Bill Cowley told the *Los Angeles Mirror*: "We don't consider Dennis a show for children. It gives adults a chance to recapture their childhood. We think a great many sophisticates watch *Dennis* for relaxation. Don't forget that Albert Einstein used to play the violin and that the late secretary Foster Dulles polished pots and pans as a hobby."[24] A disgruntled Ketcham scribbled in his scrapbook, "What has this got to do with watching a kiddie show?" This program was scheduled immediately following *Lassie* on Sunday nights, competing for audiences with *Walt Disney's Wonderful World of Color* and *The Jetsons*.

Anne Trensky has identified two icons of American childhood in nineteenth-century literature. On the one hand, there was the "saintly child" of feminine fiction, the sentimental ideal whose virtue and innocence redeems the adult world; these children are ultimately too good to live and must die in the books' melodramatic conclusions.[25] The saintly child was often a girl with "pale skin and golden curls." On the other hand, there was the "bad boy" of the masculine imagination, the puckish protagonist of *Story of a Bad Boy* (1870), *Adventures of Tom Sawyer* (1876), or *The Real Diary of a Real Boy* (1903).[26] The bad-boy books parody the "sentimental and pious child literature," pitting an aggressive, free-spirited boy against maternal authority, not to mention saintly but spoiled siblings. The bad boy was "rough and tough, quick to play and quick to fight," a shrewd judge of character, intolerant of adult hypocrisies. His pleasure often came in escaping adult control (playing hooky, going barefoot, or stealing apples).[27] If the "saintly child" stories are part of what Viviana Zelizer calls the "sacralization" of the child, the "bad boy" literature represented its carnivalization.[28] Both genres were read by children *and* adults, the saintly child aimed at female readers of sentimental fiction, the bad boy satisfying male fantasies of comic freedom.

Arguably, the two genres were responsive to the same historical shifts: specifically, the increased isolation of the middle-class home from the realm of production. As the agrarian and crafts-based economies gave way to a factory-based economy, the husband, the principal breadwinner, left the home to work, resulting in the mother's increased domestic authority. The saintly child was imagined as living comfortably within this new feminine sphere, her emotional values compensating for a loss in children's economic value. The bad boy inhabits what E. Anthony Rotundo (1990) describes as "Boy Culture," just outside the mother's watchful eyes.[29] While boys no longer had easy access to the professional world of grown men, boy culture allowed them to develop the daring, autonomy, and mastery to function apart from women. The spontaneity of boy culture contrasted sharply with the responsibility awaiting the adult male. With the shift from agrarian to urban (and later suburban) lifestyles, boys' play was structured by organizations such as the 4-H, the Little League, or the Boy Scouts, which convey adult responsibility rather than the pleasures of romping barefoot in the grass.

By the early twentieth century, more pathologized bad boys appeared in early prank films,[30] early comic strips (such as *The Yellow Kid* or *The Katzenjammer Kids*), or the popular *Peck's Bad Boy* books. If the nineteenth-century bad boys came from middle-class, rural, or small-town backgrounds, the early twentieth-century bad boys were working-class street urchins, often from immigrant families. Their pranks reflect overt hostility to adults rather than a desire to simply escape their control. As the advertising slogan for the Peck books suggested, "One such boy in every community would retard the march of civilization. One such boy in every family would drive the whole world mad."[31] In the original novel, *Peck's Bad Boy and His Pa* (1883), the bad boy sought to cause his "Pa" physical injury, expose him to public ridicule, or reveal his drunkenness, gambling, and womanizing to the moralistic mother. If such works reflect a horror at children's misbehavior consistent with prewar authoritarian parenting, George Peck saw essential masculine traits in the bad boys, whose "innocent jokes" contain the makings of "first class businessmen." However, most often, these stories end with the bad boy receiving much-deserved spankings. Lara Saguisag notes that for all their demonic conduct, adults often admired these bad boys: the comic-strip character Buster Brown was based on the premise that "mischief-making is a reassuring sign of healthy boyhood."[32] Peter Kramer also argues that the ingenuity and imagination behind such pranks was a necessary ingredient for these boy's future adult success.[33] Turning to the aforementioned Katzenjammer kids, Saguisag argues that "the American bad boy was not necessarily a figure of incorrigibility; rather he was a symbol of independence, vigor, and resourcefulness."[34] Kenneth Kidd shows how the bad-boy genre built on—and in turn, informed—popular psychological treatises of the early twentieth century that he calls Boyology: "The Bad Boy books celebrate the pre- or early pubescent boy as irrational, primitive, fiercely masculine, and attuned to nature. The evolutionary doctrine of recapitulation sustained the boy-savage comparison without insult to the boy, since he would eventually outgrow and incorporate his variously primitive tendencies."[35]

The debut of *Leave It to Beaver* on CBS's 1957 prime-time schedule signaled the emergence of a further tamed, domesticated, and suburbanized bad boy, well-suited to the comic realism of the American sitcom. Creators Joe Connelly and Bob Mosher, like Ketcham, cited inspiration from their own children that made Beaver's escapades more authentic. Both *Beaver* and *Dennis* were produced by Screen Gems, the television affiliate of Columbia Studios, then associated with family-centered sitcoms such as *Father Knows Best*, *The Donna Reed Show*, and *Hazel*.[36] The good-natured representation of the bad boy in *Dennis the Menace* or *Leave It to Beaver* had more in common with the nostalgic tales of nineteenth-century small-town life than the brutal slapstick of twentieth-century urban comedy.

Dennis was *not* a Katzenjammer kid—a malicious immigrant street urchin. A better point of comparison would be to the more middle-class characters, such as Buster Brown, also found in strips and books within the bad-boy tradition. Some of the same conditions that produced nostalgic, middle-class stories about boyish mischief in the early twentieth century were recurring during the 1940s and 1950s, leading to this new wave of stories. If Rotundo argues that boy culture represented an escape from female dominance over the domestic sphere, these later stories celebrate an irrepressible masculine spirit that flew in the face of the "momism" that social critics such as Philip Wylie saw as gaining ascendancy in the postwar period. That anxiety pushed a conservative cartoonist like Ketcham to celebrate boyhood as a force of opposition. As with the earlier bad-boy stories, *Dennis the Menace* follows a logic where disruption and transgression must be punished, though new ideas about the nature of discipline informed how adults responded to the testing of limits.

## Discipline and Punishment in the Permissive Household
### Dennis Says the Darndest Things

Dennis's disruptions are as often caused by what he says as by what he does. If the permissive paradigm celebrated children who expressed their feelings, Dennis is often shown asking questions that point to adult hypocrisies. He says what he thinks without concern for or even awareness of how others might react. And frequently, he says in public what his parents say behind closed doors. He comments on a woman's mustache[37] or the bald head of his father's boss.[38] He literalizes metaphors, asking one man about his "ball and chain,"[39] eager to see one woman stop a clock[40] and another talk the leg off a chair.[41] He blurts out family secrets, telling a random caller that his parents are arguing.[42] Dennis asks his mother, "If what I said isn't funny, why is everyone trying not to laugh?"[43] Such moments show Dennis's confusions about the meaning of adult expressions and suggest the gap between what adults say about each other in private as opposed to what goes unsaid due to social niceties. In *Problems of Parents* (1962), Benjamin Spock urges patience when such moments inevitably arise: "Avoid, if possible, interrupting or reproving a young child who, from a genuine feeling of friendliness, is spilling the beans, for instance, about some private family business. For a child to want to share interesting matters with others is the soul of good manners, and it shouldn't be turned into embarrassment unless the consequences would be really serious."[44]

As Art Linkletter, the host of the *House Party* television talk show, might say, "Kids say the darndest things!" Linkletter had brought his own children onto his show and discovered audiences were hungry for awkward revelations or baffling misconceptions. Soon, Linkletter began partnering with the Los Angeles school system to identify precocious and outspoken youngsters, selected by their teachers, prompted by their parents, and queried by the host, all with the goal of generating hysterical moments. In a 1957 bestseller, Linkletter published stories parents had shared with him, accompanied, appropriately enough, with illustrations by Charles Schulz. Linkletter explained: "Why are the thoughts of children so delightful to a grown-up? I think it's because of the vast gulf between their worlds and ours. Where we adults see the tired old commonplace of everyday life, these 'babes' see a freshness, a wonderland waiting to be explored."[45] Linkletter kept the adults offstage, allowing audiences to anticipate their reactions; Ketcham depicts adult discomfort often on the edges of his panels.

## What's So Dirty about Mud?

The grubby diaper that inspired Ketcham's wife to call his son a menace never made it into the comics or television show. Guiding his readers through Freud's stages of sexual development, Haim Ginott (1965) acknowledged that the anal phase posed particularly vexing problems for parents, who do not share the child's fascination with the "sight, smell and touching of feces."[46] Parents, however, were urged to overcome their own discomfort: "Special care must be taken not to infect him with disgust towards his body and its products. Harsh and hasty measures may make the child feel that his body and all of its functions are something to dread, rather than to enjoy."[47] Ginott found the solution through sublimation and redirection, seeking "acceptable substitute ways" to "enjoy forbidden pleasures," such as playing with sand, mud, paint, clay, and water. To prevent sex from feeling dirty, permissive writers made dirt sexy: "Dirt is pleasant, and mud feels good when it is squished between the fingers or toes. Parents don't always see it that way, especially when the stuff gets tracked into the kitchen."[48] Spock adopts a similar stance:

> A small child wants to do a lot of things that get him dirty, and they are good for him, too. He loves to dig in earth and sand and wade in mud puddles, splash in water in the washstand. He wants to roll in the grass,

squeeze mud in his hands. When he has chances to do these delightful things, it enriches his spirit, makes him a warmer person, just the way beautiful music or falling in love improves an adult. The small child who is always sternly warned against getting his clothes dirty or making a mess, and who takes it to heart, will be cramped.[49]

Here, Spock's defense of muddy boys reflects his desire for children to enjoy the natural world and his rejection of antiseptic and antisensual attitudes.

Similarly, a 1953 press release suggests Ketcham saw mud as central to the pleasures of American boyhood. "A boy is truth with dirt on its face, beauty with a cut on its finger, wisdom with bubblegum in its hair, and the hope of the future with a frog in its pocket."[50] Ketcham often drew Dennis and his friends as coated with mud and unrecognizable even to their own parents.[51] Dennis tells his mother that "if you'd get in a mud puddle once in a while, maybe you'd feel friendlier about 'em."[52] He drags another boy home just to show his mother how dirty other parents let their children get.[53] And he proclaims to his playmate, "Somethin' else I've noticed: dirty people seem happier than clean people!"[54] When he gets clean, the first thing he wants is to get dirty again before the other boys see him as a "sissy."[55] Dennis tracks mud into the house as quickly as his mother can clean it, but she smiles wistfully, knowing that she cannot remove the dirt without damaging her son's budding masculinity. Besides, as Dennis tells her, it isn't all mud—some of it is chocolate ice cream. His father boasts, "With all its soaps, detergents, antiseptics and deodorants, American industry has yet to cope with the American Boy."[56] We are back to floor wax and accommodation.

### Dennis's Nudist Colony

Dennis is comfortable in his own skin. A surprising number of the early panels depict him naked as a jaybird, or at least it would be surprising to someone who was not around children in the four-to-five age range. Dennis comes home and can't remember where he left his clothes.[57] He innocently asks his parents: "Why should I wear clothes on a hot day?,"[58] or explains that he is trying to save his mother the drudgery of cleaning his clothes.[59] One might read these cartoons in the context of the shifting ideas about children's sexuality, and in particular, the adult need to facilitate children's open exploration of their bodies. Childcare writers negotiated between extremes, offering counsel to parents who had conservative ideas about nudity and those with more liberated attitudes. Because of these conflicting values, Spock advocates regulating what the child does in public settings: "It doesn't help a child to bring him up thinking it's all right to offend the sensibilities of the community."[60] Spock responds to the conflicting social attitudes by restricting nudity and self-touching to private space. Sexual desires are too powerful to repress fully, but they can, apparently, be closeted. Others agreed: "Permissiveness in private . . . is not the same as permissiveness in public." Parents who do not caution their children against public masturbation, for example, risk "exposing the child to public scolding, ridicule and even ostracism" and thereby cause "the very confusion and anxiety modern sex education hopes to avoid."[61]

Within a suburban neighborhood, parents were unlikely to agree about the appropriate response, yet the problem became a community interest as soon as it involved children from more than one family. As one 1957 sociological study reported: "If one child persistently behaved in a manner which the other mothers disapproved of, the other children were told not to play with him. Knowing that her child would be ostracized if he did not conform . . . , a mother might teach him that he had to conform to those neighborhood standards even if his own family disagreed with them."[62] As one mother told the researchers: "I explain to him that we have to live in the group, and we have to have the respect of the group, and unless he accepts some of these things . . . they will not get along well, and they will not be happy."[63]

Parents often phoned one another, reporting incidents of sex play and reasserting community standards. Most mothers adopted "an unwritten rule that one mother must not punish another mother's child."[64] Consider an incident where Dennis organizes a nudist colony for the neighborhood kids and asks Margaret to join. It's not hard to imagine why Margaret's mother called Alice, Dennis's mother, hinting at the community policing going on behind the scenes. We can also anticipate what Alice said to her son when he barged in naked at her bridge party, transgressing borders between public and private sexuality.[65]

## Explain and Then Wham!

Spock saw himself not only negotiating competing norms within the same neighborhood but also competing norms within the same family. Contemporary parents were seen as "hesitant" about disciplining their children, torn between the spankings of their own childhood and the more empathetic model of parenting. Such uncertainties often got transferred to the child, producing rather than reducing misconduct, as the child figured out the rules, much as in several panels, Dennis brings home a word he heard sailors use to see how his mother might respond, dutifully reporting the results to other children. Here's how Spock might account for Dennis's antics: "As children grow they have to keep exploring the limits of what their parents will allow them to do, which will require the parents to make new restrictions frequently. And they have to keep testing their parents' firmness, patience, self-respect, to see how much they will be permitted to impose on them."[66] Ketcham and especially Al Williamson, who drew the comic books, were masterful at depicting Henry, Dennis's father, on the verge of completely losing it over something Dennis has said or done. Fire comes out of his mouth, his face is distorted, and he raises his fist to belt the child, only to back down. One sees this back-and-forth in the ways Dennis is disciplined, sometimes shown with his behind smarting,[67] and more often, sitting in the corner.[68]

Putting the child in the corner as a form of social isolation was advised by many experts, often going hand in hand with explaining why something was wrong. As Dennis explains to Tommy (figure 5.1), "My folks don't wham me when I do something bad. They explain to me why I shouldn't do it. Then they wham me!"[69] Often Dennis anticipates his punishment, sitting in the chair facing the wall even before anyone has heard what happened,[70] and other times he places his dog Ruff in the chair[71] or pays his friend Joey to take his place.[72] Sometimes Ketcham depicts the testing of limits Spock describes. "Who says I gotta stay in bed?" Dennis demands bravely, before quickly backing down, "Just checkin.'"[73] And other times he questions the power relations, demanding a lawyer,[74] insisting he wouldn't treat Ruff the way they treat him,[75] or simply rehearsing what he should have said when his mother ordered him to sit in the corner. And when Henry comes home, both Alice and Dennis race to tell

Figure 5.1: Hank Ketcham's *Dennis the Menace* captures the uncertainties about the best way to discipline a boy during this transitional period.

him their side. Amid this combative relationship, Dennis seems surprised and reassured in one panel: "You mean you'd love me no matter what I did? Boy, that's a load off my mind!"[76] In another, he tells his mother, "You're making me feel unloved!"[77] Read side by side, these cartoons indicate the emotional dynamics Spock described, a constant need for reassurance about boundaries and expectations. And they argue against any reading of permissiveness as a fully stable and coherent set of practices.

## Gender and Sexuality in *Dennis the Menace*
### Between Boys and Men

If the nineteenth-century middle-class small-town bad boy primarily sought refuge from his overly protective mother, and the early twentieth-century working-class urban bad boy sought vengeance on his disciplinarian father, the middle-class suburban Dennis wanted acceptance and understanding from the adult male community. If the earlier bad-boy figure responded to the isolation of adult male activity from the domestic sphere, Dennis's actions reintegrated the spaces of boys and men. Many television episodes are set in late afternoon, when Dennis's father is home.

As Jay North's Dennis barges past closed doors, he unearths much that went unsaid about the gendered experiences of early '60s "organization men." Dennis's antics reveal deep-rooted fears about the loss of heroic stature as men became corporate cogs and suburban homeowners. "The Pioneers" opens with Wilson huffing and puffing over a newspaper editorial that claims "the men of this town are a generation of weaklings" compared to their pioneer fathers. After Wilson writes a heated response, the newspaper challenges him to live off the land for a weekend and "prove to the world and our readers that modern man is not a cream puff." The episode centers on the men's clumsy attempts to hunt, fish, and survive in the wilderness. The sad truth, the episode suggests, is that suburban men might be better off staying home watching *Maverick*.

Jules Henry (1963) had warned about the loss of traditional masculine authority: "The American father can no longer stand for a Law or for a Social Order he often can neither explain nor defend sensibly against the challenges of his wife and children. . . . It seems to him better to relax and have fun."[78] A 1959 *Parents* magazine ad for childcare books summarizes the problem: "Every Dad wants to be a *Pal* as well as a good disciplinarian—but how to be *both* when your time with your child is so limited? How to win his love and respect as well as his obedience?"[79] If patriarchal authority was breaking down, permissive discourse encouraged more playful fathering. Spock notes that "a boy needs a friendly, accepting father. Boys and girls need a chance to be around their father, to be enjoyed by him, and if possible, to do things with him." Spock stressed the importance of fathers helping their sons learn how to be a man: "Give him the feeling he's a chip off the old block, share a secret with him, take him alone on excursions sometimes."[80]

Yet, as Robert L. Griswold notes, this conception of fatherhood represented a reform, rather than a radical shift, in family structure.[81] The mother still maintained primary childcare responsibilities (and in *Dennis*, she doled out most of the punishment) while the father retained primary and often exclusive responsibility as breadwinner. Men were learning to play catch with their sons and sip tea with their daughters, but still weren't changing diapers or cooking meals (aside from the occasional backyard grill). The problem is how to bridge between the father's world and the son's. The most common solution was for the father to join boy culture, as Henry and Mr. Wilson do. Jules Henry notes that fathers were most often liked because they were willing to participate in their sons' activities rather than because they included their sons in adult interests. Far from preparing the boy for manhood, permissive fatherhood reinforced adult men's retreat from "the hostility, competition and strain men experience in their occupational lives."[82]

On television, Dennis's play life bears strong parallels to Henry's professional life. Here, the world of adult men is marked by conflicts between insecure yes-men and bragging bullies. The program frequently links Henry's workplace competition against the self-important Mr. Brady and Dennis's schoolhouse feud with Johnny Brady. The adult antagonisms are staged through the boys as the two men encourage their sons to best each other at egg tosses, Little League games, and soapbox derbies. "The Club Initiation" contrasts Dennis's initiation into the Scorpions, a gang of older boys, with Mr. Wilson's potential acceptance into the local country club. Dennis's pranks, such as keeping a live goat overnight in Wilson's garage, push the adult to more erratic behavior. Dennis rejects the exclusive Scorpions to form his own club, which Wilson, having been rejected from the country club, is invited to join. Spock characterizes the desire to form and join clubs as a preoccupation of the seven-to-nine-year-old boy, suggesting that it cannot be explained in terms of making new friendships since the boys often already know each other:

> Deep inside they sense that the day will come when as adults they must be able to take their places in groups set up for honest-to-goodness purposes, whether it's to bargain collectively or combat delinquency or establish a new business. So they feel the urge to go off by themselves where parents and teachers won't bother them, to set standards of behavior for themselves and show disapproval of those who are blackballed, to prove to themselves and others that they can go through the motions of organization and administration just as cooperatively and solemnly as any grownups.[83]

Yet, the television series often show how childish adult men are in the ways they govern themselves in and through such social organizations.

Henry and Mr. Wilson hunger for something beyond the safety and security of their suburban homes. Episodes like "Dennis in Gypsyland" (where Mr. Wilson plans to run off with a gypsy caravan) or "Henry's New Job" (where Henry plans to quit his job and build bridges in the Indian jungles) cast the adult males in the ranks of Barbara Ehrenreich's "gray flannel dissidents."[84] While men faced intensified pressure to become fathers and breadwinners, they also expressed increased dissatisfaction in these roles. And the generation of war veterans turned fathers have specific memories of more exciting times to fall back on, no doubt inspiring this wanderlust. Almost any event might spark male hunger for "something more." When Wilson purchases an old chest in "The Treasure Chest," boys and men believe it is a pirate's box. Dennis and Tommy use the old coat and spyglass Wilson finds in the box to play pirate, making a pretend map and stuffing it into the vest pocket. When Wilson finds the map, he is convinced it's real and organizes a boat trip to recover the buried loot. The "practical" Alice and Martha question the men's boyish pleasure in treasure-hunting, but the men disregard them: "Women have no sense of adventure." The men are overgrown boys and their wives their nurturing and forgiving mothers. Ultimately, the men's pirate fantasy is shattered when they learn the map is fake. As Ehrenreich wrote of their contemporaries, Henry "stayed where he was because he could not think of anywhere to go. If he blamed the corporation for his emasculation, he was not about to leave his job. . . . If he blamed women, he was not about to walk away from the comforts of home."[85]

### "What Good Are Girls?"

The men in *Dennis the Menace* struggle against female encroachments. Misogynistic conflicts surface everywhere, from Mr. Wilson's ongoing antagonism with the spinster Miss Elkins and her cats, to Dennis's attempts to dodge Margaret's persistent invitations to "play house." In "Junior Pathfinders Ride Again," Dennis expresses chagrin that the troopmaster has allowed Margaret to be a "squaw" in their fire-starting demonstration: "You just stay out of the victory dance." Margaret obliges, turning around to reveal a doll papoose. "How could I dance with a little one to take care of?" Tommy, however, remains suspicious: "If the pathfinders are letting girls in, I'm going to the desert and becoming a cowboy!"

Curly-haired, pale-faced Margaret shares many attributes with the "saintly child," including piety, obedience, book learning, cleanliness, good manners, and an unwavering sense of appropriate femininity. Actress Jeannie Russell, television's version, speaks of the flouncy clothes, stiff curls, and glasses she wore as "Margaret drag," a performative femininity.[86] As Dennis grumbles to Tommy, "I sure feel sorry for girls! Dresses, hair ribbons, dolls ... Bother!"[87] Ketcham has no sympathy for Margaret's domesticating impulses:

> There is a Margaret in every man's life. . . . Threatening, bossy, superior, always pursuing, the incipient castrator. Some of us marry her, some escape, and others are rescued. . . . Perhaps she perceives his freedom in speech and action as a challenge to be met. But more likely, the vitality and disorder of his very male personality appeal to her as a Woman's Problem: an untidy room to be cleaned up and put into order.[88]

Margaret wants to be a "good girl" in a world where Dennis sees girls as good for nothing.

As Lynn Spigel notes, the Italian American girl Gina represents an alternative female identity, that of the tomboy.[89] Gina plays cowboy rather than house, wallows in the mud with the boys rather than having tea parties with the girls. "Are you sure you are a girl?" Dennis asks.[90] In *Between Parent and Child*, Haim Ginott notes that "a girl loses less prestige by being a tomboy than a boy does by being a sissy," but advises that parents help the tomboy to "find pleasure and pride in femininity": "It is appropriate for the father to compliment his daughter on her dress, looks, and feminine pursuits. It is inappropriate for him to engage her in shadow boxing or rough play, lest she conclude the father would have enjoyed her more as a boy."[91]

Ketcham's casual misogyny is one of the most troubling aspects of the strip, suggesting a fear that women sought to ensnare men. Such attitudes are closely associated with Philip Wylie's *Generation of Vipers* (1942), which, among a range of other critiques of American culture, warned of the rise of momism, suggesting that the removal of men from the home and the expansion of women's role into the public sphere had extended maternal authority in ways crippling to men: "Her policy of protection, from the beginning, was not love of her boy but of herself, as she found coming in from the disoriented young boy in smiles, pats, presents, praise, kisses and all matter of childish representations ... she moved onto possession" (201, 208–9). While Alice avoids some of the nasty stereotypes with which Wylie characterizes this mom, Ketcham celebrates the efforts of Dennis and the other boys to escape maternal control.

Dennis is all boy insofar as he embraces rough-and-tumble socializing with the other boys and minimizes contact with Margaret and the other girls. In one daily installment of the newspaper strip, Dennis ponders, "Except for being babysitters and mothers ... what good are girls?"[92] Dennis is confused upon finding his mother sitting on his father's lap or observing neighborhood men gawking when she steps outside in a sundress. Alice is so fully the mom that when actress Gloria Henry was pregnant one season, they successfully hid her behind ironing boards and sewing machines. If Margaret represents a castrating threat, the relationship between Alice and Henry helps us to understand the negotiations between being a loving (and still sexually interested) couple and being parents.

Not unlike the adult men with their outdoorsman (or treasure-hunting) dreams, Dennis escapes from the threat of domesticity into heroic male fantasies of "Cowboy Bob," who never kisses anyone other than his horse. In one television episode, Margaret complains to Alice that Dennis will only "play house" with her if she allows him to be a cowboy who must roam. An early-1960s children's record explicitly links these cowboy fantasies to male flight from commitment:

> When Margaret cries, "Dennis, let's play house,"
> I say
> "Okay"
> But I'm a cowboy with a range to ride and so I'm leavin' ya', my blushing bride
> I'm gonna ride all night
> I'm gonna ride all day
> I'll never marry, Margaret
> She won't catch me
> I'm leavin', I'm gettin' away.

We might contrast "Margaret drag" with Harriet the Spy, the protagonist of Louise Fitzhugh's popular 1966 chapter book. Harriet enjoys the same freedom of movement and the same lack of social constraints as Dennis does, spying on her neighbors, making notes about their business, and getting into trouble. Unlike Margaret with her curls, ribbons, and frocks, Harriet dresses in a boyish fashion, showing no more interest in her appearance than Dennis does, and like Gina, does not mind getting muddy during a good adventure. Fitzhugh's illustrations consistently depict Harriet in her spy clothes, a nondescript red hoodie jacket and blue jeans, carrying her notebook. Part of the book's popularity would seem to be the fantasy of escaping from the constraints of femininity and having a rough-and-tumble existence as a girl, even as the adults show distaste and sometimes outrage over her misconduct. Such books require the characters to constantly negotiate between their own desires and the expectations of proper girlhood, a set of negotiations that are rarely as explicitly stated in stories like *Dennis the Menace* that adopt a "Boys will be boys" attitude. Robin Bernstein has done a historically grounded analysis of Harriet, acknowledging the number of lesbian, trans, and gender-queer youth who have found her a "kindred spirit," even though her gender identity is treated inconsistently across the books.[93]

Stories about Pippi Longstocking, billed the "strongest girl in the world," were initially published in Sweden from 1945 to 1948 and translated and reprinted for American readers in 1950. The initial sales were slow, and many top critics of children's literature, such as those at *Horn Book*, saw her transgressive adventures as inappropriate. The author

Astrid Lindgren balances Pippi's superhuman qualities with a more maternal mission defending those who could not defend themselves. She avoids, however, the fate of other tomboy characters in children's fictions who often must accept more appropriate feminine roles in the end. Such books celebrate the character's refusal to conform and her gradual acquiescence to gender norms, suggesting that being "bad" represented a phase in her development. If boy culture was also seen as a phase on the way to adulthood, the rejection of boyish mischief occurs offstage rather than reassuring readers that the wild girls would eventually be tamed. Joey, the sissy-boy character in *Dennis the Menace*, suggests the period's limits to what counts as appropriate masculinity.

## Joey as the Sissy Boy

If permissive discourse saw gender differences as natural attributes (roughhouse in boys, domesticity in girls), it also worried that sexual identity might be negated by poor socialization (or by too much mothering). Ginott's *Between Parent and Child* advises: "Both boys and girls need help in their progress toward their different biological destinies.... Boys should not have to bear feminine names, or to wear restrictive clothes, or to grow girls' curls. They should not be expected to be as neat and as compliant as girls, or to have ladylike manners."[94] The most ambivalent figure in *Dennis*, Joey is constantly torn between playing house with Margaret and playing cowboys with Dennis. He embodies the "disoriented young boy" whom Wylie saw as the victim of momism, but even here, Ketcham holds onto a hope that he may be reclaimed for hard masculinity. In one 1964 comic book, Margaret convinces Joey to become a "little gentleman" who is "nice and polite and clean" and shuns Dennis's company. Joey rejects Dennis's play as too "rough ... an' noisy," until Dennis tricks Margaret into an anticowboy tirade. "See? She don't know nothin'! So let's play!"[95] Despite his allegiance to the cowboy mythos, Joey is a "sissy." Dennis mentors Joey about what it means to be a boy, advising the younger boy, "An' another thing! Don't ever be too good or people will think you're a girl!"[96]

*The Gesell Institute's Child Behavior* (1955) offers a description of a boy much like Joey: "This is the boy who from the beginning prefers feminine activities and shuns anything rough and tumble. He prefers to play with girls. He favors such activities as painting, singing, play-acting, dressing dolls. He himself loves to dress up in girls' clothes."[97] Permissiveness rejected the notion that scolding or ridiculing such a boy might push him back into gender-appropriate conduct: "The best treatment seems to be to permit these favored activities within certain bounds." For example, one recommendation taught the young boys how to closet their desires: "No lipstick and no flowers in the hat *outside the house.*" Ultimately, most such boys would "grow up to lead perfectly normal personal lives" and become outstanding as artists, musicians, or as actors, costume designers, playwrights. Haim Ginott similarly evokes an image much like Joey in his discussion of gender identification: "A nice, curly-haired boy may look cute to relatives, but he is sure to be a sissy to his playmates."[98] The stereotypes of the era also linked homosexuality to the presence of a domineering or overly close relationship between a boy and his mother.

We might regard Dennis's mentorship of Joey as a gentle influence on his developing identity. Dennis begs his mother, "Don't scold me in front of Joey. He thinks I'm a big shot!"[99] and later informs her, "I'm learnin' him everything I know."[100] All of this suggests that Dennis is meant to be Joey's ego-ideal, the role model he hopes to imitate on his path toward mandatory heterosexuality and normative masculinity. In turn, Joey acts as a foil for Dennis's confident "all boy" behavior, setting Dennis's fearlessness against Joey's uncertainty. A "mama's boy" like Joey confounded attempts to naturalize gender differences. Even Dennis seems confused about appropriate gender behavior in his playmate's presence: "Mom, would you explain to Joey why boys don't play with dolls? I forget." Given Joey's potential queerness, it is hardly surprising that the character appeared infrequently on the television series. His function as Dennis's pal is replaced by the more rough-and tumble, girl-hating Tommy, keeping the suburban frontier safe for "Cowboy Bob" and his posse.

## Why It Matters That Dennis Is White

Now, let's consider something that is blatantly obvious and yet rarely noted: Dennis Mitchell is white. This invisible whiteness allows him to function as a universal representative of the "all-American handful." When Ketcham describes Henry and Alice in *Merchant of Dennis the*

*Menace*, his 1990 account overflows with markers of whiteness. Henry is "a thirty-two-year-old White Anglo-Saxon Protestant who was born in a busy mill town in Central Minnesota."[101] His mother is a "Montana rancher's daughter" and his father, "a Dixie trencherman" from Social Circle, Georgia, "especially devoted to hominy grits, black-eyed peas, homemade biscuits, smoked ham, and gallons of Coke."[102] Alice is a descendant of a "pioneer family ... who emigrated westward from Pennsylvania in the 1840s, settling on the rich farmlands of the then-virgin Ohio territories."[103] Ketcham connects his characters to multiple histories of whiteness associated with the American South, the Midwest, and the West, including a healthy dose of settler mythology for good measure. The invisibility of white identity accounts for much of its potency, Richard Dyer reminds us: "White people have power and believe that they think, feel, and act like and for all people. . . . White people set the standards of humanity by which they are bound to succeed and others bound to fail."[104] Despite Dyer's reference here to "white people," whiteness is a form of discursive power that any given white person may or may not fully possess, and whiteness is a contingent, dynamic category that different groups of people possess at different historical moments and in specific cultural contexts (hence the need to apply many different myths of whiteness in characterizing the Mitchells). In Ketcham's daily comics, Dennis's whiteness amounts to a lack of black ink, but that absence becomes an overwhelming presence given the ways whiteness sets cultural norms.

Dennis and his family inhabit an all-white world. For the better part of a decade, the closest they came to engaging with racial or cultural difference was occasional dinners at a Chinese restaurant. Gina is characterized as Italian American (marked here as ethnically distinctive). Otherwise, whiteness is characterized by Anglo-Saxon or Germanic-Scandinavian descent. In the 1960s Ketcham introduced a Black boy, Jackson. One cartoon spoke of a "race problem" because Jackson could run faster than Dennis, while another notes that the only difference between them is that Jackson is left-handed.[105] Ketcham, however, acknowledges that he fell back on racial caricatures: "[I] designed him in the tradition of Little Black Sambo with huge lips, big white eyes, and just a suggestion of an Afro hairstyle."[106] For Ketcham, who by this point was a Goldwater conservative, Jackson was a means to "inject some humor into the extremely tense political climate."[107] The character was quickly dropped when to the cartoonist's apparent surprise, his reliance on racial caricature prompted a letter-writing campaign among his Black readers. Here, again, writers and artists resorted to segregation rather than rethinking racial stereotypes. By contrast, the residents of Hogan's Alley in the early twentieth-century *Yellow Kid* comic strips were multiethnic and multiracial, as were their live-action counterparts in the *Little Rascal* comedy shorts, reflecting an urban world where people from diverse backgrounds regularly bumped against each other. Irish, Jewish, Black, and sometimes Asian characters were depicted in stereotypical terms, but also as part of the community.[108]

Suburbanization had been an ongoing process in American cities since the late nineteenth century, with each generation moving further from the urban core. The postwar generation were constructing new subdivisions as the next wave of white flight (coupled with redlining) shaped who could buy into these newly populated areas. Mitchell's neighborhood is still under construction: new subdivisions are being added, new neighbors are moving in, the residents are using party lines because they can't lay phone cable fast enough, and civic institutions, such as schools, libraries, and zoos, are still being constructed. If this suburban culture is provisional, its residences are perceived as precarious, open to invasions of all kinds (burglars and bums in the comics but also imagined men from Mars and ghosts in the television episodes). The suburb became, as George Lipsitz argues, a central trope in the white spatial imaginary: "It is not that suburban whites are innately racist and consequently favor land use policies that increase the racial gap, but rather that prevailing land use policies produce a certain kind of whiteness that offers extraordinary inducements and incentives for a system of privatization that has drastic racial consequences."[109] The white spatial imaginary, Lipsitz suggests, embraces "homogeneous spaces, controlled environments, and predictable patterns of design and behavior,"[110] but also sees these values as under threat, justifying the need to police borders.

Ketcham offers narratives to justify the homogeneity of suburban culture. One *Dennis the Menace* comic book story, "The Big Cleanup," depicts the mechanisms through which white spatial norms are enforced.[111] The Mitchells and the Wilsons are frantically grooming their yards in preparation for an annual inspection from the Homeowners Association: "Our house can win a prize if it's the neatest one in the neighborhood." As "Chairman for the Block," Mr. Wilson's job is to "see that everyone else cleans up," enforcing a long checklist of ordinances and assessment standards. Dennis's efforts to help the adults produce one mess after another, intensifying the pressure to perform according to their mutual expectations—for example, an unfounded fear that the Dennis's tree house may not meet the code. Ultimately, the tree house ("So charming! So American!") tips the scale and the judges proclaim this "the best block in the neighborhood." Beneath that humor, the story never questions this push to impose homogeneous standards (or for that matter, the homogeneous nature of the people who live in that neighborhood).

These tensions surface vividly in a television episode, "Dennis and the Open House," when Henry is asked by his boss to host an "open house" party for a visiting business associate, inviting the "best people." Dennis overhears his parents complaining about the guests having difficulty finding their house and borrows an Open House sign from a local realtor, planting it in their front lawn. Suddenly, the Mitchell house overflows with guests but the "wrong kind"—workmen, farmers, and hipsters, whose crass manners, rowdy speech, blunt materialism, and overfamiliarity cause offense. The episode's humor starts from the premise that such people do not belong at a cocktail party, though underneath the surface, there is also suggestion that these people may be the next wave of suburban residents. Lipsitz notes that suburban spaces "enact a public pedagogy about who belongs where and about what makes certain spaces desirable."[112] In an already segregated world, such questions are staged around "white trash" rather than Blackness, but *Dennis* performs the mechanisms of segregation.

Dennis often puts the community's status in jeopardy. One cartoon (figure 5.2) shows a group of realtors looking at a map and remarking, "Now this area is known as the 'Mitchell Neighborhood' and it takes a REAL salesman...."[113] Much as having one Black or Jewish resident was perceived as lowering property values, Dennis's presence generates its own kind of flight as neighbors post "For Sale" signs and realtors either lie about the boy who lives next door or convince the Mitchells to keep Dennis away when they are showing homes.

Figure 5.2: In disrupting the decorum of white suburbia, Dennis the Menace potentially threatens property values.

During its final season, the television series' opening credits depict Dennis as a tornado in a cowboy hat who literally rocks and rattles a row of suburban houses. Dennis slams doors, shouts between houses, even uses a remote control to take over Mr. Wilson's television set and boost its volume so it can be heard next door. We might read Dennis as empowered to cross what Jennifer Lynn Stoever calls the "sonic color line," where Black noises—especially loud music and raucous voices, the "clang and rumble of urban life"—are policed in favor of the muted white noise.[114] Dennis consistently defies the neighborhood's desire for "peace and quiet," creating a ruckus wherever he goes, and he goes everywhere he wants, taking unauthorized dips in the neighbors' pools, barging into their bedrooms, rummaging through their closets, stealing or begging for food, crawling around in their basements. Dennis even barges into a neighboring television series in a special episode of *The Donna Reed Show*, where his efforts to help her paint her living room fray her nerves and leave her calling Mr. Wilson to take the boy off her hands. Here, the boy threatens the "controlled environments, and predictable patterns of . . . behavior" at the heart of the white spatial imaginary.[115]

Although Dennis often disrupts white middle-class decorum, he also benefits from white privilege.[116] While Dennis might display the "refreshing, naive honesty of preschool children as yet unexposed to prejudice and rancor,"[117] Jackson could forget who he was or where he came from only at his own risk. In *Racial Innocence*, Robin Bernstein points out: "Innocence was not a literal state of being unraced but was, rather, the performance of not-noticing, a performed claim of slipping beyond social categories."[118] Dennis might choose to act contrary to the community's norms but he remains safely white, as we see whenever he encounters a policeman, postman, teacher, or other agent of the state. He was often shown warring with the cops, shouting jeers, thumbing his nose, making a raspberry, or swiping their hats or badges, classic bad-boy behavior. But he always benefits from their extreme tolerance, as the big (typically Irish) cops bring him safely back home, urging his parents not to be too harsh on the spirited lad. As Lipsitz suggests, "This imaginary does not emerge simply or directly from the embodied identities of people who are white. It is inscribed in the physical contours of the places where we live, work, and play, and it is bolstered by financial rewards for whiteness."[119] In representing Dennis transgressing the rules of the white spatial imaginary and showing how the system responds, *Dennis the Menace* offers a remarkable glimpse into the prevailing social and cultural logic of whiteness. He also became the representative of a national ideal, which is why Dennis is not simply a handful, but also "all-American."

## The Bad Boy as an American Ideal

If his parents' tolerance for Dennis's misconduct reflected the empathetic understanding promoted by the Child Study movement and his proclivity to wallow in the mud embraced the new construction of childhood desire and sexuality associated with Spock's popularization of Freud, *Dennis the Menace* also absorbed the ideals of democratic family life[120] The architects of permissive culture had mostly been veterans, many involved in the management of public opinion during the war. Nicholas Sammond links *Childhood in Contemporary Cultures* (1955) to a larger project reading parenting practices as reflecting the American national character: "The child, properly studied and raised in its natural environment, would be a cold-war tool for the promotion of healthy democratic capitalism, with the power to defuse international hostilities, see past petty nationalism, and resist psychological persuasion."[121] The book's contributors drew cross-cultural comparisons among children's stories, advice literature, and parental practice in the United States, France, Germany, the Soviet Union, and other national contexts. Even as Mead stresses the "shared humanity" of all children, she is also interested in "patterns of culture" (borrowing from her mentor, Ruth Benedict) that show how constraints and freedoms are taught from the cradle. As one contemporary educator, James L. Hymes, notes in 1958: "Taking the 'Menace' out of Dennis might prove to be a real job of subversion and a truly un-American activity. . . . Dennis might be hard to live with. Free people are always harder to live with than slaves."[122] Writing about nineteenth-century paintings of "naughty boys" stealing apples, art historian Jadwiga M. Da Costa Nunes reminds us: "The creators of American culture often employed the metaphor of the child .to define the status of the new nation, which, like a child, was energetically struggling to achieve self-definition and fulfillment."[123] Such images persisted well into the twentieth century where America was trying to mask its newly discovered geopolitical influence and its intrusions into other nations' sovereignty behind a different myth of childlike innocence. America in the second half of the twentieth century was becoming the "Good Bad" nation just as Dennis was the "Good Bad Boy." Dennis's attempts to explore the adult world might cause a few problems, but, as Hymes suggested, it was "a wonderfully American kind of response:

open, trusting, friendly, cheerful." Dennis possessed qualities "inherent in the American way of life," including a strong sense of his own worth and an insatiable curiosity, "the very qualities we would prize in him twenty years from now in a laboratory."[124]

Speaking in 1958, Hymes saw Dennis as the perfect response to the Sputnik crisis and to growing anxieties about the American education system. The series came to television amid increasing American concern about children's "readiness" to compete in the space race. If the comic-strip Dennis was most closely associated with the frontier mythology of Cowboy Bob, television's Dennis was often shown playing spacemen. As Dennis remarks in "Trouble from Mars," "we've decided to desert six shooters for space-guns." NASA had rejected the idea of female astronauts, and so for the immediate future, space was one place where men could escape feminine influence. But in *Dennis*, outer space only offered pleasure for the young; space baffled adults. When they dress as astronauts in "Trouble from Mars," Dennis and his friends frighten the neighbors, who are convinced that the boys are "men from Mars." Scheduled to be photographed for *Graceful Living* magazine, Mr. Wilson accidentally gets stuck in Dennis's astronaut helmet, his adult head not suited for a space suit.

"The Junior Astronaut" opens with a dream sequence depicting Dennis as an astronaut and Mr. Wilson as mission control. Just as Dennis is preparing for a rocky reentry, his parents wake him, having fallen asleep over his math book. The post-Sputnik educational campaigns, with their emphasis on math and science, are sometimes represented as a repudiation of permissive practices. Too many American youngsters were falling asleep over their math books. Yet Dennis's dream reminds us that there were strong continuities between Sputnik-era appeals to scientific exploration and permissive appeals to play. Child-rearing articles taught parents how to turn science and math readiness into play by holding parties with spaceman themes, launching expeditions to better understand the "outer spaces" of nearby meadows, and learning to use magnifying glasses and microscopes. Appropriately enough, Dennis, the "eighth Mercury Astronaut," became the mascot for the United States Junior Astronaut program, encouraging children to buy savings bonds. If the bad boy of the nineteenth century played hooky, Dennis, the postwar bad boy, was leading the way into the classroom.

DENNIS THE MENACE, "THE ALL-AMERICAN HANDFUL" | 159

Figure 5.3: No less an authority than FBI director J. Edgar Hoover confirms Dennis's patriotism as the "all-American handful."

In mid-1960s stories, Dennis's creators allowed the Mitchell family to "see the USA," going on road trips to Los Angeles; Washington, DC; Hawaii, and various national parks. Henry dutifully lays out America's historical, geographic, and political exceptionalism to his son, who focuses his attention elsewhere or asks impertinent questions that enrage his father. Dennis wanders during a tour of the FBI Headquarters and finds himself confronting J. Edgar Hoover (figure 5.3): "It's nice to see you here. I wish ALL youngsters would see our work here at the FBI and learn that crime doesn't pay." The cartoon exaggerates their height differences so that the G-man towers over the boy. Dennis has similar encounters with Secret Service officers at the White House when he goes looking for Caroline Kennedy and with the Joint Chiefs of Staff when he explores the inner reaches of the Pentagon. He acts like he owns the place, much as he does in his own suburban neighborhood, and that renders these government officials and sacred sites more approachable to citizens.

Throughout this chapter, I have shown how the three strands of the permissive paradigm—the focus on children's emotional lives, the ideals of democratic parenting, and the Freudian rethinking of children's desires—work together to construct particular ideas about American boyhood. Ketcham sees Dennis less as a bad boy than as acting on his natural impulses, seeking to do good for others, adopting civic roles as a natural leader among a larger community of boys. Dennis exemplifies his culture's expectations about what it means to be a boy, what it means to be white, and what it means to be American. In the next chapter, I will dig deeper into narratives about children who are different because of their imaginations or their abilities, children who are misfits that the culture must find ways to assimilate or accommodate.

# 6

# Gerald McBoing-Boing and the Island of the Misfit Boys

In Gertrude Campton's *Tootle*, a young train learns to be a fast and powerful Flier.[1] Tootle must make "100 percent A+" at "staying on the track no matter what," the class for preparing young locomotives for their adult roles. But Tootle leaves the track when a black horse dares him to race to the river. Once tempted, Tootle finds more excuses for wandering into the meadow, but his trainers discover his transgression: flowers are entangled in his cowcatcher or wrapped around his smokestack. The trainers stage an intervention and he never strays again.

Sociologist David Reisman, part of Mead's circle, writes, "The story is an all too appropriate one for bringing up children in today's society. They learn that it is bad to go off the tracks."[2] A critic of mass conformity, Reisman coined the distinction between "inner-directed" and "other-directed"; he worried that adults often "lose their social freedom and their individual autonomy" in the face of social pressures that "cut everyone down to size who stands up or stands out in any direction. . . . All knobby or idiosyncratic qualities and vices are more or less eliminated or repressed."[3] In middle-class families, Reisman observed, "one must be different enough to attract attention, to be a personality, to be labeled and tagged" but "not too much" to stray outside the mass society:[4] "The parents become concerned, and understandably so, if the child's age mates reject him; they fear his differences are of the wrong sort. . . . Are they to defend their child's differences, then, at the cost of his undoubted present and possible future misery?"[5] Reisman closed his essay with reflections on what an alternative story might look like—one that allowed children to embrace their differences and pushed children toward greater autonomy from adult expectations and freedom from their peers' demands.

In *Learning from the Left*, Julia Mickenberg examines a group of midcentury writers, such as Crockett Johnson, Ruth Krauss, P. D. Eastman, Leo Lionni, Lilian Moore, and William Steig, whom she characterizes as "Lyrical Leftists" who were drawn to themes of children's play and imagination because "they believed that the imaginative, creative, artistic, and playful traits inherent to childhood represented a model for the liberation of society as a whole."[6] This chapter will explore how children's fictions helped adults and children alike to understand what to preserve within themselves even as they accepted predetermined roles within the adult order. In some ways, creativity and imagination stood for a larger range of differences that might set any individual child apart from their peer culture, including some such as race, disability, or sexuality that could not be expressed more overtly. I will use *Gerald McBoing-Boing* as the starting point for a consideration of a broader array of "misfit" boys in children's fictions. A second case study will consider Harold and his purple crayon as a way to explore theories of children's artistic expression. Third, I will look more closely at Linus as an imaginative child living in the anxious world of *Peanuts*. Such stories about "ugly ducklings" were omnipresent during my own childhood. Writers and readers were working through contradictions and uncertainties, maintaining hope that their children would remain freer than their parents felt. I am interested in how these stories served the needs of children who saw themselves as misfits and outcasts, but also in the roles they propose for adults, whether as interpreters of children's emotions or as facilitators providing the resources for their creativity.

## Misfits and Ugly Ducklings

> This is the story of Gerald McCloy
> And the strange thing that happened to that little boy.
> They say it all started when Gerald was two.
> That's the age kids start talking, at least most of them do.
> When he started talking, you know what he said?
> He didn't talk words, he went BOING instead.

Thus begins United Productions of America's 1951 cartoon *Gerald McBoing-Boing*, directed by Robert Cannon, adopted by Bill Scott and P. D. Eastman from a story written for radio by Dr. Seuss. *Gerald McBoing-Boing* set the stage for what animation historian Amid Amidi calls "cartoon modernism," an era of experimentation in animation technique inspired by modern art.[7] From the start, Gerald's substitution of sound effects for words is a problem for the everyday order of things. His doctor (even after consulting other experts) finds no explanation. He is sent to school and promptly returned home because his noise-making violates the rules. His peers reject him when he tries to join their games. And ultimately, he runs away from home, only to bump into a radio network executive who—at last—recognizes Gerald's hidden potential.

The peer culture's response (especially the boys' and girls' repeated "Nyah nyah") seems particularly poignant when read alongside Riesman's discussion of the pressures confronting the nonconforming child: "He is, as never before, at their mercy. If the peer-group were . . . a wild, torturing, obviously vicious group, the individual child might still feel more indignation as a defense against its commands. . . . [But] the peer-group is friendly and tolerant. It stresses fair play. Its conditions for entry seem reasonable and well-meaning. . . . The child is thus exposed to trial by jury with no defenses."[8] The narrator explains: "As little Gerald grew older, he found that when a fellow goes HONK, HONK, no one wants him around. When a fellow goes BOINK BOINK, he can't have any pals. And his CLANG CLANG frightened the gals." These children are not bullies or bigots; they simply want to play without distraction. The original children's record, narrated by Harold Peary (radio's "the Great Gildersleeve"), digs into Gerald's subjectivity: "What would you do, if it happened to you, if you wanted to speak but whenever you tried, a noise like CRASH came up from inside."[9] The record portrays Gerald's disruptions not as a refusal to follow rules but an inability to speak in terms the world understands. Yet, *Gerald* ends on a note of acceptance. The network owner easily discerns how the boy might contribute (not to mention how the network might profit from his labor). Tootle must sacrifice his individualism to belong (assimilation) while society learns to value Gerald's unique contributions (accommodation). Gerald's parents strut behind him, a young boy reaches out for his autograph: "Now his parents—proud parents—are able to boast that their Gerald's OO-GA is known coast to coast. Now Gerald is rich, he has friends, he is well fed because he doesn't speak words, he goes BOING BOING instead."

In the context of feminist disability studies, Rosemary Garland-Thomson reclaims the concept of the "misfit" to describe the unstable relationships between bodies and the world. Misfits are defined by their context—the material and social barriers that block their acceptance and accommodation: "A misfit occurs when the environment does not sustain the shape and function of the body that enters it. The dynamism between body and world that produces fits or misfits comes at the spatial and temporal points of encounter between dynamic but relatively stable bodies and environments."[10] The label of the misfit represents the stigma society places on the individual: "To misfit is to be rendered a misfit."[11]

Gerald and many other stories about social misfits often map these traits onto other physical and communication differences. Compare how *Gerald McBoing-Boing* treats the boy's distinctive communication style with the depiction of the mute "Ay-you" in Charles Tazewell's *Lullaby of Christmas*, read on the radio by Gregory Peck in 1949 and then popularized as a children's record (the opposite side of Loretta Young's reading of Tazewell's *The Littlest Angel*). Tazewell describes the boy's disability in language that might have been applied to Gerald: "From out of his cherub's mouth, instead of words, would come a horrible deformity of sounds, a scourging, piercing, ear-scraping babel of howls and braying gibberish." Here, there are no amusing sound effects; rather, this explicitly disabled child is described as ancient Bethlehem would have seen him. The beggar boy dreams about "all of the beautiful magic words he'd like to say" and being able to "sing with the other children when they played their games" (another reference to children's exclusion from their peer culture). Here, the unloved child confronts abjection: "And so Ay-you tried to sing, and at every tuneless howl, the crowd shouted its mockeries, and at every melody-less screech it roared its derision. At every discordant squeak, it unleashed a thunderbolt of laughter that crashed and splintered on his head. . . . His mind was fear, his body was shame, and his blood was tears." This is what Gerald might have confronted in a world less safe and accommodating than the cozy suburban realm where Seuss set his story.

As Garland-Thomson tells us about misfits in the real world, "the primary negative effect of misfitting is exclusion from the public sphere—a literal casting out—and the resulting segregation into domestic spaces or sheltered institutions."[12] Here, though, the story grants the beggar boy a triumph. Whereas Gerald is celebrated for his unique expression, this boy must be "cured" so that he can sing with a voice deemed beautiful by the Christ child. Ay-you must be changed into something that "fits." Peck's narration reassures us: "The words Ay-you spoke were as clear and melodious as the water in the brook . . . as sweet as the winds, as perfect as each raindrop and as soft as the long flowing grasses. Then Ay-you knew why he had been born never to speak until this moment." This one speech act—to the newborn Jesus—is meant to justify a lifetime of suffering and humiliation. Spock's book was one of the few guides that directly addressed the concerns of families living with disability:

> A child with a disability may need treatment for the defect. But even more he needs to be treated naturally, whether the handicap is mental slowness, crossed eyes, epilepsy, deafness, shortness, a disfiguring birthmark or a deformity of any other part of the body. This is easier said than done. . . . The important factors that make a person (with or without defects) grow up happy and outgoing are having parents who thoroughly enjoy and approve of him, who do little worrying, urging, fussing, criticizing; having opportunities to learn the give and take of other children from an early age.[13]

However accommodating Spock's advice, his references to "defects" and "deformity" sting.

Walt Disney's *Dumbo* (1941) was another popular narrative that urged the world to accommodate those who are different—in this case, a baby elephant who was rejected, almost from birth, for "ears only a mother could love." In language suggestive of the era's racial segregation, one elephant proclaims, "Frankly I wouldn't eat at the same bale of hay with him." Objecting to their snubbing Dumbo, Timothy, the mouse, sneers sarcastically, "a noble race." The elephants, indeed, speak in an accent associated with high-society whiteness. When adolescent human patrons—depicted as bucktoothed, with floppy ears and ginger hair (itself an ethnic stereotype)—laugh at Dumbo, his mother riots, spanking one boy with her trunk, and she must be locked away.

Only Timothy sees potential in the "poor little guy." Timothy is the one who discovers Dumbo can fly. With help from a flock of crows (who, infamously, jive and shuffle), he introduces the "magic feather," a transitional object that empowers Dumbo to risk falling on his face. Rejected by others of his own race, this white elephant finds acceptance and comfort from the community of others—the black crows living on the outskirts of town. While these crows have often been dismissed as hurtful racial stereotypes, which they are, less has been made of how their racial coding operates according to the logics of inclusion and exclusion within the larger film narrative. Their acceptance of the misfit pachyderm gives him the courage to gain acceptance by the circus society.

The film ends with Dumbo's triumph, his name splashed across headlines, as a prime attraction within the circus that once saw him as worthless. Such stories show how the culture spoke about the need to accept and even celebrate difference without naming any specific form of difference. We can't say Dumbo is queer, disabled, or Black, though his story might have addressed each of these issues for specific viewers. In their particularity, these stories remain abstract enough to accommodate a range of needs for children who felt different from their surrounding culture. In calling such characters "exceptional," I link them to educational terminology of the period that stressed the exceptionality of both the gifted and the disabled child as somehow falling outside educational norms and thus requiring special attention.[14] Others extended this terminology intersectionally to speak about "the exceptional minority child."[15] The term was a double-edged sword, since it provide a tool for advocating on behalf of students with special abilities or needs, but also made them an "exception" or "credit" to their race and thus implied that the normal state of being a minority child was below their white classmates. In the stories we are discussing, the misfit child produces value for the culture because of extraordinary accomplishment, which could diminish the child who is different but not exceptional.

Ronald D. Lankford Jr. (2016) described *Rudolph the Red-Nosed Reindeer*, another such narrative, as "the fantasy story made to order for American children: each child has the need to express and receive approval for his or her individuality and/or special qualities."[16] *Rudolph* originated in 1939 as a Christmas-themed coloring book, written by Robert L. May for Montgomery Ward. The core story was translated into a Fleischer Studios cartoon in 1948, and that same year was published by Little Golden Books with illustrations by Richard Scarry. Rudolph's saga was performed on the popular *Fibber McGee and Molly* radio show in 1949 and adapted into a chart-busting Gene Autry song also in

1949, which eventually sold more than twenty-five million copies. And Ranken-Bass produced a stop-motion animated version for television in 1964—still a holiday favorite. At the heart of the story is the exceptional Rudolph whom "the other reindeer won't let play in any of their reindeer games" (a classic moment of peer rejection), but then Santa (here performing the same story function as the radio network executive in *Gerald*) discovers Rudolph's unique potential and asks him to guide his sleigh. Ever after, Rudolph is celebrated for the trait that initially made him a misfit—his shiny red nose. The Fleischer cartoon puts it simply: "The bad deer who did nothing but tease him, now they would do anything just to please him."

The 1964 Rankin-Bass special introduced other outcast characters, including Hermy, the elf who would rather be a dentist, and an island of "misfit toys." When Rudolph and his companions arrive on the island, the toys present their dilemma: "How would you like to be a bird that doesn't fly. . . . Or a cowboy who rides an ostrich. Or a boat that can't stay afloat. We're all misfits." Across this segment, we are told that these toys are "homeless," that "no boy or girl loves them," that they are made "wrong" and thus cannot fulfill their functions: "A toy is never truly happy until it is loved by a child." They have formed their own outcast community, one attractive enough that Rudolph asks if he could join, but the king says that living things must return to their own world. As one of Rudolph's friends explains, "even among misfits, we are misfits," but Rankin-Bass delivers a "separate but equal" message that already must have seemed wrong when the television special was made.

As time passed, some queer audiences came to identify with the misfit toys and wanted to live in the society they created. In *The Queer Art of Failure*, Jack Halberstam finds a similar logic of exceptionalism and exclusion within more contemporary children's fictions produced by Pixar: "Failure allows us to escape the punishing norms that discipline behavior and manage human development with the goal of delivering us from unruly childhoods to orderly and predictable adulthoods. Failure preserves some of the wondrous anarchy of childhood and disturbs the supposedly clean boundaries between adults and children, winners and losers."[17] In Halberstam's account, failure is defined in terms of cultural norms, a "failure" to conform, a "failure" to accept one's place, a "failure" to embrace assigned roles, and ultimately, in this queer reading, a "failure" to reproduce. Such stories, Halberstam writes, "address the disorderly child, the child who sees his or her family and parents as the problem, the child who knows there is a bigger world out there beyond the family, if only he or she could reach it."[18] In this account, "failure" is what queers such characters before their peers.

Consider, for example, the case of Casper, the childlike ghost, unable to match ghost-world expectations that he be "frightful" and unable to get others to accept that he might be "friendly." Paramount's Famous Studios brought the character, based on an earlier children's book (1939), to the screen in 1945, and he became the focus of fifty-five theatrical cartoons over the next decade. Almost all followed the same pattern: the gentle, somewhat effeminate ghost tries to befriend mortals who react in a broad comic fashion, even as he is contrasted with the other ghosts who bully and ridicule him for his failures. Sometimes he rescues cute animals from hunters or chases away the evil banker about to foreclose on a widow, gaining temporary acceptance; even such successful integration is short-lived.

These stories were selected and often read by adults because they recognized their own children's failure to integrate into their peer culture and wanted to help them to appreciate their specialness. In an iconic sequence from *Hans Christian Andersen* (1951), dozens of children, in brightly colored clothes, have surrounded the storyteller, laughing in glee at his yarns. When he sends them to school, he notices another boy, dressed in black, peering at him wearily. The boy's head is bald, he has oddly shaped ears, his eyes are filled with suspicion. He looks remarkably like Gerald McBoing-Boing, except the world has worn him down. The storyteller sees him: "What's the matter? Are you unhappy? Would you like me to tell you a special story?" and urges him to come closer so he can learn about the "ugly duckling." At this point, the boy has said nothing, but the storyteller—another version of the "Understanding Angel"—recognizes the boy's shame. Andersen acknowledges the misfit boy because he is himself a misfit with no fixed place among adults, one who fails at constructing heteronormative relations, one who faces rebuke from the village schoolmaster and rejection by other adults, the object of ridicule but also admiration because of his exceptional abilities.

Like other stories discussed here, "The Ugly Duckling" starts at a moment when the exceptional child (in this case, a duckling) is ostracized:

> There once was an ugly duckling
> With feathers all stubby and brown.
> And the other birds said in so many words
> Pfft Get out of town
> Pfft Get out, Pfft Pfft get out, Pfft Pfft get out of town.
> And he went with a quack and a waddle and a quack
> In a flurry of eiderdown.

The ugly duckling must find his own path forward instead of staying on the tracks. "All through the wintertime he hid himself away ashamed to show his face, afraid of what others might say." The story culminates in that moment when his difference is acknowledged as valuable. The duckling becomes a swan. The boy who communicates only through sounds becomes a radio sensation. The reindeer with the shiny red nose guides Santa's sleigh. The elephant with the big ears soars above the cheering crowd. And the peer culture is forced to acknowledge that far from being an "ugly duckling," the misfit child has become "the best in town."

As Danny Kaye sings "The Ugly Duckling," the boy moves closer and closer until the two are staring intensely into each other's eyes (figure 6.1). When the story turns from the duck's humiliation to his triumph, the boy smiles and soon laughs in shared joy. The storyteller pats his head and tweaks his nose. When the song is over, he listens intently as the boy describes how he has been sick, the doctor has shaved his head, and he has been isolated from his peers. In what is meant to be a moment of reassurance, Andersen dismisses the boy's pain: "So you see, Lars, it shouldn't make any difference if the other children make fun of you and won't play with you. . . . Look what happened to the ugly duckling and that didn't matter, did it?" But the boy rejects such a utopian vision, which seemingly dismisses his current suffering as meaningless: "But it does. I want to play with them but they make fun of me, just because I was sick and the doctor shaved my head." Hans promises that someday the boy will achieve normality, all the stronger for what he endured. "The Ugly Duckling" became one of Kaye's signature songs, performed countless times around the world, making the concept of the "ugly duckling" a pervasive one in 1950s and 1960s American culture.

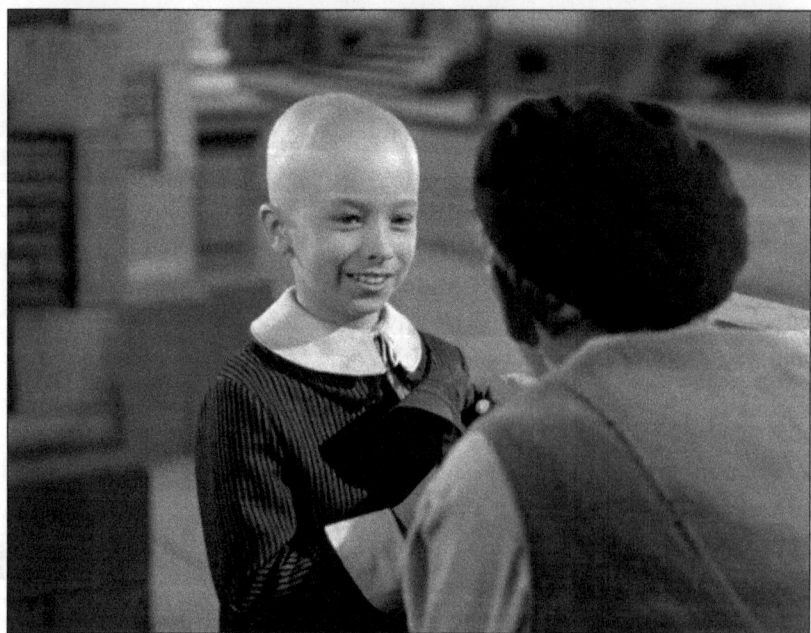

Figure 6.1: Danny Kaye as Hans Christian Andersen (1951) sings "The Ugly Duckling" to help a sickly child accept his "special place" in society.

If many of the stories discussed in this section center on the "misfit boy," the "ugly duckling," my focus in the next section is on the boy as artist, the creative child, which was very much cherished in the permissive imagination. I will be testing theories of creativity against Harold, he of the purple crayon, who appears in one of the era's most enduring children's books.

## Harold and His Purple Crayon

Published in 1955, *Harold and the Purple Crayon* offers a vivid representation of a four-year-old boy's imagination. In his joint biography of Johnson and his wife, Ruth Krauss, Philip Nel writes: "Harold lives in the existential uncertainty of the blank canvas: There is no world except that which he makes. A small god in a white romper, Harold uses art to create the heavens and the earth, dragons and apple trees, tall buildings and nine kinds of pie."[19]

Nel's evocative reference to Harold as "a small god in a white romper" would have resonated with Selma Fraiberg, who was interested in the "magic" of children's imagination as they learned to process their blurry first impressions. Fraiberg wrote *The Magic Years* while teaching at the Tulane Medical School. She saw psychoanalysis as offering the best tools for helping parents understand the inner forces shaping children's mythological narratives. She rejects any nostalgic or romantic notion that "the child lives in an enchanted world where all the deepest longings are satisfied," an idea that can be sustained only because "the first period of childhood, roughly the first five years of life, is submerged like a buried city and when we come back to these times with our children, we are strangers and we cannot easily find our way."[20] Rather, she characterizes the preschool child as "a magician—in the psychological sense," because "he believes that his actions and his thoughts can bring about events.... The magician is seated in his highchair and looks upon the world with favor.... His wishes, his thoughts, his gestures, his noises command the universe."[21]

Johnson's book opens with inchoate purple scrawls across the title, much as youngsters might sometimes draw on top of their favorite picture books (figure 6. 2) to assert ownership. Starting with a blank page, Harold takes his first tentative steps into a world of his own

Figure 6.2: Crockett Johnson's *Harold and the Purple Crayon* (1955) depicts the book itself as the object of the boy-artist's expressive gestures.

creation, drawing a moon to guide his way. Harold's imaginary world is a theater for his desires. When he is hungry, he draws a blanket covered with his favorite pies. When he is done, he draws animals to eat what he's left. In this self-centered milieu, he knows how to find his way home again because the moon stays just outside his window. Yet, Harold also draws the things he fears. He depicts a "terribly frightening dragon" to protect his apple tree, but then the boy is so afraid that he flees. He confronts his fear of falling by drawing a balloon, his fear of drowning by creating his own boat, and his fear of being lost by depicting a friendly policeman to direct him home. The book ends, like so many designed for bedtime reading, with the child fast asleep: "And then Harold made his bed. He got in it and he drew up the covers. The purple crayon dropped on the floor. And Harold dropped off to sleep."

Harold's dragon might be understood in relation to what Fraiberg describes as the "ogre problem." She writes, "It is the way in which the child manages his irrational fears that determine their effect upon his personality development. If a fear of bogies and burglars and wild animals invades a child's life, if the child feels helpless and defenseless before his imagined dangers and develops an attitude of fearful submissions to life as a result, then the solution is not a good one and some effects upon his future mental state may be anticipated."[22] Harold is blessed with enormous resources—a playfulness in the face of imagined dangers and a pragmatic response to any situation. Children create projections, such as imaginary friends or foes, as a means of externalizing parts of themselves they need to master, and they hold onto these fictions only as long as they need them to work through whatever issues they are confronting.

Miriam Lindstrom and her husband Charles Lindstrom curated the de Young Memorial Museum in San Francisco, an innovator in visual education and art therapy programs. She built on these experiences, as well as observations made at the San Francisco Museum of Modern Art's children's programs, to offer insights into drawing as "a basic process of thought."

The Lindstroms were part of a larger movement for art museums to encourage young people to see themselves as artists. Victor D'Amico, director of the Department of Education at New York's Museum of Modern Art (MoMA), adopted an approach grounded in John Dewey's experience-based pedagogy: "Toys have an important place in creative growth of the child. Through them he is introduced to the elements of design, texture, pattern, form, color and rhythms as they become the tools of his activity and his imagination."[23] Over three decades, D'Amico oversaw the New York City High School arts program, which trained teachers and provided visual aids exposing children to significant works of classical and contemporary art; the Young People's Gallery, which included pieces curated, and in some cases, created by children; the Children's Art Carnival, a series of workshops designed to free children of their clichés or imitative mannerisms and to help them discover their own way of seeing and expressing; and *Through the Enchanted Gate*, a television series jointly produced by MoMA and WNBC-WNBT to extend D'Amico's philosophy into the home. The episode titles for *Enchanted Gate* hint at D'Amico's conception of art's transformative power: "Making a Feeling and Seeing a Picture," "Discover What You Can Do with Paint," and "Paint a Picture of Sounds," among others.[24] Images from the series show children of diverse races creating art together, an integrated play space rare in children's media (or life) in the 1950s. And the opening promises children that "you will learn to paint with all of the colors of the rainbow and you will invent your own colors too. . . . You will make things no one has ever seen because they come out of your imagination."

Around this same time, Dr. Seuss was commissioned to help design the children's section of the La Jolla Museum. Sketches included in his papers at the University of California–San Diego suggest he envisioned something like an Exploratorium for the arts. Inspired by Jackson Pollock's action painting, Seuss drew a boy lying on his tummy on a swing and splattering paint onto a canvas below, suggesting a playful and imaginative conception of artistic practice.

If Fraiberg discusses children's imagination as part of their inner life, the Lindstroms describe children's mastery over that purple crayon (or whatever other color they might prefer) and over "expressive symbols": "We may not understand their early scribbling any better than we understand their infant babbling, but that does not prove there is no meaning in it for the child himself. . . . Thought and feeling not only accompany each gesture from the beginning but are themselves developed and clarified by the drawing process."[25] Their approach is more cognitive, influenced by Jean Piaget; developmental, informed by Arnold Gesell; and aesthetic, shaped by Susanne Langer. Early on, she suggests, children focus on drawing as a process rather than the drawing as the final product.[26] The drawing seems dynamic as the child improvised what will come next.

Johnson shows Harold's drawing as a process; the purple crayon's movements sometimes anticipate, sometimes respond to the boy's thoughts. The first book shows Harold's development from scribbles to more representational drawings. *A Picture for Harold's Room* (1960) suggests his progress from thinking of drawing purely as an activity to individual drawings as a product. The book starts with Harold's announcement that "I want a picture to put on my wall," but his first efforts lead to a new adventure as the drawing expands beyond borders. Only in the final pages does he return to the project of creating a picture to decorate his wall. In the end, he draws a frame and populates it with a simple landscape, constraining his free-form imagination.

The Lindstroms describes the act of a child drawing: "At any moment, one of his circles is likely to acquire a pair of dots for eyes and it will become for him a face. Or one of his straight lines will be attached to the bottom of one of his circles and he will discover that he can now make a flower or a tree."[27] Elsewhere, they summarize the cognitive growth necessary for children to move from spontaneous scribbles to recurring patterns linked to particular objects: "The squares, circles, and various lines of scribble suggest to the mind, when it is ready, images, so that with slight additions or modifications these can be converted to figures that stand for concepts in the child's own mind."[28]

Johnson's illustrations use schematic representations that are well within the range of a four-year-old. Around the age of four, children are moving from discovering only retrospectively what they are drawing toward the development of schemata that might be reused in the future. Johnson often traces the emergence of a shape across several pages so that we, like Harold, may be taken unawares as lines cohere to form the boy's imagined world, but our ability to identify what Harold is drawing depends on shared conventions.

Ezra Jack Keats's *The Snowy Day* (1962) shows how another four-year-old boy, Peter, deploys different expressive practices to leave his mark on his world. The recipient of the Caldecott Medal for its illustrations, *The Snowy Day* was one of the few popular children's books of the era to focus on a child who, in Michelle Martin's words, was "unextraordinarily black." Martin shares that what made this character so meaningful to her was bound up with the matter-of-fact way this white author presented his race:

All I knew was that someone somewhere had thought that I, a young black reader, deserved an image of a child in my bedtime stories who looked more like me than the blond-haired, blue-eyed Sallies and Billies who stared out at me from between the covers of the basal readers I read every day at school. . . . Keats's Peter was, to me, just an ordinary little black boy who loved his dog and felt surprised to find a puddle instead of a snowball in a pocket.[29]

Too young to play with the older boys, Peter finds his own ways to have fun with ice and snow. The book shares the boy's footprints in the snow, then the marks he makes by dragging a stick. Peter makes a snowman and then wallows to create snow angels. He accumulates an arsenal of snowballs and leaves a big path when he sleds down a hill. And then, he takes a bath and crawls into bed, his dreams reflecting on his adventures. Keats makes little effort to psychologize Peter's marks: they operate as traces of the boy's physical activity.

The mother does what many child-rearing experts of the period would have suggested—she listens and observes but she does not interfere with the child's efforts to express himself. In *Your Child and His Art* (1960), arts educator Viktor Lowenfeld advised, "The child has a world of his own, and the sooner we help him realize it without imposing our own adult standards on him, the better he develops."[30] Lowenfeld begins his book with explicit warnings about how badly interference might damage the child's creative and emotional development, closing him off from a needed psychic outlet and crippling the development of foundational discoveries from which later artistic skills might evolve: "His painting is not an objective representation. On the contrary . . . it expresses his likes and dislikes, his emotional relationships to his own world and the world which surrounds him."[31] By observing children's art without interfering, parents may develop vital insights. Lowenfeld held contempt for coloring books:

> It's been proven beyond any doubt that the coloring book makes the child dependent in his thinking. (It does not give him the freedom to create what he wants.) . . . It does not provide emotional relief, because it gives the child no opportunity to express his own experience and thus acquire a release of his emotions . . . and finally, it conditions the child to adult concepts which he cannot produce alone, and which therefore frustrates his own creative ambitions.[32]

Teaching a child to color in the lines represents the exact opposite of the creative freedom Lowenfeld hoped that early access to art supplies might foster.

## Margaret Mead Meets the Great Pumpkin

Harold is a master of his own solipsistic universe. Peter's mother appears only on one page where we see her remove his wet socks. Fraiberg and the Lindstroms describe adults as listeners, observers, and interpreters of children's expressive output. Parents play a more active role in Johnson's earlier comic strip, *Barnaby*, which shows the adults as skeptical of the existence of Barnaby's magical friend, Mr. O'Malley, searching for rational explanations for the pixie's disruptions of household routines.

Figure 6.3. A child psychologist interprets the boy's imaginary friend in Crockett Johnson's comic strip *Barnaby*.

Barnaby wants to introduce his "fairy godfather" to his parents, but circumstances always interfere, leaving him no way to prove O'Malley's existence. In one story the parents bring Barnaby to a child psychologist, who deploys various methods to diagnose how this magical being might have entered the boy's imagination, asking Barnaby questions and telling him to draw pictures. Offering an evolving understanding, the psychologist describes Barnaby's fairy godfather as an "imagos" from the boy's unconscious and suggests that children his age often have difficulty distinguishing between recurring fantasies and reality. When he asks the boy to draw with chalk on the blackboard, Barnaby depicts his "Pop" (figure 6.3), but at the last minute O'Malley swaps the boy's drawing with a caricature of himself: "This 'fairy godfather' your son believes he sees and speaks to is without doubt the idealized parent every child creates in his unconscious mind . . . in the case of boys it is usually patterned after the father. In some way you have failed to fulfill this ideal and Barnaby has allowed the fantasy to intrude upon his consciousness."[33] The psychologist proposes that the father spend more time with the boy, displacing the imagined fairy with a flesh-and-blood parent.

The psychologist's explanation mirrors that which Fraiberg provides for imaginary friends: "While we are enormously flattered to recognize ourselves in the child's fantasy life as a good fairy, a genie or a wise old king, we cannot help feeling indignant at the suggestion that we can also be represented as a witch, a bogey or a monster."[34]

Adults are an absent presence in *Peanuts*—depicted, if at all, by a pair of legs or the bottom of a skirt, or perhaps most famously, through the "Mwah mwah mwah" the television series used for adult voices. Cartoonist Charles Schulz wrote, "If *Peanuts* has been unique in any way, it has been because of the absence of adults. I usually say that they do not appear because the daily strip is only an inch and a half high, and they wouldn't have room to stand up. Actually, they have been left out because they would intrude in a world where they can only be uncomfortable."[35] And yet adults' influence is felt within the depicted environment in terms of the resources provided for children's play. Someone—most likely a parent—bought Schroeder his piano, supplies Charlie Brown with footballs, baseball bats, and other sporting equipment, stocks their kitchens with food, and provides the suburban homes and yards where they play. Though hidden from view, adults meet each child's distinctive needs while leaving them free to explore the world on their own.

Lara Saguisag links the series' general exclusion of adult characters to the child-centered parenting style of the permissive era.[36] Schulz often explicitly denied being influenced by the observation of actual children's lives or by child psychology: "Sometimes people ask whether our children (they range in age from six to fourteen) supply me with most of my ideas. For the most part I have to say that they do not; nor do I get many ideas from watching pets. Snoopy, you see, is more a result of reflection than of observation. You just don't see dogs lying around on top of doghouses!"[37] This disinterest in actual children was hardly the same for the adult readers who clipped strips that reminded them of their own.

Margaret Mead (1962) discusses the roles adults play in promoting, enabling, and accommodating children's creativity in a pamphlet published by the United States Children's Bureau, *A Creative Life for Your Children*. Martha Wolfenstein, Mead's sometime collaborator, had mapped how the advice given by the Children's Bureau had shifted during the pre- and postwar periods, seeing its publications as distilling the dominant thinking. Mead's advice mirrors Wolfenstein's argument that the more permissive approach to child-rearing reflected the increased affluence of middle-class families.

The ideal parent need not know answers to children's questions, but they should respect "children's need to look, wonder, recreate for themselves each new thing they encounter."[38] Assuming a suburban lifestyle, the good parent provides a constant flow of stimuli—whether access to vivid reproductions of the world's great artworks, recordings of classical music, encyclopedias, television and radio shows, and trips to the zoo, the farm, or other interesting sites around the neighborhood. While the proud parent may celebrate the child's artistic responses, Mead urged parents not to make a permanent display, suggesting that choice pieces can be preserved as a record of their child's development and others should be tossed: "Otherwise a child may start copying himself, and no child's work is worth copying. It is important just because it is free and fresh and the child's own."[39] The smart parent monitors the child's growing interests and their need for resources: "If there is no purple paint for a picture that requires purple paint, they must have purple paint."[40] Someone gave Harold his first purple crayon. But the adult does not offer help unless it is requested; adult interference can leave the child feeling "cramped and fenced in."[41]

Mead stresses the need for each child to have their own dedicated space, advice that assumes middle-class suburban homes.[42] Amy F. Ogata discusses how domestic space was being redesigned in the 1950s to provide children with room for their psychological and social development, often a playroom adjacent to the kitchen where mothers could discreetly observe what their offspring were doing as well as bedrooms decorated to foster children's curiosity and creativity.[43] As *Peanuts* itself became an omnipresent cultural reference point, it was translated into countless products designed to enhance children's lives, including the *Peanuts*-themed curtains, sheets, and blankets that adorned my own childhood bedroom. Ogata cites designer Norman Chermer (1954) on domestic space for children: "A child-conscious home should have a casual atmosphere; yet it should be clean and aesthetic. It should be an example ... to develop positive attitudes and standards for neatness and good taste."[44] These same values shape Schutz's own sparse designs.

Mead circles around the concept of accommodation, the work parents perform to create a space for the child, and individuation, seeing creativity as expressing each family member's unique personality. Creative experimentation depends on children's ability to learn from their own mistakes rather than the direct intervention favored by a more discipline-centered household.

A great deal has been written about Charles Schulz in recent years. Rather than offering an overview here, I want to focus on one example of the "creative child"—Linus—as depicted in *It's the Great Pumpkin, Charlie Brown* (1966), the third in a series of animated television specials overseen by José Cuauhtémoc "Bill" Meléndez, a Mexican American animator who had worked on *Dumbo* and *Gerald McBoing-Boing*. Schulz explained in one essay, "Linus, my serious side, is the house intellectual, bright, well-informed—which, I suppose, may contribute to his feelings of insecurity."[45] The character's distinctive way of seeing the world is suggested by a Sunday strip (figure 6.4) where a group of children are comparing the shapes of clouds.[46] Lucy announces that the clouds remind her of "balls of cotton drifting by" before asking her young brother what he sees. Linus perceives, among other things, "the profile of Thomas Eakins, the painter and sculptor. . . . The stoning of Stephen . . . I can see the Apostle Paul standing there to one side." Charlie Brown responds, "Well, I was going to say I saw a duckie and a horsie but I changed my mind." The gap between the vivid, specific, and intellectually informed way Linus interprets the clouds and the pedestrian, stereotypical images the same clouds stimulated for Charlie Brown signals Linus's exceptional brain.

And yes, such a brain is a bit fragile as suggested by the introduction of Linus's security blanket. Schulz biographer David Michaelis claims the blanket was explicitly shaped by the author's conversations with a friend about D. W. Winnicott's 1951 account of tattered rags as "transitional objects"[47]—that is, extensions of the self that help children negotiate the space between their inner life and the world beyond. The transitional object in Winnicott's account becomes a means of managing anxiety, even depression, in the young child.[48] Linus still carries the blanket in the Halloween special, using it as a tool to open a mailbox whose latch is well over his head, but the special is more interested in another famous product of Linus's imagination.

Linus has developed an elaborate mythology around Halloween in which the Great Pumpkin emerges from the "most sincere" pumpkin

Figure 6.4: Linus, Lucy, and Charlie Brown show different cognitive capacities as they read clouds in Charles Schulz's *Peanuts*.

patch and leaves gifts for children who have maintained faith in his existence. As Mead writes, "All the good stories in the world have come from people who got tired of the old ones and changed them or made-up new ones."[49] And around those stories, new rituals take shape: "Little children invent all sorts of plays of their own . . . , little girls with dolls, boys and girls with . . . toy animals or pets or other, often younger, children. They play father and mother. They play doctor and nurse. They play school. They spank and scold their children; they play that they are far away, that their parents are dead, that there is an air raid, that they are getting married."[50] Or in the case of Linus, they develop new ways to celebrate popular holidays. Mead finds in such play the spark that later informs adult creative acts: "The child is not only an actor, he is the playwright also, the creator, making up life as the play goes along, making it new, making it the way it ought to be or could be or might be."[51] Such play, Mead told parents, should be encouraged and protected from the ridicule of siblings or playmates. But Schulz and Mendez provide Linus no such safe space. Schulz noted, "The initial theme of *Peanuts* was based on the cruelty that exists among children. I recall all too vividly the struggle that takes place out on the playground."[52] In *Peanuts*, children laugh in each other's faces.

Each year, Linus identifies a worthy patch and camps out there so he can be the first to see the Great Pumpkin, and every year, he receives no reward for his faithfulness. A modern-day Job, Linus faces not only disappointment but also social embarrassment, as we see Charlie Brown tell him that it is absurd to believe in such a figure; Snoopy snickers; Lucy frets that his beliefs may also make her "the laughing stock of the neighborhood" and Violet simply dismisses the whole thing as "fake." But Sally, smitten with Linus, maintains belief in his vision and agrees to join him in waiting for the Great Pumpkin. Our expectation is that this narrative will reward Linus, but this is not what happens. He is fooled by Snoopy into believing that the beagle is the long-awaited Great Pumpkin. Sally berates Linus for making her miss Halloween, leaving the imaginative boy alone, crying out into the night, "Oh great pumpkin, where are you?" Finally, Lucy drags her brother home to bed.

We might contrast the lack of evidence in support of the Great Pumpkin with the ways that Snoopy's fantasy of being a World War I fighter pilot was enhanced by the animation and the soundtrack, especially by the heroic march that composer Vince Guaraldi created for these sequences. The camera shows us Snoopy's doghouse turn into a Sopwith Camel; we hear the distant gunfire as he passes through bombed-out buildings after he is shot down. In the comics, Snoopy's internal monologue narrates his fantasy adventures. Here Charlie Brown describes the events as they occur, giving them intersubjective validation. When Snoopy, wearing his flying-ace costume, appears at Violet's Halloween party, he leans on the piano as Schroeder pounds out sentimental war ballads. Unlike Snoopy, Linus's alternative belief structure has not been accommodated, remaining a target for social ridicule. Linus's eccentricities make it impossible for him to fully assimilate. Linus and the Great Pumpkin embody the anxiety critics have identified in Schulz's strip, which conveys the isolation each character experiences. Such alienation makes moments of collective joy—perhaps most famously, the dance scene in the Christmas special or the Halloween party here—stand out so powerfully, but even here, Schulz stresses who gets excluded from these celebrations.

Throughout this chapter, I have explored how postwar children's fictions addressed children who felt different from their surrounding culture and helped to foster children's creativity. I've considered a range of examples from Gerald McBoing-Boing to Harold and his purple crayon, from Rudolph the Red-Nosed Reindeer to Linus, which depict misfit boys and other still mostly male creatures. Margaret Mead observed concerning children's play: "Sometimes they seem to be stuck in some activity like a needle in the groove of a scratched phonograph record—and sometimes they *are* stuck. But sometimes they are just experimenting, over and over again, with all the different ways in which boys have to learn how to manage things, how to develop strength and acquire skill, and how to play by the rules of the game."[53] The same thing could be said about genre formula and repetition. The story of how a society accommodates or assimilates the creative boy was repeated endlessly because it spoke to a question at the heart of American culture—how to resolve a fundamental tension between protecting individualism and conforming to social norms. Different stories resolve these tensions in different ways—from accommodating and celebrating the exceptional boy to forcing him to conform to the expectations of his peer culture. Such stories gain their emotional resonance from moments of rejection and moments of recognition. In some cases, such as Casper and Linus, the characters are left in an indeterminate state, neither accepted by—nor accepting—the other neighborhood children.

As I conclude this chapter, I want to consider another alternative scenario, one where the society neither accommodates nor assimilates the child, but where the child becomes an irritant provoking change. Millie Goldsholl's 1969 animated short *Up Is Down* depicts the world from the perspective of a boy who walks on his hands: "Being different from other children meant that he knew there was more than one way to look at things.... But he made people uncomfortable. They thought it was somehow wrong that the boy did not see things their way, the right way. They decided he needed to be straightened out." Much as in *Tootles*, the people held a town meeting and planned an intervention that involved being diagnosed and treated by doctors, psychologists, sociologists, and educators, "whose treatment involved subjecting him to 'all kinds of tortures, from hot and cold showers to drug therapy' to 'being saturated by television commercials.'"[54] In keeping with the period's focus on art therapy, one of the many complaints directed against the boy is that "he has to paint grass pink and water purple." The film—dedicated to Martin Luther King—ends with a barrage of news images, including footage of a Ku Klux Klan rally, police brutality in Selma, the napalmed girl in Vietnam—before the boy defiantly asserts, "If you want me to stand on my feet, you will have to make some big changes." Whether this topsy-turvy fable was intended for children or parents, the film bridges between the nonconforming child and those taking to the streets by the end of the 1960s.

Plate 1: Henry's suburban boyhood was informed by an infrastructure of permissive ideas, embodied by the *Parents* magazines on the coffee table.

Plate 2: Eileen Segner and Olive W. Burt's 1941 book *God Gave Me Eyes* depicts children's sensuality as a pathway to understanding the divine.

Plate 3: Richard Sargent's "Anger Transference" (1954) depicts a cycle where bullying by adults passes down from parent to child.

Plate 4: Ruth Krauss and Maurice Sendak's *A Very Special House* (1953) imagines a utopian realm where children have license to do whatever they want.

Plate 5: Max in Maurice Sendak's *Where the Wild Things Are* (1963) acts beastly until he finds himself exiled to a land of monsters.

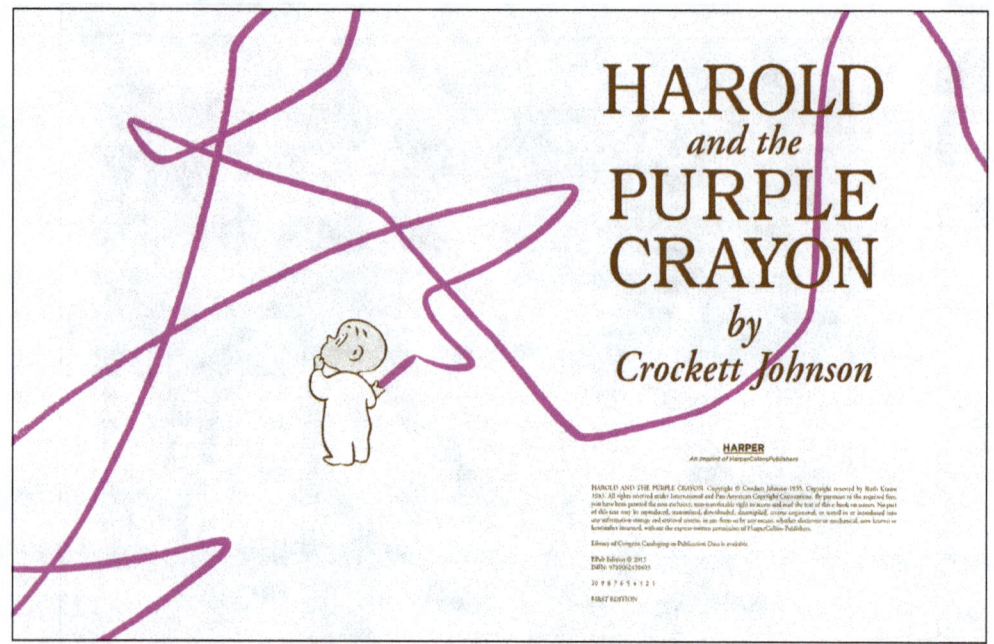

Plate 6: Crockett Johnson's *Harold and the Purple Crayon* (1955) depicts the book itself as the object of the boy-artist's expressive gestures.

Plate 7: The Junkyard Gang in *Fat Albert and the Cosby Kids* (1968) links Black boyhood with resourcefulness and creativity.

Plates 8 and 9: Cyndy Szekeres's illustrations for *What Can You Do Without a Place to Play?* (1971) (top) may have been influenced by Helen Levitt's iconic images of children's street play in Spanish Harlem (bottom).

7

"I Like You Just the Way You Are"

*Understanding Fred Rogers*

In the second season of *Mister Rogers' Neighborhood*, Fred Rogers shared a wading pool with the Black policeman Officer Clemmons (François Clemmons). In 1969 Black citizens were not allowed to use public pools in many American cities, so Rogers's gesture of cooling his feet with a Black neighbor represented defiance of segregation. As Clemmons explains, "I'll bet you there were not ten white men in this country who would share a towel with a Black man."[1] Rogers, an ordained Presbyterian minister, may have been thinking about the biblical passage where Jesus washes and dries his followers' feet.

Despite the attention paid to this moment, few have noted that Rogers invited a Black teacher, Mrs. Saunders, and an integrated group of students into his kitchen by the end of the show's first week in 1968. By that point, Rogers had gone from a job helping to produce programs for NBC, to producing and performing with his puppets on *The Children's Corner* for Pittsburgh's newly launched WQED, to hosting and producing *Mister Rogers* for the Canadian Broadcasting Corporation, and had now returned to the United States to do *Mister Rogers' Neighborhood* as part of the emerging National Educational Television network. The program, its rituals, its approach, its characters remained relatively stable during its NET years because so many of these elements had been tested in smaller markets. By the late 1960s, the idea of public television was still relatively fresh, new affiliates were launching, and federal funding for content development was precarious. One can only imagine the shock some experienced when Mrs. Saunders and her students walked through Rogers's back door, sat at his kitchen table, and began singing with him. Okay, yes, it was the back door—rarely used in the series; but as a child who grew up in Atlanta, there had never been a Black guest in my house who was not a cleaning lady, or perhaps a carpenter working for my father's construction company, both generally waiting tentatively outside the side door. At my segregated school, I would not encounter a Black teacher for several more years. In calling her Mrs. Saunders, Fred granted her a degree of respect so often denied Black people. Rogers greets each of the children—two Black, one white—by name and shakes their hands. The students are a bit camera-shy, grinning broadly, looking furtively into the lens, but Rogers seems literally at home in their presence. Rogers describes the integrated group as "mighty special people" and mentions how much he enjoys their visits, promising to feed them the next time they come. Mrs. Saunders, with or without her students, appeared on the show eight times over the next three years and Rogers visited her classroom.

I want to begin my discussion of Fred Rogers with this core question: Who belongs in *Mister Rogers' Neighborhood*? By tracing which neighbors visit his house, we may map the collaborative networks that contribute to the program's understanding of children. So often, Rogers is seen as a "singular dude" as Carvell Wallace, the host of the *Finding Fred* podcast, describes him.[2] But Rogers builds on the collective wisdom of the Child Study experts he met through his work at the University of Pittsburgh's Graduate School of Child Development. Rogers deployed these insights to identify—often via empathetic introspection—how best to address children's emotional needs. We can locate Rogers in the evolution of permissive thought and also in the history of children's television, alongside Pinky Lee, Frances Horwich, Bob Keeshan, Shari Lewis, and many others from the 1950s and 1960s. Then I will return to the issue of the imagination to better consider the role that the Neighborhood of Make-Believe plays in Rogers's address to his audience. His application of permissive ideas persisted into the 1970s and 1980s, even as this approach was no longer the dominant one, which is why Rogers, today, is seen as a unique rather than representative figure—in some ways, a man out of his time.

## Who Belongs in *Mister Rogers' Neighborhood*?

Consider a few of the guests that first season. Dancer Paul Draper was asked to demonstrate how tap dance and its rhythms express a range of emotions. Lady Aberlin—part of the royal family in the Neighborhood of Make-Believe—describes him as "one of the world's foremost interpreters of the dance." The virtuoso performer had first gained attention for his tap interpretations of classical music on CBS's *Toast of the Town* in 1950, but he was accused of communist leanings and blacklisted for more than a decade. Draper brought a defamation suit against his accuser, but negative press made it impossible for him to book gigs in the United States; he eventually moved to Switzerland for three years. He had just returned to Pittsburgh when Rogers featured him. The sympathetic conversation he has with King Friday XIII seems particularly poignant, as Draper shares the passion and hard work he brought to dancing and Friday speaks of his loneliness. Friday's desire to express his darker feelings leads Draper to show how dance might be deployed therapeutically. Vija Vētra, a dancer featured on fourteen episodes, had been born in Latvia but primarily focused on Indian classical dance. On the program, she represented an émigré artist who could perform a broad range of interpretive dances, playing everything from domestic animals to cleaning ladies.

One memorable 1968 episode had Lady Aberlin bring together a multiracial mix of talented teens, including gymnast Bernard Jessol, scientist Charlotte Yeh, electric guitar player Johnny Lively, African dancer Akeba Blazia, and majorette Lynda Martha. These young people were aspirational figures for viewers, suggesting what they could accomplish if they practiced their skills. At the same time, Rogers celebrates diverse forms of knowledge and expressive practices:

> I really wanted to offer kids a kind of smorgasbord of ways that people could say who they are. For me it was the puppets and music, but for someone else it might have been dance or sculpting or architecture or bricklaying. I wanted to expose kids to as many different creative people as possible and that's been a joy for me. I wanted kids to realize that there isn't simply one way to be and that we are OK.[3]

There is some implicit stereotyping in having Blazia perform an "African tribesman" dance to drumbeats, his body and face painted with white markings, donning a zebra-skin loincloth and a feather headdress.

Was this an early acknowledgment of African culture or did it reduce the Afro-American dancer to primitivism, or perhaps both? Friday encourages the boy to remove the "silly" headdress and to not wear face paint anymore.

Black teachers, blacklisted dancers, émigrés, African performers, and female scientists, not to mention white majorettes, are among the many people Rogers counted as neighbors. At a time when zoning limited who could live where, Rogers modeled a more inclusive community. Fred Rogers calls his episodes "visits," suggesting the intimate relationship he establishes with each viewer as he enters *their* homes via television and as he invites them into his own with his opening song "Won't You Be My Neighbor." Neighbors are people who help each other, who share what they know, despite or perhaps because of their differences. He thus focuses on the interests of the individual and on the goals of the larger community. Such a vision surfaced in his 1996 essay on Pittsburgh: "Each time I stroll these familiar streets, many of the houses remind me . . . about someone who lived there once—or lives there still. To me, a neighborhood is the weaving made from those stories, a living tapestry of personal experiences, family lore and neighbors' tales."[4] Biographer Maxwell King suggests that Rogers's neighborliness responded to the increased alienation of contemporary life, where "the grocer down the street doesn't know the young boy walking by on the way to school and the matrix of helpful cousins, aunts, uncles and close friends have scattered across the country."[5] Instead, many turn to television for familiar patterns, solace, and connection.

Margaret Mead wrote about the importance of neighborhoods in providing security through familiarity. Children, Mead argued, need a community that is "child-scale, some place where children can walk about. . . . Even the young baby, growing up to live in a city, needs to have windows on the unknown world. . . . The child needs the grass plot, the protected walk, and the nursery school where everything is close and familiar. Only in this way can the small child achieve the autonomy that is necessary at every stage of development."[6]

Far from a place where everyone knew your name, Mead called for neighborhoods where children met strangers: "From the point of view of human experience, segregation is equally damaging for the privileged, who are cut off from experiencing others—and themselves—as full human beings."[7] *Mister Rogers' Neighborhood* with its recurring characters and fresh visitors deployed television as such a "window" onto the world.

*Who Is My Friend?*, published by Wonder Books in 1959, adopts a notion of the civic defined by the roles community members perform for each other.[8] The book operates like a guessing game where the child is encouraged to anticipate who the person is based on familiar objects and clothing: the fireman's helmet, the mailman's pouch, the policeman's whistle, and so forth. The cover shows a boy in a green striped shirt, a girl in a yellow dress, and a cocker spaniel looking out their door anticipating visitors (figure 7.1). And in the end, they invite "you" into their house. *Mr. Rogers' Neighborhood* depicts these same occupations, though it moves from a focus on the functions characters like Mr. McFeely ("speedy delivery") or Chef Brockett perform to their personality quirks, Mr. McFeely's relentless forward motion or Brockett's insistence that people not talk while he is cooking. We get to know them as individuals, looking past Brockett's shushing to see someone who takes pride in making food for others.

Rogers sees a supportive community that listens to children as fundamental to the development of democratic citizenship. Dorothy Baruch would certainly have embraced the "real world" segments, the parts where actual people and animals enter Mr. Rogers's home, where he experiments with familiar objects or the Picture Picture screen shows how things are made. Yet, Rogers rejects this constraint to "here and now" realism, also stressing the value of imaginative works.

### What Child Study Taught Mister Rogers

Sometimes the show's visitors offer a glimpse into the larger networks that shaped its production. Rogers first met Emilie Jacobson when he was producing *The Children's Corner* in the mid-1950s for the local Pittsburgh audience. There she was known as Emilie the Poetry Lady. In one interview, Rogers notes that she was a local actress who lectured on Shakespeare's women or the works of George Bernard Shaw.[9] In one 1955 episode, she interacts with both the program's host, Josie Carey, and early incarnations of King Friday (who shares his love of wordplay by reciting an elevated version of "Twinkle Twinkle Little Star") and Daniel Striped Tiger (whom she encourages to be the best "cloth tiger" he can be).

Figure 7.1: *Who Is My Friend?* (1959) helps children identify the different civic roles performed by the people in their neighborhood.

When she visited *Mister Rogers' Neighborhood* in 1968, she was in the last year of her life. Rogers acknowledges that she has been "very ill" but always has a poem for him when he pays a hospital visit. She reads a poem about the joys of wandering to unfamiliar places but also the pleasures of returning home again. Rogers suggests that his house constitutes a "second home" for her. The segment has a retrospective tone, as if both knew that her days of visiting were over. As she departs, Rogers exclaims, "What a great lady! I am so glad she is well again!" Emilie tells Daniel, who has brought her a tiger lily, "You never will know how many times I thought of you when I was sick." Daniel says it has been a "long time" and Emilie adds "a hard time" as she refers to the doctors who have cared for her. Much has been made of how Rogers helped children confront grief; this episode hints at what's to come.

Another interesting visitor was Judith Rubin, "Judy" or simply "the arts lady." She stopped by often in the early seasons, modeling things children could make using household materials and suggesting that creating art might help them work through hurt or mean feelings. Rubin had a BA in art from Wellesley College and an MA in education from Harvard. She became a teacher in the Cambridge school system and then moved to Pittsburgh to study children's art at a local Child Study Center. She contacted Margaret McFarland, the director of the Arsenal Family and Children's Center, who introduced her to art therapy. In 1965 she met Fred Rogers, appearing on the show across its first three seasons, before publishing influential textbooks and founding Expressive Media, which circulates arts-education resources. In an essay about her career, Rubin discusses art as a bridge between childhood and adulthood:

> The forbidden touching, the delight in the sensory pleasures of body and earth, put aside as part of the price and privilege of growing up; these were preserved . . . in the joy of kneading clay or smearing pastel. Not only is art a path to permissible regression, but it was a way to acceptable aggression as well. The cutting up of paper, the carving of wood, the representation of hostile wishes; these were available to me as to others in the many symbolic meanings inherent in the creative process.[10]

The "art lady" was introduced in the second week sharing birds produced by her young "friends" from diverse materials, from kitchen vegetables or tinfoil to construction paper and string. She carefully names each artist, all between four and six years old, before asserting that "most children can have very special ideas when they have enough things [raw materials] to have ideas from." Here, she emphasizes the diverse strategies different artists apply to the same theme: "You could never think up so many different ideas by yourself." Mr. Rogers pulls out some materials to extend the project: "I like to keep things like these on hand in case creative people like you come by." Rubin returns several weeks later to share how her "young friends" made windmills, again foregrounding how each child artist tackles the same creative prompt.

While he was studying at the Pittsburgh Theological Seminary, Rogers was advised to seek formal training in Child Study if he wanted to minister to children and was referred to Margaret McFarland, who would become a lifelong mentor and regular consultant on his programs. McFarland founded the abovementioned Arsenal Family and Children's Center in Pittsburgh, a nursery and counseling center for low-income families, in 1953 along with Benjamin Spock and Erik Erikson. By observing children play, make art, and interact with their families Rogers learned "what a child's real concerns are."[11] His biographer Maxwell King describes Arsenal as "a teeming petri dish of the most progressive thinking in the developing field of child development."[12]

McFarland threw herself fully into mentorship, teaching, therapy, and administration, publishing little traditional scholarship, but she was widely recognized for translating child-psychology insights into storytelling. She would often bring a mother and child into her classroom to observe their interactions and to model how analysis might help them to better address their issues: "Margaret talked about how the child interacted with the mother. 'Did you see her face and the baby's face? And what about when he started to fuss? How did the mother handle it?' I learned so much from just watching her ... describe to the class what was going on between the mother and the baby."[13]

Rogers often drew explicitly on theories about children's emotional, ethical, and expressive lives as he spoke about his creative choices. For example, Rogers wrote about the "comfort" adults bestow upon the young when they read together, memories of which persist into adulthood: "I'm convinced that as we ourselves read we read not only to get ideas but also to recreate ... the good feelings we had when we sat close to those who read to us."[14] McFarland amplifies such ideas in a 1969 article:

> The visual contact Mister Rogers makes with the viewing child, by looking directly into the television screen while making some explanation or inviting the child's participation, may provide a longed-for experience in one-to-one relationship with an adult.... The gentleness of Mr. Rogers's

presentation, his warm invitation to the children to watch and listen, gives children day-to-day support in the development of confidence in the goodness of visual and auditory attention to adult educators.[15]

McFarland suggests that the program develops "real communication" with its child viewers. Rogers responds, "I never felt I needed to wear a funny hat or jump through a hoop to have a relationship with a child.... I am an adult in relationship with the child, not working out some of my old needs in front of a group of children."[16] As the two speak in one video, the camera pans across psychology books and a bulletin board full of children's drawings, including several representations of Black children. McFarland adds, "The minute the television artist becomes a child before the screen, then the adult-child relationship is lost."

The philosophy undergirding the series was a composite of many concepts traced across this book—the empathetic reflection of the Child Study movement, Spock's emphasis on sensuality, Mead's celebration of the creative child, some notions of democratic family life, and above all, a recurring emphasis on children's needs for security, support, and recognition. In his own variant of the Child Study Association's template, Rogers often asks questions directly to the camera, pausing to allow the child viewer to reflect:

> Did you ever have a scary dream? What did you do about it? Did you tell the people you love about it? The people who love you? When I was a little boy and I had a scary dream, sometimes I'd get some paper and crayons, and I would draw pictures about my dream. Sometimes that would help so much that I was able to get back to sleep real soon. It really helps to talk about the way you feel.[17]

Open and uncensored communication, McFarland argued, was essential, stressing that "anything human is mentionable, and anything mentionable is manageable."[18] She, like Rogers, felt that children could be trusted to confront difficult conversations as long as the adult spoke calmly and honestly. Rogers noted, "For her, learning could only take place in the context of love. She believed that if a child doesn't sense that the teacher cares for him or her, then that child will not be able to learn very much."[19]

While *The Good Neighbor* stresses what Rogers learned from McFarland, he also learned from other Arsenal researchers. Spock, for example, was conducting his own advice program for parents at WQED at the time Rogers was first producing *The Children's Corner*. King notes, "Like Fred Rogers later, Ben Spock tried to influence parents to treat their young children as individuals and to have the confidence to be flexible and responsive with them."[20]

Erik Erikson was the third founder of the Arsenal Family and Children's Center, along with McFarland and Spock. In *Children and Society* , Erikson analyzed the basic conflicts a developing child must resolve to enter the next stage of their potential. The children watching *Mister Rogers' Neighborhood* might be struggling to act upon their own initiative and to ease the guilt they sometimes feel when they see their goals as inappropriate by adult standards. Older children are seeking approval for their "industry," and at the same time they are turning inward to develop a sense of themselves. The themes Erikson identifies surface often on *Mister Rogers' Neighborhood*, whether it is through the emphasis on industry in songs like "You've Got to Learn Your Trade," "Children Can," or "You've Got to Do It" or the focus on individuation in songs like "You Are You." When Rogers tells children that he likes them "just the way you are," he addresses their worry over their own failures and imperfections, and when he speaks about the importance of practice, he models how they might move from initiative to industry. Erikson stressed play as a means of mastering the rules and roles of adult society. Play can be a powerful site of learning, and thus play is work; but it is sometimes important that play not be work, that its pleasure comes from escaping adult expectations and just enjoying life.[21] Often, Rogers plays with things before he buckles down and uses them to perform some tasks, whether it is everyday materials in Rubin's art projects or musical instruments in the case of the many orchestra members who visit.

Rogers took what he observed interacting with real families and from various theories of child development and applied the insights to regular production for child viewers. To watch Mr. Rogers explain sexual difference to preschoolers using a rotary and push-button phone, and sing that "Some are fancy on the outside, some are fancy on the inside," is to take a master class in child psychology. Rogers would reassure children that they were accepted and cherished even as they made mistakes and struggled to control their emotions: "What do you do with the mad that you feel when you feel so mad you could bite.... Do you punch a bag? Do you pound some clay or some dough? Do you round up friends for a game of tag? Or see how fast you go?"

Much like Dr. Seuss asking children whether they should keep secrets from their parents, Mr. Rogers gave them permission to feel what they could not help feeling. Rogers's presence is felt through his puppetry when Daniel Tiger proudly proclaims, "I don't growl anymore . . . I don't prowl anymore," having become a "gentleman, not . . . a beast." X the Owl sometimes displays the know-it-all qualities of a school-age child lording over his siblings. Each puppet targeted children at different stages of development.

## How Television Learned to Talk to Children

To fully understand his contributions to children's television, we need to situate Rogers in a larger history that takes us back to the 1950s and early 1960s, when he first entered the scene. Rogers described his inspiration: "I saw this new thing called television. And I saw people dressed in some kind of costumes, literally throwing pies in each other's faces. . . . And I thought: this could be a wonderful tool for education, why is it being used this way?"[22]

In the early 1950s, when Rogers would have first encountered the medium, much content *was* slapstick. Local television networks were buying syndicated packages of short subjects, such as Laurel and Hardy, *The Three Stooges,* or *The Little Rascals*. Local children's hosts would incorporate such shorts and cartoons, around which they might perform skits or play games with their live studio audience. The major networks were turning former circus clowns loose to do what they did best. Consider the case of Pinky Lee who toured the vaudeville circuit as an eccentric dancer, acquiring skills he would later bring to radio (where he played childish and incompetent men) and later children's television. On *The Pinky Lee Show* (1954), his opening song stressed his transgressive energy:

> My name is Pinky Lee.
> I skip and run, bring lots of fun
> To every he and she.
> It's plain to see
> That you can tell it's me
> With my checkered hat
> And my checkered coat,
> The funny giggle in my throat
> And my silly dance
> Like a billy goat.

As Lee sings at a frantic pace, he rocks back and forth, kicking and mugging for the camera. Soon he directs attention to the studio audience, whom he incorporates into his act, sometimes sitting in the mothers' laps, often getting them to dance with him. Given the rigid suit-and-tie formality of 1950s adulthood, these moments can be transfixing as scowling faces turn into smiles and Pinky allows the grown-ups to clown in front of their children.

Martha Wolfenstein's *Children's Humor: A Psychological Analysis* (1954) uses Freudian vocabulary to interpret examples of children's joking:

> Children are little and they greatly long for bigness and the powers of adults and their marvelous prerogatives; they feel often oppressed by adult superiority and adult moral rules. . . . From an early age children avail themselves of joking to alleviate their difficulties. They transform the painful into the enjoyable, turn impossible wishes and the envied bigness and powers of adults into something ridiculous, expose adult pretensions, make light of failures, and parody their own frustrated strivings.[23]

Wolfenstein discusses the recurring figure of the moron—the adult who acts like a child and thus allows the child a momentary sense of superiority: "Children at that age are peculiarly preoccupied with the issue of who is smart and who is dumb. . . . The figure of the moron represents all that the child repudiates in his aspirations to smartness."[24] Wolfenstein traces the moron through fairy tales about fools and sillies and through the tradition of clowns and buffoons, all of whom functioned historically as truth-tellers. She notes the amusement children take in "his unexpected movements, his alternative collapses and surprising hypertension."[25] Lee tests adult roles, often failing, or acts out his appetites: exaggerated hunger forces him to eat the fruit in a bowl as an artist is painting a still life. Lee intuitively reveals the childishness of grown-ups while Rogers insisted that adults remain adults.

On the other end of the spectrum was Frances Horwich, or Miss Frances as she was called on *Ding Dong School* (1952–56). Each episode opened with the ringing of a school bell welcoming children into her classroom. Like Rogers who is sometimes credited with developing this technique, Horwich spoke slowly and directly to the lens, asking questions and pausing to allow the imagined audience to respond. Horwich, who had a doctorate in education from Northwestern, brought decades of experience teaching elementary school or supervising other teachers. She saw *Ding Dong School* as modeling schooling for anxious preschool children: "The child prepares for school long before he is of school age. When he is a toddler just learning about things in the world, he learns the words school, teacher, playground, class. As he grows, he absorbs more and more. . . . He learns about school from you, from the books you are reading to him, from the stories you tell him."[26]

In *Ding Dong School*, Horwich introduces the child to schedules and routines, reads appropriate books, plays records, does art projects and science experiments, appreciates musicians and singers, and socializes the homebound child to group interactions. The camera may hold for minutes on the schoolmarm's face or hands as she works through a project. At the end of each episode, she asked children to bring their mothers into the room and for five minutes offered parenting advice, discussed the day's lessons, and encouraged the children to gather materials for the following day's project: "Young children (like many grownups) want at least one program with a day-to-day sequence—a program with which they identify themselves and which gives them a sense of being participants in what is taking place. The best kind is one that gives them many ideas for activities which they may carry on after the program is finished."[27] Rogers, who rejected all attempts to sell directly to children, would have been outraged by the ways Horwich delivered pitches in the same calm, loving voice as her lessons.

Somewhere between the two would be *Captain Kangaroo*, which ran weekday mornings on CBS for almost three decades starting in 1955. Bob Keeshan describes his program as "designed to meet the emotional and educational needs of children while attending to the serious business of entertaining them."[28] Keeshan's memoir outlines his core assumptions: "The show's aim has always been to help develop that intelligence and good taste, to make that one child at home know he or she is unique, special and valued. It all came down to nurturing a child's self-esteem through the intimate medium of television."[29]

Much like Fred Rogers, Keeshan was a sharp critic of the commercial imperatives driving children's programming: "The problem with children's television is that too few people respect the child as an individual of potentially great taste. To the TV industry he is a statistic to be added to a ratings sheet; to many of the sponsors he is a consumer to be gulled; to many performers he is a tone-deaf, sadistic little animal whose attention cannot be held by anything more subtle than a pie in the face."[30] *Captain Kangaroo* was broadcast on a commercial network and as a result, had to balance market imperatives alongside the social values and educational goals. Otherwise, there are strong resemblances to *Mister Rogers' Neighborhood*; the captain invites the viewer into his home (the Treasure House) with repeated routines (involving the captain unlocking the door with a big ring of keys, feeding the fish, winding the clock, etc.), with frequent visitors, with a strong focus on animals, music, stories, and art. The captain slowed things down, spoke to the camera, and rejected having a live studio audience who might compete with the home viewer for his attention. Captain Kangaroo, modeled initially after Geppetto in Walt Disney's *Pinocchio*, was a grandfather figure for a generation growing up within nuclear families. Margaret Mead wrote often about the loss of connections to that older generation, explaining:

> Where we used to depend on grandparents for a fixed experience that could be passed on, we now depend on them to give young people a sense of perspective, a sense that you can get from there to here and from here to somewhere else.... Having experienced so much that is new, they can keep a sense of wonder in their voices as they tell their grandchildren how something happened, what it was like the first time, and open their grandchildren's eyes to the wonder of what is happening now and may happen soon.[31]

Himself a new father in his late twenties when the series began, Keeshan plays the captain as an easygoing figure who can transmit culture (for instance, introducing children to opera and classical music). Those moments when he sat in his rocking chair and read brought a particular warmth because each title, such as *Curious George, Make Way for Ducklings, Stone Soup, Caps for Sale, Mike Mulligan and His Steam Shovel*, and *Never Tease a Weasel*, was selected with love. Although he lacked Fred Rogers's formal training in Child Study, he read deeply across popular and academic writing about children's lives. Keeshan also stressed the lack of male teachers and the opportunities to demonstrate a more nurturing masculine presence: "It takes strength to be gentle and to solve problems through thoughtfulness and kindness."[32]

In other ways, the series differed substantially from *Mister Rogers' Neighborhood*. Fred Rogers was careful to maintain sharp distinctions between the real world and the Neighborhood of Make-Believe; *Captain Kangaroo* offered an eclectic mix of elements: "It was a fairyland, and the children were invited to make believe with us. Or was it real? There was no line drawn between fantasy and reality, for such a line didn't exist for me during that enchanted hour."[33] Keeshan had begun his career playing Clarabell the Clown on *Howdy Doody*: "I flopped around in my huge shoes and squirted a seltzer bottle right at Buffalo Bob, to the delight of the children in the Peanut Gallery."[34] Keeshan introduced a gentler version of such madcap antics through scenes with Bunny Rabbit, who never spoke but somehow tricked the captain into giving him carrots, or Mr. Moose, who punctuated jokes by raining ping pong balls on Keeshan's head: "Bunny Rabbit is, in some ways, allegorical and represents the triumph of children over authority figures. . . . If children realize that grown-ups are fallible, that they too make mistakes, it is easier for them to accept the mistakes they themselves make in exploring their environment. It also makes it easier for them to accept advice and guidance and to work cooperatively in the effort to achieve the ultimate goal, self-discipline."[35]

*Captain Kangaroo* regularly hosted a trained chimp, Zippy, who had also been a regular on *Howdy Doody*. One 1962 episode featured Zippy on roller skates as the captain tried to catch him. A picture book (figure 7.2) shows Zippy in overalls and a green striped shirt stacking blocks, eating breakfast, and drawing on a blackboard, even as it also

Figure 7.2: *Captain Kangaroo* often surrounds Zippy the Chimp with images and practices associated with the "boy in the striped shirt" figure.

stresses that Zippy dreams of "the time when he used to live in the jungle ... sleeping in the treetops, with jungle noises all around him."[36] Zippy was a bit wild, somewhat domesticated, not unlike the young boys whose iconic dress he imitated. The image of a chimp in a striped shirt coexisted with the more earnest and educational encounters with wild things facilitated by Mr. Green Jeans, who was ahead of his time in warning about the ways some animals were endangered and that their loss posed risks for human survival.

*Captain Kangaroo* also incorporated cartoon segments, but unlike the local hosts who repurposed studio animation, the program commissioned new cartoons from Terrytoons, whose creative director Gene

Deitch had worked at UPA. Deitch's best-known character Tom Terrific wore a magical funnel-shaped thinking hat that shot out steam as he generated ideas, and could transform himself into various objects or vehicles in the service of his creative problem-solving. He and Manfred the slow-witted Wonder Dog outsmarted Crabby Appleton who bragged he was rotten to the core. The whimsical episodes were written by Jules Feiffer who would win the Academy Award for *Munro*, a later collaboration with Deitch, about a young boy who is drafted and has to explain why he doesn't belong in the army. Tom Terrific was a kindred spirit to Barnaby, Gerald McBoing-Boing, and Harold—that is, a creative and eccentric child who has found his place.

## But What about the Puppets?

For those who see Rogers as a "singular dude," his use of puppets to speak with children often gets presented as one of his more idiosyncratic traits, but in fact, puppets were, like slapstick, a constant on children's television and indeed the two were historically intertwined.[37] Punch and Judy shows were often rambunctious and transgressive, including ample themes of sexuality and violence.[38] They also encouraged active participation as spectators shouted their reactions.[39] By the early twentieth century, puppet shows were seen as ideal entertainment for children's birthday parties. They were an activity for families to engage in together and a vehicle to stage their emotions, even during church services.

As early as 1939, the *Christian Science Monitor* interviewed puppeteer Remo Bufano who predicted that, "because [puppets] are characteristically small enough so that really authentic theatrical effects can be got with them on the really small area of the television screen," television would become an "ideal" medium for this craft.[40] As television networks and local stations saw children as an important audience, puppets were a useful means of holding youngsters' attention. *Parents* reported in 1947 that "marionettes are already favorites on many programs," describing everything from puppet shows performed by children to more professional network series such as *Howdy Doody*: "Good children's programs often use circus themes, pantomime, actors and puppets."[41] Broadcaster Frederick Rainsberry wrote in 1950:

> CHILDREN LOVE PUPPETS! The child can comprehend a dramatic experience with puppets more easily and achieve a greater degree of empathy than with a live performer. Puppet characters can be manipulated within the child's realm of fantasy. He can objectify the dramatic action and take it in at the level of his own emotional comprehension without being overwhelmed. . . . The abstract quality of the puppets enables the child to fill in his own conception of the characters.[42]

The advice literature encouraged children to stage their own dramas, casting dolls and puppets as teachers, parents, siblings, or other family members.

Puppets often coexisted with games or syndicated cartoon or slapstick comedy packages. For example, in Atlanta we had *The Popeye Club* with Officer Don; every episode featured a sequence involving the Orville the Dragon puppet, a Popeye cartoon, and a pseudopoliceman who played games with a live studio audience. Burr Tillstrom's *Kukla, Fran and Ollie* was a daily series on Chicago's WMAQ (the NBC affiliate that also produced *Ding Dong School*) starting in 1947. Largely improvised, the show aired every weekday with episodes manifesting an adult sophistication and often starting with Ollie the One-Toothed Dragon or Kukla the Clown reading magazines and discussing topics with the other characters (a format it might have borrowed from radio's Fred Allen). Fran Allison was the mother figure who interacted with the puppets. The show's lessons were not always age-appropriate: one episode introduced concepts such as public opinion polling and cultural distinctions before insisting, in the end, that everyone has their own tastes. *Time for Beany* also went on the air in 1947, introducing characters who would eventually be animated as *Beany and Cecil*, a Saturday-morning series starting in 1962. The original series was overseen by former Warner Brothers animator Bob Clampett with voice acting by Daws Butler and Stan Freberg.

Shari Lewis and her puppets were among the many regular visitors Captain Kangaroo greeted. While Lewis had been gradually entering the television landscape on various variety and children's shows throughout the early 1950s, her most well-known and beloved puppet, Lamb Chop, debuted in a 1956 *Captain Kangaroo* episode. Shari, Lamb Chop, Charlie Horse, and Hush Puppy starred in their own show in the early 1960s, NBC's *The Shari Lewis Show*.

Not unlike Fred Rogers and Daniel Tiger, Shari Lewis mapped what she understood about child psychology onto her sock-and-cloth puppets. Lamb Chop, Charlie Horse, and Hush Puppy interacted as though they were siblings with all of the rivalry that might imply:

> "Hush Puppy is a real middle child. He makes peace between the older and the younger. He is less secure than the others. Plays by himself.... Charlie Horse is very much like me. I have to watch myself with Charlie Horse because he wants what he wants and he is very self-centered and self-focused.... And Lamb Chop just stomps her little foot and wants what she wants and she's the baby and used to being indulged. I'm an old child so I guess I'm a combination of all three."[43]

One 1961 episode ("Charlie Horse's Birthday") centered on Lamb Chop's rising suspicions when Charlie Horse reforms his ways and becomes more generous and supportive of those around him. Shari Lewis and Mr. Goodfellow acknowledge that "if Charlie Horse offered to mow your lawn, he's covering up for something." They sing a duet, "What Did Charlie Horse Do?," speculating about the motives behind his good deeds: "Did he shatter a window with his ball? Splatter ink upon the wall?" or some other form of rule breaking, opening space for Lewis and her puppets to explore manners. As a combination friend–mentor figure, Lewis guides the puppets through conflict and provides calming support. She often gently admonishes Charlie Horse for his chicanery and Lamb Chop for her cheeky backtalk, and regularly demonstrates her love through caring songs and stories. The sweet and sentimental aspect of the Lewis and Lamb Chop dynamic is like that of Lady Aberlin and Daniel Tiger—full of affection. While Rogers remained visually absent from the Neighborhood as he voiced all his puppet characters, Lewis utilized ventriloquy to voice, animate, and engage her puppets at the same time.

Fred Rogers's version of the television puppet show relied less on slapstick and more on empathy:

> As a child I always liked puppets.... Often, our puppets allow us to express those parts of our personalities that we might not be quite comfortable expressing all by ourselves. There seems to be quite a feeling

of safety created by the distance between our heads and the puppets in our hands. When we talk to someone through a puppet, that person can never be quite sure whether what the puppet says is what we really feel or it's just something such a puppet character might feel. That allows us to take risks."[44]

If Keeshan's intermixing of reality and fantasy was consistent with a romantic conception of childhood enchantment, Rogers's interest in child psychology led him to wall off the Neighborhood of Make-Believe from the here and now: "We make great use of fantasy in our Neighborhood of Make-Believe in *Mister Rogers' Neighborhood*, but we are also very careful to keep the difference between reality and fantasy as clear as we can. Parents can do that too by encouraging their children to engage in make-believe play as much as they want to, but by reinforcing, at the same time, that some things are *only* pretend."[45]

Here's how Rogers described the function of the Trolley: "First of all, we wanted to have a way of separating our Neighborhood (where things happen in a real way) from Make-Believe (where things can happen by pretending or by magic). Secondly, we wanted to show that we could all go together to another place—the Neighborhood of Make-Believe—by pretending."[46] Many characters, such as Chief Brockett, Lady Aberlin, or Handyman Negri, move back and forth between worlds. For practical reasons, Fred Rogers cannot since he must operate and voice the puppets. Rogers maintains awareness of what's happening in the Neighborhood of Make-Believe, watching through his telescope, listening through a tin-can telephone, and gossiping. Mark Wolf suggests that organizing the program around the two different realms allowed educational content to be delivered in different ways: through observation and experimentation, through direct address and reading books in the real-world segments, through empathetic introspection and interpretation, through fables and "operas" in Make-Believe.[47]

## Exploring the Neighborhood of Make-Believe

Dorothy Baruch insisted on only realistic stories for children under five: "We, as humans, have many difficulties in facing realities. Why should further difficulties deliberately be put in the way? And why should any avoidable weight be placed on the burden of the many things a child needs already to be keeping straight and clear? . . . More than ever in this day and age, children need to face realities, to grow up without hamperings from unfounded beliefs and superstitions."[48] Fred Rogers used fantasy, as storytellers long have, to teach us to see the real world through new eyes, even as he uses the plausible deniability fantasy offers to take risks.

By the second episode in 1968, Rogers was using the Neighborhood of Make-Believe to address volatile issues. King Friday—frightened of changes in his community, goaded by the wicked pranks of Lady Elaine Fairchilde—wants to build a wall to protect his castle, drafts a border guard, regulates his citizens, and otherwise places a demand for security over neighborliness. King Friday sends Rogers a "gift," a punch-card machine, which our host uses playfully before discovering the repressive functions it has assumed in the Neighborhood of Make-Believe. X the Owl and Henrietta Pussycat worry that war may be coming. As the tensions mount, people are no longer visiting each other. Daniel, X, and Lady Aberlin organize a peace protest, attaching protest messages to balloons they float over the wall. And the good king is forced to recognize the errors of his ways, removing the barbed wire around his castle and ending the War on Change: "All that separation—it's been a hard time for everyone." Such a protest—and its specific "peaceful coexistence" message—must be read in relation to stories the parents were watching on the news regarding the Vietnam War protests. Making the most beloved characters into protesters signaled the value of dissent at a time when some neighbors saw things differently. As Wolf notes, such conflicts rarely surface in the reality segments that demonstrate how diverse neighbors get along together, but arise in Make-Believe, often as "the result of a misunderstanding, selfishness, a personality conflict, or characters' plans or schemes affecting others."[49]

What a community gains from working together across differences often surfaces when the Neighborhood of Make-Believe produces an "opera." Rogers studied music at Dartmouth and at Rollins College as an undergraduate, and helped to stage the popular children's opera *Amahl and the Night Visitors* during his rookie days at NBC. When Handyman Negri, Lady Aberlin, and Daniel Tiger decide to perform *Goldilocks and the Three Bears*, X the Owl agrees to participate only if he gets to play

Ben Franklin, a historical figure with whom X strongly identifies. Much drama surrounds Henrietta's desire to be Goldilocks. By the time the opera reaches the stage, its title has expanded further to *King Friday, Goldilocks, Benjamin Franklin, and the Three Bears,* remixing the original to find room for everyone who wants to participate.

Throughout this chapter, I have explored the ways Fred Rogers was in conversation with other Child Study advocates, children's fiction writers, and children's show hosts as he considered how television might address children's needs. Rogers shaped his scripts in response to the insights of McFarland and others at the Arsenal Center, and he invited these experts onto his program to model how they interacted with children. In his advice book, Rogers summarized the relationship between television content and child psychology:

> The inner dramas of early childhood are perhaps the hardest for us adults to understand. They are subtle and deep and, of course, young children do not have the concepts or words yet to talk very clearly about them.... But they are there, a part of every child, and somewhere, a part of us. That's why those of us who make television programs—for adults or for children—have a responsibility to do our work with the greatest of care. Those of us who are parents have an equally great responsibility for knowing what our children are wishing and for helping them cope with the inner dramas those programs may arouse.[50]

Rogers sees television producers and parents as part of a therapeutic process that allows expression of intense emotions and provides reassurance that the child is accepted and safe.

# 8

# Permissiveness and the Black Child

Turning his attention to racism, Benjamin Spock addressed his *Redbook* readers in October 1964:

> I certainly can't claim to know specifically what Negro parents would say to their children about prejudice having never had to talk with my own children about anything so difficult. How do you break the news to a small child who trusts you and who still trusts the world that he'll be considered second class and objectionable all his life, no matter how admirable he is, because of the color of his skin? It must seem like hitting him in the face. It's also admitting you can't protect him and that must seem ignominious.[1]

Spock enters a blind spot in the permissive paradigm. Leave aside the implication that white parents do not need to speak to their own children about "prejudice." The permissive writers encountered Black children working at inner-city clinics, such as the Arsenal Center, but often they simply folded these observations into their assumption that child psychology was universal, resulting in the normalization of white experience. Erik Erikson was a notable exception, who wrote explicitly about the experiences of the Black child as he encounters popular media produced with white children in mind:

> I know a colored boy who, like our boys, listens to Red Rider. Then he sits in bed, imagining that he is Red Rider. But the moment comes that he sees himself galloping after some masked avenger and then he notices that in his fancy Red Rider is a colored man. He stops his fantasy. When a small child, this boy was extremely expressive, both in his pleasures and in his sorrows. Today, he is calm and always smiles; his language is soft and blurred; nobody can hurry him or worry him—or please him. White people like him.[2]

If white characters like Gerald McBoing-Boing force society to embrace them for who they are, Erikson imagines the Black child in a white society settling for a second-class status. Black children, as this example suggests, would have consumed much media aimed predominantly at white audiences and their parents may well have also read Spock and other advice books. But there are also signs that they felt such advice did not fully apply to their circumstances. And permissive ideals were often used to demonstrate the inadequacies of the Black child, even by or perhaps especially by white liberals.

In his 1965 report *The Negro Family: The Case for National Action*, Daniel Patrick Moynihan used permissiveness to critique what he saw as the sources of Black poverty:

> The white family has achieved a high degree of stability and is maintaining that stability. By contrast, the family structure of lower-class Negroes is highly unstable, and in many urban centers is approaching complete breakdown. . . . A very large percent of Negro families are headed by females. While the percentage of such families among whites has been dropping since 1940, it has been rising among Negroes. . . . It has been estimated that only a minority of Negro children reach the age of 18 having lived all their lives with both of their parents.[3]

Moynihan points to rates of illegitimacy, divorce, and the psychological harm caused by boys being raised without strong father figures: "In essence, the Negro community has been forced into a matriarchal structure which, because it is too out of line with the rest of the American society, seriously retards the progress of the group as a whole and imposes a crushing burden on the Negro male and, in consequence, on a great many Negro women as well."

Moynihan seems to be reraising the issue of momism that worried white parents a decade earlier. His report has been the subject of heated critiques since it was first published, including suggestions that however well-intentioned, it provided ammunition for racist depictions of the Black family as a poor environment for raising children. Psychologist William Ryan wrote an entire book debunking the report, *Blaming the Victim*. Moynihan certainly did not invent the discourse of the absent Black father and the over-present Black mother, but he lent it authority.

Although much of the present book has been shaped by memories of my own childhood in an all-white world, this chapter considers what it might have been like to be a Black child during this same period. I will begin this discussion with the advice Black parents would have received from James P. Comer and Alvin F. Poussaint's *Black Child Care: How to Bring Up a Healthy Black Child in America*, not published until 1975 but based on columns the authors contributed to *Ebony* starting in the late 1960s. In this more targeted book, the tensions around race and permissiveness are explicitly addressed as the two authors negotiate conflicting expectations within the Black community about what parenting practices best prepare children for a racist society. Then I will consider *The Quiet One*, a liberal documentary from 1948—roughly contemporary with *The Boy with Green Hair* and *The Littlest Angel*—that gives us some glimpses into how social reformers thought about the "problem" of the Black child through an explicitly permissive lens. Finally, I will consider some texts from the late 1960s and early 1970s—*Fat Albert and the Cosby Kids*, *Wee Pals*, and *Sesame Street*. By this point, permissiveness was under critique from multiple directions and these texts are often seen as the emergence of a new set of "relevant" images of American childhood. Here, my focus will be on urban childhoods with an emphasis on forms of street play. Each case study helps us to see some of the fault lines in how permissiveness related to the Black child. I avoid using the term "Black boys" because of its dismissive role in white supremacist discourse, but the children central to these texts, like those discussed elsewhere, are overwhelmingly male.

Like Spock, I worry that I am not the best guide for these issues, that these are not <u>my</u> stories to tell. And yet, at the same time, *Where the Wild Things Were* will be inadequate if it bows to segregationist logics. So, this chapter considers how advocates of a more permissive approach saw Black families and how Black authorities understood permissiveness, often in rather antagonistic terms.

## *Black Child Care* (1975)

"This book is for all people who are involved in the important job of helping black children develop in a healthy way," write James P. Comer and Alvin F. Poussaint in the opening lines of *Black Child Care*.[4] Comer, a professor of psychiatry at the Yale University Child Care Center, served on the Board of Advisors and Consultants for the Children's Television Workshop, which produced *Sesame Street*. Poussaint, an associate professor of psychology at Harvard Medical School, was a consultant for *The Cosby Show*. Both had previously published their insights in *Ebony* and *Redbook*. Their experiences as Black psychologists convinced them that generic advice for "all children" did not address the specific challenges Black children faced in a white-dominated society: "The responsibility of all parents is to help their children develop in a way that equips them to function well as individuals, family members, and citizens. . . . In America, however, racist attitudes and actions deny blacks a oneness with society and the security that comes from this feeling. Racism forces blacks to fight for the respect that whites take for granted."[5]

Martin Luther King's 1963 "I Have a Dream" speech anticipates a day when "down in Alabama . . . little black boys and black girls will be able to join hands with little white boys and white girls as sisters and brothers." As Shari Goldin notes, "The speech conflates an ideology of childhood innocence and a utopian fantasy that casts children as bearers of cultural transformation," but such images coexist with "more dystopian accounts of . . . children waiting for the school bus early in the morning that will take them away from their home and neighborhoods to an unfamiliar community or images of federal agents escorting black youths into the supposedly integrated schools in 1957 Little Rock."[6] By the time *Black Child Care* was published, the utopian images were wearing thin. Black parents had mixed feelings about helping their offspring assimilate into white society. Written as a series of frequently asked questions, Comer and Poussaint capture the multiple conflicting voices in the Black community:

> "Do some child-care experts think that black babies are understimulated?"[7]
>
> "Isn't it true that some child-care experts feel that black parents tend to be too strict?"[8]
>
> "Don't many black parents feel that middle-income white parents are too permissive?"[9]

"Traditional African culture valued cooperation and opposed competition for individual gain. Shouldn't we teach black school-agers to be less competitive and more cooperative?"[10]

"Because blacks have been the victims of unfair competition and exploitation, shouldn't black children learn to be more competitive and better exploiters than anyone else?"[11]

"Shouldn't black children learn the realities of life rather than being indoctrinated by 'white' ritual and fairy tales?"[12]

At stake here was the question of what it would mean to be Black in a future society that they hoped would be more just, what Black families need to do to remain true to their roots. At the same time, the book surfaces nagging questions about whether Black children were cognitively deficient, whether they were less capable of abstract thought or otherwise "inadequate" when read by white standards. Comer and Poussaint stress that there is no single "right way," that there are multiple kinds of Black families, including those where the father is absent, those where an older generation cares for the young, and those where white couples adopt Black children.

While parenting books by white writers generally focus on psychology, these authors turned to sociological perspectives. They could not consider how to raise "normal" Black children without asking core questions about the society where they were coming of age: "How to deal with our feelings of aggression and to what extent we should adapt white standards are further issues of great concern to black parents. Many blacks feel that in the past we have been too passive; that we are going to have to fight more aggressively for the rights, respect, and opportunity we want for ourselves and our children. We ask ourselves to what extent is adaptation compatible with black needs."[13] The two Black psychologists acknowledge their doubts that white models apply to Black families: "The need to preserve our culture and community springs from a desire to maintain a real and psychological place, where we are accepted, respected, and protected. For this reason, we are concerned about whether 'white psychology and child-rearing approaches' will change us, hurt us, destroy our culture."[14] If Moynihan saw the absence of Black fathers as the source of the problem, Comer and Poussaint saw strong Black families as key to addressing ongoing issues of racism and poverty.

Comer and Poussaint view themselves as negotiating a middle path between tough love and permissiveness. Unlike Mead, they do not assume parents with infinite resources: "Food, clothes, shoes and other basic items are often scarce. Such aids to a child's motor and intellectual development as toys, books, and play areas are frequently unattainable. Because they cannot afford to buy toys and games for their children, some black parents have had to invent activities to teach and amuse them."[15] Parents were advised to speak with children about race, much as they might speak about sex, at an appropriate age, when they seemed ready to listen, and only to the degree they seemed capable of processing:

> It is not helpful to try to explain the concept of race to an infant. But you can discuss color and race-related issues in a natural way. For example, you can talk about body parts and functions to your child in a way that includes skin color.... Providing your infant with both black and white dolls helps to make black, brown and white normal—like in the real world. When the question of color arises later, it can be discussed in a positive, relaxed manner because you have not previously ignored or overdramatized it.[16]

Permissive writers often celebrated children as "wild things," but Black parents question what might happen to a Black child seen as too wild: "Because of their rude behavior, adults sometimes respond to them in a negative manner, and they, in turn, respond negatively. This negativity can lead to learning and discipline problems."[17] Asked whether "destructive" behavior might be permissible, they again offered concrete advice: "Children love to tear up newspapers, magazines, and anything else they can get their hands on. Some black parents feel this is messy and destructive behavior, but it is really a safe release of aggression, an exercise for the hand muscles, and a learning experience. Let them sit on the floor and tear up things you don't want."[18] Black parents need to teach children "self-control . . . to accept responsibility for their behavior."[19] Like Baruch, Comer and Poussaint worry that some parents use spanking as an outlet for their own pent-up aggression and rage: "There is a difference between being strict and being excessively harsh, arbitrary, and unfair. It is these latter developments that are likely to create problems. They promote rage, anger, unruly and otherwise undesirable behavior in children. . . . Inconsistent responses—strictness one time and permissiveness the next for the same kind of offense—add confusion, doubt, and suspicion to the child's feelings of anger and rage."[20]

Comer and Poussaint's model pulls some Black parents toward a less discipline-centered approach, while curbing the extremes of permissiveness: "You help your child gradually to develop skills. You give children increased freedom, independence, and opportunity to function on their own as they demonstrate the understanding and ability to do so. You may occasionally have to back up and permit less when they demonstrate they can't handle the situation."[21] Again and again, they return to the concept of self-control as their cornerstone: "The development of internal control, direction and motivation does not start at five or at fifteen years. It begins with the way you help your child to wait for his bottle or stop taking the toy of the boy next door."[22] Feeding on demand, rather than on a fixed schedule, had been an early breakthrough for permissive parenting. But for Comer and Poussaint, feeding according to a fixed schedule might be more manageable in the context of working mothers and may help children learn patience: "Some people have argued that black children will face greater hardships in life than whites, and therefore that soothing and comforting them after falls, fights, or frustrations is not good for them."[23] Pushing discipline too far may also have negative effects, hobbling the child's ability to think for themselves, much as Black children were taught passive acceptance of their plight under slavery:

> In the past, because aggressive black males were likely to be in danger, some parents tried to suppress normal aggressive behavior in their preschool children. In order to survive in a hostile world, youngsters were taught to obey authority figures, right or wrong, fair or unfair. . . . Patient, firm and fair management of a young child's angry, aggressive behavior is necessary. When properly managed, the child is still free and better able to choose his own value system, so as an adult he will have the ability to work within the political and economic system he believes in, through the methods of his choice. He will still be able to be aggressive, when necessary, but will be able to control his aggression.[24]

*Black Child Care* rejects core precepts of permissive culture, even as it also encourages the empathetic, introspective, and psychological understandings that motivated that philosophy.

### *The Quiet One* (1948)

*The Quiet One* was a scripted documentary about an emotionally disturbed Black child's escape from what were then perceived as the pathologies of the Black family into a more healing world. A Black psychologist draws Donald Peters out of his shell through empathetic introspection, democratic decision-making, and art therapy, offering the child appropriate outlets to express the conflicted feelings boiling inside him.

*The Quiet One* opens with lyrical images of a magical afternoon. The wind is rustling through the leaves as boys playfully spy on each other. The sunlight forms flickering patterns on their faces. A Black child in an iconic striped shirt lies on his back, chewing gum and blowing bubbles.

But a voice-over complicates this picture of childhood innocence:

> When I watch them playing, they seem like ordinary children. By all rights, they *are* ordinary children. But circumstances have deformed them. Some of them have serious delinquency records and nearly all of them are sick enough to need my help as a psychiatrist. The root of most of their troubles is that nobody has ever wanted them. Here we try to show them they are wanted.
>
> This is the story of one of those 80 boys—Donald Peters, 10 years old—how he lost his way and how at last he began to find it. We learned this story very slowly by bits and pieces. . . . In all these months, Donald has never made any friends. We have never seen him smile. He has barely spoken.

The scene occurs on the grounds of the Wiltwyck School for Boys in Esopus, New York. Begun in 1936 by the Episcopal Church as "an experimental summer camp for Protestant African-American juvenile delinquents and potential juvenile delinquents," the school had fallen into secular hands by the late 1940s, offering education and therapy to help students process their emotional issues.[25] Eleanor Roosevelt was on the oversight committee. *The Quiet One* was produced to raise money and promote awareness of the school's mission.

The film depends on the contrast between this healing community and Donald's dysfunctional family, "the vanished father whose face he can't even recall, the mother who has no room for him in her life . . . a home he hates so much that even at night he seldom comes back." Such traumatic memories are anchored to a photograph showing Donald and his family on a visit to the beach—the father's head is cut off altogether, the mother and grandmother are partially obscured. Across the film, his grandmother calls him "a good-for-nothing" and his mother (and a man who may or may not be his father) treat him coldly. Donald spends his time sulking in the streets, watching other children playing, and throwing rocks through windows: "Of course the streets of a city can be a wonderful school, freedom is wonderful too, but if you are as lonely as Donald is, all you learn is more loneliness. . . . Everybody else has some place to go, some definite thing to do. And after a while, you even want to go home. But home is no refuge. Home is a place of unutterable boredom, sadness, wild daydreams, vengefulness, rebellion."

In contrast to the glistening sunlight in the opening scenes, the urban world is captured in a film noir style. Here, the film taps tropes about the failure of the Black family and the "'toxicity' of the 'inner city'" without acknowledgment of white flight that blocked Black families from suburban life. The only solution offered is to help the children learn to cope but never to address structural and systemic racism. By the end, the narration has broadened to an indictment of the social conditions that led to Donald's emotional turmoil:

> The most we can hope to do here at Wiltwyck for any of the boys who lie sleeping here, is to clear away some of the great harm they suffered in the difficult world they came from, to make them a little better able to take care of themselves in the difficult world they must return to, a little better able to live usefully and generously in that world, a little better able to care for the children they will have than their parents were to care for them, lest the generations maimed in childhood each making the next in their own image create upon the darkness like mirrors locked face to face, an infinite corridor of despair. To keep open a place of healing, care, and hope for as many as we can afford to care for, among the thousands of children who lie sleeping tonight in impoverished little rooms and in poor fugitive derelict holes in the rotten depths of the city, whom poverty,

bewilderment, anger, pride, fear, loneliness may drive into sickness and crime and who in the world that disfigures them cannot be cared for and are not wanted.

In contrast to this bleak depiction of the Black experience, Wiltwyck is a permissive haven where children express themselves freely and participate in the decisions that impact their lives. They receive attention from concerned adults—not only the white therapist but also a Black counselor, Clarence, and the attentive Black teacher Mrs. Johnson:

> Mrs. Johnson has very good reasons for not keeping order. Her boys are very backward in their reading.... They have failed so often that they are afraid to even try anymore. Before they can even begin to trust their intelligence, they have to be sure they are liked, no matter how stupid they seem or what they do. Before they know they are liked, they can't like you. Until they like you, they cannot even begin to learn.

The words are those of James Agee, an important film critic, journalist, novelist, screenwriter, and activist. Agee was a major force helping to organize the production and he brought to it the emotional insight that shapes his autobiographical novel *A Death in the Family* and informs his best-known work *Let Us Now Praise Famous Men*. Agee's collaborator on *Famous Men*, documentary photographer Walker Evans, had embraced Helen Levitt as his protégé and pushed her to create the city sequences. In an earlier collaboration with Agee, *In the Streets* (1948), Levitt captured the vibrancy of street life in Spanish Harlem, though here she constructs a darker image of Harlem through the eyes and ears of this troubled boy. The Wiltwyck sequences were captured by Richard Bagley. Shot as a silent film with music, sound effects, and off-screen dialogue recorded later, every choice demonstrates intentionality. For example, when we hear shattering glass after Donald throws a rock through the window, the image is juxtaposed with the rippling surface of Wiltwyck's stream, Donald having returned to his place of comfort. And Ulysses Simpson Kay's score conveys Donald's shifting emotions. The filmmakers are observant of the small details of Donald's life. We watch him form a cat's cradle with string only to have the angry grandmother snatch it from his hands. Donald looks around furtively before using his finger to scoop peanut butter out of the jar. In one of the few shots where we see him smile, he watches two older males parody the melodramatic images on movie posters. A defining example of his growing normality is that he is reading a comic book with obvious pleasure, sharply contrasting with the more pathological understanding of comics in *Little Fugitive*.

Donald's handcrafted bowl is key to his emotional progression. As the narrator explains, "One day in crafts class Donald was making a little bowl. He wanted to make it look like a seashell, he couldn't say why. He just wanted it to be a seashell. Donald seemed to be doing fine. Suddenly the hands that were working in the damp clay of the unborn shell drew him into a deep quicksand." Under the sounds of ocean surf, his hands working the clay dissolve into his hands playing in the sand, and the boy plays at the feet of his father, mother, and grandmother (the moment from the cherished photograph). Donald crumples the clay and then stomps away; in a later scene he is urged back to finish his project: "Even the failure with the shell is the beginning of a victory for with it he has begun to make something tangible with his hands out of the depths of his past unhappiness. . . . Most importantly for Donald, he goes back to the little sea shell and keeps at it until he finishes it. That gives him his first real sense of accomplishment." Donald, later, realizes that he has made the bowl for his estranged mother and asks his teacher to deliver it, a broad toothy grin on his face as he places his handiwork in her hands. She brings it to the psychologist, who explains the harsh truth that the grandmother does not know where to find his mom. When Donald feels jealous of the attention Clarence is paying to another youth, Donald smashes the pot.

Edith Kramer, a pioneering figure in art therapy, had freshly arrived at the school in 1947 and would write a 1958 book, *Art Therapy in a Children's Community*, documenting how the school thought about such craft projects: "Artistic sublimation begins as the artist replaces the impulse to act out his fantasies with the act of creating equivalents for his fantasies through visual images. . . . The instinctual energy which is not discharged . . . is used in the development of skills and accomplishments which give the individual greater mastery over his environment and improve his capacity for positive object relationships so that he becomes a more valuable member of society."[26] Donald's seashell-pot thus represents the distillation of a flood of mental images brought under his control and permitted expression through his art. If documentary pushes for us to know all and the melodrama for us to feel all, the remarkable moment where we first start to grasp what the shell means to Donald tries to do both at once—knowing through feeling. The Wiltwyck faculty recognize the importance of Donald's autonomy: "It was a question of whether Donald needed to talk out what was disturbing him or live it out first. The director and I agreed that we better give him a chance to work it out his own way. There are things you can only find out for yourself and by yourself." Here, we see permissive principles at play, with the adults observing the smallest gesture and responding when the child seems ready to accept their help. Between the white filmmakers and the Black child stood committed Black educators, who had internalized the insights of Child Study and art therapy.

The role of Black educators is more directly celebrated in *Bright Road*, a 1953 MGM production made on a B-movie budget with a mostly Black cast and based on Mary Elizabeth Vroman's semiautobiographical short story "See How They Run." Vroman, a schoolteacher in rural Mississippi, was the first Black woman admitted to the Screen Writers Guild. *Bright Road*, which offered Dorothy Dandridge and Harry Belafonte their first major screen roles, deals with an idealistic teacher's struggle to help an intelligent, curious, and creative Black lad, C. T. Young, discover and achieve his hidden potentials. When we first encounter him, we learn that C. T. has long ago been given up as a lost cause by the other teachers whose tough-love approach has resulted in this "backward child" repeating each school year so far. He seethes with resentment against the poor schooling he receives, disrupting class as often as he dares. His teacher first recognizes that he needs to be put on the school lunch program because of his impoverished background; he has been too proud to ask. The film shows the audience, but not the teacher, that he is a budding young scientist who listens to and observes birds and caterpillars. His knowledge as a young beekeeper who sells honey to support his family allows him to clear a swarm out of a classroom. On the last day, he brings a tree branch where a butterfly is just about to hatch from its cocoon and the whole class gathers to watch. Miss Richards draws parallels between the butterfly's first flight and the young man's fledgling steps toward academic achievement, "a wonderful promise of things to come."

*Bright Road* shows that the Black community already possesses the resources to save itself—if the Black teacher, who also doubles as a Sunday-school teacher, and the Black principal, who gives her cover to bend the rules to help the child, can only dig deep enough to understand and heal his emotional wounds. The film, strikingly, refuses to pathologize his family: his father is an unskilled laborer without much education, but he is a loving presence. A Christmas scene shows how much his large family look after each other's needs as they say grace over a table piled with biscuits and fried chicken. If *The Quiet One* moved beyond the suburban world depicted in most permissive-era children's fictions to consider the urban Black experience, *Bright Roads*, along with William H. Armstrong's novel *Sounder* and Gordon Park's film *The Learning Tree*, explores the rural experience as we watch young Black children come of age within segregated communities, struggling to overcome the effects of poverty and racism.

## *Fat Albert and the Cosby Kids* (1972)

Bill Cosby, who would become progressively more conservative through the years, modeled how to discipline Black minds and bodies through street play. In her account of the Black comedians of the Civil Rights era, Bambi Haggins notes, "Cosby embodied the optimism of the integrationist New Frontier—his squeaky-clean likability and universalist comedic approach won over audiences regardless of race, creed, or color."[27]

Let me briefly address the elephant in the room: Bill Cosby has been thoroughly discredited as a human being as a result of the many accusations (and subsequent legal battles) regarding his drugging and sexual assault of women of various races over a prolonged period of time. I believe the victims. That said, if we attempt to erase him, we will leave a large gap in our understanding of the evolving representation of Black culture on American television. Much like W. Kamau Bell's outstanding docuseries *We Need to Talk About Cosby*, I aim not to rehabilitate Cosby but rather to explain why he was such an influential voice.

Cosby had developed a crossover following based on his top-selling LPs and performances as a stand-up comic at Vegas nightclubs. The highlights of his comedy records included stories about his friends growing up in North Philadelphia. Though Cosby rarely explicitly spoke about race, his stories offered a window on Black childhood and family life in the mid-twentieth century. Fat Albert was based on an actual person in his neighborhood, Albert Robertson. Bill Cosby introduced Fat Albert on his 1967 album *Revenge* as part of a routine about "Buck Buck," a game where groups of youth, organized into teams, tested their strength and power: one holds onto a street pole or some other stable structure, five others hold onto each other, bent over so that their backs are exposed. The other team, one at a time, runs and jumps on their backs until the structure collapses under their weight. Cosby and his gang are proud of their reputation until they confront a rival gang from "the rough part of town": "They have toothpicks hanging out of their mouths, their hats are on sideways, they have their pants on backwards, you know, just rebelling against everything." I find it hard to quote this passage today without seeing connections to Cosby's later demands on Black youth to pull up baggy pants. The convicted serial rapist consistently cast himself as the voice of Black respectability politics. Cosby exaggerates the competition, which results in four hundred or so players piled up to the sky. And it is then that Fat Albert enters as "the baddest Buck Buck breaker in the world": "Fat Albert weighed two thousand pounds. . . . The ground was trembling, trees were falling over, buildings losing pieces of brick, parents taking kids off the street." And the other team quits rather than bear his weight.

Fat Albert with his deep-throated "Hey, hey, hey" became an instant pop culture phenomenon, the basis for a prime-time animated special in November 1969 and the protagonist of a Saturday-morning cartoon series, *Fat Albert and the Cosby Kids*, that ran from 1972 to 1985. Cosby reflected on the character in his 1976 dissertation for his education degree from the University of Massachusetts–Amherst:

> Fat Albert is . . . a sympathetic hero that children, especially black children, can empathize with as he struggles with the value conflicts and the peer group problems that confront children today. As he moves through these perplexing situations, he teaches. Children learn by following Fat Albert as he solves his dilemmas: What to do about the big kid who uses little kids? What to do about a liar? A braggart? . . . What needs to be understood is that these issues are very real and vital to young children. They are part of the growing-up process.[28]

In a little under a decade, Fat Albert evolved from a "Buck Buck" folk hero into a Black everyman, whose core decency and natural leadership placed him at the center of "lessons" helping children, "especially black children," navigate growing up. Cosby saw him as ideal for pedagogical interventions designed to foster greater emotional intelligence. In the opening credits, the viewer was promised: "This is Bill Cosby coming out with music and fun. If you're not careful, you may learn something before it's done!" Across his dissertation, Cosby made the case that formal schooling was failing Black children, arguing that television—with its different modes of storytelling—might respond to this crisis. Cosby cites an early CBS planning document: "Fat Albert is concerned with the concepts and precepts involved in that vital learning process—growing up. Ethics and values, Personal Responsibility. Judgment. Concepts of personal and public cleanliness, and the risks of neglect. . . . Ganging up on a kid because he is different . . . . Frustration and anger."[29] Their curriculum closely parallels the issues Comer and Poussaint had addressed for Black parents. And Cosby, for his part, amplified the lessons implicit in the stories, speaking directly to the camera, offering advice about how viewers might handle similar situations in their own lives:

> No other show previously on television has concerned itself so much with identifying with black children. . . . The program provides a powerful block to reverse racism, and to establish in the minds of millions of television viewers and educators that black children are not by nature stupid or lazy; they are not hoodlums; they are not junkies. They are you. They are me. The fact that the "kids" are black is neither minimized nor exploited. They are people. Their problems are universal.[30]

Incidental details—for example, references to corn bread and greens or the Southern accent of visiting relatives—remind us of the Great Migration and as we will see, the series taps into a tradition of Black verbal culture and street games that have local particularities. The primary characters are most often shown outside of school, playing games together especially in the local junkyard that provides ample resources to solve their problems. In an episode on the Junkyard Gang's origins ("Creativity"), the "boys" do everything they can to raise the money they need to buy instruments at a local music store, a plot that reflects their

Figure 8.1: The Junkyard Gang in *Fat Albert and the Cosby Kids* (1968) links Black boyhood with resourcefulness and creativity.

poverty. In the end, they construct their own instruments from what they can find in the junkyard and learn to create percussive sounds to express what they are feeling. They make music from drumming on a trash can, hitting a string of tin cans, strumming on an old bedspring, and the like (figure 8.1) This resourcefulness reflects what Comer and Poussaint had written: "Popsicle sticks, packing material, string, paper cartoons, you name it can become anything you want them to be with scissors and paste. Toys are just props or things to encourage the imagination. If the object you or your child cut out is called an airplane, it will fly to Nigeria or China just as well as one that costs ten dollars or more."[31] That the series speaks so often to the issues raised by *Black Child Care* should not be surprising. Cosby wrote a blurb praising it as "a book that must be read by parents and teachers of Black children." Later, Cosby would invite Poussaint to serve as an adviser for his sitcom and they would coauthor a book, *Come on People: On the Path from Victims to Victors*, about reclaiming pride and resilience in the Black community. His connection with Poussaint was among many other collaborations between Black educators from the UMass faculty and the team of mostly UCLA-based consultants who advised the production of *Fat Albert*.

"Buck Buck" resurfaces as the core plot of one first-season episode, "Moving." Another neighborhood gang challenges the regulars to the "Buck Buck championship of the world," and the group decides to donate their lunches to Fat Albert to further increase his body mass, but he is too stuffed to participate. This backbreaking activity constituted a prime space for young Black youth to prove their toughness and stoicism. This coupling of physical stress and trash talk would make "Buck Buck" the logical extension of the forms of play Lawrence Levine discussed in his 1978 book *Black Culture and Black Consciousness*: "From the time of slavery, self-control under certain circumstances, the ability to 'take it' when necessary, have been highly praised virtues. . . . Developed at a time when black Americans were especially subject to insults and assaults upon their dignity to which they could not safely respond, the Dozens served as a mechanism for teaching and sharpening the ability to control emotions and anger; an ability which was necessary for survival."[32] Levine's focus was on "the Dozens," a form of joking relationship among Black children—mostly same-sex groups—that involves the ritual insult of mothers, but the same basic mechanism was true of physical competitions like "Buck Buck." The colorful nicknames the characters give each other—Fat Albert, Dumb Donald, Weird Harold, and the like—suggest the role insult humor plays in Black culture. *Fat Albert* frequently depicted another form of insulting wordplay—"sounding"—where the boys came up with puns to justify belittling nicknames.

Cosby's world resembles the photographs of street play Helen Levitt produced in the 1930s and 1940s. Levitt, who taught art and photography classes to children through the Federal Works Project, became intrigued with the street drawings of New York children. Her book *In the Street*, finally published in 1987, cataloged many such pictures from 1937 to 1947. Her best-known book *A Way of Seeing*, published in 1965, starts with the chalk drawings but expands outward to depict boys and girls playing in the streets of Harlem and Spanish Harlem. Levitt was aware of the ways children were playing in crowded and seemingly inhospitable urban environments. Her work is a celebration of children's resourcefulness, whether children are wrenching open fire hydrants on a hot day and frolicking in the spray or transforming stoops and window ledges into playgrounds or using discarded boxes as toys. Regardless of the efforts of middle-class reformers to police street culture, Levitt evokes a world of public sociality that was a rich environment for Harlem children.

Kathryn Hitte's 1971 picture book *What Can You Do Without a Place to Play?* offers an ambivalent account of such urban environments.[33] Published by the editors of *Parents* magazine, the book stresses the plight of children who have just moved to the city as they investigate where they might be allowed to play, only to be displaced by adults who find their choices inappropriate. Cyndy Szekeres's illustrations show children hanging from fire escapes, playing hide-and-seek in a laundromat, cramming into a deserted bathtub, and making elaborate constructions from cardboard boxes (figure 8.2). Here, as in Levitt's images, these street games involved mixed-race groups contrasting with white, middle-class, suburban images or the Black neighborhood gang in *Fat Albert*.

Our efforts to understand the period's fascination with the Black child bring us to another key work: *Poems by Kali* (1970), which featured the words of eight-year-old Kali Grosvenor and photographs by Columbia anthropology graduate student Joan Halifax and Black activist Robert Fletcher. I cannot do justice to the richness of Katharine Capshaw's multilayer analysis of this book, its relationship with the Black Arts Movement, and its liberatory politics, but her account persistently stresses the "ingenuity" and "exuberance" through which Grosvenor asserts her possession of urban space as a playground that stood in opposition to what she describes: "This world is wite.... Wite Book, Wite Milk, Wite Dolls, Wite Everything." Discussing the role of photographs in this collection, Capshaw explains, "The photographs place Kali in relationship with an urban context, insisting on her ability to shape that landscape.... Photographs aim to capture Kali and, in doing so, ... her body in motion. Because physicality—in handshakes, hairstyles, clothing, and so on—was ideologically revelatory during the Black Arts Movement, photography took on particular significance."[34]

This fascination with how and where urban—especially Black—children play also informed the design of *Sesame Street*. Disturbed by Carnegie Foundation research on the lack of reading preparedness

Figure 8.2: Cyndy Szekeres's illustrations for *What Can You Do Without a Place to Play?* (1971) (top) may have been influenced by Helen Levitt's iconic images of children's street play in Spanish Harlem (bottom).

among Black children, the producers sought a format that might speak to their targeted audience. In *Street Gang*, an HBO documentary, producer Jon Stone explained its urban setting:

> Our target audience were inner-city children, and the bull's eye of that target audience were inner-city Black children. But the traditional children's show setting was always a cute little tree house, or a club in the backyard, or something fairy-land and fanciful, and so we had struggled with the idea of the setting, the home base for this for a long time. And it came into focus for me when I saw a commercial for the Urban League which was shot on location in Harlem out on the sidewalk. . . . I wanted to capture that New York energy because for the three-year-old who is cooped up in the room upstairs, the action is on the street.[35]

While this decision feels preordained for a generation that grew up watching Oscar pop out of his trash can, children stop by the corner shop, Muppets talk on stoops, and adults stick their heads out of brownstones, the producers were initially uncertain how middle-class viewers would react. *Sesame Street* would become a familiar location where children felt safe to learn and experiment, supervised by adults but surrounded by loving, cuddly Muppets. The opening episode depicted a new girl's introduction into the neighborhood, providing the first-time viewer a way to see and think about the multicultural community. As Gordon, the black man showing the girl around the neighborhood, explains, "Sally, you've never seen a street like Sesame Street. Everything happens here." The original opening-credits sequence starts with grainy footage of two Black boys climbing on a jungle gym with an urban skyline behind them. The opening song, asking how to get to Sesame Street, stresses the pleasures of belonging to an urban community: "Sunny day, sweepin' the clouds away. . . . Everyone's A-OK. Friendly neighbors there. . . . Everything will be open wide to happy people like you." Sesame Street is an integrationist utopia where Black, Latino, white, and Asian children jump ropes, living alongside affable monsters of all colors (including green!).

Cosby imagined *Fat Albert* as a Black counterpart to the Charlie Brown specials. Much like *Peanuts*, the central conceit was a world where children played freely with limited adult interference, unlike the friendly neighbors on *Sesame Street*. The children are raising themselves in a state of benign neglect, the primary adult influences being a black schoolteacher (Miss Berry) and an old vagrant (Mudfoot). Cosby saw television as displacing the street corner as a source of advice and insight for Black children.

On *Fat Albert* there are no fatherless children. When the gang goes to summer camp in one episode, there is an image showing all the moms and dads seeing the boys off. In another episode, Fat Albert lifts some money from his sleeping father, and in another, the Cosby father visits Russell and Bill in the hospital when they have their tonsils out. And in a second-season episode, the teacher asks everyone to share what their father does for a living with no hint of why this might be an awkward issue. We get limited sense of the parenting style these fathers might deploy, though here and in the stand-up comedy routines, Cosby hints at frequent "whuppings," a common slang term for spankings.

We might see this focus on the Black nuclear family as part of a larger project of depicting Black life while ignoring the realities of racism. Many episodes deal with the challenges of the group accepting children who are different—because they are girls who are good at sports ("The Tomboy") or because they wear glasses ("Four Eyes"). In the summer-camp episode ("Fish Out of Water"), the Black kids confront a second bus of campers who are overwhelmingly white (except for one East Asian child). The white and Black children work through their differences and bond, without either side acknowledging what is really in dispute.

Cosby's ignoring of racism stands in contrast to the work of groundbreaking Black cartoonists of the 1960s and 1970s. Morris Turner, who served in the famed all-Black 477th Bomber Group in the US Air Force during World War II, launched his comic strip *Wee Pals* in 1965, and by 1969, when the first segments were published in book form, his strip was carried by thirty-two newspapers. *Wee Pals* depicts a multiracial group of children living together in a suburban community.[36] The book's introduction was written by Charles Schulz. Racial politics are foregrounded from the first. The initial panels depict a Black child, Nipper, wearing a

Johnny Reb cap and waving a Confederate flag, ending with the comment of his Black older brother to a white friend: "Obviously American history is not a required subject of the kindergarten class!" Turner's characters include Black, white, Asian, Chicano, and Native American children who constantly debate the politics of the civil rights and Black Power movements and question stereotypical assumptions about each other. Another panel shows a Black child on one side of a tree reading a book on the history of the American Indian and a Native kid on the other side reading a book of Black history, before clenching hands together in solidarity: "Soul brother!" "Blood brother!" (figure 8.3) Another shows a series of child-run "soul food" stands selling what passes as such for several of the characters—chitlins and neck bones, gefilte fish, tacos and refried beans. *Wee Pals* foregrounds racism to model how the next generation might transcend it.

Rebecca Wanzo has written about the struggles of Black cartoonists to construct new representations from the racial stereotypes that have been the legacy of cartooning and caricature. The artist Randy Hollar designed each of the Cosby kids with distinctive personalities and ways of moving through the world. Their images tap histories of Black hair and fashion, and they embody actual people Cosby knew as a child. Wanzo describes the Black-comics characters as "black infantile citizens that push audiences to remember, as opposed to improbable white child ideals that encourage the nation to forget racism."[37] Cosby's characters assert the normality of Black family life, but they also want to forget the obstacles between these children and full citizenship.

Across this chapter, I have suggested the fault lines around Blackness and permissiveness. In *Black Child Care*, two Black psychologists negotiate a space between what they see as the strictness of Black parenting and the permissiveness of white culture. In *The Quiet One*, an emotionally disturbed and socially alienated Black child needs to be removed from his toxic family life and placed in a therapeutic environment where he can release his anger through art therapy. Both works stress the raw rage experienced by many Black men in a culture where, as Robin Bernstein has noted, Black children have never been allowed to be innocent. Bill Cosby (along with *Sesame Street*) offers a sanitized version of these same realities: a Black culture depicted without open acknowledgment of racism, one that celebrates community life without addressing the

Figure 8.3: Newfound understanding across racial differences informs Morris Turner's groundbreaking comic strip *Wee Pals* (1969).

challenges this community confronts. Cosby's desire to normalize the Black family and universalize Black childhood was groundbreaking at the time, yet fifty-plus years later, its silences stand out. Fat Albert and the gang enjoy freedom and autonomy, even if they lack the resources and space allocated white suburban childhoods.

PART III

The Spaces of the Permissive Imagination

# 9

## Between Backyards and the Great Outdoors

In an essay exploring the success of Walt Disney's *Davy Crockett* series in the mid-1950s, Sean Griffin portrays "the king of the wild frontier" as a compensatory fantasy for children growing up within the "crabgrass frontier."[1] As Griffin notes, the suburbs were being sold, in large part, as a preferable place for families to live, allowing children more room and greater safety. But parents, Griffin suggests, often remained concerned about children wandering into the streets when they played. Griffin documents the choices suburban parents made to fence in their backyards and thus limit children's mobility."[2] He asks, "Did the television western help to keep children contained within the frame of the screen or did it open young viewers to a frontier of possibilities beyond parental control?"[3] Griffin's focus on the fence as a constraint reflects a large literature, produced from the 1950s forward, which describes the limits of suburban life—the cookie-cutter floor plans, the "keeping up with the Joneses" competitiveness, women limited by their domestic roles, the "rat race" jobs of the men in the gray flannel suits, and here, the entrapment of children. Whether or not baby-boom-generation children were contained in their backyards, the relationship between the lived space of children's culture and the imagined space of children's fictions should be explored. Another popular representation—boys on their bikes, racing down subdivision streets—offers a less constrained perspective.

We have already seen many examples of how children's play in the context of the American Western (and frontier mythology more generally) was represented in the postwar period: Cowboy Bob in *Dennis the Menace*, the gun-toting boys in "Bang! You're Dead," and the Coney Island pony rides in *Little Fugitive*, each offering glimpses into how adults imagined what their children were doing with such stories. The next three chapters will explore three other genres—stories about animals (*Flipper*) and outdoor adventures (*My Side of the Mountain*), stories about international adventures and cross-cultural friendships (*Jonny Quest*, *Maya*), and stories about outer space (*Lost in Space*), each of which represented alternative spaces for children's fantasy lives. These three chapters are organized as a movement from near to far, from familiar to alien. These genres spoke to adult concerns—environmentalism, globalization, and the space race—but also reflected children who were, in theory, being granted greater freedom and autonomy.

This chapter starts with a consideration of backyard culture as it was understood by sociologists and anthropologists of the era. I will consider the case of Flipper, the trained dolphin, and his relationship to the boys in his life. Here, I am interested in the space represented by the Florida nature preserve, the setting for the television series—a space extensive enough to allow exploratory play and risk-taking, but small enough to be supervised by the boy's father, the park's warden. I will contrast the nurturing role of the father in the television series with the more oppressive father in the original film, another dramatization of shifting styles of parenting. I also will explore the domestication of frontiers in the novel *My Side of the Mountain*, where a boy demonstrates his wilderness skills, building a home in the Catskills and surviving alone through a harsh winter. The author invites us to "run away with the book," seeing reading as itself an adventure.

## Backyard Culture and Children's Imaginative Play

New approaches to researching children's relationships to physical spaces emerged during the 1950s and 1960s but would only be fully achieved in the early 1970s when a generation of researchers (some British, some American) applied ethnographic approaches to mapping how children played within everyday spaces.[4] We have multiple accounts of children's play cultures from just beyond this book's period. Their conceptual frame and some of their direct observations are suggestive for understanding the backyard as "childhood's domain." What follows is necessarily speculative (supplemented by my own memories) but suggestive regarding how children's play intersected with the popular narratives this book discusses.

A key figure in this emerging literature on children's spatial exploration, Edith Cobb was part of the circle Margaret Mead assembled around her Contemporary Cultures Research Group at Columbia.[5] Mead helped to get Cobb's book *The Ecology of Imagination in Childhood* published in 1977 following Cobb's death. In her introduction, Mead describes Cobb as "a woman from a world in which orderly nannies ruled the nursery,"[6] and discusses Cobb's decision to enter a master's program at the New York School of Social Work late in life. Mead tells how Cobb came alive in a circle of other children's culture scholars, including Wolfenstein, Erikson, and Mead, leading Cobb to once again redefine herself: "She had shifted from the thought of doing actual social work, to the observation of children's play constructions and spent time in systematic observation of individual children and children on playgrounds and schools."[7] The final version of her book, alas, contains few details of what she observed, having translated these insights into a more abstract philosophical argument:

> The landscapes in which I observed children's world-building included playgrounds, both the stony and sterile and the lushly vegetative, the empty and littered city lot or backyards, the country garden and the open fields, as well as the beautiful world of sea and sand in which child or man can revel in the wonders of unstructured beauty and movement that released the desire to create in terms of one's particular vision of the nature of things in time and space.... "Privileged" or "underprivileged," every child tries to structure a world.[8]

Kenneth T. Jackson describes a gradual transition from a nineteenth-century conception of the yard as a space of domestic labor to the mid-century conception of a recreational space for adults and children alike; the functional vegetable garden was replaced by the decorative flower garden and the backyard was now dedicated to children's play and outfitted with jungle gyms, tree houses, and play forts.[9] Given a rise in pet ownership, the fences Griffin discusses were both a means of containing the family dog and of constraining children. Parents could let their offspring romp and shout without adult supervision. Smaller children clung to their parents, playing mostly in their immediate orbit, but as they grew older, they ranged further, seeking greater autonomy, a process Erik Erikson (1964) described.[10]

In 1970, Frederick Donaldson introduced the widely adopted distinction between the "home base," a secure, familiar space that individual children could call their own, and "home region," a still uncharted space of exploration and social interaction that children negotiated.[11] John and Elizabeth Newson explain:

> The home base—not just the house itself, but its immediate surroundings, the people, animals and artifacts it contains, and the well-worn ritual of the daily round associated with it—provides a comfortable framework within which the child can be spontaneous and feel free to cope with new ideas and experiences at his own pace; separated from home base, he is also cut off from his frame of reference, and this may initially have a disorienting and disturbing effect.[12]

Such scholars speak of the child's range, the terrain across which children may comfortably explore and play—some well-trodden paths, some frontiers being incorporated, some (such as the backyard) for private play and some shared with other children. Remember that the fence is only one element in a larger regulatory structure that shaped where and when children could play. The Newsons, for example, write:

> He may have to traverse several streets and a busy road on the journey to school; is he allowed to do so in the course of his play? Does his mother expect to keep a check on him at all times, so that she always knows just where to find him? Once he has told her his destination, may he go as far as he likes, or are there definite boundaries—and do those boundaries allow for the crossing of main roads? What happens if he has express permission to go to a friend's, and the friend wants to move on to a third child's house? What about the time between leaving school and reaching home? Does he have to report home first before playing out and is there in fact someone there to report to or does his mother fetch him herself from school?[13]

In 1970s suburban America, boys enjoyed far greater mobility and range than girls of the same age and class. Across an afternoon's play, a typical ten-to-twelve-year-old boy traversed 2,452 yards, while the average ten-to-twelve-year-old girl only traveled 959 yards.[14] For the most part, girls expanded their geographic range only to perform chores while parents often turned a blind eye to a boy's movements into prohibited spaces. Boys were more likely to move beyond their homes in search of "rivers, forts and treehouses, woods, ballfields, hills, lawns, sliding places, and climbing trees," while girls were more likely to seek commercially developed spaces, such as stores or shopping malls.[15] One study found that parents were more likely to describe boys as being "outdoors" children and girls as "indoor" children.[16] Margaret Mead captures gender differences in her writing, informed by her conversations with Cobb:

> Boys play with the complexities of machinery, radios or rockets. Sometimes a boy builds a small scene in which he himself is the engineer constructing the bridge; sometimes he builds models or acts out whole scenes. If boys are given space and materials, their creativity can begin to relate itself to what is going on in the world around them. Girls, as they daydream and talk and read about horses, are thinking about growing up and moving away and being in command of their lives; sometimes they are the horses, and sometimes the riders. So, too, boys, as they think about rockets and atomic submarines, are thinking about what they are going to be, as males and as men, as they are older.[17]

The fenced-in backyard may intensify the security children feel within their home base in possession of their own places, things, and fantasies. For older children, what mattered most was not the fence but the gate, which allowed them to invite friends in while locking out bullies. As the suburban neighborhoods of the 1950s and 1960s were constructed and gradually occupied, they constituted transitional spaces—vacant lots, construction sites, and woods and fields. And these spaces offered room for exploration, intensifying children's fantasies of wild frontiers. Children in the same neighborhoods could have different relations to shared spaces, cutting their own paths, giving their own names to environmental features.

For Cobb, the act of mapping and naming one's environment ("worldmaking") was essential to children's creative lives. I still remember almost every inch of *my* backyard and its adjacent spaces, the ways my brother, our friends, and I mapped them, naming certain environmental features (for example, we named a low space that was dry most of the time, but overflowed with water during the rainy spring season, "Lemonade Lake" after a space in the Candyland board game). We shared a grassy side yard with our neighbors so that this would be one area for collaborative play (impromptu wrestling matches), whereas my tree house was a private space where I would retreat to nurse my wounds, to read and reflect, to draw and write. On one side of the house was a lot that remained undeveloped for most of my childhood and became an overgrown "jungle" where we could climb trees and swing on vines. On the other side was another untended area where bamboo grew wild and fast; it was especially exotic in my mind (and dangerous, at least when we stepped barefoot on a hornet's nest one time). And across the street behind the house was a woodland I would explore with my Golden nature handbooks in hand.

However small and contained such spaces might have seemed, however safe they were perceived to be by grown-ups, these spots were the "wild places" in my imagination. The book *Childhood's Domain* offers this description of children's "adventure play," which constituted roughly a quarter of the time that the children its author, Robin C. Moore, observed spent in recreation: "To wander through a diverse terrain is to feel the surroundings pass through one's body as the body passes through the surroundings—at one with each other. Like the rambler, one experiences a floating state of mind, drugged by a wealth of sounds, of smells, of sights and textures."[18] Adventure play, Moore recounts, includes climbing, rolling in the grass, making fires, camping, playing with pocketknives, building forts, damming creeks, and other activities through which boys demonstrate mastery.

How might we connect this literature on children's physical play space to the adventure spaces introduced through children's fictions? We might start with Griffin's suggestion that adventure stories play a compensatory role of expanding the child's access to space within their conceptual terrain, albeit space they cannot physically act upon. The recurring themes of journeys, quests, wanderings, and adventures in uncharted space would amplify children's spatial exploration of their actual neighborhoods, reflecting a tension between the security of home and the excitement of wandering further afield. As Mead makes clear in her discussion of young girls' fantasies about horses, "Of course, very few of them have real horses to ride, but they have little glass or pottery horses, pieces of riding costumes, or books about horses. The spurs one girl hangs on the wall, the copy of *National Velvet* another keeps by her bedside, the four little Chinese pottery horses another stands on her desk— all are part of one great shared daydream for American little girls."[19] Here, fan engagement with fictional narratives, such as *National Velvet* or *My Friend Flicka*, provide raw material for a rich fantasy life.

Drawing insights from reformist literature from the 1930s and 1940s, Scott Higgins has reconstructed how movie serials provided narratives children acted out through their play. Higgins cites this passage from Alice Miller Mitchell's 1929 *Children and Movies*: "The movie has become a new backyard for the after-school-hours child.... Not only is it a better and a more interesting playground to the child, but it makes more attractive to him his own playland, for when he returns from the movie to his 'back-yard' he has new ideas of what to play and how to play it. He and his little companions congregate and begin to re-enact the film they have seen."[20] Higgins notes that these serials depicted the characters acting on their physical environment as children staged these sagas in their real-world play spaces. He describes these films as having ludic potentials: "Rope bridges, fiery pits, buzz saws, crushing rooms, flooding shafts, and sacrificial altars are physical traps with clear operational boundaries: story potential is embedded within concrete space."[21]

All of this is to say that "adventure play" was fueled by the adventure stories we consumed, whether about a boy and his pet exploring the American wilds, American boys having exotic adventures in Africa or India, or boy scientists getting "lost in space." Such stories spoke to the "snips and snails and puppy dog tales" fantasies that Americans had about boys as natural and untamed, free of spirit. Throughout this chapter, I am interested in a tension between domestic and wild spaces: boys respond to a "call of the wild," venturing beyond fenced areas, but even as these stories offer alternatives to their "home base," this new terrain also becomes domesticated—a safe place to play and ultimately a familiar place to perform mastery.

## They Call Him Flipper

"I've lived all of my life on the sea. So did my father. So will my son." The father's first line in *Flipper* (1963) already establishes the film's central tension. Delivered in Chuck Connors's gruff voice, the line raises the issue of the father's expectations and whether he can dictate what his son <u>will</u> become. The son, Sandy, has a deep commitment to the sea: the opening shots show the two working the nets, the twelve-year-old eager to impress his father. But as the film continues, Flipper comes between them as the boy spends more time playing with the dolphin and less time doing chores: "Pa doesn't think you're a good influence."

As this conflict intensifies, Porter, the father, delivers a devastating critique: "What's wrong with you, boy? How old are you? 12? Almost in your teens? Or are you 9 or 7 or 5? A child who doesn't have the sense to know what his next meal depends on? . . . Are you growing up or down? Aren't you getting any sense of responsibility, obligation, discipline? Or are you holding onto a 'feed me, dress me, blow my nose' childhood?" Contrary to the permissive-era ideal of the Understanding Angel, the father's tough love reflects his sense of what is required to prepare a boy for the fisherman's life. The mother tells Porter he was too rough with Sandy: "He's hurt. He's crying." He responds, "I grew up with the sea. The sea is never soft." Connors spends much of the film shirtless, displaying his muscular physique and leathery skin. Porter must learn how to express his affections. "Men just don't talk that way," Porter says. "Maybe you should," his wife responds, and by the end, Porter has learned to become a more permissive and loving father.

Porter sees the ocean as a dangerous place where massive beasts clash and where the fishermen must be responsible for each other's survival:

> I've seen the giant creatures of the deep, the great whales making their passage to the northern feeding grounds, and the last herds of the sea elephants. I've watched the cunning maneuvers of killer whales as they leaped into the air and hit the sea with the sound of a cannon shot chasing the seals and the sea elephants into the water where they would become easy prey. The shark, lacking this cleverness, prowls after what smaller fish he can find.

In the opening, Sandy and his father race back to shore in a raging storm, while the women and children sheltered inside a post office ask anxiously about the missing men. The tempest may rip apart their boats or destroy homes. Sandy races along the rocky shore as waves crash around him.

The father's opening monologue also suggests that the dolphins have a curious status, closer to man yet still wild and unknowable: "But the dolphins, the dolphins always seem to come right up to the fisherman's boat and ride the bow wave with the speed of a torpedo. Curiously, they seemed at times to be talking to each other and looking at us. . . . I didn't really understand the dolphins, until my son . . . led me to an understanding of their kind." Sandy has formed a bond with Flipper that bridges land and sea. From here, the story reconciles father and son, helping the man see Flipper as Sandy does.

The film's catchy theme song conveys how Sandy regards his remarkable animal friend. The familiar refrain is withheld until a sequence, midway through, where Sandy has the dolphin performing tricks for the neighborhood children:

> Everyone loves the king of the sea,
> Ever so kind and gentle is he,
> Tricks he will do when children appear,
> And how they laugh when he's near!

These lyrics celebrating Flipper's playfulness are linked with images of him chattering, laughing, splashing, and gliding. We might contrast such visuals with how Porter describes the threat dolphins pose: "If the dolphins come, they tear our nets, they eat our fish, they chase the rest away. He may be your friend but when the fish are scarce, they are our deadly enemy. We will kill them. We have no choice." The father sees Flipper eat from his catch, but he does not see the dolphin direct Sandy to hidden abundances where the men have never found fish before. What convinces him in the end—seconds before he was ready to kill the dolphin—is the discovery that Flipper has protected Sandy from a shark attack. Sandy has earlier rescued Flipper when he has been speared by another boy and nursed the animal back to health, doing hired labor in the village to earn fish to feed the dolphin. By the end, Flipper has fully repaid his debts, protecting Sandy and providing for his family.

The film's initial premise sprang from the minds of Ricou Browning (the actor who had played the Creature of the Black Lagoon) and his writing partner Jack Cowden. Browning had been impressed by his experiences working with "Flippy, the Educated Porpoise" from Marineland of Florida in *Revenge of the Creature*. *Flipper* was dedicated to Captain Adolph Frohn who had trained the first porpoise only thirteen years before the film went into production. Stories about porpoises rescuing humans lost at sea date back to ancient mythology, but they enjoyed new currency because of several documented instances where these creatures had protected sailors from shark attacks during World War II. Douglas Burton, a founder of Marineland, commissioned Frohn, a veteran circus trainer who had previously worked with seals and sea lions, to see if the same techniques might be successful with other marine mammals. Frohn spent three years training Flippy, who became a star attraction. *Popular Mechanics* wrote that: "Flippy, who is a bottlenose dolphin, is not just a trick animal like a trained seal. . . . He is one of a host of marine experiments being conducted at the world's most remarkable deep-sea zoo, where scientists peer through portholes to watch the private lives of marine denizens. Flippy is proving that porpoises have a brain development so advanced that it may compare with that of the dog and chimpanzee."[22]

Richard O'Barry, who was earning his living capturing and training dolphins for the Miami Seaquarium, was approached about casting the part of Flipper. *The Cove* (2009) shows a more contemporary O'Barry deeply remorseful, now an animal rights activist, calling attention to the cruelty of removing these animals from their habitats. At the time, though, Browning had been fascinated by the relationship between Flippy and his trainers. Inspired by *Lassie*'s television popularity, Browning brought his concept to producer Ivan Tors, who was then enjoying ratings success with *Sea Hunt*. Tors produced the original *Flipper* film and a 1964 sequel. *Flipper's New Adventure* (1964) was designed to kindle interest in the television series launched a few months later. *Flipper's* success led to Tors's subsequent nature-themed projects—*Zebra in the Kitchen* (1965), *Clarence the Cross-Eyed Lion* (1965), *Gentle Giant* (1967), and *Africa Texas Style* (1967).

*Flipper* was watched by many who had heard about but had not yet witnessed performing porpoises. The theme song's lyrics celebrated the animal's agility ("faster than lightning"), his intelligence ("No one, you see, is smarter than he"), and his exotic habitat (he "lives in a world full of wonder . . . under the sea"), all topics of curiosity for the filmgoing public. While Flippy's name was meant to call attention to his tricks (doing flips), Flipper's name emphasizes his mobility—the limbs the dolphin uses to swim—but also the parallels to the boy's own freedom to explore his environment using his rubber flippers.

We might compare *Flipper* with *Lassie*.[23] If *Flipper* deals with wild spaces, *Lassie* was more domestic, centering on the virtues of the family farm.[24] Most of the episodes centered on everyday mishaps: Jeff and Porky babysit for a six-year-old brat who causes them endless trouble; Lassie brings home a litter of kittens, but the Millers can't get them to eat; Timmy accidentally breaks Uncle Petrie's guitar and has to raise money to fix it. Many stories could have been told just as well on any domestic sitcom. Here, Lassie, not the father, knows best. Where more serious incidents occurred, offering opportunities for Lassie's curative powers, they tended to come from outside the core family—escaped convicts, bankrupt traveling circuses, blinded Korean War returnees, Japanese American families hoping to settle in the community, crop dusters down on their luck, or deer poachers, to cite only examples from *Lassie*'s first seasons. With the virtues of rural living as its ideological bedrock, *Lassie* confronts the threats posed to this traditional culture by the city (which, throughout the American sentimental tradition, has been cast as the source of evil) and by technology (which is often seen as threatening organic communal bonds). City folks are either so green that they get into trouble (falling into wells, sliding off cliffs, getting lost in the woods) or they bring crime and violence (kidnapping Lassie, hitting her with a car, organizing pit-bull fights). Throughout the Jeff and Timmy years, Lassie remains close to home, having adventures on or around the family farm. The ever-watchful Lassie goes into the woods with Timmy and ensures he doesn't get into trouble. As Cully explains to Timmy, "Lassie's always looked after you like her own puppy."

While Lassie represented a maternal presence as Timmy and the other boys rambled, Flipper was more of a playmate who might lure Sandy from his chores. Timmy may be Lassie's "puppy" but Sandy is

Flipper's friend. "Flipper, we've got a problem," Sandy says more than once across the series, though the resourceful pair always find their own way out of dangers. Flipper can scarcely be called a pet, since he is free to go where he wants, exploring the depths and interacting with the humans on the surface. The same could not be said for the animal actor who played the part, whose movements were contained and whose body was disciplined—in ways that O'Barry came to regret.

Luke Halpin played Sandy across the two films and the television series, allowing audiences to watch him mature. He assumed new responsibilities when the television series introduced his ten-year-old brother, Bud (Tommy Norden), who would now have the more intensive relationship with Flipper. For boys of the period, Sandy and Bud were aspirational figures, taking off on a motorboat, swimming and scuba diving. Occasionally helping their father, the television variants were less burdened with responsibilities than Sandy was in the original film. While the film takes place within the rough-and-tumble world of the fisherman, the series offers a more welcoming environment for two young boys. By the time the series opens, the parkland has become their "home base" as they learn every underwater cave or coral reef. For the viewer this is a space of adventure, but for the two boys it represents a space they have mastered, though there are always unexpected risks. Throughout, there are many threats: the park may be forced to close, Flipper may be shipped to a research center, he may be kidnapped by a traveling circus, he is injured and may die, but the emotional bonds between the boys and Flipper remain unbreakable. Just as Flipper is a "wild" animal who interacts with humans, Coral Key represents a "wild" space that is also the Ricks' backyard.

Animal-centered adventure series were consistently panned by the National Association for Better Radio and Television and other such groups. In 1956, for example, the group condemned *Rin Tin Tin* as one of the "most objectionable" programs on television: "Tense situations exist throughout the program and unbelievable problems are solved by this incredible dog. . . . Whole-some episodes are the exception."[25] The Child Study Association's Anna W. M. Wolf feared that suspenseful storylines, especially those involving children in jeopardy, overstimulated children's imaginations.[26] *Flipper*, for example, was condemned for "story themes [that] abound in crime and involve youngsters in extremely dangerous situations."[27] One television producer cited *Lassie* in 1967 as an example of how the vividness and immediacy of television added luridness to classic boys' adventure stories: "*Lassie* is one of the scariest shows for kids. They see a real kid and a real dog in real danger."[28] *Flipper* walks a thin line between satisfying the child viewer's desire for daring exploits and reassuring parents that the children will be safe under Flipper's supervision. Flipper is both wild and domesticated, childlike and mature, nurturing and tempting, allowing him to become everything a growing boy might desire—except perhaps satisfying the fantasy of running away from home altogether, a central theme of *My Side of the Mountain*.

## Domesticating the Wild: *My Side of the Mountain* (1959)

In the late 1960s, Margaret Mead published a series of essays addressing the need of children and adults alike, especially those living in the suburbs "where people live too close for freedom and too far apart for the richness of community," to spend more time engaging with the natural world.[29] Mead's writings on the wilderness, parks, summer camp, and family camping were no doubt informed by her conversations with Edith Cobb, whose work she was then actively preparing for publication. Cobb's advocacy for children's exploratory play in the natural world bridges between Mead's ongoing interest in children and America's growing ecological awareness in the wake of Rachel Carson's best-selling *Silent Spring* (1962).[30] In a 1969 essay, Mead advocated expanding the amount of federally protected land to reflect the population density of America's growing cities and the creation of a youth-based conservation corps as a form of public service paralleling the Peace Corps and Vista:

> The work would help us to re-establish the links between the man-made and the natural world, as the young people themselves would come to understand better the cycles of growth and decay and the deeper attachment of human beings to outdoor life. . . . Play on the land, vacations from city living, will be true recreation for all of us when we can respond with wonder to a world we know, a world that nourishes our imagination as it claims our care.[31]

Mead could have been describing the experiences of fourteen-year-old Sam Gribley, who runs away from an overcrowded New York City apartment to live off the land on his great-grandfather's abandoned upstate farm in Jean Craighead George's 1959 chapter book *My Side of the Mountain*. The book was adapted as a feature film in 1969, the same year Mead published her essay. George's family regularly took her camping in the woods, where she climbed trees to study owls, gathered edible plants, made fishhooks from twigs, and captured and raised animals, starting with a turkey vulture. She published more than a hundred books, a mix of fiction and nonfiction, mostly for children, mostly dealing with the relations between humans and animals. For *My Side of the Mountain*, she translated her own adventures into those of a male protagonist, perhaps, again, reflecting the sense that girls would read books about boys but boys resisted female protagonists. Her best-known book, it is at once a novel recounting a boy's adventures living in the woods in the tradition of Henry David Thoreau and a handbook teaching skills and lore necessary to do so. She wrote in the preface: "Almost everyone I know has dreamed at some time of running away to a distant mountain or island, castle or sailing ship, to live there in beauty and peace. Few of us make it, however."[32] Her preface addresses those who only vicariously enjoy Sam's adventures: "Perhaps Sam will fulfill your dreams, too. Be you writer or reader, it is very pleasant to run away in a book."[33]

In another 1968 essay, Mead argued for the value of children spending time outside the city or beyond the suburbs, where they could make their own choices about what they wanted to do, where they encountered new people outside the "confined circle of family, neighbors, and schoolmates."[34] Summer camps were more likely to be the places where the young tried the skills and practices George described. I recall reading *My Side of the Mountain* by flashlight at a Boy Scout camp when I was just a bit younger than Sam. Rereading the book brings a rush of sense memories, including the smell of the cooking fire, the chill of lake water, and the taste of fiddlehead ferns, just as George uses multisensual descriptions to bring Sam's story alive.

*My Side of the Mountain* begins with a tour of Sam's place, a ritual he performs multiple times. This passage recalls the ways suburban kids might open the backyard gate for chosen friends: "I am on my mountain in a tree home that people have passed without ever knowing that I am here. The house is a hemlock tree six feet in diameter and must be as old as the mountain itself. I came upon it last summer and dug and burned it out until I made a snug cave in the tree that I now call home."[35] Sam's language demonstrates his pride in his own accomplishments.

My analysis is informed by, among others, the writings of the cultural geographer Yi-Fu Tuan, who helped to conceptualize the differences between space and place.[36] Space represents a territory that is unknown, undifferentiated, unexplored, uninhabited, and/or unpossessed, while place is familiar and intimate, defined by the memories and meaning we attach to it. Tuan links space with freedom and mobility, place with security. He describes the process by which children develop a conception of their surrounding environment, coming to see more and more of the world as part of their home, which he discusses as an "intimate place," while the maturing child becomes fascinated with spaces not yet fully known.[37] Tuan uses the process of settling a frontier as an example of how spaces become places:

> At first there is wilderness, undifferentiated space. A clearing is made in the forest and a few houses are built. Immediately differentiation occurs; on the one side there is wilderness, on the other a small vulnerable man-made world. The farmers are keenly aware of their place, which they created themselves and which they must defend against the incursion of wild nature. To the passerby or visitor, the fields and houses also constitute a well-defined place, obvious to him as he emerges from the forest to the clearing.[38]

This passage maps well onto George's novel: Sam claims a place (or home base) he must increasingly defend against various encroachments. Writers of the period saw the settling of the frontier as a core American myth and the desire to settle the wilderness as fundamental to the national character. No wonder the book's characters compare Sam to such historical figures as Daniel Boone and Henry David Thoreau. Much like Thoreau, Sam does not ultimately live alone. Not only does he gather animal companions but also adults he trusts. When Sam runs away from his urban apartment, he is searching for land settled and farmed by his great-grandfather. Sam's father had been a sailor who felt discontent with his new life as a dockworker: "Dad didn't like the land.

He liked the sea, wet and big and endless."[39] The father laughs at his son's bold proposition of living on the family homestead. When Sam finds the Gribley Farm, it is a ruin—"a few stones in a square, a slight depression for the basement, and trees growing right up through what had once been a living room."[40] If Tuan describes how wilderness becomes a place, George suggests how an abandoned place may be reclaimed as space. George evokes the vulnerability Sam feels that first night: "I had made my hemlock bed right in the stream valley where the wind drained down from the cold mountain top.... I didn't have enough hemlock boughs under me, and before I had my head down my stomach was cold and damp.... I curled up in a ball and was almost asleep when a whippoorwill called."[41] Sam stresses his need for "a house that could not be seen" by passersby who might threaten his solitude and freedom: "People would want to take me back where I belonged if they found me."[42] Something intuitively guides him toward what will become his new home: "I looked at that tree. Somehow, I knew it was home but I was not quite sure how it was home."[43] He develops a plan, scraping away the "old rotten insect-ridden dust": "With most of the dust out, I could crawl in the tree and sit cross-legged. Inside I felt as cozy as a turtle in its shell."[44] Such imagery contrasts with the earlier description of curling up in a ball for protection.

Only a few pages later, Sam acknowledges his growing security: "Five notches into June, my house was done. I could stand in it, lie down in it, and there was room left over for a stump to sit on. On warm evenings I would lie on my stomach, and look out the door, listen to the frogs and nighthawks, and hope it would storm so that I could crawl into my tree and be dry."[45] This is *his* home because *he* found it and he made it, because it accrues *his* memories. As the story progresses, he names the animals he sees most often, and this act of naming also contributes to his sense of possession. He captures and trains a peregrine falcon who hunts for him, and this process of making the falcon his pet parallels the process of creating a home inside a tree. The mountain becomes *his* through a process of acquiring knowledge: "Not a cloud passed unnoticed, not a wind blew untested. I knew the moods of storms, where they came from, their shapes and colors."[46]

George makes this a "place" for her readers too through her detailed descriptions, her helpful instructions for the skills Sam deploys. She illustrated the book with her pencil sketches of edible plants, the tree and its furnishing, drawings intended to be studied and perhaps applied by her readers. And when she writes about practices, such as how to build a fire or how to make fishhooks, she offers them more in the form of advice than as narrative description: "If you ever eat cattails, be sure to cook them well. Otherwise, the fibers are tough, and they take more chewing to get the starchy food from them than they are worth. However, they taste just like potatoes after you've been eating them a couple of weeks, and to my way of thinking are extremely good."[47]

Her second-person address feels like a passage from the *Boy Scouts Handbook* or *Boy's Life* magazine, both highly popular with those fantasizing a space beyond their own backyards. Scouting's ranks had grown from two million members at the end of the Second World War to 6.5 million by the early 1970s, with the book's publication and the film's release both demarking key moments in this dramatic growth.[48] Norman Rockwell offered heroic images of the scouting life in the *Saturday Evening Post* and *Boy's Life*, not to mention on the covers of various handbooks. Mischa Honeck describes the vision Rockwell brought to his boy-scouting pictures: "Portrayed in the company of proud parents, devoted scoutmasters, former presidents, and foreign Scouts, the boys represent all that is right and virtuous about a nation that lived with the threat of nuclear annihilation."[49] Honeck stresses how scouting functioned in this Cold War context, promoting a nationalist ideology and a civic religion. By the late 1960s, however, the organization was encountering pushback against wearing uniforms or being required to pledge to the flag. The back-to-the-land dimensions of the hippie movement offered an alternative version of what it might mean to live on your own side of a mountain. This countercultural concept was reflected in the film version by the more consistent references to Thoreau (whose writings had been embraced by hippies who wanted to "march to the beat of a different drummer"), the casting of antiwar folk singer Theodore Bikel as the boy's mentor, and the inclusion of a scene where some townie boys make fun of Gribley's long hair and buckskin. The story captured the imagination of dedicated Scouts and the organization's critics alike.

In writing to parents, Mead (1971) suggests that the value of summer camps lies not simply in time spent apart from the family but also in the emotional reconciliation upon the child's homecoming:

Looking ahead, parents can be very sure of only one thing: the returned camper (even the child away from home for no more than two weeks) will be different.... The child has met a challenge and has found his or her own way of coping with the unknown and the strange, something no one could tell the child how to do.... Daring to walk alone in the dark past shadowy trees may have meant conquering a very private set of fears. The discovery that every plant has a name and can be classified may have been extraordinarily exciting—the first step into a new world of how to think about things.[50]

But she also acknowledges that the family will have undergone changes of its own to which the returning camper must adjust: "A father may perhaps realize how often he compared his own son with other boys, not always to his boy's advantage, and now with nostalgia wonder whether he wouldn't prefer to have his son home again quite unchanged."[51] I have pulled out this passage about the father from Mead's longer discussion of adjustments—physical and emotional—in the lives of other family members because in *My Side of the Mountain*, what matters most is how Sam gains the respect of adult men—both his actual father and Bando, a schoolteacher who becomes an alternative father figure. When Bando is first invited into Sam's realm, he observes what the boy has built: "He arose, turned around and around, and looked at his surroundings. He whistled softly when I kindled a spark with the flint and steel."[52] Bando asks, "Am I dreaming? I go to sleep by a campfire that looked like it was built by a boy scout, and I awaken in the middle of the eighteenth century,"[53] a comment linking the boy's accomplishments with the larger frontier mythology. Sam describes various wild foods he offers his guest and how the man eats them from a turtle shell. Later, when Bando returns for a Christmas visit, he brings an unexpected guest, Sam's father, whose presence signals his acceptance of the boy's decision to leave home: "I thought maybe you'd pick a cave.... I never would have thought of the inside of a tree. What a beauty! Very clever, son, very, very clever."[54] The father spends many days in the encampment, but reluctantly returns to civilization.

Sam encounters more and more people who become aware of where he is living: some stumble upon him, some he invites. Their presence impacts how he perceives this place: "I was no longer hiding in the wilderness. I was living in the woods like anyone else lives in a house. People drop by, neighbors come for dinner.... I felt exactly like I felt when I was home. The only difference was that I was a little harder to visit out here, but not too hard."[55] Another visitor warns him, "Let's face it, Thoreau, you can't live in America today and be quietly different. If you are going to be different, you are going to stand out and people are going to hear about you."[56] Across the final two chapters, "I Cooperate with the Ending" and "The City Comes to Me," readers watch Sam prepare for his inevitable homecoming. When Sam hears his father calling to him along the pathway, he faces a final choice: "For a long moment I stood wondering whether to meet Dad or run forever. I was self-sufficient. I could travel the world over, never needing a penny, never asking for anything of anyone. I could cross to Asia in a canoe via the Bering Strait. I could raft to an island. I could go around the world."[57] As we will see in the next chapter, these imagined adventures in other lands (and the potential for friendship with people from other cultures) were also being depicted in children's fictions.

This is the moment Sam realizes that he is ready to engage with his family again. Mead writes: "Coming home from camp is a rehearsal for something that will happen again and again and become more important through the years as the absences grow longer and visits home shorter. What parents and children succeed in making of this first venture out of the home circle will affect all the reunions in later years—the return from college, from summer jobs, from trips abroad, with a wife or a husband, with a first baby."[58] The family has come to stay, the father constructs new shelters for the others, and the mother reasserts her supervision. As the mother explains, "Well, if he doesn't want to come home, then we will bring the home to him."[59] Sam has gained his father's respect *as a boy*, still not quite a man, but he has also lost the freedom that makes his story so compelling.

Across this chapter, I have discussed two different spatial fantasies: the story of a dolphin who serves as a mediator between humans and the natural world, sometimes a "bad influence" and sometimes good, as his story takes him from the wild sea to a protected nature reserve; and a story where a boy enters a wilderness and makes it his home, gradually finding natural counterparts to the creature comforts of his old neighborhood. Each offered readers an alternative to their fenced backyards.

These stories provided risk and reassurance, wildness and domestication to bridge between the worlds they depicted and those where these stories were read. My generation "ran away" through books consumed in our tree houses, or perhaps by flashlight at camp. In the following chapter, I will discuss how fantasies of freedom and mobility were reflected in adventures on a global scale, such as those found in *Jonny Quest* and *Maya*. If such stories addressed the child's need to move further from their "home base," these fictions also spoke to adult desires for a generation more open to global perspectives.

10

*Jonny Quest*, *Maya*, and the Promise of "World Brotherhood"

Newly returned from army service in Korea, Ken Heyman, then an undergraduate studying to be a social worker, enrolled in one of Mead's classes at Columbia. Fascinated with the role visual media might play in ethnography, Mead encouraged students to include photographs with their assignments. Heyman shared a photo-essay of boys he was mentoring at a Harlem settlement house. Mead invited him to accompany her on a return to Bali, where she had done her earliest fieldwork, and later she collaborated with him on *Family*, a 1965 book in which she penned her own perspectives on family life around the globe. Writing to Mead from an Israeli kibbutz, Heyman described how his perspective shifted when he photographed a young mother breastfeeding her newborn, as the father and their ten-year-old son looked on:

Almost for the first time, do I have the feeling of the universality, or "world." In the past I have only concentrated on family, not really being concerned that the book (my part, that is) has not only to say family, but must also give the reader the feeling that all peoples have been accounted for. . . . I have already been to Sweden, Germany, Austria, Turkey, Egypt, Pakistan, India, Iran and Israel. I'll leave the day after tomorrow for Greece, then Italy, Spain and Portugal.[1]

*Family* was inspired by *The Family of Man*, the epic photographic exhibition organized a decade earlier by Edward Steichen, then the director of photography for the New York City Museum of Modern Art. Steichen assembled 503 photographs representing 68 countries through the work of 273 photographers. The exhibit toured the world thanks to support from the recently formed United States Information Agency. Its focus on universal humanism was perhaps most vividly stated by Carl Sandburg: "There is only one man in the world and his name is All Men. There is only one woman in the world and her name is All Women. There is only one child in the world and the child's name is

All Children."[2] Jerry Mason adapted the photographs and texts into a best-selling book, which has remained in print for decades. Mason also followed with a second volume, *The Family of Children*, in 1977 as part of the United Nations' celebration of the "Year of the Child." *Family* differed from *The Family of Man* in several important ways: Heyman took all the images and Mead's text is substantial, intended to make an important statement about global interconnectedness: "These pictures are held together by a way of looking that has grown out of anthropology, a science in which all peoples, however contrasting in physique and culture, are seen as members of the same species, engaged in solving problems common to humanity" (10). Mead's introduction acknowledges how families protect their members, even as they confront the atomic age: "As men must now irrevocably perish or survive together, the task of each family is also the task of all humanity. This is to cherish the living, remember those who have gone before, and prepare for those who are not yet born."[3] Mead's contributions to *Family* included short essays on such themes as "Mothers," "Fathers," "Brothers and Sisters," and "Friends."

Across two decades, Mead linked the threats posed by nuclear war with the importance of global consciousness, buoyed by the success of the allies during the Second World War, the formation of the United Nations, the images of the Earth created by the Soviet and American space programs, and the recognition that television was exposing people to the perspectives of those living across the planet. Heyman's images of children playing, doing chores, cuddling with their parents, interacting with pets, showed readers what needs to be protected from the threat of war while Mead's writings characterized the emerging generation as the last great hope for human survival. Her writings also addressed domestic concerns about racism so often elided by others who celebrated global citizenship: Mead hoped that children might overcome historical divides if parents and teachers protected them from prejudices.

In a 1967 *Redbook* article, Mead summarized her hopes for her own daughter:

> I wanted her to feel at home and welcome anywhere in the New World, where all the great races of man have mingled, and in the Old World,

where so many groups have lived apart from one another.... I wanted her to know members of other groups so that she would not classify individuals by such categories as skin color, language, or religion, but would be able to respond to each of them as a person whom she liked or found uncongenial for individual reasons. I wanted her to experience living with others as full human beings.[4]

Here, Mead endorsed a cosmopolitan perspective that had not yet been fully achieved by her readers, advocating a progressive transformation of American culture that merged permissive ideas about childhood with advocacy for global citizenship.

Mead asked in a 1962 *Parents* article, "How can we bring up our children so that they will be patriotic and devoted Americans and at the same time, true world citizens?" For her, the answer lay in the concept of a global community:

> Even today, we do not yet have world citizenship—citizenship implies the existence of a responsible government with sanctions. But we do have, today, a world in which the act of any one person anywhere may affect the well-being of people on the opposite side of the globe.... Our children are natives of the new age. The more clearly we realize this, the more we can help our children respond intelligently to the conditions they were born to, the better chance we have of bringing up children who know that they belong to and must take responsibility for a planetary community of interconnected human lives.[5]

Mead consistently linked struggles to bridge nations with the similar difficulty of embracing marginalized peoples within the United States:

> Will the people of such countries, as India and China, for instance, or of Ghana and New Guinea, be able to make the necessary adaptations? ... For that matter, we must ask whether our own people can catch up— the white children in Appalachia, the Negro children in big-city ghettos, the Indians boxed in on their own reservations, and all those who have been deprived, for whatever reason, of the social experiences that make new forms of adaptation easier. Can they become full participants in 20th-century living?[6]

Mead saw the spread of mass media as exposing children in one country to the lives of their peers elsewhere. She told delegates to the Seventh International Congress on Mental Health in August 1969, "The first generation to be reared on TV. . . . No matter where they live, they are watching fragments of life in every part of the world."[7] Mead had no illusions that Marshall McLuhan's concept of the global village could describe the new awareness that television fostered:

> In a village everyone knows everyone else. . . . True villagers speak the same language, laugh at the same jokes, share the same expectations, and remember the same past. . . . The news media brings the peoples of the earth within view of one another. But the sheer numbers of people of whom we are made aware diminish the possibility of any feeling of closeness and community. Seen from space, our planet may look like a little, blue, spinning top. But the world is not, nor is it likely to become, a global village.[8]

Children, she felt, did not naturally ascribe meaning to racial differences, but rather, acquired prejudice through parental influence. So, if they could be exposed to diversity from an early age, children might develop greater respect for those from different backgrounds. Mead's support for integrated education was consistent with other opinions she expressed in her *Redbook* columns, supporting interracial marriage even as she insisted that racial differences should be acknowledged rather than erased.

### It's a Small World After All

Mead was not alone in stressing the need to raise children with a desire to engage with the world. Henry H. Goddard began his 1948 book *Our Children in the Atomic Age* with a concise summation of the problem: "We know now we cannot live isolated from the rest of the world and we do not know how to live together. . . . Eventually we must have men who were born and bred since 1945, men who will be unhampered by the old disproved traditions. This means that we must start with the children and give them better care, better bringing-up, better schooling."[9]

Many educators shared this belief that schools could be a vehicle for fostering global consciousness and breaking down racial prejudice, though most seemed more invested in the former than in the latter. In *Bringing the World to the Child*, Katie Day Good traces a succession of new media (from magic-lantern slides to films, radio, television, and the internet) that were promoted as "technologies of global citizenship," addressing Americans' persistent lack of interest in world events and knowledge of geography.[10] This pedagogical approach, Good argues, was "ethnocentric insofar as it positioned the United States and white, Anglo-American identity at the center of mediated lessons on the international world, and exhibited cultural differences in ways that reinforced, in ways subtle and overt, colonial, Euro-American ideologies of racial and national superiority and progress."[11] This ideal of global citizenship was at its core apolitical, based on commonality and friendship among individuals while ignoring the economic and geopolitical factors that made it challenging for nations to interact on equal terms.

As early as 1901 Swarthmore College and the Modern Language Association organized an exchange to match American youth with pen pals in other countries. Children of immigrants were encouraged to bring relatives as classroom speakers or to share meaningful objects reflecting other cultures. And in some cases, these children dressed in traditional garb and performed ethnic identities as part of school pageants. Yet, even if such practices encouraged youth to take pride in where their families had come from and form friendships with children from other lands, many found it easier to deal with diversity on the other side of the planet than in their own backyards. As one educator reported in 1929, "An international pageant was observed on a playground to which colored children were never admitted; but some of them got near enough to watch it over the railing. No one in that neighborhood seemed to recognize anything incongruous about the situation."[12]

Mischa Honeck and Benjamin René Jordan have traced similar hypocrisies in the ways the Boy Scouts claimed support for a "brotherhood of all mankind," embodied by rituals at international jamborees where white and nonwhite boys joined hands and sang together, or ennobled by the Scout Law, which proclaimed equality among all boys.[13] Yet, at the same time, Scout troops remained racially segregated across much of America, and in some Southern states Blacks were not allowed to participate. Such contradictions are not surprising when we consider that the Boy Scouts originated in the service of preparing British boys to play active roles in sustaining colonial rule. But, despite or perhaps because of this troubled history, this push for global brotherhood had gained new urgency for the Boy Scouts in the Cold War era.

In 1953, the Boy Scouts of America introduced the World Brotherhood Merit Badge (later renamed the Citizenship in the World Badge and made a core requirement for the coveted Eagle rank). The badge's first requirement asks the boys to identify on a map at least thirty countries with scouting organizations: "You have brother scouts in every continent—more than 5,000,000 of them altogether. Every one of them would be glad to shake your hand, using the familiar left hand international Scout handclasp. . . . Of course, if you ever had the opportunity you would want to visit another country not just to 'see the sights' but to see how other people live."[14] The requirements offer scouting's characteristic mix of knowledge (explaining different forms of government, identifying cultural heroes, and explaining the operation of the United Nations) and applied skills (translating a passage or conducting a conversation in a "modern foreign language," hiking or camping with boys from other nations, collecting relief supplies, or making friends with "new arrivals from abroad"). But at heart, there is a general set of assumptions about globalization: "Tell briefly how modern transportation and communication have 'shrunk' the world during the past hundred years and have made nations more dependent upon one another. . . . Tell how natural resources, commerce, and trade affect a nation's economy and relationships among nations."[15] The rationale for the badge adopts Cold War concepts, starting with the need to defend capitalism and democracy from "enemies of the American way of life,"[16] the notion that America's economy and government made it a "natural leader" among nations, and the argument that "nations that trade freely with one another tend to establish peaceful relationships."[17]

The Boy Scouts was only one of the youth-centered organizations trying to cement sentimental ties between children across national borders. For example, in 1949, Mary Emma Allison, a school librarian living in a suburb of Philadelphia, started to collect pocket change for UNICEF rather than candy on Halloween. Her husband, Reverend Clyde Allison, introduced the concept through Presbyterian churches in 1950, and in 1953 the US UNICEF committee made it an official fundraising practice. The first Model United Nations Conference, hosted at Swarthmore College in 1947, assembled 150 students from over forty-one colleges to role-play as delegates to the General Assembly. The Model UN, paralleling earlier efforts at student-led simulations of the League of Nations in the 1920s, soon spread across American high schools.

Children and youth played key roles in Dwight Eisenhower's People2People initiatives through the US Information Agency, which had emerged from a Geneva summit where Nikita Khrushchev had expressed enthusiasm for cultural exchange. Among the People2People efforts were programs to place foreign exchange students in American homes and to organize trips for US students to visit their counterparts overseas. Walt Disney was inspired by his experiences as one of the initiative's founding directors to launch the "It's a Small World" attraction first at the 1964 New York World's Fair, where all of the proceeds for the ticket sales went to UNICEF, and later as an attraction at Disneyland. Mary Blair's colorful and whimsical designs feature more than three hundred animatronic children, dressed in traditional clothing and engaging in locally specific pastimes, as tourists ride past in boats and get the Sherman Brothers' theme song stuck in their heads:

> It's a world of laughter
> A world of tears
> It's a world of hopes
> And a world of fears
> There's so much that we share
> That it's time we're aware
> It's a small world after all.

Popular culture was being recruited in the service of this diplomatic and pedagogical agenda. Consider, for example, the *CBS Children's Film Festival*. Starting in early 1967 and continuing off and on in various formats and time slots through 1984, the program brought an international flavor to Saturday mornings, with screenings of award-winning children's films from the United Kingdom, Russia, France, Bulgaria, Japan, Sweden, Italy, China, Australia, South Africa, Czechoslovakia, and other countries, initially introduced by Kukla, Fran, and Ollie. Many of the films, such as Japan's *Skinny and Fatty*, dealt with unlikely friendships, including several films—notably the British *Hand in Hand*—that dealt with cross-cultural or interfaith bonding. The program sought to encourage American children's curiosity about international cinema (at the peak of adult interest in European art cinema) and a greater awareness of how children in other countries played, went to school, and enjoyed family life.

Such explicit efforts at cosmopolitanism were rare on commercial television, but the adventure genre might more subtly introduce depictions of cross-cultural and international friendship. The rest of this chapter will consider two examples—Hanna-Barbera's animated series *Jonny Quest* (1964), and the live-action prime-time drama *Maya* (1967–68), both of which dealt with friendship between a white American boy and a brown boy from India. These adventure series tap themes of mobility, risk-taking, and autonomy believed to have strong appeal to boys and linked in the permissive imagination to younger children's urge to explore their immediate environment. Insofar as permissiveness linked wildness to the child's quest for autonomy, such adventure stories became another means of giving boys a chance to "run away" through fictions. I will explore how these two series negotiated with the conventions of a genre deeply rooted in the colonialist project, shedding light on the concept of global citizenship. Much as schools found it easier to deal with global friendship while ignoring inequalities between the races in the domestic context, these programs depicted cross-racial friendships at a time when there were still few Black children represented in children's fictions.

Writing in *Family*, Mead stresses the central roles friendship plays in every culture, encouraging children to develop a greater sense of autonomy beyond the family and forge interconnections with other families:

> Friendship with its symmetry is at the root of those tendencies that, with many different shades of meaning, we call democratic—the desire for others to have the same opportunities as oneself, and the demand that one be granted the same treatment accorded others.... As the world widens, friendship can include greater differences within its essential symmetry, differences of education, nationality, race, and sex, and boys and girls and men and women can find in each other both likeness and contrast.[18]

Heyman's images are not as cosmopolitan as Mead's prose. Across twenty-three images representing clusters of children playing and hanging out together, none of them represent integrated groups. Friendships, Mead argues, often start by children sharing some activity—most often play but also shared tasks. Adventure series dealing with young boys as traveling companions gave frequent opportunities for shared activities.

## Case Study: *Jonny Quest*

In 1963, comic book artist Doug Wildey, best known for his work on adventure stories such as *The Outlaw Kid* and *Journey into Unknown Worlds*, was hired by Hanna-Barbera to develop an animated series focused on the exploits of long-standing radio character Jack Armstrong. The serialized adventures of Jack Armstrong—an "all-American boy" who traveled the world with his Uncle Jim, an industrialist—had been a radio success from 1938 to 1951. Jack Armstrong was still a known brand in the early 1960s, and despite the success Hanna-Barbera was then enjoying as the leading producer of television cartoon series, the company was unable to secure the rights. Asked to rework the genre elements into an original property, Wildey rapidly developed the core concepts for *Jonny Quest*. Up until that point, Hanna-Barbera had been associated with a more cartoonish visual style and broad character-driven comedy, going back to their role in the development of the Tom and Jerry cartoons for MGM and their subsequent success with series such as *Huckleberry Hound*, *Yogi Bear*, *The Flintstones*, and *The Jetsons*. Rather than the garishly colored animal characters, Wildey adopted a visual style inspired by adventure comic strip artists such as Milton Caniff. Prior to working for Hanna-Barbera, Wildey had worked at Columbia on the 1962 animated series *Space Agent* under the direction of adventure comic veteran Alex Toth. Toth would eventually be hired by Hanna-Barbara to work on subsequent series, including *Space Ghost*, *Super Friends*, *The Fantastic Four*, and *Birdman*.

While Jonny, his scientist-adventurer-superspy dad, and their silver-haired bodyguard all sprang more or less fully developed from Wildey's concept art, Hadji, Jonny's friend and adopted brother, first appears—without much ceremony or explanation—in the second episode. One would love to see the producer's notes telling Wildey that what this

Figure 10.1. Jonny and Hadji literalize the ideals of "world brotherhood" in Hanna-Barbera's *Jonny Quest* (1964–65).

otherwise promising series really needs is an Indian orphan. Years later, Wildey offered this explanation: "Hadji was supposed to be a child of the streets. I wanted to use a minority character other than the typical black kid from the ghetto which so many others had used in comic strips and comic books at the time. . . . I wanted a clear difference between these two kids who were roughly the same age, a different perspective and lifestyle to spice things up."[19] Here, there's an acknowledgment that casting Hadji was about displacing Blackness, shifting from a civil rights frame to a global-brotherhood one, which somehow felt less stereotypical. Throughout this section, I want to resist the temptation to read Hadji as Jonny's sidekick, as he is so often seen (figure 10.1). Instead, I will center him in my analysis.

Writing in 1948 about the ways many classic works of American literature fell loosely under the category of boys' adventure stories, Leslie Fielder maintained that what unified works as diverse as *Moby-Dick*, *The Adventures of Huckleberry Finn*, *The Last of the Mohicans*, and *Two*

*Years Before the Mast* was a fascination (bordering on the homoerotic) with "the mutual love of a white man and a colored."[20] He explains: "The white boy and the black we can discover wrestling affectionately on any American sidewalk, along which they will walk into adulthood, eyes averted from each other, unwilling to touch even by accident. The dream recedes; the immaculate passion and the astonishing reconciliation become a memory, and less, a regret, at last the unrecognized motifs of a child's book."[21] Jonny and Hadji represent a juvenile version of Ishmael and Queequeg.

Christina Klein argues that America's involvement in the Cold War depended on two interwoven, if sometimes contradictory, imperatives: containment, which held that "since cooperation with the Soviets was impossible and all communist governments were subservient to Moscow, the expansion of communism anywhere in the world posed a direct threat to the U.S. share of world power,"[22] and integration, bringing other countries into alignment with US interests through the global spread of "the American way of life." Such integration required strengthening affectionate and sentimental ties between America and the world, goals that were pursued through cultural and citizen-based diplomacy. Klein discusses the adoption of war orphans as one mechanism of integration—first European children in the wake of the Second World War, and subsequently, the cross-racial and cross-cultural adoption of Asian children in the context of the Korean and Vietnam Wars. Welcome House, a nonprofit established by Pearl Buck in 1949 with support from James Michener and Oscar Hammerstein II, helped to place Asian war orphans in American families because, in Klein's words, "hybrid Asian and American families created through adoption could eventually facilitate better political relations between the United States and Asia."[23] As Klein explains:

> These families offered a way to imagine the U.S.-Asian integration in terms of voluntary affiliation: they presented international bonds formed by choice (at least on the part of the American parents), rather than by biology. In doing so they foregrounded the idea of alliance among independent parties—the model of postwar integration—rather than the idea of an empire unified by blood and force. These mixed-race families also offered a way to imagine Americans overcoming the ingrained racism

that so threatened U.S. foreign policy goals in Asia. In part because the family balanced emotional unity with internally structured hierarchies of difference based on age, it served as a model for a "free world" community that included Western and non-Western, developed and underdeveloped, established and newly created nations. The family became a framework within which these differences could be both maintained and transcended and offered an imaginative justification for the permanent extension of U.S. power, figured as responsibility and leadership, beyond the nation's borders.[24]

Between 1953 and 1963, Americans adopted 8,812 children from Asia, a practice that followed from the 1952 Immigration and Nationality Act, which lifted restrictions on Asian immigration. While this number is relatively small, the involvement of so many from the creative community meant it was disproportionately represented in popular fictions. The idea of cross-cultural integration through adoption would have been highly topical when *Jonny Quest* went into production. Klein stresses the parent–child relationship as justifying American paternalism toward Asia. *Jonny Quest* suggests another possibility—the brotherhood between children of different races adopted by shared parents.

So, why an Indian boy as opposed to children of China, Korea, or the South Pacific, those most commonly adopted?

Few details are provided about Hadji's life in India before joining the Quest family. Though he first appears in the second episode, "Arctic Splashdown," no real attempt is made to provide him with a backstory until episode 7, "Calcutta Adventure," where he is shown to be a "beggar boy" who earns his living snake-charming outside Calcutta University. Dr. Quest has come to India to lecture about the benefits and risks to mankind represented by sonic waves, but also to investigate reports of nerve gas being deployed in the Bharat Mountains two hours north of the city. After the Indian boy saves the American scientist from an assassination attempt, Hadji tells the Quests that he has been taught English and judo by an American marine. As they dodge attacks from militant nationalists, the Quests are aided—for a profit—by Hadji's "old and venerable friend" the Pasha Peddler, who further embodies the Americanization of Indian culture. The Peddler plays jazz on the sax and speaks American slang—"Hadji, baby," "What's shakin', man," "A-OK," and

"Daddy-O." The colorful character tells them he has no conscience, only a cashbox, having embraced capitalism as a "spiritual practice." When Dr. Quest agrees to bring Hadji to America, the Pasha Peddler greases local palms: "It's not a question of how—it's how much!" The Peddler's profiteering is treated in a good-natured fashion, largely because he is so sympathetic to American interests.

Having dedicated an entire episode to recounting Hadji's origin story, these details are quickly forgotten. In a subsequent episode ("Double Danger"), Hadji grumbles "I should have stayed in Bombay," and in "Monster in the Monastery," the urchin recalls being educated at an elite school. Similarly, Hadji is referred to more than once as a "Hindu boy" though his turban and Punjabi last name, Singh, imply he is Sikh. In "Riddle of the Gold," he complains about missing American hamburgers while on a return visit to his "native land," a line that is either oblivious to Hindu taboos or perhaps implies how much Hadji has assimilated. And in "Shadow of the Condor," Jonny and Hadji are shown saying Christian prayers. Different writers filled in Hadji's background to serve plot functions. Consequently, his Indianness comes in spurts, with one episode referring to his belief in reincarnation, another his strengths at chess and science, another the ruby in his turban, a resource beyond the means of a slum kid. While the series won praise for its geographic and ecological particularity, setting its adventures in countries that children might locate on a map and populating its wilds with specific tribes or animal species they might read about in *National Geographic*, there is far less explicit interest in what it might mean for Hadji to come from a particular region.[25]

If, as Klein suggests, adoption was a means of assimilating Asian children into American family life, the process was only moderately effective here. While Hadji has a relatively easy rapport with his adopted father, he still calls him "Sir" and "Dr. Quest" and in one episode ("Riddle of the Gold") he is introduced by Dr. Quest as "Johnny's friend" rather than his brother. In "A Small Matter of Pygmies," when the bodyguard, "Race" Bannon, asks Hadji if he can use his ruby to signal a rescue helicopter, Hadji tells him, "You can have anything I have," signaling the indebtedness the Indian boy feels toward his adopted family. Dr. Quest stresses the boy's alienness by jokingly calling him an "Indian turbanfish" during an underwater sequence in "Skull and Double Crossbones." Hadji exists on the fringes of his adopted family, a state no doubt shared by other Asian adoptees; their racial difference makes them visibly different from white children who share the same parents.

The adopted Hadji bridges between "western and non-western, developed and underdeveloped, established and newly created nations."[26] India was playing a similar bridging function in America's global imaginary. By the beginning of the 1960s, the Indian Army dislodged the Portuguese from Goa, marking the first time in four hundred years the country was fully independent of colonial presence. Under the charismatic leadership of Jawaharlal Nehru, India seemed to be on the verge of tremendous economic growth. Nehru was positioning his country as a free agent dealing with both the United States and the Soviet Union and thus able to be a mediator between warring factions. As Manu Bhagavan writes, "India played a very important role in tamping down violent situations, bringing down the temperature in hot conflicts like the Korean War, and with numerous peacekeeping operations around the world."[27] Nehru was seen as "uniquely positioned to be able to intervene, to calm things down and keep a steady hand on the wheel" when Cold War frictions intensified. The key moment is the Bandung Conference in Indonesia in 1955, at which Nehru mapped an alternative way of orienting the world neither toward Washington nor Moscow. As the USSR and America both wooed India, television depictions of friendship between children from the two nations possessed a particular geopolitical urgency. Hadji's Nehru jacket combined elements of Western design and traditional Indian tailoring, a constant reminder of India's international aspirations. A Chinese child would be aligned in the American civic imagination with enemy powers, always held in suspicion, whereas an Indian child embodied the future potential of a closer American relationship.

Children, India's Ashis Nandy wrote, often became ideological lynchpins in the restructuring of postcolonial society, shaped not only through adoption but also through "civilizing" education that severed them from their roots:

> Throughout the Southern world, children are being made a means of reconciling the past and the present *of* their societies. And now, with the accelerating pace of social change, even in many modern societies children

are expected, as a matter of course, to help their elders cope with the contradictory social norms introduced into a society or a family by large-scale technological and cultural changes, and to vicariously satisfy their elders' needs for achievement, power, and self-esteem.[28]

Hadji is a mediating figure with one foot in Western modernity and one in a more traditional society.

While Jack Armstrong's uncle traveled the world as an American industrialist pursuing his own private interests, Dr. Benton Quest's travels are defined in terms of the "national interest." The pilot starts with government agents flying to the scientist's private island to ask for his assistance. Race Bannon is referred to as "our man," Government Agent 0-37, assigned to guard "the doctor's boy" around the clock. As the mission leader explains, "Since Jonny lost his mother, the government is taking no chances with the boy's security. If Jonny fell into the hands of enemy agents, Dr. Quest's value to science would be seriously impaired." Across his adventures, Benton often participates in the international scientific community, but he also pursues covert governmental missions—sometimes a diplomat courting unaligned countries, sometimes a spy in more overt struggles to contain communism. Dr. Quest oversees the mining of a precious metal they hope will give Americans an advantage in the space race in "The Fraudulent Volcano," seeks to prevent a hallucinogenic plant from falling into the wrong hands in "Turo the Terrible," and is sent by an unnamed American intelligence agency to investigate a foreign power, the Maharajah of Jalalpur, in "Riddle of the Gold."

Such missions often pit Benton's Western rationality against "childish superstition," which the villains deploy to manipulate fearful local populations.[29] Benton offers a concise summary: "Sometimes native superstitions are just as powerful as scientific proof." In "The Dreadful Doll," Korbay, a local Haitian leader and self-styled witch doctor, claims to be using voodoo to overthrow a sympathetically portrayed French family that has been running a plantation on the island for twenty-five years. Dr. Quest uses Western medicine to overturn the enchantment, reverse engineering an antidote for the poisoned darts Korbay uses to control his people. Of course, the Americans are prepared to use superstition and mythology when it serves their interests. In "The Pursuit of the Po-Ho," the Po-Ho are an Amazonian tribe consistently described as "savages" having no knowledge of the outside world. The images of the Po-Ho tap adventure-story stereotypes—war paint, nose bones, spears, loincloths, tribal drums, firepits, and ritual tests of manhood, and the Americans pass modern technology off as magic to protect their culture from contamination.

In "The Curse of Anubis," the Quests head to Egypt to visit Dr. Amid Kareem, who turns out to be a treacherous nationalist leader determined to create "unity among Arab nations" under his control.[30] Seeking to trigger an international incident, Kareem plans to frame Benton and Race as part of a "foreign plot" to steal a jackal-headed statue of the god Anubis. Kareem is contemptuous of his own people, suggesting that Egypt's cultural traditions are what keep them from assuming a place among the modern nations, and justifying his own violation of local jurisdictions; "in the Middle East borders are fluid affairs." Ultimately, the nationalist leader is overthrown by the mummy whose curse was unleashed when his tomb was robbed and the roof collapses on his head, allowing the Americans to escape his clutches. Here, Hadji situates himself somewhere between Egypt, which he describes as "a very ancient country like my own India," and the West, making fun of the accents with which the Egyptians speak English.

Hadji uses traditional magic to distract Kareem's henchmen while Jonny shows his greater technological capacities by stealing a motorcycle. And later, Hadji uses his snake-charming to control the adders Kareem directs against the Americans. Hadji's loyalty to his adopted family takes precedence over any residual loyalty he might feel toward another developing nation.

Hadji seems especially in his element when the team visits Thailand in "Double Danger," noting that the country is "covered with much jungle like my country," reflecting on his belief in reincarnation, referring to a native thug as "sahib," and riding an elephant. Yet, other times, he characterizes India as a superstitious country. Hadji is equally at home deploying science or magic. The series also depicts Hadji as the intellectual superior to his white sibling, outperforming Jonny in school.

Above all, Hadji's Indian origins counterbalance the series' frequent "yellow peril" discourse, especially as represented by Dr. Zin, a Fu Manchu–like scientist whose thin mustache and garishly yellow skin signal his Chinese descent. Dr. Zin is first introduced in an Indian context in "Riddle of the Gold," where he is aligned with a group of Muslim followers seeking to manufacture synthetic gold. In "Turo the Terrible," he has brainwashed an army that will be "totally without will," a "flock of sheep awaiting instructions." And in "The Fraudulent Volcano," Dr. Zin develops "the greatest destructive force known to man," which he plans to sell to "those who can pay." By contrast, Benton is developing the technology to extinguish oil fires and when he defeats Dr. Zin's plans, he marks it as "another bull's-eye for science." Dr. Ashida, another Asian menace character, has made himself a "new god" among the native tribes with whom he shares his island, walking a pair of Komodo dragons on leashes. He warns Dr. Quest that his "Western stomach" may not allow him to witness the cruelty the dragons inflict on their prey, suggesting that his Asian background gives him a "different perspective." Dr. Ashida forces Race to fight his manservant, a Sumo wrestler, whom Ashida dares to "wipe that superiority" off the Westerner's face. Dr. Zin and the other Asian characters are depicted with jaundiced skin, thick accents, and traditional clothing, and they engage in traditional practices from fireworks to dragon parades, all of which contribute to the association of evil with Chinese communism or, perhaps, with an implicit pan-Asian conspiracy. Hadji's role in this context is to remind viewers that a different relationship with Asian peoples is possible, assuming they are willing to assimilate into an American-controlled world, and to absolve the producers, at least somewhat, of their racist imagery and white saviorism.

Nothing in *Jonny Quest* signals the desirability of the American way of life so much as the permissive family structure. All of the boys' emotional needs are met by caring adults while they are given the space to grow and mature. They are homeschooled by their scientist father mostly through flying around the world on a private jet. For the most part, they are treated as equals of the adults and allowed access to Benton's high-tech vehicles and futuristic weapons, all in the service of promoting democracy, goodwill, and Western knowledge. Their natural intelligence and curiosity sometimes get them into trouble, especially when they disobey adult edicts, though such restrictions are few and far between. Race grumbles, "Take your eyes off them for two seconds and they are gone," but he admires their boyish high spirits. The only time we see them punished comes in "Terror Island" when their father grounds them. Frequently, the adults permit them to make their own mistakes and lead them through their shared sense of adventure. The boys' perceived innocence allows them to enter spaces the adults could not, discovering information about the enemy's plans.

Often, their resourcefulness and courage enable them—always working as a team—to rescue the adults. The risks are acknowledged in "Treasures of the Temple": "We have the boys and there is no use kidding yourself, there is danger all around here," but Benton recognizes that the boys "have good heads on their shoulders" and can take care of themselves. They seem to be at home anywhere in the world, much as Margaret Mead might wish, interacting with all kinds of people. Their emotional understanding allows them to intuit others' needs, even where they can't speak local languages. Here, the series most fully embraces the potentials of cross-cultural adoption as a way of intensifying sentimental bonds between Asia and America. Hadji belongs in this world, perhaps not as fully as his white brother, but he earns his place by deploying Indian cultural practices to outsmart the bad guys. If the adult–child relationship bears traces of paternalism, modeling how America guides the developing world into maturity and prosperity, the brother–friend relationship implies reciprocity. In *Family*, Margaret Mead wrote about the relations between biological siblings once they have come to accept each other: "Now there are two who can run away together and hide, wade in the brook, dig their toes in the wet sand, reach out for the fireflies that evade their fingers, or roll like happy puppies on the grass. . . . Companionship born by such an alliance never can be quite lost."[31]

## Case Study: *Maya*

In the opening moments of the 1966 feature film *Maya*, a young white boy, Terry Bowen (Jay North), gets off a train somewhere in rural India, newly arrived from Wyoming. Finding no one to greet him, the teen walks miles through bush, forming relations with various locals, to get to the father he has never known. Having filled a scrapbook with clippings about his dad's exploits as a "great white hunter," the boy soon learns his father does not want him. Viewers learn, though Terry does not, that his father has been mauled by a tiger and has lost his courage. Ram Singh, a family servant, hopes the boy's presence will force his master to recover. The father constantly calls Terry a "boy," suggesting that "it takes more than a dish of hot curry to make you a man." He sends his son back via train, but Terry hops off, setting out across the jungle in search of adventure. Terry rides a straw raft down rapids and is rescued by Raji, a Hindu youth. Raji's father—a dying holy man—sends his son to deliver a white baby elephant to a distant temple. Terry's father and Ram pursue the boys throughout the film, which brings the adults once again into the Valley of the Tigers. Having lost his gun, Terry's father must confront the beasts unarmed, creating a spear from a knife and a wooden stick. Maya the elephant also battles two tigers to protect the boys. Terry is reconciled with his father who invites him to stay in India; the two boys deliver the elephant to his sacred home.[32]

Although neither the film nor the 1967 television series, which lasted only one season, is well-known today, *Maya* constitutes a remarkable epic of postindependence India: the friendship between the white and brown youths helped American audiences to understand India's struggles to build democratic institutions and practices. Their journeys allow viewers a glimpse into many different aspects of Indian society—sometimes through larger-than-life adventures with outlaws, bandits, runaway princesses, and tigers, but more often through the struggles of rural villagers to improve their lives.

*Maya*—as both film and television series—was produced by King Brothers Productions, an independent film studio active from 1951 to the late 1960s. The King Brothers built their reputation in the gangster and film noir genres, were perhaps best known for *Gun Crazy* (1949), and are remembered as producers willing to buy scripts in the 1950s from uncredited blacklisted writers, such as Dalton Trumbo who wrote their only other children's film, *The Brave One* (1968). In the case of *Maya*, they hired John Berry, who also had been blacklisted after refusing to name names to the House Un-American Activities Committee. Berry, the son of a Polish Jewish father and a Romanian mother, had a remarkable career, working as a comedian and master of ceremonies in Catskill resorts, acting for Orson Welles's Mercury Theatre, directing his first Hollywood movies under John Houseman, and going into self-exile when his Hollywood career ended. He directed *Maya* to test the waters for a reentry into American cinema.

A title on the feature film conveys some of the benefits of producing *Maya* in India: "The King Brothers and Metro-Goldwyn-Mayer Inc. express their sincere appreciation to the government and to the People of India whose cooperation made it possible to photograph this motion picture in its entirety on location in the jungles and in the remote villages of this stirring land." The Kings also produced the television version on location. While the directors and writers were all American or British, the series cast character actors from the Bollywood cinema such as Iftekhar, Prem Nathand, I. S. Johar, and Sajid Khan. Khan, who played Raji, had made his screen debut in the iconic *Mother India*, which had been directed by his adopted father. Johar, another Bollywood veteran, was along with North and Khan the only film cast member to carry over to television—in this case, in the recurring role of the scheming One-Eye.

Television's *Maya* foregrounds the mutual dependence among Terry, Raji, and Maya the elephant. Terry dismisses reports that his father was killed in a hunting accident and is searching for a man believed to have been a witness. Whereas, in the film, Terry accompanies Raji on his own quest, in the television show Raji assists Terry in his search for answers. The quest allows them to enter a new town each week before moving down the road again. As a white American, Terry has access to the highest levels of society, but his situation leaves him evading authorities who want to send him back to the States. Only his gun gives him power and he lacks the skills to shoot effectively.

Much like Hadji, Raji is a "street urchin," an orphan, but he knows India, its customs, its geography, its language, all of which allow him to guide Terry on his journey. Raji is a strong swimmer, can navigate hostile terrains, feed the elephants and himself, barter with the villagers. Terry mocks Raji for his "Indian superstition," but the trope of the hot-blooded, all-American, white hero is constantly subverted when he gets captured and rescued by Raji or when his various "white savior" projects fall apart. Raji lovingly teases his friend, "He who leaps upon a naked sword is neither brave nor wise, but mad." Terry insists that he does not "change my mind with every passing wind like some people." The series and its characters constantly wink at Terry's ideas of American superiority in a classic "Pride comes before a fall" setup. Yet, Raji remains willing to subordinate himself to Terry's quest. Terry promises to reward Raji's loyalty by having his father adopt him. Raji realizes that Terry's friendship is the "treasure" Raji's father had promised him.

Raji is given some exotic elements—his curses ("May there be serpents in your hair"), his prayer to Krishna, his tendency to call Terry "Little Brother," his traditional clothing. Though he claims to be a pacifist, Raji concedes that "my temper and my beliefs are at odds." Terry calls him "the most independent person in the world," though Raji questions whether independence is a good thing at the cost of his family. As one character comments in "Raji's Ransom," "There is a spirit of love between Maya and Raji that few people have. Often, she knows what he wants without any spoken words." A son of India, Raji's memories of his mother include a blue sari, an amber necklace, and a gold anklet. Indian childhood is shown as dangerous (the flash flood that took Raji's parents, the tiger that kills an anonymous young girl) and no one cares about a lone Indian boy wandering the countryside, though a white American boy consistently attracts notice.

Terry's journey takes him from an all-white world (on board the ship and before that, as a boy of the West) into a world where his whiteness needs to be masked. Terry makes a tempera paste from earth, water, and eggs, and Raji paints the American boy's face and body brown. This moment of racial masquerade is staged as a christening: "I, Raji, son of Maya, create you in my own image." The brown boy transforms the white boy's identity and, in the process, constructs a new family to replace both boys' birth parents who have been lost, one of many places where the series signals that bonds that are actively sought are stronger than those formed by blood ties (figure 10.2).

North's brownface performance confounds many traditional associations with racial masquerades: it is a gesture of brotherhood, not meant as mocking; the white boy achieves reciprocity by lowering his status and in some cases, experiencing the poverty and exclusion of colonial subjects. Above all, this ritual certifies the relationship the two achieve across differences in race, class, and nationality. In "The Witness," Terry sums up their relationship: "We have adopted each other as brothers," claiming kinship outside blood ties.

To be sure, the transformation allows the white child a comforting fantasy of transcending race, much as liberal texts, *Black Like Me* (1961) and *Gentleman's Agreement* (1947), which depicted whites passing for

Figure 10.2: Terry and Raji declare each other blood brothers in *Maya* (1967).

other racial or ethnic groups, did for adults a few years earlier. Becoming brown constitutes Terry's final liberation from the Western world, another way of becoming a "wild thing," but it also renders him responsible for what is happening in India's struggle to build an independent nation. Hadji enters Johnny's world on Western terms; Terry becomes vulnerable in shedding his world to enter Raji's as not quite a white savior figure. Whiteness, as an unmarked category, could become "other" when "marked," in this case by a crude tempera paint. Raji would have enjoyed much less fluidity, due to his color, accent, and class markers, in crossing the color line in the other direction. The gesture thus calls attention to racial and national borderlines even as it imagines the possibilities of transcending them.

As Terry imperfectly tries to pass for brown, *Maya* also offers a rich metaphor for white privilege recognized by some, ignored or unrecognized by others. In "Caper of the Golden Roe," the brownface, coupled with their ragged clothing, blocks them from entering the upscale Taj Hotel. The doorman dismisses the idea that Terry is an American, claiming that the accent is an elaborate ruse by the Mumbai street urchins ("You feed one, you feed a hundred"). Other times Terry marches forward with entitlement and white characters treat him as their own. And there are moments where Terry's whiteness shows, as when his head covering slips to reveal his blond hair, allowing One-Eye to recognize who he really is. In "The Allapor Conspiracy," Mukherjee the village elder cools the American boy's fevered forehead with a towel and accidentally wipes away the stain: "You are not one of us, you are a sahib. You are not of this land." Later, in that same episode, village elder Jang Bahadur spots a white torso under Terry's brown tempera. The two boys' racial and class differences allow them to travel between contrasting worlds, with Raji talking with the villagers while Terry aligns himself with the white authorities, but the series remains interested in the difference.

Often, the series falls back on classic adventure tropes created by authors such as Rider Haggard, Rudyard Kipling, Joseph Conrad, Edgar Rice Burroughs, Jules Verne, and others. Such empire-era tropes were now deployed in a transitional period of nation-building where India was confronting long-standing problems in the wake of its independence. *Maya* displays this process of negotiating with—and actively rethinking—a genre, stripping away (if never fully) racist assumptions and telling different stories about India in a postcolonial context. We have already seen some ways in which *Maya* addresses this challenge—strengthening Raji's voice, questioning white privilege and American superiority, respecting the particularity of local culture, and with only a few exceptions, avoiding gothic devices of the supernatural and its association with an ancient world largely unknown to the West. The residual materials of the adventure genre shape "The Khandur Uprising," an episode depicting the heroic stand of British major Walker and his men against a next-generation Khanduri leader terrorizing local villages. The major has spent more than forty years fighting in the hill country, grumbling about the lack of courage he has observed—"Never could get them to stand up and fight like men"—but he also underestimates the Khanduris, telling the villages to refuse them tribute. An Indian officer is convinced that the new leaders may be harder to beat than the major imagines, but the "insolent young pup" (in the major's words) does not remain to fortify the major's men, paving the way for an extended battle. Throughout, the contemptuous major describes the rebels as "pigs," "scum," "filth," "jackals," "blasted devils," and "cowards." The boys are treated as men who must contribute actively to the battle. Raji disguises himself, slips through enemy lines, steals a horse, and uses grenades against the combatants whereas Terry shows his improving skills with firearms. In the end, Raji delivers a message to the Indian Army while Terry and the major fight to their last bullet. Here is another story where local knowledge trumps the expertise of the former empire. But this is a rare episode that reinforces such stereotypical battles between the good (if racist) British officers and the bad local rebels.

"Tiger Boy" also has its roots in the British adventure story—in this case, taking its core premise from Rudyard Kipling's Mowgli, the man-cub, and other myths about feral children raised without human contact. Walt Disney's version of *The Jungle Book* was released in 1967, the same year that the *Maya* television series premiered. Kenneth Kidd has discussed the persistence of what he calls "feral tales," stories about boys—almost always boys—raised by wild animals: "Whether the 'wild child' originates in India, Germany, or a Native American community, the lesson this creature's career is usually taken to impart is about the white, middle-class male's perilous passage from nature to culture, from bestiality to humanity, from homosocial pack life to individual self-reliance and heterosexual prowess—that is, from boyhood to manhood."[33]

While Mowgli must ultimately battle Shere Kahn, the powerful tiger, to protect those he cares about, Kuma, the boy, in this episode has been raised by a tiger. The child is heartbroken when Terry kills his feline protector; the boys must tame this "wild child" before finding him a new home. Much of the dialogue involves an ongoing nature vs. nurture debate. Raji takes Kuma's relationship with his adopted mother more seriously than Terry does, understanding the tiger as nurturing the boy, and later cites the boy sobbing over the tiger's lifeless form to highlight the cruelty of attempts to "civilize" what one does not understand (language that could be applied to the entire colonialist project). Terry seeks to surface the boy's humanity, which he locates in Kuma's loyalty, his ingenuity and capacity for moral reasoning. Humanity, for Terry, also emerges from recognizing oneself in a mirror, learning to use tools, trimming one's nails, and smiling. Terry initially names the boy

"Heathcliff" in what is surely a parody of the British civilizing project. When Terry tries to teach the boy to hunt, Kuma subverts the lesson, using the same skills to trap Maya. Raji expresses little to no interest in Terry's civilizing project, seeing no reason to remove Kuma from the wild since the boy has the capacity to care for his own needs. The debate persists to the end, where Terry tells the boy, "At heart, you are not an animal. You are a human being," while Raji notes, "He may stay in the village, but his heart is in the jungle."

The British and American presence is gradually being pushed aside. Remnants of a crumbling empire are ever present—often in corrupted or moribund form. These issues arise in "Twilight of the Empire," which explores two intersecting stories: that of an American poacher (and his Indian guide) who are killing elephants for ivory, and that of an embittered British colonel preparing to leave since India has no more use for him. The boys seek the colonel's help after the poacher wounds Maya. In the first story, the poacher threatens to kill the boys to protect his operation and his Indian guide refuses to obey. In the second, the orderly Thapa questions the colonel's courage when he turns Terry away with some words on paper and a kukri. In some ways, the colonel's story parallels that of Terry's father and his Indian tracker with the servant entitled to question the white man's valor. Ultimately the colonel saves the boys, and they nurse Maya back to health. The American poacher's ruthlessness and racism ("Elephant or Indian makes no difference") are shocking, especially for a children's program. The kindly colonel's last efforts to help India represent a romantic conception of the white man's burden.

Lansing, a hard-bitten fugitive American in "Deadly Passage," is confused by Terry's story: "Why would a kid from the States pick Indian living?" to which Terry responds, "I didn't pick it," though by this point he clearly has. This question of which white colonizers chose to stay, on what terms, and for what reasons gets restaged often across the series. Terry is working through whether he will, in the end, return to the States or remain in this land that he is helping to achieve its own future. "The Allapor Conspiracy" uses a rural village as a microcosm for struggles between dictatorship and democracy. The village is ruled by Jang Bahadur, who killed the "great white hunter" to gain control over his weapon. The struggle over the gun offers a metaphor for power in the postcolonial world, where those who had been close to the colonizers still threaten the freedom and independence of their countryfolk. Jang now claims the village's resources, and none dare stand against him. Terry awakens the conscience of several villagers, but they only stand up for themselves when Raji develops a plan that requires the villagers to burn their own crops. ("I will pay with an empty belly if once again I may hold up my head.") The episode ends with fireworks and dancing: "Freedom, freedom from fear, that's what we are celebrating."

A number of *Maya*'s characters are seeking, however imperfectly, social justice, technological development, education, and legal processes for a more democratic India. "Roots of India" centers on an Indian cop investigating the theft of a Hindu statue and the murder of a priest by Muslims, intensifying religious tensions. When the priest dies, the boys, strangers in the community, are accused of the crime. The cop protects them from mob violence: "We are not savages—we will deal with them legally."

In its final episode, "The Legend of Whitney Markham," *Maya* returns to the core question of why white people might stay in India even after its independence, making a final case for cross-cultural friendship. Worried about his friend, who is listless and feverish, Raji brings Terry to see the British-born village doctor, recognizing him instantly as wise and kindhearted. The doctor asks Terry to stay and help for a week, telling Raji "a broken spirit is like a broken bone, Raji—it mends but slowly." Terry breaks down and shouts, "They're right! I don't belong here! I hate this country! I hate it! . . . I have to get out of here. I'm going home." Raji prays to Krishna to relieve his friend's pain: "Give all his worries to me. . . . Give back his happiness, his smile." The doctor recounts how he came to India to "gather trophies for my den" but learned to love its people. Terry tells the doctor that he is "the first grown-up who has not tried to make me give up." Throughout, the doctor represents a potential father figure for Terry, completing the family he has constructed with Maya and Raji. Helping the local villagers gives both boys a purpose and the doctor's own declining health suggests a need for a replacement. And this episode comes close to resolving things, but because of the need of episodic television to maintain the journey structure, the series' final shot shows Terry, Raji, and Maya riding off, waving goodbye.

*Jonny Quest* and *Maya* offer compelling images of potential friendship between an American boy and his Indian counterpart, holding the promise of "world brotherhood" through emotional bonds—whether of friendship or family. At the same time, the television writers were working through core contradictions in America's global mission in the Cold War era. Friendship and brotherhood, as Mead's writings suggested, required notions of reciprocity and equality that were at odds, often, with assumptions of American technological superiority and white dominance. The power dynamics between the two boys represent alternative models for how the two countries might relate to each other. *Jonny Quest*'s producers show limited interest in the cultural specificity of Hadji's Indian upbringing. Hadji is an afterthought, literally, since he was added after the initial pilot and his backstory is even more so. He is an adopted son of Dr. Quest, but also an outsider still making the cultural adjustments expected to fully belong in this American family. The show's tentative embrace of Hadji's Indianness coexists with its anxious relationship with the Asian world. *Maya* makes a greater attempt to ground Raji's backstory in the larger saga of India's transformation into a modern democratic society. Raji and Terry work through their differences, debating alternative responses to India's core issues. Terry must shed his white privilege, masked behind brown tempera, and must learn to serve rather than save India. He discovers his own reasons to remain and help build a better future for this emerging nation-state. Both series tap the genre conventions of the adventure story, linking them to permissive culture's emphasis on freedom, mobility, and autonomy from adult control. *Maya*, more than *Jonny Quest*, sometimes works against its tropes to imagine a different kind of cross-racial relationship, hard to find elsewhere in 1960s American popular culture.

## 11

# "Danger, Will Robinson"

*Accommodating the Boy Scientist in* Lost in Space

Will Robinson, who already possesses remarkable knowledge in science and engineering, travels aboard an alien spacecraft and undergoes accelerated intellectual growth. This is the premise of "A Change of Space," a first-season episode of *Lost in Space*. Will's parents do not know what to do with the boy's changed disposition. When his mother Maureen asks if he is okay, Will responds with a cold analysis: "She was just expressing her momentary emotional anxiety in rhetorical terms. Certainly, the state of my physical well-being should be apparent to all." Maureen is puzzled over his distant response, and again, he questions her assumptions: "I'm sorry if the operation of my mind doesn't please you. But it happens to be the way I am." Will tells his father, himself a world-class scientist, that his explanation for how faster-than-light-speed space travel works "might be a little hard for you to understand." His mother worries that his accelerated intellectual development will leave him more socially isolated.

For a series about a family of scientists, this episode is surprisingly ambivalent about how a child's intellectual development may undermine the boy's "normality" and turn him into a "far-out supergenius." As Arnold Gesell and his collaborators at the Institute of Human Development began doing clinical tests to measure mental development, some parents worried that they were raising an "egghead." Margaret Mead (1964) warned *Parents* magazine readers: "Our unwillingness to have anyone stand out from the rest and our guilt about robbing a child of his playtime, conspire to perpetuate a fundamental hostility to the gifted child." Parents should find ways to help each family member feel "special" and call out more humanizing traits—such as "having ears that stick out or hair that is straight as a string"—to help gifted children feel "cherished" as a whole person and not simply because of their "gifts." Mead notes: "The brightest is bright in mathematics but has no talent for human relations, and so on."[1]

Writing for *Redbook* a few years later, Mead warned that many parents felt diminished by their children's accomplishments because ideally, children were better prepared to confront space-age challenges: "Today all adults are immigrants in a changing world. And in the same measure all children . . . take for granted the thinking toward which their parents can only grope."[2] She observed that the "knowledge gap" was as vast between different generations in the same family as between so-called developed and undeveloped countries. Across these two articles, Mead moves from anthropological observations about the accelerating rate of change—what Alvin Toffler would famously call "future shock"[3]—to advice about how to deal with unequal mental capacities within a family.

The Robinsons were not the only family on American television facing this dilemma. "Dennis Is a Genius" opens with a parent-teacher conference as the teacher, Mrs. Perkins, tells the Mitchells that Dennis's cognitive potential surpassed her other students: "The intelligence tests were given to every child in his class and they were graded electronically by machine." The Mitchells confront the news with disbelief, asking the questions many other parents would ask in the same situation: Why haven't we seen signs of this hidden intelligence before? Why does he have trouble with his schoolwork? What should be done to help him achieve his full potential? Mrs. Perkins explains, "Unfortunately, under our system of education, the abilities of exceptional children—particularly the young ones—go unnoticed far too long." A child psychologist visits and confirms the diagnosis, impressed by Dennis's original solutions to the puzzles he uses to test his development. The doctor browbeats Dennis's parents: "Boredom is often the plight of the gifted child who needs to be surrounded by minds of his own intelligence level, to go to school with equally superior children, to live in a more mentally stimulating atmosphere." Henry huffs, "Why that egghead was trying to tell us we are too stupid to be around our own child!" Dennis is bemused to learn he has "brains I didn't even know I had," but is distressed when the other children avoid him. Margaret warns that most geniuses have "tragic lives" and suggests he start wearing glasses. And in the end, everyone is relieved to discover that a glitch resulting from the machine's failure to process bubble gum stuck to Dennis's exam led to misleading results. Everyone wants a bright child but no one wants a know-it-all.

The first-time viewers of *Lost in Space* saw Will in the pilot episode as he was strapped to a doctor's chair, wires connected to his head, undergoing the "final testing" to determine whether he could join his parents and siblings as the first family sent into deep space. "Did I pass?" Will eagerly asks while the Robinsons express relief, though they claim to have never doubted his suitability for the mission. A newscaster explains that the Robinson family displayed a "unique balance of scientific achievement, emotional stability, and pioneer resourcefulness." In an unaired pilot, "No Place to Hide," the narration goes further, designating the expertise each family member possessed. Judy, one of Will's two sisters, is described as having "heroically postponed any hope of a career in the musical comedy field for the next two centuries"; Will graduated from the Campo Canyon School of Science at nine with "the highest average in the school's history." And Penny, his other sister, is defined in terms of her interest in zoology. The announcer reports that this is the "first time in history that anyone other than an adult male has passed the international space administration's grueling physical and emotional screening for intergalactic flight."

So terrifying in "It's a Good Life" and "Bang, You're Dead," Bill Mumy plays Will as a child of great maturity, intellect, and courage, and yet also well-adjusted and good-natured. The early episodes show Will making repairs to the complex technology that supports their space colony, consulting with the adult men on scientific matters, and gathering soil and rock samples. In her book *Innocent Experiments*, Rebecca Onion evokes the figure of the boy scientist: "It was the boy in the basement with the chemistry set who was hailed as the closest thing the family had to a connection to the world of science and industry. In his individual fumbling, adults saw the grand possibilities of the future."[4] Will represented the fulfillment of that promise, no longer playing with test tubes in his basement, now experimenting on an alien world.

In the early episodes the adults are dominant, but as the series progresses, *Lost in Space* increasingly centers on Will and his companions, Dr. Zachary Smith (Jonathan Harris) and their talkative Robot. Its child-centered narratives make *Lost in Space* a bad object among science fiction fans, especially when compared with the more adult-focused adventures *Star Trek*, *Twilight Zone,* and *Outer Limits*. For decades fans struggled against the stigma that science fiction was "kid stuff," insisting that the genre could command adult interest and deserved literary respect. An episode of PBS's *Pioneers of American Television* contrasts *Star Trek* and *Lost in Space*: "For his new television series Gene Roddenberry aimed to move the science fiction genre in an entirely new direction. He didn't want monsters or giant grasshoppers. Instead Roddenberry was developing a show which explored ideas and values. . . . The polar opposite of Gene Roddenberry, Irwin Allen, wasn't interested in political issues or character development. Instead, his signature was action and excitement." Nichelle Nichols insists that Roddenberry "wanted to write about the human condition." Angela Cartwright (Penny) grumbles about Allen's series, "It is hard to keep a straight face when you are looking at a piece of celery that is talking to you." Marta Kristen (Judy) expands, "I think he had a vision of the show being colorful, being kind of eccentric, having these monsters, breaking new ground, having lots and lots of rocks and meteors and falling and laser guns and that was his vision—more like a comic book." *Lost in Space* is often dismissed as "juvenile." I want to suggest here that *Lost in Space* was not just a show *for* children but also often a show *about* childhood.[5] In particular, it was a story about a family trying to maintain normality under extraordinary circumstances, pushing the culture's ideas about family life to their breaking point, surfacing ambivalences in a period of dramatic social transformations. *Star Trek* sometimes—but rarely—told stories dealing with children's lives ("Miri") but always from the perspective of its adult protagonists, while Will was allowed to have his own adventures. Such episodes explore what it felt like to be a boy in a world without peers or playmates. They offer us glimpses into late permissive-era ideas about democratic family life and, in particular, the contradictions in how the culture saw masculinity and femininity at a moment when traditional gender norms were questioned by feminist writers. Many in the post-Sputnik era saw science fiction as a means of getting boys invested in scientific careers, offering a mix of intellectual problem-solving and outdoor adventures, but science fiction was more than that—a window on contemporary society, asking questions rarely addressed elsewhere.

## Boys and Scientific Education

In the late 1950s, Margaret Mead and Rhoda Métraux were engaged in a long-term research project to understand how American youth perceived scientists. Writing in 1959, Mead worried about the gap between the American and Soviet educational systems: "While we have been rearing happy, well-adjusted, unafraid children, we have lagged behind in creating conditions out of which come first-rate achievement in the sciences, in the arts, in politics. Children who are always active and occupied, who have lots of friends and get on well with the group, become people who work well in big organizations and apply knowledge that is already known. Rarely do they contribute original thinking or unique achievement."[6] Métraux is often described as Mead's editor, secretary, sometimes ghostwriter, housemate, and perhaps lover, but she was also an accomplished anthropologist, having studied voodoo in Haiti and done fieldwork in Latin America and Papua New Guinea. Mead, Métraux, and their students gathered toy catalogs and monitored science fiction television programs. They recruited teachers to ask their students to write short essays about their perceptions of scientists, and later, following the launch of Sputnik, they used these same connections to gather children's pictures and writings about space travel, forming a composite picture of how this emerging generation thought about science (figure 11.1).

Reporting their initial findings, Métraux noted:

> Where girls are unwilling to have anything to do with scientists who work in laboratories because, spending all their time there ("day and night, eating and sleeping science,") they neglect their home life, boys strenuously object to laboratory work because they cannot bear the idea of sitting down in one place all day, doing the same thing over and over ... ("pouring things from one test tube into another").... For girls, the laboratory is already too remote and far removed from home; for boys it is the antithesis of the action and distance they dream about, as the scientist in the laboratory—too tall or too small, with too little or too much hair, wearing glasses, stoop-shouldered, hollow-chested, fatigued—is the antithesis of the masculinity toward which they are growing.[7]

Figure 11.1. Rhoda Métraux read children's art as depicting male scientists trapped in their labs and longing for more outdoor adventure. (From the Métraux collection at the Library of Congress.)

For decades, Onion notes, girls had been represented as "spectators" of male scientific accomplishments, an assumption that also shaped Mead and Métraux's research. The women asked boys to respond to the question, "If I were going to be a scientist, I should like to be the kind of scientist who . . ." Girls, on the other hand, had the option of answering the question, "If I were going to marry a scientist, I would like to marry the kind of scientist who . . ." At least one boy crossed off "for girls" and described the kind of scientist he wanted to marry: "I would like my scientist wife to have lots of knowledge but not show it around other people so that it would embarrass me as I probably wouldn't know as much about certain things as she would." Many girls inserted themselves into fantasies of future scientific exploration through imagined roles as nurses, lab assistants, or other helpmates. "If possible I would like to work alongside of him," one girl wrote. Another wrote, "I am very much interested in this field (Archeology) and I could be a help to my husband." Not quite full participants, not merely spectators, these girls imagined how they could reconcile intellectual curiosity and their future roles as wives and mothers "if possible."

Speaking at the Northwestern Science Seminar for Public Information Officers in 1962, Métraux resorted to blistering sarcasm about the consequences of feminine disinterest in science: "We throw out at the very beginning about half the people who might do something, be something. . . . We cut out a lot of boys who are curious about physics, or math or space or chemistry and so on. Why? Because their girls, who have a dim view of science, also have a dim view of most forms of science as occupations for possible husbands."[8] Métraux hoped to generate role models for the next generation that linked an openness to new experiences with the courage to take calculated risks, but her research discovered the exact opposite, a sense that scientific work was dull, plodding, and routine. In another talk, she linked these perceptions to the regimentation of formal education: "Children, of course, get some ideas about scientists, just sitting in school, immovable, while their teacher performs experiments . . . and they are dreaming how nice it would be to go outdoors and move around. Pictures of scientists and science laboratories are full of barred windows that you can't see out of. . . . Space, of course, can be different. It can be outdoors; it can be exciting."[9]

Sputnik's launch created new "excitement" about science-oriented careers. Reviewing children's representations of Sputnik, Métraux and her team found striking gender differences in how the satellite was represented:

> Looking at a characteristic boy's drawing, the satellite appears to rush through space. If it is rising above the emergent earth, "rise" lines may be shown; if it has an orbiting rocket, this has an upward tilt; its fiery tail curves or streaks out. . . . In contrast, girls' pictures tend toward ornamentation (rather than functional machinery, as in some boys' pictures) and balanced formality of design. . . . So where boys appear to be moving out into space, in the more complex pictures, girls turn all of space into a bright but motionless still.[10]

Those who studied toy catalogs discovered that adults were having difficulty keeping up with these shifts in how young boys perceived space science. Most scientific toys were designed to be used in prescriptive ways—devices for which children followed instructions and the mechanical device unfolded with little to no control other than winding it up: "The mechanical space toys, precisely because they are mechanical and highly realistic, can be used in only a few stereotypical ways. They are not 'let's pretend' toys. A cowboy gun and holster can be used in many different kinds of plots. A rocket launcher can only launch rockets."[11] Researchers noted the absence of toys (space suits or space dolls) that allowed children to imagine themselves as part of a space mission (at least in the 1958 Sears catalog): "There seems to be a reluctance to encourage children to use their imaginations freely in space play."[12] Adults regarded the competition with the Soviets as a knowledge gap and thus responded by increasing educational content. On the other hand, science fiction writers (and the children they addressed) understood the problem as one of imagination: if they could dream it, scientists and engineers could build it.

Métraux and her team found that students writing about Sputnik often described the real mission as "science fiction come to life." Adults were just now entering space in reality that these children had long explored through "space cadet" stories. "Boys have fantasies about space," she wrote. These fantasies might take an array of different shapes, "from an interest in learning about atoms and nuclear physics to an interest in working on rockets and missiles, from a wish to become a test pilot or to help build space ships to a fantasy of being 'the first one to go to the moon,' from talking about astronomy to wondering about the possibilities of life on other planets." And interest in space sometimes shaded into curiosity about bombs as well as rockets or, alternatively, into a wish to work on "peaceful uses of the atom" instead of "for the destruction of mankind."[13]

These fantasies had many origins: some young boys experimented with blasting off rockets in their backyards or participated in science clubs with names such as "The Curiosity Club," "Explorers Society," and the "Riley High Mad Scientists" that linked science with adventure and exploration.[14] Schools launched science-fair competitions where young people—again, especially boys—demonstrated scientific mastery. Westinghouse generated media coverage when it sponsored a national competition to identify the best "future scientists.".

But above all, these fantasies emerged from science fiction. The most passionate lovers of space fantasy engaged with fandom, which had first taken shape in the late 1930s around Hugo Gernsback's pulp science fiction magazines. Librarians, many of them fans, were encouraging young boys to read science fiction and publishers were releasing science fiction books written specifically for the juvenile market by authors such as Robert Heinlein, Ray Bradbury, Isaac Asimov, and Ursula K. Le Guin. Asimov told the American Institute of Biological Sciences that science fiction was an "entire branch of popular literature which is given over to the proposition that brains are respectable." He continued, "Scientific research is presented. . . . as an exciting and thrilling process; its usual ends as both good in themselves and good for mankind; its heroes as intelligent people to be admired and respected."[15] Heinlein argued: "The romance of space flight will grip the imagination of the rising generation of boys in the same fashion as did air flight for the generation that just passed."[16] And this fascination spread to television: stripped of scientific speculation, these shows offered thrilling serialized adventures where scientists were portrayed as men of action fearlessly confronting alien threats. As Cynthia J. Miller and A. Bowdoin Van Riper recount, "To be a rocketman's fan was to be part of something much bigger—a Cold War identity that united knowledge and imagination, discipline and integrity, nation and individual—all wrapped in fantastic science and the promise of a universe waiting to be explored."[17] *Tom Corbett, Space Cadet*, one of the most popular of these series, was based on Heinlein's *Rocket Ship Galileo* and was developed in consultation with Willy Ley, one of America's most influential space advocates.[18]

Such programs offered young viewers affiliation, interactivity, and participation in something larger than themselves, tapping early television's liveness and immediacy.[19] Experts, such as Frank Forrester of the Hayden Planetarium, described the value of stimulating children's curiosity about space, suggesting that reading and watching science fiction be accompanied with trips to local science museums and planetariums. Bell Telephone sponsored science documentaries, such as *Our Mr. Sun* (1956), which was directed by Frank Capra, aired on broadcast television, and used in the nation's schools. Walt Disney also produced several space-themed documentaries, working with animator Ward Kimball and space experts Willy Ley and Wehrner von Braun, and including accurate renderings of current proposals for manned space flight. These documentaries, aired during the "Tomorrowland" segments of his *Disneyland* series, were so popular that the studio released them theatrically.[20]

Starting with his 1953 documentary film *The Sea Around Us*, based on the writings of Rachel Carson, Irwin Allen's began his career as a producer of science-themed documentaries, though his works, such as *The Animal World* (1956), were more terrestrial than the movie *Our Mr. Sun* or the "Man in Space" episode of *Disneyland*. Allen's showmanship pulled him toward more fantastical adventures, such as *The Lost World* (1960), *Five Weeks in a Balloon* (1962), and *Voyage to the Bottom of the Sea* (1961). *Lost in Space* was the only Irwin Allen series with a strong focus on a child protagonist. His other television series, *Voyage*, *Time Tunnel*, and *Land of the Giants*, all focused on adult adventures. *Lost in Space* was not initially centered on the boy scientist, and its stellar cast of adult actors, including Guy Williams (the star of Walt Disney's *Zorro*), Mark Goddard (*Johnny Ringo*), and June Lockhart (*Lassie*), were each promised more central roles. Allen saw *Lost in Space* as building on the success of Disney's *Swiss Family Robinson*, realizing that the source material was in the public domain. The idea was seemingly in the air since he would later encounter legal battles with Dell Comics, which had released a *Space Family Robinson* comic book series. CBS had a strong reputation for family-oriented programming, so Allen felt a constant pressure to ensure that *Lost in Space*'s action and suspense elements were child-friendly. The children, literally and figuratively, took a back seat in the original pilot, which included intense action scenes. What was then called the Gemini 12 (later renamed the Jupiter 2) was launched into space, blown off course by a meteor shower, and then landed on an unknown planet; they then battled a cyclops, made a trip by water and through a frozen wasteland on their rover, discovered an underground city, and finally found themselves in a lush tropical landscape, all within an hour's time. There are hints of a budding romance between Judy Robinson, the oldest daughter, and second in command Don West, but few suggestions of how central Will would become. CBS asked that Allen remake the pilot, relying heavily on the original footage to save money but remixed to incorporate Dr. Zachary Smith (a saboteur and unwilling stowaway) and Robot (originally Smith's sinister henchman but later reprogrammed by Will) as two new characters who would introduce conflict. And as the producer observed the chemistry among Will, Smith, and Robot, they assumed progressively larger roles, with the boy scientist motivating many stories. The pulpy and fantasy elements also expanded and with the introduction of color in the second season, *Lost in Space* developed a pop aesthetic, dressing the cast in Easter Egg–colored uniforms alongside aliens with green, red, silver, or orange skins. *Lost in Space*'s genre commitments fluctuated, sometimes doing speculative fiction, sometimes pure fantasy. The constant was the focus on the family.

## Meet the Robinsons

Researchers closely studied the finalists in the Westinghouse science competition to identify shared traits. Among the finalists in 1959, 57.5 percent of them had scientists elsewhere in the family. Another researcher reported that their families were "stable, cultured, educated; enjoyed economic advantages, [had] leisure time; ... were often 'democratic' and 'permissive.'"[21] All of these are attributes we might ascribe to the Robinsons. Will is the youngest of three children. As the only boy, he often joins the adult males on adventures while his two sisters remain closer to home, helping their mother to raise and harvest vegetables, prepare food, and do the laundry (using a massive washing machine that somehow made the exacting weight requirements for space flight). NASA at that point had considered and rejected the idea of female astronauts, so their inclusion in the program, however marginalized, represented a step beyond reality.

In "The Sky Is Falling," the Robinsons encounter an alien family—Taurons—who have come to scout the planet for future colonization. At first, the adults are fearful and uncertain about their Tauron counterparts. John warns his son, "Will, their emotions could be the direct opposite of our own. A laugh could be deep hatred while a frown could be the friendliest of expressions." When Will goes missing, John expresses his uncertainty about how to respond: "If we were on Earth, I would know exactly how to handle the situation. But this alien world, with alien people, and alien morality—it'd be just too easy to make mistakes. And I wouldn't want to do anything we'd all be sorry for later." Will, on the other hand, walks right up to the alien boy and announces, "Hello there. I'm William Robinson from planet Earth. I'm a friend. Can't you talk? Is there anything you want me to do for you?" The initially skittish alien boy soon brings out his ball and the two play together. Will reports to his family later, "I don't think we have anything to worry about. The boy was really friendly. I could tell we liked each other." The alien family is just like the Robinsons in almost every way, but especially in the worry the mothers and fathers exhibit regarding the missing boys. Maureen notes the shared maternal instincts, while John observes the male's desire to protect his family. The Robinsons don't have much to fear, but the aliens confront near-lethal consequences when Will sneezes on the Tauron boy and infects him with a cold. Will nurses the boy and returns him to his parents. Will's emotional intelligence allows him to instantly understand the aliens' perspectives, and viewers are left with the two family units, identical in composition, coexisting in not simply global but universal brotherhood.

Nina C. Leibman regards domestic comedies and family melodramas, such as *Leave It to Beaver*, *Father Knows Best*, *The Donna Reed Show*, and *Dennis the Menace*, as "fairly bursting with advice and directives on how the new American family was to see itself."[22] She might also be describing John Robinson: television dads are "loving and stoic, deeply involved with [their] children's lives, attentive to their needs, and physically available. The narrative issue here is for fathers to manipulate their children into making upstanding choices on the basis of a set of moral precepts founded on capitalism, consumerism, and quasi-religious notions of good and bad."[23] Though the problems Will faces are often different from those Beaver Cleaver encounters, there are many moments where John pulls his son aside and gives him what Leibman calls "living room lectures" about how the world works. In "There Were Monsters on Earth," after Will has just saved the day by killing a giant cyclops with a laser gun, John tells his son: "So you thought you would come and save us. And you *did* save us. Now I want you to promise something on your word of honor. When I tell you to stay and protect the family, don't you ever leave your post again, understand? If we are going to survive in this place, we must follow orders. And that goes for all of us. There may be other giants around."

In true permissive fashion, John confronts a disobedient boy in a way that acknowledges his accomplishments but also asserts the importance of listening to what his parents tell him. Here, we see the central negotiations that must occur within the Robinson family, given Will's extraordinary knowledge and abilities. Consider the father–son conversation in "The Wreck of the Robot," where aliens have dismantled the beloved Robot. "The Robot isn't just a machine to me, Dad," Will shares with his father. "We've special feelings for each other—like we were brothers." John offers Will some insight into the nature of death: "I understand what you're trying to say, Will. And when the aliens send Robot back, we'll do our best to reassemble him. But, if we don't, you're going to have to adjust to the loss. Nothing is permanent, son. . . . Not man or machine."

Lynn Spigel argues that the fantastic sitcoms of the 1960s, such as *The Munsters*, *The Addams Family*, or *I Dream of Jeannie*, defamiliarize the contemporary American family, offering alternative ways of framing conflicts, especially those concerning race and integration, that were difficult to depict within familiar formulas.[24] *Lost in Space* often adopts broadly comic tones, casting over-the-top performers such as Hans Conried and Wally Cox while the plots resemble those of *Gilligan's Island*: some stranger visits the Robinsons with the potential to satisfy Smith's oft-stated desire to return to Earth, but when they depart, the family is still stranded in this barren world. And the episodes, as in the case of "The Sky Is Falling," sometimes model how white America might deal with racial others. For example, in "The Girl from the Green Dimension," an alien turns Will's skin Green, asserting that Green is beautiful. But, unlike in *The Boy with Green Hair*, the family embraces Will regardless of his color. John confidently tells Will that Penny and Judy will not laugh at him, while Maureen offers, "Will, dear—don't you think that the sooner they see you, the sooner they'll get accustomed to you? Besides, you haven't really changed, you know." Nevertheless, his mother scrubs him aggressively. The Robot comforts him: "Anyone could be Green. Not as desirable or exclusive as a sturdy, silver-gray, but acceptable." While the show objects to the alien's assumption that Green is the ideal, *Lost in Space* assumes that color is skin-deep.

In "The Hungry Sea," Don asks his girlfriend, "Can't you ever conceive of your father being wrong?" and the answer is a resolute no. John

Robinson bears unquestioned moral authority, a man of firm convictions as well as a world-class scientist who knows the best way to cope with alien conditions. As with his earthly counterpart, father knows best. John explains why he was so demanding: "It's just that we do not have time for philosophical discussions. We've got to get that shelter built before that sun comes blazing over." In *Children: The Challenge*, Rudolf Dreikurs explains, "When each member of the family insists on doing as he pleases . . . the result is constant tension. . . . An atmosphere of constant conflict, stress, and strains produces tension, anger, nervousness, and irritability."[25] On television, the result is good drama, and the producers acknowledge that they deployed Smith as a constant irritant, disrupting the harmony that might otherwise exist among the Robinsons. Sometimes, the young lack a full picture: "Well-defined restrictions give a sense of security and a certainty of function within the social structure. . . . To help our children, then, we must turn . . . to a new order based on the principles of freedom and responsibility. Our children can no longer be forced into compliance; they must be stimulated and encouraged into voluntarily taking their part in the maintenance of order."[26]

For Dreikurs, "one of the most important tools for dealing with troublesome problems in a democratic fashion" is the family council, a weekly meeting where all family members sit together and make collectively agreed decisions.[27] The set designers built a large conference table into the Jupiter 2 for frequent family meetings. All family members, including Don West as prospective son-in-law, sit around the table, with the father at its head. The estranged Smith often sits apart, eyeing the proceedings with smug skepticism, determined to pursue his own interests even if they mean betraying this loving family. Yet, the series dramatizes the differences between a fully democratic structure and a more authoritative one: the Robinson family also constitutes a semimilitary crew with its own chain of command. When push comes to shove, everyone is expected to follow John's orders. Dad proclaims in "There Were Giants in the Earth": "We only know that we must depend on ourselves for survival. Starting tomorrow, we are going to turn this immediate area into a self-sufficient community. And that means everyone is going to have his job to do." While the father may grumble and lecture, Will is never punished for his actions, since the outcomes are almost always helpful to the larger mission. John offers gentle guidance, nudging the boy in line.

## Friends and Father Figures

In "Follow the Leader," John shares his regrets for bringing the boy on this mission: "Instead of being lost out here in space, you should be leading the life of a normal boy, playing with youngsters your own age, going to ball games, doing all of the things a boy needs to do before growing up." The original script gave Will an older brother; Don absorbed many of that character's roles, except he does not play with the boy. Will spends time with Dr. Smith, assisting his various quests, schemes, and hobbies.

Actor Jonathan Harris describes his perceptions of his character: "I drew Dr. Smith based on every kid I'd ever known.... I did a lot of stuff as Smith that was absolutely childlike and childish, like nobody would notice how bad I am—kids are that way. Or I would cover it up or blame somebody else as all kids do."[28] Smith lacks adult restraint over his emotions and desires. While Will braves his way through situations beyond his years, Smith cringes and cowers. Smith shirks all responsibilities, grumbling constantly when asked to do his fair share of the chores. Will functions as the older brother to a childish adult. Will excuses Smith's behavior in "The Prisoners in Space" when he says, "I knew he was wrong. But that's Dr. Smith. You can't expect him to act like anyone else." However frustrated they are, the adults act bemused as they might be with the antics of a child.

Robot sometimes performs adult responsibilities such as overseeing Will and Penny's schooling, but Will often treats him as a playmate. Robot jokes about Smith's faults and openly expresses pleasure in Will's company. *The Invisible Boy* (1957) featured the friendship between a robot and Timmie, the middle-school-age son of an American scientist, offering prototypes for some of the core relationships in *Lost in Space*. Robot was designed by the same production team that had designed Robbie the Robot, first used in *Forbidden Planet* but featured again in *The Invisible Boy*. In *Invisible Boy*, Timmie adjusts the robot's programming so that he no longer protects the boy from potential harm. To Timmie's mother's horror, the robot builds a giant kite enabling Timmie to fly above his suburban home. As the story progresses, the robot is torn between his affection for the boy and his commitment to his fellow robots who seize control of the planet. He ultimately betrays his own kind to protect those he loves. Robot in *Lost in Space* is similarly converted by the boy's affections (and reprogramming) into a playmate.

Will's desire to connect with other men leads him to forge relationships with the sultans and cowboys, gamblers and above all, aliens who pass through their world. And often, his naive trust touches these characters, reforming them at least temporarily. Consider the case of Alonso P. Tucker in "The Sky Pirate" and "Treasure of the Lost Planet," a character designed to parody Robert Newton's Long John Silver in Walt Disney's *Treasure Island*. Actor Albert Salmi, best known as Fess Parker's sidekick on *Daniel Boone*, portrays the character as a man-child who has so much fun playing at being a buccaneer that he cannot abandon the pirate's life, but who sees a different potential through Will's eyes. He has Will swear a pirate's oath in blood, much like a boys club initiation. "Do pirates have to wash behind their ears and take lessons and mind their older sisters?" Will asks. When Will tells him that it is "wrong" to be a pirate, Tucker reassures him that he is the "honest" pirate. Tucker risks his own life to protect Will, something Dr. Smith would never have done.

What happens when a boy's innocence is betrayed is explored in "The Questing Beast." For more than forty years, an aging knight, Sir Sagramonte (Hans Conried, Dr. Terwilliker in *The 5,000 Fingers of Dr. T*), has pursued Gundemar the dragon (June Foray, best known as a voice actor on *Rocky and Bullwinkle*) across the universe. Will is drawn to the knight's larger-than-life saga, agreeing to be a squire in return for his mentorship: "I shall teach you knightly manners, the use of arms, the language of courtesy, the art of equitation, and I shall only beat you when it is required to sharpen your wits." Penny, meanwhile, befriends the dragon who is fond of the knight, using her magic to allow him to pursue but never best her. As the story progresses, Will discovers that Sagramonte is a coward. And as his knight-in-shining-armor fantasy collapses, Will excuses Smith who was caught in a deception: "You were just trying to make yourself out to be a big hero. . . . Don't people do it all the time? Brag and elaborate and build themselves up?" Smith asks whether his father or Major West might be an exception and Will disappointedly says, "How do I know they are so special? Maybe there's a time when you have to get rid of illusions the way you outgrow fairy tales." Smith is crushed: "Oh for the first time in my miserable life I regret every lie I've ever told." Ultimately, Smith conspires with the knight to restore the boy's faith. Harris's performance suggests how Smith's disillusionment shapes his actions. Such moments represent *Lost in Space* at its best, perhaps not commenting on adult issues, but despite the papier mâché rocks, offering emotional truths.

## Gender in Crisis: Benjamin Spock vs. Betty Friedan

Despite the infinite possibilities, only occasionally does *Lost in Space* suggest that gender roles might operate differently in alien cultures. In "The Colonists," the Jupiter 2 crew encounters a scout ship full of Amazon warriors seeking a new base. In this thinly veiled response to "women's lib," the warrior women proclaim, "The women of my nation have had many sons. They are of little worth to us. What we need is your male animal strength. That is all." And they convert Penny to their cause. The men are quick to dismiss women with Will grumbling, "I don't see why you have to be a female warrior when there's so many men around." Smith, always kowtowing to authority, poses as a sensitive artist: "What an agreeable man you are!" When she is outwitted by the men, the female commander fears that she will be "sentenced to a lifetime of degrading drudgery—cooking, cleaning, laundry, [taking care of] squalling, sniveling children." The characters argue that this hardline ideology of female empowerment and male subservience constitutes a threat to the earthly social order. Maureen suggests, "It isn't a defeat to acknowledge that men are just as good as women. Why, the equality of the sexes has advantages you may have overlooked."

Betty Friedan's *The Feminine Mystique* (1963)—a founding text for second-wave feminism—had launched a full-frontal attack on advice literature—the "theorists of femininity"—as a force that robs women of meaningful choices.[29] Writing in a September 1960 issue of *Good Housekeeping*, alongside articles asking, "What in the World Will He Get Into Next?" or promising advice on "discipline for Danny," Friedan proclaims, "Women Are People Too!" She summarizes her core argument:

> They tell us—the psychologists and psychoanalysts and sociologists who keep tracing the neuroses of children back to mother—that all of our problems and dissatisfactions and frustrations—and the problems of

our husbands and children—were caused by education and emancipation, the striving for independence and equality with men, which made American women unfeminine.... For a woman to have such aspirations, interests, goals of her own, the experts keep telling us, impairs not only her ability to love her husband and children but her ability to achieve her own sexual fulfillment.[30]

She cites the advice given by magazines like *Good Housekeeping* (though not by name) for drowning women's own voices beneath suggestions about "how to breast feed our children and handle toilet-training, sibling rivalry, adolescent rebellion . . . how to keep our husbands from dying young and our sons from growing into delinquents." One generation of women had seen improving the rights of children as fundamental to improving the rights of women. But Friedan was asking for something more and to attain that, women needed freedom from domestic obligations, less focus on motherhood and more attention to other identities.

Unlike the sense of adventure the series offered boys who could do science and still explore the great outdoors, *Lost in Space* offers a painfully limited range of activities for its female characters, taking as given the domestic containment of women even in this unlikely setting. Dr. Maureen Robinson is "a distinguished biochemist of the New Mexico College of Space Medicine," but she spends most of her time cooking soup. This shift in status might have been suggested by the image of John kissing his wife as the announcer describes her intellectual credentials. Even here, she is a wife first and scientist second, much as the girls in Métraux's study saw their future as helpmates for their scientist husbands. Judy's function is to be Don's love interest, to help her mother manage their spaceship home, and to scold her younger sibling. The one episode dedicated to her, "Space Beauty," has her entered, despite her resistance, in an intergalactic beauty pageant. When the women meet a female android in "The Android Machine," their first impulse is to give her a makeover. She protests, "I have been created to be useful. It is not my function to look nice." And yet, despite such programming, the android is pleased with her new appearance and more closely bonded to the women. When the men leave the women in charge, circumstances always force the men to rescue them.

Spock wrote in raw anger in *Problems of Parents* (1962) defending his own positions against such critiques: "The women called feminists, who are resentful of men's advantages, grant that there are certain anatomical differences, but they believe firmly that the supposed differences in temperament and capability are bogus. They think that men have staked out a claim to certain characteristics and privileges by brute strength and bluff and have simply got away with it."[31] This caricature of what second-wave feminists believed suggests just how threatening they were to Spock as they questioned a logic that granted children much greater respect than ever before but often at a cost to women. Spock's writing assumes that women place their roles as mothers above any other ambitions, much as Maureen's doctorate is, well, lost in space. Can we imagine that Maureen experienced what Friedan called "the problem that has no name"?[32] Did she wake up in the middle of the night wondering if there should be more to her life than childcare, or does she remain eternally smiling, watching her son get into and out of trouble, teaching her daughters how to please their future husbands?

Spock became increasingly brittle and paternalistic in response to feminism, before working through and ultimately reversing his own position about how gender is reproduced. He persisted in his belief that

> a human being is a creature who *must* have a father and mother, in his feelings, and will create them if necessary. Of course, a real father who's a good one will be a lot more satisfactory than an image, on many scores. But if there isn't a real one, the mother's job is not to try to be one, and not necessarily to try to find one, but to maintain a wholesome environment for her child so that he can create one in his imagination.[33]

Will would have experienced the years that Spock felt were most essential for the formation of male character before he ever left Earth:

> It's between two and three years that a boy begins to realize more consciously that it's his destiny to become a man. From then until six he really sets to work to pattern himself after his father particularly, after older brothers if he has any, after other friendly males. He watches to see what occupations they are interested in, how they go about them, what

they think is right and wrong in behavior, what their attitudes are to each other and to women, how they talk, what mannerisms they use, what feelings they have, which ones they express freely and which they try to conceal, what they are scared of. He plays all day at manly occupations, pushing toy cars, building structures, riding a horse, shooting pistols, driving a car or a plane, acting the father when he plays house.[34]

The boy might test different models for masculinity as embodied by men other than his father or through his imagination—for example, characters in a television program.

Will is already treated as one of the men, going out with his dad, Don, and sometimes Smith on critical missions, wielding a weapon when needed. Yet, more than once, episodes show Will testing his masculinity, often under circumstances closely related to violence. For example, in "The Challenge," Quanto (played with swagger by Kurt Russell) arrives without warning, threatening Will with a spear: "I am twelve years old. I am very brave and strong. Would you like to fight to see who is a better man?" When the good-natured Will says he would rather be friends, Quanto says bluntly, "You are a coward." Angered by these fighting words, Will soon has his fists raised. Quanto wants nothing to do with "weak and worthless girls." He has been sent to prove his manhood by confronting a beast in his lair. Throughout, the dialogue returns to the idea that masculinity needs to be proven, often defined in opposition to femininity. Will is repeatedly called "unmanly," accused of "doing the work of women" and otherwise failing to meet the expectations of mature masculinity: "You should build up your strength, test your courage." When Will accepts the challenge, John has to explain to Maureen: "I don't care how primitive or civilized a man is, he welcomes a challenge. It's part of his nature to test his intelligence and skill as well as his strength. And without these things we'd be living in caves, eating out of stone bowls." Will explains, "It's like I am representing every boy from Earth against every boy from another planet." In the end, not only does Will prove his courage but the usually calm and reasonable John is pitted in a sword fight against the alien ruler, allowing the actor best known for playing Zorro a chance to show his swashbuckling chops.

Spock offered advice to parents about how to deal with a similar situation:

> Well-adjusted children get into occasional mild fights from the time they begin playing with others.... This is one of the ways they learn to respect each other's rights and to stand up for their own.... I would not interfere in ordinary brief scraps as long as the children were fairly evenly matched in spirit, were doing each other no serious physical or emotional harm, and were generally friendly characters. If I had to interfere, I'd do it casually, rather than with shaming.[35]

Spock does not see fighting as a "test" of manhood, but he does normalize such disputes as an inevitable consequence of growing into a man and he links fighting with being prepared to stand up for your rights, an ideal of the democratic childhood tradition. The need to hold your ground, the need to prove your manhood through physical action are a shared masculine code across the universe.

Margaret Mead stressed in 1959 that fathers, whom she jokingly calls "the Children's Mother's Husband," were embracing more child-rearing responsibilities and noted that women were more apt to work outside the home. Like Spock, Mead was struggling: "These are upsetting times when men feel less like husbands because their wives work outside the home, and women feel less like wives because their husbands do so much work inside the home. These are dangerous changes because we don't know what effects they will have on men's sense of themselves as men, as well as husbands."[36] Mead describes the father's role as bridging the family and "the outside world," encouraging his son to "move out of the home, into the world." And she ends with a distinction between masculinity and manhood:

> Masculinity is that part of a male's behavior which distinguishes him from a female—in his sex relations, in fighting and in sport.... But manhood is that part of a male's behavior which makes him a responsible human being, able to control his sexuality, bridle his aggression, protect and provide for his wife and children and make some positive contribution to the world. If taking care of children is seen as playing a woman's part, being a sucker, being dominated by women, it will be looked at one way. If it is seen as an extension of manhood, as an exercise of strength, imagination, and tenderness, it will be looked at the other way.[37]

Spock and Mead were adjusting to the challenges of "raising children in a difficult time," as the pediatrician titled one of his final books. They had come out of the Second World War determined to build a new model of American family life, grounded in democratic principles, based on permissive practices, yet there were also limits to how much change they (and others of their generation) could absorb, how prepared they were to reimagine the work of mothers and fathers.

*Lost in Space* as science fiction offered the possibility of representing radical alternatives given the alien contexts in which many of these stories are set, yet most often retreated to earthly models. Will Robinson embodies many of the values permissive parents hoped to foster in their boys: he is deeply curious about the world, even if that curiosity sometimes leads him to disobey his parents; he is a budding young inventor, engineer, and scientist; he has empathy that leads him to try to understand other perspectives, including those of alien species; he has a grounded sense of what is fair and is willing to stand up to powerful beings when an injustice has been committed; and he is all boy, embodying a natural "manhood." He is at once exceptional in his abilities and yet typical in his boyishness. Will exemplified the fantasies of the space-age boy, the hopes that science and adventure might be merged, the goal of escaping the confinement of the schoolroom and running free, whether conquering their own side of the mountain or wandering across India looking for their missing father or encountering alien visitors in remote corners of the universe. These were the shows baby boomers watched in their living rooms, stories they played in their backyards.

# Coda

In April 1972, *Redbook* organized a conversation between two longtime contributors, Margaret Mead and Benjamin Spock. Asked whether she would participate, Mead responded, "If we can do it about babies—yes—I'd like to try out some questions on Ben. But politics—No."[1] The exchange represents a rich time capsule allowing us to see two key architects of permissive culture discuss what they had achieved.

> DR. MEAD: I think we had the best parents we've ever had during the 1950s. Mothers had your *Baby and Child Care*, and it relaxed them.... That's one of your great contributions, Ben; you helped mothers relax. Once they were relaxed, they became confident. And that confidence was passed on to their children, who are the young mothers of today.... Incidentally there have been some remarks made about you lately as having been a champion of permissiveness. Of course, it isn't true. People who say that could never have read *Baby and Child Care*.
>
> DR. SPOCK: No, I never championed permissiveness. The ideal parent, to my mind, is one who has considerable control and who is quite firm and clear in telling the child what is expected of him. I've always believed that. A reasonable amount of parental control and guidance is not restrictive in any way to a child. I realize that this isn't stylish doctrine nowadays, especially among the young. When parents are overly conscientious and afraid of imposing on their children—a fairly common pattern among college-educated parents today—I think this leaves the children more in the lurch, especially during the period of youthful rebellion.... On the other hand, if the parents are hesitant, guilty, easily intimidated by their child, his rebelliousness may erupt like a volcano, making life hell for his parents and himself. In fact, if a child knows that he is behaving

unreasonably and getting away with murder, he instinctively goes from bad to worse in the unconscious hope of provoking his parents into cracking down.[2]

This exchange captures the back-and-forth nature of childcare trends: both Mead and Spock saw themselves as centrists, seeking initially to nudge postwar parents to new approaches, such as feeding on demand and being less strict in regulating children's bodies. Mead regarded adjustments in family structures as preconditions for other social change. The deeper they got into the 1960s, the more worried they became about an "'Everything goes" attitude. In "A New Understanding of Childhood," an unpublished manuscript, Mead reflected:

> Looking back, our descendants will regard as one of the great accomplishments of our age the discovery of the nature of childhood and our attempt to put this new knowledge to work in the upbringing of our children. . . . We have growing up around us—here and in many parts of the world—a whole generation whose lives have been deeply affected by our initial efforts to put into practice (as well as, for far too many children, our failure to put into practice) this new knowledge. We cannot know how it will all turn out, for nothing on so large a scale and with so many variations has been tried before. . . . In our first attempts to bring up at least part of a generation in the light of new insights and a growing understanding of how a human being becomes a person, our efforts have suffered from all the difficulties of transition—inconsistencies, reversals, misunderstandings and the discouragement of hopes set too high.[3]

*Where the Wild Things Were* has offered an account of the permissive imagination as shaped by a process of cultural negotiation around an emergent set of ideas about parenting. We have seen the Child Study movement popularize expert insights into child development and spread those ideas through parent education. During the war, Baruch, Wolf, and others articulated a vision of more democratic family life and sought to promote a more racially just culture for the postwar era. When Spock's book became a bestseller, "permissiveness" became the dominant paradigm informed by Freudian approaches to sexual development. By the end of this period, pushback emerged on multiple fronts, two of which I have already discussed—feminist backlash against the idea that women should be focused primarily on their children; and the idea that permissiveness represented white middle-class norms inappropriate for Black children. The third I will discuss more fully here: the efforts of cultural conservatives to blame "permissiveness" for the rise of the counterculture.

My generation was shaped by what Mead described as "inconsistencies, reversals, misunderstandings and the discouragement of hopes set too high." Our parents were trying to figure this out as they went along, cut off from their extended family through suburbanization and corporate transfer, applying advice from books and magazines, inconsistently, imperfectly, in various contexts. The permissive paradigm would have operated differently in the city or the countryside than in the suburbs, in the South than in the North, and would have fit oddly in Black households where stricter parenting styles remained the norm. This cultural transition moved forward in jolts and lurches, as once radical beliefs were normalized, even as parents sometimes had difficulty translating them into consistent practices. These same transitions were being modeled in children's fictions across a range of genres—from the whimsy of Dr. Seuss or the bad-boy comedy of *Dennis the Menace* to adventure stories such as *Jonny Quest*, *Flipper*, or *Lost in Space*. The deeper we get into the 1960s, the more likely it was that children's programs were coupled with explicit pedagogical models as in *Mister Rogers' Neighborhood*.

The permissive imagination is a configuration of ideas about parenting, child psychology, social change, and cultural negotiation. Permissiveness:

- Uses empathetic reflection to take stock of children's hidden motivations with adults assuming the role of the "Understanding Angel" who seeks clues about why children react the way they do.
- Values children's sensuality, pleasure, curiosity, and passion as motivating them to explore their environment.
- Defends the rights of children to find their own voices, articulate their own sense of justice, and participate in democratic processes within their families and schools.

- Offers expressive means, such as drawing pictures, playacting stories with dolls or their own bodies, singing songs, and so on as a means of working through intense, sometimes overwhelming emotions.
- Encourages parents to minimize orders or authoritative statements in favor of explanations and discussions and to provide resources so children can map their own course.

Above all, permissiveness is known for what it permits and accommodates, rather than what it disciplines, limits, regulates, or thwarts. These ideas broadly inform the advice parents heard and followed in the era from 1948 to 1968. No one figure embraced all these ideas. Spock, for example, is more permissive about children's sexuality than about discipline. Mead writes:

> Two things in particular changed all this drastically and brought into focus many attempts to think about childhood in another way—not as a stage or state but as a process based in human biology and shaped by the child's relationships to the world of people and things. One was our growing recognition that although there are extraordinarily different routes from childhood to adulthood, there are also regularities in children's growing—regularities of timing, for example, within wide individual limits, of when children begin to walk or begin to talk. . . . The other discovery grew out of the explorations carried out by the psychoanalyst Sigmund Freud with his patients in which they traced the paths of experience back to childhood—to long "forgotten" memories, fantasies, and conflicts. . . . So for the first time we are beginning to see and understand the relationship between the child's developing capacities and what he experiences from day to day and from month to month, responding to and initiating responses from the people around him.[4]

Mead sees two key strands to this new understanding—one through child development (pointing toward the work of the Gesell Institute) and the other through child psychology (especially through Spock's work popularizing Freud). Mead and her circle played vital roles in promoting these changes in how the postwar generation thought about children, their minds, their bodies, and their self-expression. They thought about children and the arts, the image of scientists, their exploration of geographic space, global brotherhood, and mass conformity. Mead as a public intellectual translated seminar-room discourse into more readerly spaces such as the pages of *Redbook*. Her pediatrician was right beside her, publishing his own insights on the choices confronting parents. Betty Friedan may have read these women's magazines as offering an impoverished diet for women, trapped at home and wanting to be anywhere else, but to look at these magazines now is to see a space crackling with ideas. To ask about the nature of the child is to pose core questions about what kind of world people want to inhabit.

This model would not work for us today; it is very much of its period. The approach assumed, for example, a mother fully dedicated to raising children and not working outside the home. The approach largely excluded (and was never fully embraced by) Black people. It is rife with contradictions and ambivalences born of the clash between democratic aspirations and antidemocratic impulses, especially regarding racism, nationalism, colonialism, sexism, and homophobia. But, that said, there is much we could learn from Spock, Mead, Baruch, Frank Ginott, Dreikurs, McFadden, and so many others. Despite several decades where the right has celebrated a "Ward and June Cleaver" lifestyle, the writers of this period mostly saw themselves as progressive, trying to change the structure and goals of the American family and pave the way for larger changes in the national culture. They wanted to raise children who would be more open to diversity, more willing to embrace democratic citizenship, better prepared to deal with a rapidly changing world, more capable of embracing global brotherhood, and more comfortable with their own bodies. They embraced the idea that children have rights. They saw play and learning as closely related. They sought to better understand children's emotional lives. And they sought to persuade rather than discipline children as they helped to shape the person they would become.

> DR. SPOCK: It's only recently that I've begun to question some of my own earlier assumptions, under prodding from the Women's Liberation Movement. They have said I'm a sexist, a chauvinist. In *Baby and Child Care*, I emphasized that little boys should be encouraged to be masculine and little girls to be feminine. Well, liberated women made me realize that ... whether a boy or girl will grow up with a sufficient

sense of maleness or femaleness and how different the sexes are obviously varies from society to society. So, I've promised to revise *Baby and Child Care*. I'll say that boys of themselves will identify predominantly with their fathers and girls with their mothers, especially after they get to be three years old or older. It isn't necessary for a father to keep saying, "now, watch me, boy and do as I do, because I'm male and you're male."

DR. MEAD (abruptly): Now, look here, Ben, I'm not going to put up with your reluctance to defend yourself against these attacks on you as a sexist. [Both laugh] After all, you were writing during a period when we defined maleness as not being female and people had a lot of superficial ideas about what makes a male or a female. Little boys were being brought up by mothers who spent their time trying to make them masculine, often in very silly ways. They'd say to their little boys, "Men don't cry" . . . and they'd put two guns on the hips of a little boy. And all you were saying, Ben, was "let each child *accept* his own sex." Well, we are still going to have to accept our own sex. That isn't any great conclusion, and to say that someone is sexist because he wanted children to be certain of their gender, their sex, is rubbish.

DR. SPOCK (Smiling): Well, I think I am a little guilty. For example, I was sexist in assuming that when a couple had a baby it would be the mother who would have to make the compromises with her career—cut down to a part-time job, for instance—in order to take care of the child. I agree with the feminists now. Why shouldn't the father equally have to consider whether he should compromise his career in order to help take care of the child?

DR. MEAD: But we didn't know in 1946, when the first edition of your book appeared, that fathers could take care of children to the same degree mothers had always done. . . . The fathers had been taught to believe that they weren't capable of caring for babies. Now we know that males do respond to tiny infants. . . . And we saw that fathers had tremendous capacity to care for young children.

Spock's memoir described his shock when, sometime in the late 1960s, he was publicly confronted by Gloria Steinem: "Dr. Spock, I hope you realize that you have been a major oppressor of women in the same category as Sigmund Freud." Spock describes the self-reflection that followed: "It hurt my feelings to be called an enemy of women, after so many women had called me a friend and helper. But it is indicative of my sexism that it took me three years of discussion with many patient women before I fully understood the nature of my sexism. . . . I am not saying that there's no trace left—my wife Mary still has some reservations."[5] In the *Redbook* exchange, Spock acknowledged past mistakes, including a new stress on the role of culture in defining gender roles, a growing recognition that his approach placed an unfair burden upon mothers, and some questioning of the values ascribed to masculinity. Mead, on the other hand, defended Spock's earlier views against what she saw as the more self-centered perspective of current mothers, insisting on understanding Spock's writing and her own as having emerged in response to dominant attitudes of their time. Spock agreed: "This is one of the problems for people who have lived as long as you and I. Nobody looks at the context in which we say things."

T. Berry Brazelton, who along with Spock, Erikson, and McFarland had helped to define Arsenal's research agenda, took the project of revising permissive parenting ideas in response to feminist critiques much further. One mother was cited on the back cover of Brazelton's *Toddlers and Parents* (1974): "Dr. Spock was always my Bible. With your book I now have an Old and New Testament." Brazelton factors diverse family configurations into his advice, more comfortably addressing the adjustments working mothers made:

> As we develop better caretaking situations, such as day-care centers, it would help concerned mothers and improve the planning at the centers if we knew when infants can best afford separation from a single caretaker. . . . I have noticed that if a mother leaves during or soon after the first grueling weeks, she leaves before she has begun to reap the rewards of a three- or four-month-old baby. This is such a peaceful, rewarding time that it might be seen as the reward for having lived through the big adjustment period of the first two months. . . . She has only the memory of ambivalent feeling to cement her to her baby in the stress periods which are bound to come.[6]

Here, it is not a question of whether women should work, but when they should return to their jobs. Brazelton noted that "Women's Liberation groups are working hard to free women of these incapacitating guilt feelings. I hope they will be successful." At the same time, he acknowledged that such conflicting feelings were natural and common among the generation of new mothers trying to raise their children according to feminist principles.

In an unpublished essay, "Changing Family Styles," from the early 1960s, Mead stressed that the extended family structure common to early twentieth-century America had allowed broader options for caring for children: "The future, if expressed in new designs for cities and housing clusters and new expectations of how young people will elect to live, should free people for choice—to marry or not to marry, to have children or not, and if they choose to have children, to take parenthood seriously."[7] Spock raises a similar argument during the *Redbook* conversation:

> The worst thing we can do as a society is to isolate the family. And we've done that. Young families are often far from relatives and grandparents, even far from neighbors, in the sense that they do not share in each other's lives. Many young people think the only alternatives are either to live in larger groups in communes or to put the young children into daycare centers so that the mothers and the children can escape from the tensions of the nuclear family. But I think we should first try to bring families closer together in the community—through richer social relations, recreation and neighborly work projects.[8]

Mead reiterated her long advocacy for day care but also states dismissively, "Who's going to run the day-care centers—these ambitious young women who don't want to look after their own children? People who want children only in order to turn them over to a day-care center had better not have them in the first place." Spock had further reflections about his earlier misguided thinking about gender.

> DR. SPOCK: I'm convinced that we make our children anxious and less effective when we scold them for not being all boy or all girl. For example, when I was a boy I was ashamed of seeming at times to be a sissy. So I tried to make my older son ashamed of being a sissy too. I thought I was encouraging him to be a good male. But if

I achieved anything, it was to make him less sure of himself and of his acceptance by me. Well, I'll continue to write for parents that as children grow older they tend to identify more with the parent of the same sex, and that is good. But I'll also remind parents that children identify to a lesser degree with the parent of the opposite sex too. How a man or a woman gets along in marriage will depend in part on how well he or she identified with the parent of the opposite sex during childhood. I want to make parents see that some boys will want to be gentle and can make a better adjustment in life by being allowed to be gentle. They should not be coerced or shamed, just as girls should not be shamed for wanting to be a baseball player or to drive a tractor. Then you'll end up with a more flexible array of jobs for both men and women.[9]

For all their progressive impulses, Spock and Mead struggled with inherited constructions of gender we would question today. They may be debating the relative balance of nature and nurture and how much elasticity there is across cultures. Yet they do not ever question the heterosexual imperative and are not prepared to think about gender in nonbinary terms. In another passage cut from the finished interview, Mead ranted, "If you make them [the genders] genuinely parallel so that children know who they are and aren't forever denying it, pretending they're the other sex, or frightened that they're the other sex, or dreadfully competitive with the other sex. . . . We mustn't let the contemporary emphasis jettison all that we've learned about the importance of people being clear about who they are." Spock's discussion of steering his son away from choices he regarded as "sissy" shows similar assumptions about the values of working within shared gender and sexual norms.

> DR. MEAD: I'm very anxious to get your response to the relationship between physical affection and breast-feeding. We had a slight controversy about this in the 1950s when breast-feeding was considered to be more beneficial to the child than the bottle. But we felt the important thing was not that the baby was breast-fed but that the mother should hold her baby lovingly in her arms, caress him and let him feel the warmth of her skin. Mother love could be supplied

perfectly well with a bottle too. Well, in the next generation lots of women put their babies on bottles, and now I'm beginning to notice that something is happening to the second generation of bottle-fed children. These young people are demanding to be touched. When they occupy college administrative buildings during a demonstration, what they really enjoy is sitting close together. (Laughter.) . . . I don't think it is accidental that they're demanding closer physical relationships with people. They never had the amount of touch they needed as babies. . . .

DR. SPOCK: . . . I'm skeptical about your thought that bottle-fed babies may demand touching later and that breast-fed babies don't. Most of the American babies born to college-educated parents back in the 1920s and 1930s weren't breast-fed either, yet they didn't ask for touching when they grew up.

It is easy to connect what Dorothy Baruch wrote about raising a generation of young people who questioned authority, could stand up for their own rights, and would oppose any future Hitlers to the generation of students who protested on behalf of free speech at Berkeley, practiced free love at Woodstock, stood up for Black voting rights in Selma, embraced feminism, and protested the Vietnam War. And we can see the irony that they called their parents "fascists" when this postwar generation had wanted so hard to build an antifascist world for their children. Yet, as Spock stressed, such connections are easy to assert and difficult to prove. Speaking in late 1970, Vice President Spiro Agnew drew links between what alarmed him about the counterculture and Spock's parenting advice:

Let me give you some everyday examples of the kind of permissiveness that has insinuated its way into our behavior. A permissive parent sees his child come to the dinner table wearing dirty clothes, his hands unwashed and his hair unkempt. The parent finds this offensive and turns to Dr. Spock's book—which has sold over 25 million copies in the past generation—for guidance. He reads this on that subject: "As usual, you have to compromise. Overlook some of his less irritating bad habits, realizing that they are probably not permanent." The thing to be carefully avoided, says our foremost authority on children, is "bossiness."[10]

Spock did set limits in regard to the issues Agnew identified. Spock (1962) criticized "children who come late to meals or leave early without permission or apology, who mess up their food at the table on purpose, who regularly interrupt the parents' conversations and ignore their requests, who brush by visitors as though they did not exist, who make demands in imperious tones . . . who regularly talk back to their parents and others."[11] He adds, "I don't think any well-trained, experienced professional leader in any of the children's fields has ever advocated full self-expression or total lack of repression." The same book explains: "If my child were rude to me I wouldn't put up with it, nor yell at him as an equal, nor act as if he had committed an unforgivable sin. I'd just tell him, seriously and as calmly as I could manage, that I don't want him to speak that way to me; it isn't polite; it isn't right."[12] Spock got his revenge in his memoir: "Well, I certainly can't be blamed for Agnew who was forced to resign from office because of criminal charges against him—he was much too old to have been raised by me!"[13] This conservative backlash against Spock was aimed at discrediting his highly publicized participation in the antiwar movement, but it also justified more traditionalist advice for parents by the early Reagan years.

Dr. James Dobson, associate clinical professor of pediatrics at the University of Southern California Medical School, launched Focus on the Family as a fundamentalist Christian media empire in 1977. An early force in conservative talk radio, Dobson hosted stadium lecture series for parents and published magazines and books promoting a more discipline-based model. My mother, who raised me according to Spock, wanted me to attend Focus on the Family classes when my own son was born. Dobson's 1970 bestseller *Dare to Discipline* attacked permissiveness as "an unworkable, illogical philosophy of child management."[14] Dobson argued that parents had been overly concerned about the perceived psychological consequences of too much discipline and in the process had lost sight of self-discipline: "In a day of widespread drug usage, immorality, civil disobedience, vandalism and violence, we must not depend on hope and luck to fashion the critical attitudes we value in our children. That unstructured technique was applied during the childhood of the generation that is now in college, and the outcome has been quite discouraging. Permissiveness has not just been a failure. It's been a disaster!"[15]

Decades later, a 2007 episode of *Fox & Friends* blamed Fred Rogers for the perceived flaws of contemporary youth: "'This evil, evil, evil man has ruined a generation of kids. . . . These experts are saying the kids of today who grew up with Mr. Rogers were told by him, 'you're special just for being who you are.' . . . The idea of working hard and making something of yourself has been discounted." Nancy from Tallahassee emailed her reaction: "I do believe that the combination of Mr. Rogers (you are special), *Sesame Street* (You need to be entertained to learn), and Dr. Spock (Lax discipline, no spanking) were three of the worst influences on child rearing."[16] Some myths die hard.

I am often asked who today's Dr. Spock is. Spock never spoke in isolation from the broader movement of Child Study advocates, even if the media liked to see him (or Rogers, later) as a unique personality. Mead and Spock gained prominence in an age of mass media, writing bestselling books, publishing in popular magazines, speaking on network television, and so forth. Today's landscape is too fragmented and diversified for such figures to emerge. There is also no contemporary equivalent of *Parents* or *Redbook*, and children's fictions address increasingly niche audiences in a multicultural and ideologically polarized society. Contemporary parenting advice is being shaped by the emergence of blogs and podcasts, where a cacophony of voices articulate different approaches and values, many of which nevertheless incorporate some residual permissive ideas (or a conservative backlash). It is often said that the conflicts that define our contemporary culture wars reflect the disputes of the 1960s around the Vietnam War, feminism, the sexual revolution, and the civil rights movement. Yet, there persists the conservative idea that these conflicts were themselves the acting out of a generation that had been given too much freedom as children. The American right now posits a generational sense of "entitlement," decrying the "pampering" of these youth in a world where everyone was a "special snowflake." The *Collins English Dictionary* made "snowflake" one of its words of the year in 2016: "The young adults of the 2010s, viewed as being less resilient and more prone to taking offence than previous generations."[17] Whereas the permissive imagination saw the snowflake as a metaphor for the unique combination of traits that made any individual child who they were, the right uses it to describe the performative fragility they associate with the push for "safe spaces" and "political correctness."

The fragmentation of parenting styles is yet another source of political polarization in the 2020s: permissive ideas have persisted even as more autocratic models have reasserted themselves. Consider the Free-Range Kids movement, spearheaded by mommy blogger Lenore Skenazy, who has reacted against what she sees as the extremes in how our culture seeks to protect children from the world: "Do you ever . . . let your kid ride a bike to the library? Walk to school? Make dinner? . . . If so, you are raising a Free-Range Kid! Free-Rangers believe in helmets, car seats, seat belts—safety! We just do NOT believe that every time school age kids go outside, they need a security detail. . . . Here's to common sense parenting in uncommonly overprotective times!" Skenazy's argument often rests on a nostalgia for the world of her childhood where greater respect was paid to the autonomy and resilience of children, who were allowed to make more choices for themselves:

> A Free-Range Kid is a kid who gets treated as a smart, young, capable individual, not an invalid who needs constant attention and help. . . . Free-Range Kids are sort of old-fashioned. They're kids who are expected to WANT to grow up and do things on their own. And then, when they show us they're ready, we allow 'em to. . . . In just one generation, what was considered a normal, happy, HEALTHY childhood has become considered WILDLY dangerous.[18]

Her Discovery Channel reality series, *World's Worst Mom*, intervenes in families that have reached their breaking point due to overly protective parents. Contemporary popular culture, responding to similar nostalgia, has generated a whole subgenre of "kids on bikes" adventure stories, *Stranger Things* and *Paper Girls* for example, as neighborhood children find themselves encountering and overcoming aliens, monsters, and other invaders.

If the Free-Range Kids movement stresses freedom, autonomy, mobility, and risk-taking as core permissive values, other parents, especially those working with LGBTQ+ kids, have reclaimed the practices associated with empathetic engagement and the values of accommodating the desires of children who are different from their peers. When Marlo Mack's four-year-old son announced one day, "Mama, I'm a girl," she pulled out a tape recorder to capture the conversation and continued to document the child's transition in "How to Be a Girl," a podcast that went on to be a finalist for a Peabody Award.[19] Even though Spock, Mead, and many other permissive writers had fairly rigid ideas about gender identification, they might have recognized something of their own approach in the ways that this mother respected the child's knowledge of her body, sought to understand why the girl felt this way, amplified the child's voice through the podcast, and otherwise helped other parents to accept the realities of transgender lives.

Almost every day one can find the clash of permissive and conservative norms in the newspaper. At an event in the school library, Toby Price, an assistant principal in Mississippi, read a book out loud that he knew his own children had enjoyed.[20] Written by Dawn McMillan and illustrated by Ross Kinnaird, *I Need a New Butt* was one of the top one hundred best-selling children's books on Amazon. It depicts a young boy who discovers that his butt has a crack and fears it may be broken. This whimsical story—in which the protagonist imagines a range of possible solutions to this perceived problem—speaks to children's curiosity (and need for reassurance) about their bodies, a theme that would have spoken to Spock and Rogers alike. But in a hotly contested case, Price lost his job because of outraged parents.

Florida governor Ron DeSantis has risen to national prominence on the back of such controversies, doing battle with Disney over his so-called "Don't Say Gay" legislation, tightening state control over books in school libraries, banning drag shows to protect children from their gender-confusing messages, and repressing the rights of transgender children, all in the name of exerting control over institutions he claims are imposing too much "wokeness." Conservative commentators—such as Joe Rogan—have made claims about schools where children were allowed to drink milk from a bowl and use a litter box in the classroom because they saw themselves as cats, a hyperbolic response to a current culture that is increasingly respecting children's perceptions of their own gender identities.[21] One wonders what they would say about a boy who speaks only in noises (such as Gerald McBoing-Boing), that is, a child who fails to conform. If the permissive imagination was defined by what parents permitted, accommodated, and even facilitated, then this antipermissive discourse is defined by what it refuses to understand, or tolerate.

If by the early 1970s Spock and Mead were taking pains to deny charges of permissiveness, they were reacting to the first waves of this culture war. This is one of the many reasons why it seems urgent to reconsider the cultural negotiations taking place around childhood in America from 1946 to 1968, since doing so might arm us to deal with the contested space of contemporary parenting. Permissiveness provides progressive models of family values and encourages us to imagine—as Mead and others of her generation had—how we might build a better world for our children with children understood as civic agents capable of promoting global brotherhood and racial bonding, not to mention resisting fascism and promoting democracy. From the start, the advocates of permissiveness worked at the grass roots, through parents' education and Child Study programs in local communities, to inform how parents understood their relationships with their children. Collectively these researchers formed an intellectual rationale for their approach and wrote in mass market publications to translate those insights about child psychology into practical advice parents came to trust. Creative artists responded to Mead's call for "the symbol-makers, the writers, the artists, the radio broadcasters and the filmmakers" to rethink the American family in more democratic terms. These children's fictions persist, still consumed and remembered today, and their progressive values became normalized. If we often do not see these stories today as progressive, it is because, despite reactionary backlash, we now more or less live in the world they imagined. Spock, Mead, and the other advocates of the permissive imagination made plenty of mistakes and had blind spots, but they refused to cede the ground to conservative perspectives, and these changes had consequences in terms of how the young understood their place in the world. We certainly would want to rid these ideas of the gender-normative, white-centric view of the world that sometimes undercut their best intentions, but there is much here worth reclaiming and updating to confront the challenges of a world still undergoing changes that first became apparent during the permissive era.

ACKNOWLEDGMENTS

*Where the Wild Things Were* is the result of more than twenty-five years of research and reflection, starting in the early 1990s when I was still an early-career scholar. The first impulse to write such a book came in 1991 following the death of Dr. Seuss, when I organized a salute to his works, including a screening of *The 5,000 Fingers of Dr. T*, at MIT. For almost twenty years, my annual Salute to Dr. Seuss remained an MIT institution, as I read and contextualized his works to a lecture hall full of students. This led me to want to place him in a larger frame and thus to research other children's culture of the period. *The Children's Culture Reader* (1998) was a by-product of this initial phase of research, incorporating both primary and secondary materials emerging from the project. This early effort was strongly encouraged by five scholars, three of whom have now passed away: Richard DeCordova, Nina C. Lieberman, Anne Friedberg, Lynn Spigel, and Nick Sammond, each of whom modeled what a more robust history of children's media might look like. Lynn Spigel resurfaced near the end of this project as one of the readers assigned by the press to review the manuscript. Her comments and suggestions, along with those of Philip Nel, and a third anonymous reader, were enormously helpful in refining the final drafts of this book.

I have actively reworked and reconceptualized some of the materials published during this phase. Among them:

"'The All-American Handful': Dennis the Menace, Permissive Childrearing and the Bad Boy Tradition," in *The Revolution Wasn't Televised: Sixties Television and Social Conflict*, ed. Lynn Spigel and Mike Curtin (New York: Routledge, 1997).
"The Sensuous Child," in *The Children's Culture Reader*, ed. Henry Jenkins (New York: New York University Press, 1998).
"'Her Suffering Aristocratic Majesty': The Sentimental Value of Lassie," in *Kids' Media Culture (Console-ing Passions)*, ed. Marsha Kinder (Durham, NC: Duke University Press, 1999).

"'Complete Freedom of Movement': Video Games as Gendered Play Spaces," in *From Barbie to Mortal Kombat: Gender and Computer Games*, ed. Justine Kessell and Henry Jenkins (Cambridge, MA: MIT Press, 1998).

"'No Matter How Small': The Democratic Imagination of Doctor Seuss," in *Hop on Pop: The Politics and Pleasures of Popular Culture*, ed. Henry Jenkins, Jane Shattuc, and Tara McPherson (Durham, NC: Duke University Press, 2003).

The first phase of this project bogged down and got put on hold when I was asked to establish the MIT Comparative Media Studies program. When I was invited to spend a term as the chair of modern culture at the Kluge Center of the Library of Congress in 2018, I was able to rekindle this initiative via extensive research in the Margaret Mead Papers and in the Comic Book Collection, not to mention the library's large collection of vintage child-rearing books. Each chapter here is animated by discoveries made during this phase of the research. I also want to acknowledge the support I received from the Fred Rogers Archive and the Geisel Archive at the University of California–San Diego.

This more recent phase of writing benefited from the support of many of my University of Southern California colleagues (among them Sasha Anawalt, Sarah Banet-Weiser, David Craig, Nicholas Cull, Larry Gross, Becky Herr-Stephenson, Susan Kresnicka, Josh Kun, Nancy Lutkehaus, Christine Panuschka, Lisa Pons, Howard Rodman, Joe Saltzman, Sangita Shresthova, Sarah Taylor, and the folks at the Los Angeles Institute for the Humanities who heard the earliest presentation of this material). Other early audiences included conferences on "Lonely Are the Brave: The Western and Post-War America" in Norwich, UK, "Horrifying Children" at York University, and "Media Literacies" at the University of Wisconsin–Madison. Thanks to Lynda Corey, Clausson Director of Special Collections and Archives at the University of California, San Diego, for last minute help fact checking materials in the Doctor Seuss collection.

Chapter 7 benefited enormously from the research assistance provided by Lauren Sowa, who helped me think through the relationship of *Mister Rogers' Neighborhood* to other early children's programs and wrote the discussion here of Shari Lewis's career. Shari Goldin was generous enough to root around in her attic and dig out old papers she had written about the history of puppets on early television, which also proved foundational for this chapter.

Chapter 9 is dedicated to the memory of Paromita Gupta, who was my doctoral student at USC. Gupta—raised in Calcutta—served as my research assistant for this chapter, watching and discussing the complete runs of *Jonny Quest* and *Maya* with me. She left detailed notes that have served as the basis for the ideas and some of the language in the chapter. Unfortunately, she passed away unexpectedly before this project could be completed.

Other students whose work contributed to my thinking for this project include Meryl Alpert, Sam Close, Briana Ellerbee, Sam Ford, Neta Kligler-Vilinchik, Diana Lee, Ioana Literat, Andres Lombada, and Joan Miller.

Shari Goldin also proved to be an important reader and critic of the book, as did my longtime friend and colleague Peter Kramer. Both worried every sentence across the manuscript, pushing for greater precision in my argument and my historical periodization, and otherwise holding me accountable for the highest standards of history writing. Amanda Ford, my longtime assistant, has been tireless in helping to prepare this manuscript for publication, having a special interest in the theories of childhood and the practices of parenting, especially in the Montessori tradition. Becky Pham was responsible for reviewing all of the citations for the book to ensure consistency and accuracy, which is almost by definition a thankless task, but I am thanking her anyway.

Thanks go to the various MDs who have held me together during a challenging period of my life.

Cynthia Jenkins, my friend, my co-parent, my thinking partner, has always been a huge influence on my work. It has been painful to live apart the past few years as she has heroically provided care for her mother.

I am dedicating this book to my son, Charlie, which had been my intention from the start. I saw the book as an answer to the question of what the world had been like when I was a child. I started this research when he was still in middle school and as I am finishing it, he is releasing his own first novel. Cynthia and I raised him using our own modified version of the permissive paradigm and could not be more proud of the result.

# NOTES

## INTRODUCTION

1. Haim G. Ginott, *Between Parent and Child* (New York: Three Rivers, 1965).
2. Ginott, *Between Parent and Child*, 11
3. Ginott, 22.
4. Ginott, 23.
5. Ginott, 71.
6. Ginott, 93. Here, he echoes earlier formulations that sought to introduce children to definitions that are grounded in use, such as Lucy Sprague Mitchell's "A table is to eat off. A spoon is to eat in" or Ruth Krauss's "A mirror is so you can make faces." For fuller discussion of the roots of these formulations in perceptual and cognitive psychology, see Kenneth B. Kidd, *Freud in Oz: At the Intersection of Psychoanalysis and Children's Literature* (Minneapolis: University of Minnesota Press, 2011).
7. Ginott, *Between Parent and Child*, 23.
8. Ginott, 48.
9. Ginott, 93–94.
10. Ginott, 94.
11. Ginott, 109.
12. Jack Halberstam, *Wild Things: The Disorder of Desire* (Durham, NC: Duke University Press, 2020), 8.
13. Robin Bernstein, *Racial Innocence: Performing American Girlhood from Slavery to Civil Rights* (New York: New York University Press, 2011).
14. Benjamin Spock, *The Common Sense Book of Baby and Child Care*, rev. ed. (New York: Duell, Sloan & Pearce, 1957), 13.
15. Michelle Ann Abate, *Funny Girls: Guffaws, Guts, and Gender in Classic American Comics* (Jackson: University Press of Mississippi, 2019).
16. Elizabeth Segal, "'As the Twig Is Bent . . .': Gender and Childhood Reading," in *Gender and Reading: Essays on Readers, Texts, and Contexts*, ed. Elizabeth A. Flynn and Patrocinio P. Schweickart (Baltimore: Johns Hopkins University Press, 1986).
17. Raymond Williams, *Marxism and Literature* (Oxford: Oxford University Press, 1977), 121–27.
18. Nicholas Sammond, *Babes in Tomorrowland: Walt Disney and the Making of the American Child, 1930–1960* (Durham, NC: Duke University Press, 2006), relies

heavily on these two sources and thus reproduces the idea that scientific parenting went largely unchallenged during this prewar period.

19. Dorothy W. Baruch, *Parents and Children Go to School: Adventuring in Nursery School and Kindergarten* (Chicago: Scott, Foresman, 1939), 213.
20. Ginott, *Between Parent and Child*, 221.
21. Alan Petigny, *The Permissive Society: America, 1941–1965* (Cambridge: Cambridge University Press, 2009), 2.
22. Mike Ryan, "Won't You Be My Neighbor? Director Morgan Neville Tries to Explain Why People Keep Crying over Mr. Rogers," *Uproxx*, June 13, 2018, accessed October 1, 2023, https://uproxx.com/movies/wont-you-be-my-neighbor-morgan-neville/.
23. Maxwell King, *The Good Neighbor: The Life and Work of Fred Rogers* (New York: Abrams, 2018).
24. Ginott, *Between Parent and Child*, 83.
25. Susan Stewart, *On Longing: Narratives of the Miniature, the Gigantic, the Souvenir, the Collection* (Durham, NC: Duke University Press, 1993).
26. For more on the concept of civic imagination, see Henry Jenkins, Gabriel Peters-Lazaro, and Sangita Shresthova, eds., *Popular Culture and the Civic Imagination* (New York: New York University Press, 2020).
27. Bill Goodykoontz, "Won't You Be My Neighbor? Director: Never Another Mr. Rogers," *Arizona Central*, June 7, 2018, accessed October 1, 2023, https://www.azcentral.com/story/entertainment/movies/billgoodykoontz/2018/06/07/morgan-neville-interview-mr-fred-rogers-and-wont-you-my-neighbor/680468002/.
28. No such scene exists in the original 1934 novel. There, we only learn:
    Mr. Banks went off with his black bag, and Mrs. Banks went into the drawing-room and sat there all day long writing letters to the papers and begging them to send some Nannies to her at once as she was waiting; and upstairs in the Nursery, Jane and Michael watched at the window and wondered who would come. They were glad Katie Nanna had gone, for they had never liked her. She was old and fat and smelt of Barley-water. (P. L. Travers, 1934, 4–5)
29. Rudolf Dreikurs and Vicki Soltz, *Children: The Challenge* (New York: Plume, 1964), 153.
30. Ada Hart Arlitt, *The Child from One to Six* (New York: McGraw-Hill, 1930), quoted in Dan Beekman, *The Mechanical Baby: A Popular History of the Theory and Practice of Childraising* (Westport, CT: L. Hill, 1977).
31. John B. Watson, *Psychological Care of Infant and Child* (New York: W. W. Norton, 1928), 82.
32. Arlitt, *Child from One*.
33. Watson, *Psychological Care*, 9–10.
34. Watson, 142.

## 1. "MAKING A NEW PATTERN"

1. I use the term "baby boom" here with some caution, recognizing that there has been some disagreement about the dates that define its boundaries (with the years 1946–66 most often used) and that demographic framings of this generation are not necessarily aligned with the discursive framing of the permissive paradigm. This paradigm is often associated with the 1946 publication of Spock's *Common Sense Book of Baby and Child Care*.
2. Ann Hulbert, *Raising America: Experts, Parents, and a Century of Advice about Children* (New York: Random House, 2003), 225–27.
3. Judith Sealander, "Families, World War II, and the Baby Boom (1940–1955)," in *American Childhood: A Research Guide and Historical Handbook*, ed. Joseph M. Hawes and Ray N. Hiner (Westport, CT: Greenwood, 1985), 166.
4. Sealander, "Families, World War II," 165.
5. Sealander, 164.
6. Sealander, 164.
7. Sealander, 163.
8. Sealander, 163.
9. William Schneider, "The Suburban Century Begins," *The Atlantic*, July 1992, accessed October 1, 2023, https://www.theatlantic.com/past/docs/politics/ecbig/schnsub.htm.
10. Schneider, "Suburban Century Begins," 166.
11. Wikipedia, "History of Religion in the United States," accessed October 1, 2023, https://en.wikipedia.org/wiki/History_of_religion_in_the_United_States.
12. Georgia Vital Statistics, 1958, https://oasis.state.ga.us/VSR_1950_1993/1958_GA_Vital_Statistics_Report.pdf, 38
13. Jennifer Ritterhouse, *Growing Up Jim Crow: How Black and White Southern Children Learned Race* (Chapel Hill: University of North Carolina Press, 2006).
14. My focus on images from my family album is inspired by the writings of Annette Kuhn, *Family Secrets: Acts of Memory and Imagination* (London: Verso, 2002), who directed her own analytic focus at the construction of British girlhood during roughly this same period.
15. Petigny, *Permissive Society*, 37–38.
16. The statistics already shared make clear that white suburban parents were still a minority in the United States, even if they were central to the self-representations of this period. Suburbanization was only one of several migrations taking place, all of which would have led to the possibility of reconfiguring American family life
17. Benjamin Spock, *The Common Sense Book of Baby and Child Care* (New York: Duell, Sloan & Pearce, 1946).
18. Benjamin Spock, *A Better World for Our Children: Rebuilding American Family Values* (Bethesda, MD: National Books, 1994), 27, 29.

19. Daniel Thomas Cook, *The Moral Project of Childhood: Motherhood, Material Life, and Early Children's Consumer Culture* (New York: New York University Press, 2020).
20. Spock, *Common Sense Book*, 13.
21. Spock.
22. Johanna Johnston, "Only Johnny Knows," *CBS Radio Workshop*, August 10, 1956, https://www.youtube.com/watch?v=f7FZGp3kTEI.
23. Margaret Mead and Martha Wolfenstein, eds., *Childhood in Contemporary Cultures* (Chicago: University of Chicago Press, 1955).
24. Mead and Wolfenstein, *Childhood in Contemporary Cultures*, 168.
25. Mead, "Implications of Insight," in *Childhood in Contemporary Cultures*, ed. Margaret Mead and Martha Wolfenstein (Chicago: University of Chicago Press, 1955), 145.
26. Leonard S. Marcus, *Golden Legacy: The Story of Golden Books* (New York: Golden Books, 2017).
27. Marcus, *Golden Legacy*, 146.
28. Margaret Mead and Ken Heyman, *Family* (New York: Ridge Press Books, 1965).
29. Margaret Mead, "Beyond the Nuclear Family," paper presented at "The Future of the American Family: Dream and Reality," Child Study Association of America, March 4, 1963. Later condensed for publication in *Children*, March–April 1963, 24.
30. Margaret Mead, "Correspondence with Benjamin Spock," Margaret Mead Papers, December 8, 1939, Library of Congress.
31. Mary Catherine Bateson, *With a Daughter's Eye: Memoir of Margaret Mead and Gregory Bateson* (New York: Harper Perennial, 2001), 28–29.
32. Bateson, *With a Daughter's Eye*, 29.
33. Bateson, 29.
34. Margaret Mead, "Youth in an Uncharted Landscape," *Junior Bazaar*, November 1945, 91.
35. Mead, "Youth in Uncharted Landscape," 91.
36. Margaret Mead, "Youth Needs New Models," unpublished, 1945, Margaret Mead Papers, Library of Congress.
37. Margaret Mead, "What's the Matter with the Family?," *Harper's*, April 1945, 393–99.
38. Mead, "What's the Matter."
39. Mead, "Implications of Insight III," 455.
40. Jacqueline S. Rose, *The Case of Peter Pan: The Impossibility of Children's Fiction* (London: Macmillan, 1984).
41. Rose, *Case of Peter Pan*.
42. Mead and Wolfenstein, *Childhood in Contemporary Cultures*.
43. Katherine M. Wolf, *The Controversial Problem of Discipline* (New York: Child Study Association of America, 1953), 6–7.
44. Wolf, *Controversial Problem*.
45. Wolf, 34.

46 Mead and Wolfenstein, *Childhood in Contemporary Cultures*, 16.
47 Benjamin Spock, *Problems of Parents* (Boston: Houghton Mifflin, 1962), 52.
48 Spock, *Problems of Parents*, 22–23.
49 Spock, 287.
50 Martha Weinman Lear, *The Child Worshipers: A Book about Parents Who Are Making the Child a New Status Symbol and Parenthood a Competitive Sport* (New York: Crown, 1963).
51 This is not to say there was not another field—social work—that continued to focus on the problems of poor, inner-city, and minoritized children; only that they were not the primary focus of the Child Study and child-development literature and did not appear with any frequency in the children's fictions of the postwar period.
52 The category of "whiteness" and what it includes was, then as now, under constant change, with some groups, such as the Irish or the Germans, that would have been seen as "ethnic" at some points in American culture increasingly falling into popular understandings of who constituted white children, and other groups, such as Hispanics or in many accounts, Jews, falling outside that construction.
53 Child Study Association of America, *Children in Wartime: Parents' Questions* (New York: Child Study Association, 1942), quoted in Henry Jenkins, ed., *The Children's Culture Reader* (New York: New York University Press, 1998), 477–79.
54 Child Study Association of America, *Children in Wartime*.
55 Pearl S. Buck, "At Home in the World," in *Our Child Today: A Guide to Their Needs from Infancy through Adolescence*, ed. Sidonie Matsner Gruenberg and the Child Study Association of America (New York: Viking Press, 1952), 340.
56 Buck, "At Home in the World," 341.
57 Dorothy W. Baruch, *Glass House of Prejudice* (New York: William Morrow, 1946), 15.
58 Baruch, *Glass House of Prejudice*, 36.
59 Christina Klein, *Cold War Orientalism: Asia in the Middlebrow Imagination, 1945–1961* (Berkeley: University of California Press, 2003).
60 Baruch, *Glass House of Prejudice*, 170.
61 Baruch, 171–72.
62 As reprinted in Julia Mickenberg and Philip Nel, eds., *Tales for Little Rebels: A Collection of Radical Children's Literature* (New York: New York University Press, 2008).
63 Ruth Benedict and Gene Weltfish, *The Races of Mankind* (New York: Public Affairs Committee, 1943).
64 Mickenberg and Nel, *Tales for Little Rebels*, 269.
65 Mickenberg and Nel, 273.
66 Philip Nel, "Children's Literature Goes to War: Dr. Seuss, P. D. Eastman, Munro Leaf, and the Private SNAFU Films (1943–46)," in *Journal of Popular Culture* 40, no. 3 (June 2007): 468–87.

67 Nel, "Children's Literature Goes to War" offers a somewhat different reading of the racial politics of P. D. Eastman's postwar children's books in comparison with those of Dr. Seuss and Munro Leaf.

## 2. THE UNDERSTANDING ANGEL

1. Rick Caulfield, "'Trust Yourself': Revisiting Doctor Spock," *Early Childhood Education Journal* 26, no. 4 (1999): 263.
2. Margaret Mead, "Theoretical Setting—1954," in *Childhood in Contemporary Cultures*, ed. Margaret Mead and Martha Wolfenstein (Chicago: University of Chicago Press, 1955), 5.
3. Shari L. Thurer, *The Myths of Motherhood: How Culture Reinvents the Good Mother* (New York: Penguin Books, 1994), 248–55.
4. Dorothy Canfield Fisher, *The Home-Maker* (London: Persephone, 1924; reprint: Kessinger, 2004),
5. Fisher, *Home-Maker*, 3.
6. Fisher, 11.
7. Kathleen W. Jones, *Taming the Troublesome Child: American Families, Child Guidance, and the Limitations of Psychiatric Authority* (Cambridge, MA: Harvard University Press, 1999), 5.
8. Fisher remains a controversial figure having recently undergone critiques because of her possible connections to the eugenics movement.
9. Fisher, *Home-Maker*, 35–37.
10. Fisher, 144.
11. Fisher, 12.
12. Fisher, 141–42.
13. Fisher, 72.
14. Dorothy Canfield Fisher, *A Montessori Mother* (New York: Henry Holt, 1912), 118.
15. Fisher, *Montessori Mother*, 121.
16. Fisher, 131.
17. Gerald L. Gutek and Patricia A. Gutek, *Bringing Montessori to America: S. S. McClure, Maria Montessori, and the Campaign to Publicize Montessori Education* (Tuscaloosa: University of Alabama Press, 2016), 47.
18. Fisher, *Home-Maker*, 161.
19. Dorothy Canfield Fisher, *Mothers and Children* (New York: Henry Holt, 1914), 10.
20. Fisher, *Home-Maker*, 180–81.
21. Fisher, *Mothers and Children*, 175.
22. Fisher, *Home-Maker*, 256.
23. Fisher, *Mothers and Children*, 143.
24. Fisher, 143.
25. Fisher, *Montessori Mother*, 53.
26. Fisher, 54.
27. Fisher, *Home-Maker*, 198–99.
28. Fisher, 255–56.

29  Federation for Child Study, "Statement of Purpose," 1913, Social Welfare History Project, accessed October 1, 2023, https://socialwelfare.library.vcu.edu/programs/child-welfarechild-labor/child-study-association-of-america-statement-of-purpose-1913/.
30  Kathleen W. Jones, *Taming the Troublesome Child: American Families, Child Guidance, and the Limits of Psychiatric Authority* (Cambridge, MA: Harvard University Press, 1999), 17.
31  Jones, *Taming the Troublesome Child*, 94.
32  Jones, 149.
33  Alice Boardman Smuts, *Science in the Service of Children, 1893–1935* (New Haven, CT: Yale University Press, 2006), 1.
34  Julia Grant, *Raising Baby by the Book: The Education of American Mothers* (New Haven, CT: Yale University Press, 1998), 38.
35  Benjamin C. Gruenberg, ed., *Outlines of Child Study* (New York: Macmillan, 1922), accessed October 1, 2023, https://archive.org/details/outlinesofchidsoochil/page/n9, ix–x.
36  Child Study Association of America, *Child Study Groups: A Manual for Leaders* (New York: Child Study Association of America, 1926), 5.
37  Margaret J. Quillard, *Child Study Discussion Records: Development—Methods—Techniques* (New York: Child Study Association of America, 1928), 42.
38  Smuts, *Science in the Service*, 224.
39  Quillard, *Child Study Discussion Records*, 12.
40  Quillard, 12.
41  Sidonie Matsner Gruenberg, "Changing Patterns of Family Living," in *Our Child Today: A Guide to Their Needs from Infancy through Adolescence*, ed. Sidonie Matsner Gruenberg and the Child Study Association of America (New York: Viking, 1952), 13.
42  Sidonie Matsner Gruenberg, *Your Child Today and Tomorrow* (Philadelphia: J. B. Lippincott, 1913), 18.
43  Gruenberg, *Your Child Today*, 103.
44  Gruenberg, 151. This issue of informal neighborhood gangs is explored charmingly in *Penrod and Sam*, the 1922 silent-film adaptation of the beloved Booth Tarkington novel, which depicts the various ways this boy culture gets entangled with adult interference. Penrod's status as leader of the local gang gets threatened when his parents insist that the brattish son of a wealthy banker be included in their activities, or when the father sells off the undeveloped land on which the boy has built his ramshackle clubhouse. The film's resolution requires the father dad to recognize why the gang's status structure is important for his son, bringing him to buy back the clubhouse at an inflated price and give the deed to Penrod.
45  Gruenberg, *Your Child Today*, 152–53.
46  Gruenberg, 154.
47  Anna W. M. Wolf, *The Parents' Manual: A Guide to the Emotional Development of Young Children* (New York: Simon & Schuster, 1943), 84.

48  Wolf, *Parents' Manual*, 68.
49  Anna W. M. Wolf, *What Makes a Good Home? The Beginnings of Emotional Health* (New York: Child Study Association, 1951), 3.
50  Wolf, *Parents' Manual*, 73.
51  Sidonie Matsner Gruenberg et al., *Parents' Questions*, rev. ed. (New York: Harper & Brothers, 1947), 34–35.
52  Wolf, *Parents' Manual*, 187.
53  Quillard, *Child Study Discussion Records*, 42.
54  Frank, as quoted in Ken Quattro, "The Comics Detective: Josette Frank: Alone against the Storm, Part 1," *The Comics Detective*, February 7, 2014.
55  Frank, as quoted in Quattro, "Comics Detective."
56  Josette Frank, *Television: How to Use It Wisely with Children* (New York: Child Study Association of America, 1959), 13.
57  Gruenberg et al., *Parents' Questions*, 183.
58  Gruenberg et al., 181.
59  Frank, as quoted in Quattro, "Comics Detective."
60  Gruenberg et al., *Parents' Questions*, 149.
61  Josette Frank, "New Arts of Communication," in *Our Children Today: A Guide to Their Needs from Infancy through Adolescence*, ed. Sidonie Matsner Gruenberg and the Child Study Association of America (New York: Viking, 1952), 316.
62  Gruenberg et al., *Parents' Questions*, 146–47.
63  Wolf, *Parents' Manual*, 73.
64  Charles Tazewell, *The Littlest Angel* (Nashville, TN: Ideals Children's Books, 1946; reprint, 2006).
65  Wolf, *What Makes a Good Home?*, 18.
66  Here, we see one of the multiple examples of the transitional object running through children's fictions, with the implication that adults should respect objects that are meaningful to children even if the adults do not really know how to make sense of the junk items they have mapped meaning onto.
67  In the 1969 television dramatization, the boy Samuel is given his own guardian angel, Patience (a name signaling what the writers saw as the highest virtue in a parent). Patience is himself imperfectly assimilated into the adult order. He is prone to daydreams, has a tendency to break the rules, and behaves impulsively. He is threatened with punishment if he does not transform this unruly boy into a perfect angel.
68  Olive W. Burt, *God Gave Me Eyes: My Five Senses* (New York: Samuel Gabriel Sons, 1942).
69  Jane Werner Watson, *My Little Golden Book about God* (Racine, WI: Golden Inspirational, 1952), 120.
70  Anna W. Wolf, *Our Children Face War* (Boston: Houghton Mifflin, 1942), 1.
71  Wolf, *Our Children Face War*, 3.
72  Child Study Association of America, *Children in Wartime*, 478.
73  Wolf, *Our Children Face War*, 98–99.

74 In popular representations of the era, red hair was often associated with being Jewish, and in older stories Judas was depicted as having red hair. So, this scene is one of many in the film that link the protagonist to the history of Jewish refugees from Europe during and following World War II.

## 3. "NO MATTER HOW SMALL"

1 Seuss, November 1960, Dr. Seuss Collection, University of California–San Diego, MSS 230 https://library.ucsd.edu/speccoll/DigitalArchives/mss0230/m230b18f8.pdf. While representations of brats were common in children's fictions starting in the early twentieth century, Seuss uses the term here to refer, jokingly, to the readers of his books more than to the characters. In this formulation, every child is a bit of a brat, and Seuss is displaying a certain irreverence toward his own creative output.
2 Dorothy W. Baruch, *Parents Can Be People* (New York: D. Appleton Century, 1944), 113.
3 Katie Ishizuka and Ramón Stephens, "The Cat Is Out of the Bag: Orientalism, Anti-Blackness, and White Supremacy in Dr. Seuss's Children's Books," *Research on Diversity in Youth Literature* 1, no. 2 (2019): 113, https://sophia.stkate.edu/rdyl/vol1/iss2/4/.
4 Judith Morgan and Neil Morgan, *Dr. Seuss and Mr. Geisel: A Biography* (New York: Random House, 1995).
5 Henry Herbert Goddard, *Our Children in the Atomic Age* (Mellott, IN: Hopkins, 1948), ix.
6 Mauree Applegate, *Everybody's Business: Our Children* (Evanston, IL: Row, Peterson, 1952), 59.
7 Julia Mickenberg, *Learning from the Left: Children's Literature, the Cold War, and Radical Politics in the United States* (New York: Oxford University Press, 2006), 17.
8 Andrew Patner, *I. F. Stone: A Portrait* (New York: Pantheon, 1988).
9 Larry Ceplair and Steven Englund, *The Inquisition in Hollywood: Politics in the Film Community, 1930–1960* (Garden City, NY: Anchor Books, 1980).
10 Max Lerner, "Preface," in Roy Hoopes, *Ralph Ingersoll: A Biography* (New York: Atheneum, 1980), viii.
11 Michael Denning, *The Cultural Front: The Laboring of American Culture in the Twentieth Century* (New York: Verso, 1996).
12 Richard H. Minear, *Dr. Seuss Goes to War: The World War II Editorial Cartoons of Theodor Seuss Geisel* (New York: New Press, 2001); Edward Connery Lathem, "Interview with Dr. Seuss," undated transcript, Seuss Papers, Box 18, File 14, 141., Geisel Library, University of California–San Diego.
13 Lathem, "Interview with Dr. Seuss."
14 It's interesting that Frank Capra and Ted Geisel, who served together during the war, would create two of the most beloved holiday classics of the postwar era: *It's a Wonderful Life* and *How the Grinch Stole Christmas*.
15 T. S. Geisel, "Memo to Chief, Army Inform. Branch, IED," Seuss Papers, December 7, 1944, Box 230, File 29, Geisel Library, University of California–San Diego.

16 T. S. Geisel, Seuss Papers, February 5, 1945, Box 1, File 34, Geisel Library, University of California–San Diego.
17 T. S. Geisel, "Final Continuity Script, Your Job in Gemany," undated. Seuss Papers, Box 9, File 9, Geisel Library, University of California–San Diego.
18 Dr. Seuss, lecture notes, "Mrs. Mulvaney and the Billion Dollar Bunny," Seuss Papers, University of Utah Workshop, July 1947, Box 19, File 7, Geisel Library, University of California–San Diego.
19 Dr. Seuss, "Mrs. Mulvaney."
20 Dr. Seuss.
21 Ishizuka and Stephens, "The Cat Is Out."
22 Philip Nel, "Breaking Up with Racist Children's Books," *Washington Post*, May 16, 2021, accessed October 1, 2023, https://www.washingtonpost.com/education/2021/05/16/breaking-up-with-racist-childrens-books/.
23 Dr. Seuss, "Mrs. Mulvaney."
24 Dr. Seuss.
25 Dr. Seuss.
26 Dorothy W. Baruch, *New Ways in Discipline: You and Your Child Today* (New York: McGraw-Hill, 1949), 14.
27 Wolf, *Our Children Face War*, 198.
28 Wolf, 198.
29 Dorothy W. Baruch, *Parents Can Be People* (New York: Appleton-Century-Crofts, 1944), 90.
30 Dorothy W. Baruch, *You, Your Children, and War* (New York: Appleton-Century, 1942), 111.
31 Baruch, *Parents Can Be People*, 120.
32 Elizabeth A. Boettiger, *Your Child Meets the World Outside: A Guide to Children's Attitudes in Democratic Living* (New York: Appleton-Century, 1941), 9.
33 Baruch, *Parents Can Be People*, 113.
34 Boettiger, *Your Child Meets the World*.
35 George B. de Huszar, *Practical Applications of Democracy* (New York: Harper & Brothers, 1945), xiii.
36 De Huszar, *Practical Applications*, 52. For more on the democratization of children's lives, see Jennifer S. Light, *States of Childhood: From the Junior Republic to the American Republic, 1895–1945* (Cambridge, MA: MIT Press, 2020).
37 De Huszar, *Practical Applications*, 52.
38 Mary Elizabeth Byrne Ferm, *Freedom in Education* (New York: Lear, 1949).
39 Goddard, *Our Children*, iv.
40 Howard A. Lane, *Shall Children, Too, Be Free?* (New York: Anti-Defamation League of the B'nai B'rith, 1949), 11.
41 Goddard, *Our Children*, 135, iv.
42 Darnton argues that many of the classic fairy tales originated with the desperation of the peasant classes—their hunger, poverty, powerlessness, infant mortality—even if they are passed down to us in a form that reflects bourgeois

and aristocratic tastes and interests. See Robert Darnton, *The Great Cat Massacre and Other Episodes in French Cultural History* (New York: Basic Books, 1984).
43 Robert L. Griswold, *Fatherhood in America: A History* (New York: Basic Books, 1993).
44 Baruch, *New Ways*, 115.
45 Baruch, 123.
46 Dr. Seuss, "The Ruckus," *Redbook*, July 1954, 84.
47 Dr. Seuss, *Yertie the Turtle and Other Stories* (New York: Random House, 1950).
48 T. S. Geisel, "Some Notes by the Professor," Seuss Papers, undated, Box 7, File 13, Geisel Library, University of California–San Diego.
49 T. S. Geisel, "5,000 Fingers of Dr. T," first draft script, Seuss Papers, Box 7, File 19, November 1951, San Geisel Library, University of California–San Diego.
50 Dick Williams, "Roaming the Sound Stages," *Los Angeles Mirror*, March 7, 1952, in *5,000 Fingers of Dr. T* clipping file, Margaret Herrick Library, Academy of Motion Picture Arts and Sciences, Los Angeles.
51 Dorothy W. Baruch, *You, Your Children and War* (New York: Appleton-Century, 1943), 114.
52 Geisel, "Loose Notes," Seuss Papers, undated, Box 7, File 13, Geisel Library, University of California–San Diego.
53 Zlabadowski's insistence on making money raises an interesting question—was this a residual stereotype of the "money-grubbing" Jew (even though the part is played by a WASP actor) or does it simply reflect the materialism as American culture shifted toward a culture of consumption as the veterans returned home from the war?
54 Baruch, *Parents and Children*, 291.
55 Mary Phelps and Margaret Wise Brown, "Lucy Sprague Mitchell," *Horn Book Magazine*, May–June 1937.
56 Lucy Sprague Mitchell, *Here and Now Story Book: Two- to Seven-Year-Olds* (New York: E. P. Dutton, 1921), 2. See also Kidd, *Freud in Oz*, for a deeper discussion of Mitchell's rationale.
57 Baruch, *Parents and Children*, 271.
58 Mitchell, *Here and Now*, 16.
59 Carol Kismaric and Marvin Heiferman, *Growing Up with Dick and Jane: Learning and Living the American Dream* (New York: HarperCollins, 1996), 78.
60 John Hershey, "Why Do Students Bog Down on the First R?," *Life*, May 24, 1954, 136–44; see 138.
61 Margaret Mead, *A Creative Life for Children* (Washington, DC: US Children's Bureau, 1962), 30.
62 Mead, *Creative Life*, 33. The anthropologist anticipated the argument that psychologist Bruno Bettelheim would later make for the "uses of enchantment": the value of fairy tales for helping children make sense of their own antisocial impulses and anxieties about the world.

63 Something of this same debate between realism and fantasy can be witnessed in the 1947 Christmas classic *Miracle on 34th Street*, as a mother who has sought to raise her daughter in a rational, scientific fashion locks horns with a man claiming to be Santa who wants to help the girl learn to imagine.
64 Dr. Seuss, *The Cat in the Hat* (New York: Random House, 1957).
65 *The Ultimate DICK & JANE Storybook Collection: 1946 thru 1956* (New York: Grosset & Dunlap, 1984), 256.
66 Kismaric and Heiferman, *Growing Up*, 37.

## 4. "SOMETIMES MY KIDS SEEM LIKE A BUNCH OF KANGAROOS"

1 Watson, *Psychological Care*, 47.
2 Watson, 9–10.
3 Marvin R. Weisbord, "Let's Not Stifle Our Children's Creativity," *Parents*, October 1961, 106.
4 Gladys Gardner Jenkins, "Watch Your Child's Mental Growth," in *The Child Care Guide and Family Advisor*, ed. Phyllis B. Katz (New York: Parents Institute, 1960), 144.
5 Spock, *Common Sense Book*, 19–20.
6 Spock, 217–19.
7 Spock, 20.
8 Aline B. Auerbach, *How to Give Your Child a Good Start* (New York: Child Study Association of America, 1951), 18.
9 Auerbach, *How to Give*, 18.
10 Spock, *Common Sense Book*, 204.
11 Jules Henry, *Culture Against Man* (New York: Vintage Books, 1963); Vance Packard, *The Hidden Persuaders* (New York: Penguin Books, 1957).
12 Lear, *Child Worshipers*, 100.
13 Dorothy W. Baruch, *One Little Boy* (New York: Julian, 1952), 237–38.
14 Nancy C. Lutkehaus, *Margaret Mead: The Making of an American Icon* (Princeton, NJ: Princeton University Press, 2008).
15 Benjamin Spock, "Personal Correspondence with Margaret Mead," October 26, 1940, Box C44, Margaret Mead Papers, Library of Congress.
16 Mead, "Correspondence with Benjamin Spock."
17 Spock, *Common Sense Book*, 300–304.
18 Spock.
19 Spock, 145. For a fuller discussion of the roots of recapitulation theory in evolutionary discourse, see Kenneth B. Kidd, *Making American Boys: Boyology and the Feral Tale* (Minneapolis: University of Minnesota Press, 2004), 16–18.
20 Dorothy Ross, *G. Stanley Hall: The Psychologist as Prophet* (Chicago: University of Chicago Press, 1972).
21 Domnick Cavallo, *Muscles and Morals: Organized Playgrounds and Urban Reform, 1880–1920* (Philadelphia: University of Pennsylvania Press, 1981), 77.
22 Kathryn Hitte, *I'm an Indian Today* (New York: Little Golden Books, 1961).

23 Dustin Tahmahkera, *Tribal Television: Viewing Native People in Sitcoms* (Chapel Hill: University of North Carolina Press, 2014).
24 Margaret Mead, "Are Children Savages?," *Mademoiselle*, July 33, 1948, 33.
25 Mead, "Are Children Savages?," 110.
26 "When Children Have Bad Dreams," *Parents*, 1950 (quoted in Sammond, *Babes in Tomorrowland*, 289).
27 Chandra Mukerji, "Monsters and Muppets: The History of Childhood and Techniques of Cultural Analysis," in *From Sociology to Cultural Studies: New Perspectives*, ed. Elizabeth Long (London: Blackwell, 1997).
28 Quoted in Betsy Bird, Julie Danielson, and Peter D. Sieruta, *Wild Things: Acts of Mischief in Children's Literature* (Somerville, MA: Candlewick, 2014), 23. Sendak may, however, be underestimating the tradition of "bad boy" books that were popular in the early twentieth century and would be reinvented by Sendak, Seuss, and as we will see in the next chapter, Hank Ketcham among others.
29 Philip Nel, *Crockett Johnson, and Ruth Krauss, How an Unlikely Couple Found Love, Dodged the FBI, and Transformed Children's Literature* (Jackson: University Press of Mississippi, 2012), 5–6.
30 Baruch, *New Ways*, ix. Even as late as 1975, when the influence of permissiveness had waned, Bruno Bettelheim, the psychoanalyst known for his work with disturbed children, stressed the value of fairy tales as resources for children to work through their emotions: "Children know they are not always good; and often, even when they are, they would prefer not to be. This contracts [[AU: contradicts?]] what they are told by their parents, and therefore, makes the child a monster in his own eyes. The dominant culture wishes to pretend, particularly where children are concerned, that the dark side of man does not exist."
31 Baruch, *New Ways*, 53.
32 Baruch, 51–52.
33 Bill Moyers, "Maurice Sendak, 'Where the Wild Things Are,'" *NOW on PBS*, 2004, accessed October 1, 2023, https://billmoyers.com/content/bill-moyers-talks-maurice-sendak/
34 Jack Halberstam, *Wild Things: The Disorder of Desire* (Durham, NC: Duke University Press, 2020), 130.
35 Halberstam, *Wild Things*, 125.
36 Kidd, *Freud in Oz*, 113.
37 Golan Y. Moskowitz, *Wild Visionary: Maurice Sendak in Queer Jewish Context* (Stanford, CA: Stanford University Press, 2021), 5.
38 Dorothy Haas, *Christopher John's Fuzzy Blanket* (New York: Whitman, 1959).
39 Spock, *Problems of Parents*, 55.
40 Martha Wolfenstein, "The Image of the Child in Contemporary Films," in *Childhood in Contemporary Cultures*, ed. Margaret Mead and Martha Wolfenstein (Chicago: University of Chicago Press, 1955), 277.
41 For background on Engel and Orkin, see Stefan Cornic, *Morris Engel, and Ruth Orkin, Outside: From Street Photography to Filmmaking* (Paris: Carlotta, 2014).

42  Abrashkin also wrote the Danny Dunn series of children's books, sometimes with illustrations by Ezra Jack Keats, author and illustrator of *The Snowy Day*.
43  Wolfenstein, "Image of the Child," 258.
44  Wolfenstein, 89.
45  Frank, *Television*, 8.
46  Frederic Wertham, "What Parents Don't Know about Comic Books," *Ladies' Home Journal*, November 1953, 50–54, 215.
47  Does Joey's rejection of Superman in favor of the cowboy suggest a path toward a more wholesome form of hero worship, one free of the taint of comics and reflecting the persistence of the Western as part of the national character?
48  Wolf, *Controversial Problem*.
49  Julie Beck, "The Comic Strip That Explains the Evolution of American Parenting," *The Atlantic*, June 28, 2023, accessed October 1, 2023, https://www.theatlantic.com/family/archive/2023/06/goofus-and-gallant-american-parenting-highlights/674536/?utm_source=newsletter&utm_medium=email&utm_campaign=atlantic-daily-newsletter&utm_content=20230628&utm_term=The%20Atlantic%20Daily.
50  Lear, *Child Worshipers*, 12–13.
51  Henry, *Culture Against Man*, 145.
52  Henry, 305.

## 5. DENNIS THE MENACE, "THE ALL-AMERICAN HANDFUL"

1  Hank Ketcham, *The Merchant of Dennis the Menace* (New York: Abbeville, 1990), 101.
2  "Dennis the Menace Is Big Business," press release, Hank Ketcham Papers, Box 69, Boston University; "Ketcham's Menace," *Newsweek*, May 1, 1953, 57.
3  Mike Berenstain, *Child's Play: Cartoon Art of Stan and Jan Berenstain* (New York: Abrams, 2008).
4  Hank Ketcham, "There Are Millions of Menaces," *McClurg Book News*, November 1953, Hank Ketcham Papers, Boston University.
5  Ketcham, *Merchant of Dennis*, 24.
6  Ketcham, 110.
7  Leslie Fiedler, "The Eye of Innocence," in *No! In Thunder: Essays on Myth and Literature* (Boston: Beacon, 1960), 263.
8  Henry, *Culture Against Man*.
9  Hank Ketcham, *Complete Dennis the Menace 1953–1954* (Seattle: Fantagraphics, 2006), 3-5-59.
10  Hank Ketcham, *Complete Dennis the Menace 1951–1952* (Seattle: Fantagraphics, 2005), 6-7-51.
11  Ketcham, *Complete Dennis 1951–1952*, 2.
12  Ketcham, 4.
13  Ketcham, 12.
14  Ketcham, 27.
15  Ketcham, 36.

16  Ketcham, 32.
17  Ketcham, 57.
18  Ketcham, 4-10-52.
19  Ketcham, 6-5-51.
20  Ketcham, 6-10-51.
21  Donald Freeman, "Dennis the Menace to Make TV Debut with Fall Series," *San Diego Sunday Morning*, 1959, Hank Ketcham Papers, Boston University.
22  Ketcham, "There Are Millions."
23  Hank Ketcham, *Complete Dennis the Menace 1957–1958* (Seattle: Fantagraphics, 2007), 9-18-57.
24  Hal Humphrey, "Dennis Is Only a Menace to Maverick," *Los Angeles Mirror*, January 27, 1960, Hank Ketcham Papers, Boston University.
25  Anne Tropp Trensky, "The Saintly Child in Nineteenth-Century American Fiction," *Prospects: Annual of American Cultural Studies* 1 (1975): 389–413.
26  Anne Tropp Trensky, "The Bad Boy in Nineteenth-Century American Fiction," *Georgia Review* 27, no. 4 (1973): 503–17.
27  See also John Hinz, "Huck and Pluck: 'Bad' Boys in American Fiction," *South Atlantic Quarterly* (1952): 120–29; Jim Hunter, "Mark Twain and the Boy-Book in the 19th Century," *College English*, March 1963, 430–38; Evelyn Geller, "Tom Sawyer, Tom Bailey, and the Bad-Boy Genre," *Wilson Library Bulletin* 51 (1976): 245–50.
28  Viviana Zelizer, *Pricing the Priceless Child: The Changing Social Value of Children* (Princeton, NJ: Princeton University Press, 1985).
29  E. Anthony Rotundo, "Boy Culture: Middle-Class Boyhood in Nineteenth-Century America," in *Meaning for Manhood: Constructions of Masculinity in Victorian America*, ed. Mark C. Carnes and Clyde Griffen (Chicago: University of Chicago Press, 1990).
30  Tom Gunning, "Crazy Machines in the Garden of Forking Paths: Mischief Gags and the Origins of American Film Comedy," in *Classical Hollywood Comedy*, ed. Kristina Karnack and Henry Jenkins (New York: AFI/Routledge, 1994).
31  George Peck, *Pa's Bad Boy and His Pa* (New York: Dover Books, 1958).
32  Lara Saguisag, *Incorrigibles and Innocents: Constructing Childhood and Citizenship in Progressive Era Comics* (New Brunswick, NJ: Rutgers University Press, 2019), 85.
33  Peter Kramer, "Bad Boy: Notes on a Popular Figure in American Cinema, Culture and Society, 1895–1905," in *Celebrating 1895: The Century of Cinema*, ed. John Fullerton (Sydney: National Museum of Photography, Film and Television, 1998).
34  Kramer, "Bay Boy," 46.
35  Kidd, *Making American Boys*, 53.
36  Nina C. Leibman, *The Living Room Lectures: The Fifties Family in Film and Television* (Austin: University of Texas Press, 1995).
37  Ketcham, *Complete Dennis 1951–1952*, 5-23-51.
38  Ketcham, 10-20-51.
39  Ketcham, 5-18-51.
40  Ketcham, *Complete Dennis 1957–1958*, 9-7-57.

41  Ketcham, 5-5-58.
42  Ketcham, *Complete Dennis 1951–1952*, 10-29-51.
43  Ketcham, *Complete Dennis 1953–1954*, 5-25-53.
44  Spock, *Problems of Parents*, 44.
45  Art Linkletter, *Kids Say the Darndest Things!* (New York: Crown, 1957), viii.
46  Ginott, *Between Parent and Child*, 149–50.
47  Ginott, 150.
48  Constance J. Foster, "Why Children Misbehave," in *The Child Care Guide and Family Advisor*, ed. Phyllis B. Katz (New York: Parents Institute, 1960), 247.
49  Spock, *Common Sense Book*, 263–64.
50  Alan Beck, press release, New England Life Insurance Company, later circulated in publicity materials for *Dennis the Menace*, Hank Ketcham Papers, Boston University, 1953.
51  Charles Schulz's Pig-Pen character is obscured by clouds of dust wherever he goes, a drier version of the same thinking.
52  Hank Ketcham, *Complete Dennis the Menace 1961–1962* (Seattle: Fantagraphics, 2009).
53  Ketcham, *Complete Dennis 1957–1958*, 6-19-58.
54  Hank Ketcham, *Complete Dennis the Menace 1959–1960* (Seattle: Fantagraphics, 2009), 5-5-61.
55  Ketcham, *Complete Dennis 1957–1958*, 3-15-58.
56  Ketcham, *Complete Dennis 1961–1962*, 1-25-61.
57  Ketcham, *Complete Dennis 1951–1952*, 6-12-53.
58  Ketcham, 8-2-54.
59  Ketcham, 12-17-54.
60  Benjamin Spock, *Dr. Spock Talks with Mothers: Growth and Guidance* (Boston: Houghton Mifflin, 1961), 169–70.
61  Stella Chess, Alexander Thomas, and Herbert G. Birch, *Your Child Is a Person* (New York: Viking, 1965).
62  Robert A. Sears, Eleanor A. Maccoby, and Harry Lewin, *Patterns of Child Rearing* (Evanston, IL: Row, Peterson, 1957), 205–6.
63  Sears, Maccoby, and Lewin, *Patterns*.
64  Sears, Maccoby, and Lewin.
65  Ketcham, *Complete Dennis 1959–1960*, 2-12-59.
66  Benjamin Spock, *Raising Children in a Difficult Time* (New York: W. W. Norton, 1974), 111.
67  See, for example, Ketcham, *Complete Dennis 1951–1952*, 5-10-51, 6-5-51, 8-30-52.
68  First shown in Ketcham, 7-19-51.
69  Ketcham, 5-4-53.
70  Hank Ketcham, *Complete Dennis the Menace 1955–1956* (Seattle: Fantagraphics, 2006), 9-16-55.
71  Ketcham, *Complete Dennis 1957–1958*, 3-25-57.
72  Ketcham, *Complete Dennis 1955–1956*, 1-11-56.

73 Ketcham, *Complete Dennis 1959–1960*, 4-24-59.
74 Ketcham, *Complete Dennis 1955–1956*, 12-15-56.
75 Ketcham, 1-28-55.
76 Ketcham, *Complete Dennis 1959–1960*, 4-25-59.
77 Ketcham, *Complete Dennis 1961–1962*, 1-31-61.
78 Henry, *Culture Against Man*, 132.
79 Advertisement, *Parents*, April 1959, 150.
80 Spock, *Problems of Parents*, 254–55.
81 Griswold, *Fatherhood in America*.
82 Henry, *Culture Against Man*, 143.
83 Spock, *Problems of Parents*, 138–39.
84 Barbara Ehrenreich, *The Hearts of Men: American Dreams and the Flight from Commitment* (New York: Anchor Books, 1983).
85 Ehrenreich, *Hearts of Men*, 39–40.
86 *Dennis the Menace*, Season 1, directed by Charles T. Barton, DVD Extra.
87 Ketcham, *Complete Dennis 1957–1958*, 5-9-57.
88 Ketcham, *Merchant of Dennis*, 136.
89 Lynn Spigel, "Innocence Abroad: The Geopolitics of Childhood in Postwar Kid Strips," in *Kids' Media Culture*, ed. Marsha Kinder (Durham, NC: Duke University Press, 1999).
90 Ketcham, *Complete Dennis 1951–1952*, 4-25-54.
91 Ginott, *Between Parent and Child*, 172.
92 Ketcham, *Complete Dennis 1961–1962*, 5-17-61.
93 Robin Bernstein, "The Queerness of Harriet the Spy," in *Over the Rainbow: Queer Children's and Young Adult Literature*, ed. Michelle Ann Abate and Kenneth Kidd (Ann Arbor: University of Michigan Press, 2011).
94 Ginott, *Between Parent and Child*, 171–72.
95 "Miss Behavior," *The Best of Dennis the Menace*, no. 21, Fawcett, 1964.
96 Ketcham, *Complete Dennis 1959–1960*, 6-25-59.
97 Francis L. Ilg and Louise Bates Ames, *The Gesell Institute's Child Behavior: From Birth to Ten* (New York: Harper & Row, 1955), 62–64.
98 Haim Ginott, *Between Parent and Child* (New York: Macmillan, 1965), 172.
99 Ketcham, *Complete Dennis 1957–1958*, 1-30-58.
100 Ketcham, 1-31-58.
101 Ketcham, *Merchant of Dennis*, 116.
102 Ketcham, 118.
103 Ketcham, 120.
104 Richard Dyer, *White* (London: Routledge, 1997), 9.
105 Dyer, *White*, 210.
106 Dyer, 210.
107 Dyer, 210.
108 I have discussed this project with Black boomers, and they have shared that they enjoyed watching the *Our Gang* comedies, widely shown in the 1950s and 1960s,

because they were where Black children could see someone who looked like them on American television.
109 George Lipsitz, *How Racism Takes Place* (Philadelphia: Temple University Press, 2011), 35.
110 Lipsitz, *How Racism Takes Place*, 29.
111 "The Great Cleanup," in *Dennis the Menace Television Special*, Fawcett, 1966.
112 Lipsitz, *How Racism Takes Place*, 15.
113 Hank Ketcham, *Complete Dennis 1961–1962*.
114 Jennifer Lynn Stoever, *The Sonic Color Line: Race and The Cultural Politics of Listening* (New York: New York University Press, 2016), 11.
115 Lipsitz, *How Racism Takes Place*, 29.
116 Stoever, *Sonic Color Line*, 33.
117 Ketcham, *Merchant of Dennis*, 210.
118 Berenstein also pointed out in *Racial Innocence*: "White children became characterized as tender angels while black children were libeled as unfeeling, noninnocent nonchildren," 6.
119 Lipsitz, *How Racism Takes Place*, 6.
120 For more, see Jenkins, Peters-Lazaro, and Shresthova, *Popular Culture*.
121 Sammond, *Babes in Tomorrowland*, 255.
122 "Educator Cites Comic, Sees No 'Menace' in Dennis," *Honolulu Star-Bulletin*, July 23, 1958, Hank Ketcham Papers, Boston University.
123 Jadviga M. da Costa Nunes, "The Naughty Child in Nineteenth-Century American Art," *Journal of American Studies* 21, no. 2 (1987): 225–47; see p. 229.
124 "Educator Cites Comic."

## 6. GERALD MCBOING-BOING AND THE ISLAND OF THE MISFIT BOYS

1 Gertrude Crampton, *Tootle* (New York: Little Golden Books, 1945).
2 David Reisman, "'Tootle': A Modern Cautionary Tale," in *Childhood in Contemporary Cultures*, ed. Margaret Mead and Martha Wolfenstein (Chicago: University of Chicago Press, 1955), 240.
3 David Reisman, Nathan Glazer, and Reuel Denney, *The Lonely Crowd: A Study of the Changing American Character* (New Haven, CT: Yale University Press, 1950), 72.
4 Reisman, "'Tootle,'" 236–37.
5 Reisman, 236–37.
6 Mickenberg, *Learning from the Left*, 33.
7 Amid Amidi, *Cartoon Modern: Style and Design in Fifties Animation* (San Francisco: Chronicle Books, 2006).
8 Reisman, Glazer, and Denney, *Lonely Crowd*, 73.
9 Seuss's "What would you do, if it happened to you" would be recycled for *The Cat in the Hat* (1957).
10 Rosemarie Garland-Thompson, "Misfits: A Feminist Materialist Disability Concept," *Hypatia* 26, no. 3 (2011): 591–609; see 594.

11  Garland-Thompson, "Misfits," 593.
12  Garland-Thompson, 594.
13  Spock, *Common Sense Book*, 493–94.
14  William J. Arn, "Integrating Another Minority: Exceptional Children," *American Secondary Education* 6, no. 2 (1976): 37–38.
15  Philip C. Chinn, "The Exceptional Minority Child: Issues and Some Answers," *Exceptional Children* 45, no. 7 (1979): 532–36.
16  Donald D. Lankford, *Rudolph the Red-Nosed Reindeer: An American Hero* (Dartmouth, NH: Dartmouth University Press, 2016).
17  Jack Halberstam, *The Queer Art of Failure* (Durham, NC: Duke University Press, 2011), 27.
18  Halberstam, *Queer Art*, 27.
19  Nel, Johnson, and Krauss, *How an Unlikely Couple*, 15.
20  Selma H. Fraiberg, *The Magic Years: Understanding and Handling the Problems of Early Childhood* (New York: Scribner, 1959), xv.
21  Fraiberg, *Magic Years*, 103.
22  Fraiberg, 5–6.
23  "Exhibition of Toys at Museum of Modern Art," *MoMA*, October 14, 1953, https://www.moma.org/documents/moma_press-release_325917.pdf.
24  Michelle Harvey, "Channeling Creativity: A Trip through the Enchanted Gate," *MoMA*, December 20, 2017, https://stories.moma.org/channeling-creativity-a-trip-through-the-enchanted-gate-15568ee940e.
25  Miriam Lindstrom, *Children's Art: A Study in the Normal Development of Children's Modes of Visualization* (Berkeley: University of California Press, 1959).
26  Lindstrom, *Children's Art*.
27  Lindstrom, 7–8.
28  Lindstrom, 21.
29  Michelle H. Martin, *Black Gold: Milestones of African American Children's Picture Books, 1845–2002* (New York: Routledge, 2004), xviii.
30  Victor Lowenfield, *Your Child and His Art: A Guide for Parents* (New York: Macmillan, 1960).
31  Lowenfield, *Your Child*, 5.
32  Lowenfield, 14.
33  Crockett Johnson, *Barnaby: Volume One* (Seattle: Fantagraphics, 2013), 84.
34  Fraiberg, *Magic Years*, 13.
35  Charles Schulz, "The Theme of Peanuts," in *My Life with Charlie Brown*, ed. M. Thomas Inge (Jackson: University of Mississippi Press, 2010), 160–61.
36  Lara Saguisag, "Consuming Childhood: Peanuts and Children's Consumer Culture in the Postwar Era," in *The Comics of Charles Schulz: The Good Grief of Modern Life*, ed. Jared Gardner and Ian Gordon (Jackson: University Press of Mississippi, 2017).
37  Charles M. Schulz, "Peanuts as Profession of Faith," in *My Life with Charlie Brown*, ed. M. Thomas Inge (Jackson: University of Mississippi Press, 2010b), 24.

38  Schulz, "Peanuts as Profession," 19.
39  Schulz, 26.
40  Schulz, 34.
41  Schulz.
42  Mead, *Creative Life*.
43  Amy F. Ogata, "Building Imagination in Postwar Children's Rooms," in *Studies in the Decorative Arts* 16, no. 1 (Fall–Winter 2008–09): 126–42.
44  Norman Chermer, *How to Build Children's Toys and Furniture* (New York: McGraw-Hill, 1954).
45  Charles Schulz, "What Can You Do with a Dog That Doesn't Talk?," in *My Life with Charlie Brown*, ed. M. Thomas Inge (Jackson: University of Mississippi Press, 2010), 174.
46  Schulz, "Theme of Peanuts," 28–29.
47  David Michaelis, *Schulz and Peanuts: A Biography* (New York: Harper Perennial, 2007), 254.
48  D. W. Winnicott, *Playing and Reality* (London: Routledge, 1971), 7.
49  Mead, *Creative Life*, 26.
50  Mead, 31.
51  Mead, 34.
52  Schulz, "Theme of Peanuts," 147.
53  Mead, *Creative Life*, 47.
54  Lynn Spigel, "Designs for the Small Screen," in *Up Is Down: Mid-Century Experiments in Advertising and Film at the Goldsholl Studio*, ed. Amy Beste and Corinne Granof (Chicago: Block Museum of Art, 2018), 119.

## 7. "I Like You Just the Way You Are"

1  This iconic incident gained new prominence in the documentary *Won't You Be My Neighbor?*, and the podcast *Finding Fred* (2019) devoted its entire second episode to its interview with Clemmons.
2  *Finding Fred*, 2019, episode 1.
3  "Each One of Us Is Special," undated clipping, Fred Rogers Archive, Pittsburgh.
4  Fred Rogers as told to Marvin J. Wolf, "Why I Live where I Live: Mister Rogers' Neighborhood," *Ambassador*, November 1996, 19, Fred Rogers Archive, Pittsburgh.
5  Rogers, "Why I Live," 19.
6  Margaret Mead, "The Knowledgeable Young," in *Progress in Mental Health: Proceedings of the Seventh International Congress on Mental Health*, ed. Hugh Freeman (London: Churchill, 1969).
7  Mead, "Knowledgeable Young," 36.
8  Louise Corum and Birdice McLaughlin, *Who Is My Friend?* (New York: Wonder Books, 1959).
9  "Emily Jacobson: Lecturer, Actress, Journalist," undated clipping, Fred Rogers Archive, Pittsburgh.

10  Judith A. Rubin, "An Ugly Duckling Finds the Swans or How I Fell in Love with Art Therapy," in *Architects of Art Therapy: Memoirs and Life Stories*, ed. Maxine Borowsky Junge and Harriet Wadeson (Springfield, IL: Charles C. Thomas, 2006).
11  Door Wittenberg, "Some Interviews: Mr. Fred Rogers," June–July 1977, 15, Fred Rogers Archive, Pittsburgh.
12  King, *Good Neighbor*, 132.
13  Sally Ann Fleckner, "When Fred Met Margaret," *PITTMED*, Winter 2014, https://www.pittmed.health.pitt.edu/story/when-fred-met-margaret.
14  Fleckner, "When Fred Met Margaret."
15  Margaret McFarland, "The Educational Significance of Mister Rogers' Neighborhood," *WQED Close Up*, September 1969, 7–10, Fred Rogers Archive.
16  *Mister Rogers' Neighborhood*, https://www.misterrogers.org/articles/margaret-mcfarland/.
17  Quoted in *Finding Fred*.
18  McFarland, "Educational Significance."
19  Lauren Vinopal, "5 Lessons from Margaret McFarland, the Scientist behind Mister Rogers," *Fatherly*, October 25, 2019, https://www.fatherly.com/health/margaret-mcfarland-science-mister-rogers.
20  King, *Good Neighbor*, 131–32.
21  Erik Erikson, *Childhood and Society* (New York: W. W. Norton, 1964).
22  King, *Good Neighbor*, 35.
23  Mead and Wolfenstein, *Childhood in Contemporary Cultures*, 12.
24  Mead and Wolfenstein, 93–94.
25  Mead and Wolfenstein.
26  Frances Horwich and Reinald Werrenrath, *Have Fun with Your Children* (New York: Prentice-Hall, 1954), 206–7.
27  Horwich and Werrenwrath, *Have Fun*, 64.
28  Bob Keeshan, *Growing Up Happy: Captain Kangaroo Tells Yesterday's Children How to Nurture Their Own* (New York: Knopf Doubleday, 1989).
29  Keeshan, *Growing Up Happy*, 101.
30  Keeshan, 51.
31  Mead, "Beyond the Nuclear Family," 1963.
32  Keeshan, *Growing Up Happy*, 113.
33  Keeshan, 94.
34  Keeshan, 54.
35  Keeshan, 130, 180.
36  Lee Ecuyer, *Zippy the Chimp* (New York: Rand McNally, 1953).
37  This following section could not have been written without the generosity of Shari Goldin, who shared with me several unpublished papers she wrote dealing with the history of puppets and television at the University of Wisconsin–Madison under the direction of Lynn Spigel.
38  Dina Sherzer and Joel Sherzer, eds., *Humor and Comedy in Puppetry* (Bowling Green, OH: Bowling Green University Popular Press, 1987).

39 Frank Proschan, "The Co-Creation of the Comic in Puppetry," in *Humor and Comedy in Puppetry*, ed. Dina Sherzer and Joel Sherzer (Bowling Green, OH: Bowling Green University Popular Press, 1987).
40 Evelyn Roe, "Remo Bufano, a Puppeteer from Childhood, Discovers that the Smaller Figures Are Useful in Television Plays," *Christian Science Monitor*, June 3, 1939, 4–5.
41 D. L. McFadden, "Television Comes to Our Children," *Parents*, January 24, 1949, 26–27.
42 Frederick Rainsberry, "The Social Responsibility of Children's Television," *Child Study*, Summer 1960, 1319–23.
43 Nat Segaloff and Mallory Lewis, *Shari Lewis and Lambchop: The Team That Changed Children's Television* (Louisville: University of Kentucky Press, 2022), 41.
44 Fred Rogers and Barry Head, *Mister Rogers Talks with Parents* (Pittsburgh: Family Communications, 1983).
45 Rogers and Head, *Mister Rogers Talks*, 111.
46 Quoted in Mark J. P. Wolf, *The World of Mister Rogers' Neighborhood* (New York: Routledge, 2017).
47 Mark J. P. Wolf, *The World of Mister Rogers' Neighborhood* (New York: Routledge, 1917).
48 Baruch, *Parents and Children*, 318.
49 Wolf, *World of Mister Rogers' Neighborhood*.
50 Rogers and Head, *Mister Rogers Talks*, 169–70.

## 8. PERMISSIVENESS AND THE BLACK CHILD

1 Spock, *Raising Children*.
2 Erikson, *Childhood and Society*, 241.
3 Daniel Patrick Moynihan, *The Negro Family: The Case for National Action* (Washington, DC: Office of Policy Planning and Research, US Department of Labor, 1965).
4 James P. Comer and Alvin F. Poussaint, *Black Child Care: How to Bring Up a Healthy Black Child in America* (New York: Simon & Schuster, 1975), 11.
5 Comer and Poussaint, *Black Child Care*, 11–12.
6 Shari Goldin, "Unlearning Black and White: Race, Media and the Classroom," in *The Children's Culture Reader*, ed. Henry Jenkins (New York: New York University Press, 1998), 136.
7 Comer and Poussaint, *Black Child Care*, 42.
8 Comer and Poussaint, 57.
9 Comer and Poussaint, 57.
10 Comer and Poussaint, 123.
11 Comer and Poussaint, 124.
12 Comer and Poussaint, 117.
13 Comer and Poussaint, 12.
14 Comer and Poussaint, 12.
15 Comer and Poussaint, 9.
16 Comer and Poussaint, 17.

17 Comer and Poussaint, 44.
18 Comer and Poussaint, 28.
19 Comer and Poussaint, 46.
20 Comer and Poussaint, 56.
21 Comer and Poussaint, 56–57.
22 Comer and Poussaint, 58.
23 Comer and Poussaint, 36.
24 Comer and Poussaint, 63–64.
25 *Archival Collections*, Wiltwyck School for Boys records, 1942–1981, bulk 1964–1982, accessed October 1, 2023, https://findingaids.library.columbia.edu/ead/nnc-rb/ldpd_6262245#:~:text=The%20Wiltwyck%20School%20for%20Boys,delinquents%20and%20potential%20juvenile%20delinquents.
26 Edith Kramer, "Art as Therapy," in *Architects of Art Therapy: Memories and Life Stories*, ed. Maxine Borowsky Junge and Harriet Wadeson (Springfield, IL: Charles C. Thomas, 2006).
27 Bambi Haggins, *Laughing Mad: The Black Comic Persona in Post-Soul America* (Rutgers, NJ: Rutgers University Press, 2007), 24.
28 William Henry Cosby, "An Integration of the Visual Media via "Fat Albert and the Cosby Kids" into the Elementary School Curriculum as a Teaching Aid and Vehicle to Achieve Increased Learning," doctoral diss., University of Massachusetts, 1976, https://scholarworks.umass.edu/dissertations/AAI7706369, see p. 64.
29 Cosby, "Integration."
30 Cosby.
31 Comer and Poussaint, *Black Child Care*, 129.
32 Lawrence W. Levine, *Black Culture and Black Consciousness: Afro-American Folk Thought from Slavery to Freedom* (Oxford: Oxford University Press, 1978), 358.
33 Kathrynn Hitte, *What Can You Do Without a Place to Play?* (New York: Parents Magazine Press, 1971).
34 Katharine Capshaw, *Civil Rights Childhood: Picturing Liberation in African American Photobooks* (Minneapolis: University of Minnesota Press, 2014), 170.
35 Ironically, Stone had effectively reversed the message of the original Urban League spot that inspired him; it had denounced the dangers of playing and dodging cars in dirty streets, demanding better play space for children.
36 Morris Turner, *Wee Pals* (New York: Signet, 1969).
37 Rebecca Wanzo, *The Content of Our Caricature: African American Comic Art and Political Belonging* (New York: New York University Press, 2020), 169.

## 9. BETWEEN BACKYARDS AND THE GREAT OUTDOORS

1 Kenneth T. Jackson, *Crabgrass Frontier: The Suburbanization of the United States* (New York: Oxford University Press, 1987).
2 Sean Griffin, "Kings of the Wild Backyard: Davy Crockett and Children's Space," in *Kids' Media Culture*, ed. Marsha Kinder (Durham, NC: Duke University Press, 1999), 108.

3   Griffin, "Kings," 109.
4   Roger Hart, *Children's Experience of Place* (New York: Wiley, 1979); Robin C. Moore, *Childhood's Domain: Play and Place in Child Development* (Berkeley: MIG Communications, 1986); M. H. Matthews, *Making Sense of Place: Children's Understanding of Large-Scale Environments* (Hertfordshire, UK: Harvester Wheatsheaf/Lanham, MD: Barnes & Noble, 1992); John Newson and Elizabeth Newson, *Seven Years Old in the Home Environment* (London: Allen & Unwin, 1976).
5   Sally Schauman, "The Genius of Childhood: The Life and Ideas of Edith Cobb," *Children, Youth and Environments* 23, no. 2 (2013): 194–207.
6   Edith Cobb, *The Ecology of Imagination in Childhood* (New York: Columbia University Press, 1977; reprint, Thompson, CT: Spring Publications, 2015), 198 (reprint edition).
7   Cobb, *Ecology of Imagination*, 244.
8   Cobb, 245.
9   Jackson, *Crabgrass Frontier*.
10  Erikson, *Childhood and Society*.
11  Frederick Donaldson, "The Child in the City," mimeograph, University of Washington, 1970; cited in Matthews, *Making Sense of Place*.
12  Newson and Newson, *Seven Years Old*, 68.
13  Newson and Newson, 77.
14  Hart, *Children's Experience*.
15  Hart.
16  Newson and Newson, *Seven Years Old*.
17  Mead, *Creative Life*, 32.
18  Moore, *Childhood's Domain*, 57.
19  Mead, *Creative Life*, 31.
20  Quoted in Scott Higgins, *Matinee Melodrama: Playing with Formula in the Sound Serial* (New Brunswick, NJ: Rutgers University Press, 2016), 16.
21  Higgins, *Matinee Melodrama*, 19.
22  Quoted in Joyce Slaton, "Day of the Dolphin: How Vintage Florida Kitsch Masked a Grim Reality," *Collectors Weekly*, January 31, 2019, accessed October 1, 2023, https://www.collectorsweekly.com/articles/day-of-the-dolphin/.
23  Henry Jenkins, "'Her Suffering Aristocratic Majesty': The Sentimental Value of Lassie," *The Wow Climax* (New York: New York University Press, 2006).
24  Ace Collins, *Lassie: A Dog's Life* (New York: Cader Books, 1993).
25  "The Most Objectionable," *Newsweek*, July 30, 1956, 78.
26  Anna W. M. Wolf, "TV, Movies, Comics: Boon or Bane to Children?," *Parents*, April 1961, 46–48.
27  Frank Orme, "TV for Children: What's Good? What's Bad?," *Parents*, February 1964, 54.
28  "The Mini-Wasteland," *Newsweek*, January 23, 1967, 92–94.

29. Margaret Mead, "What Kind of Park?," *Science Service*, November 19, 1968. Draft found in Margaret Mead Papers, Box 177, Library of Congress.
30. Rachel *Silent Spring* (New York: Houghton Mifflin, 1962).
31. Margaret Mead, "Where Is the Wilderness?," in *A Way of Seeing*, ed. Margaret Mead and Rhoda Métraux (New York: McCall, 1969), 143.
32. Jean Craighead George, *My Side of the Mountain* (New York: Puffin, 1959), xii.
33. George, *My Side*, xiv.
34. Mead, "Where Is the Wilderness?"
35. George, *My Side*, 1.
36. Yi-Fu Tuan, *Space and Place: The Perspective of Experience* (Minneapolis: University of Minnesota Press, 1977).
37. Tuan, *Space and Place*, 144.
38. Tuan, 166.
39. George, *My Side*, 8.
40. George, 27.
41. George, 17.
42. George, 29.
43. George, 29.
44. George, 38.
45. George, 45.
46. George, 132.
47. George, 36.
48. Mischa Honeck, *Our Frontier Is the World: The Boy Scouts in the Age of American Ascendancy* (Ithaca, NY: Cornell University Press, 2018), 207.
49. Honeck, *Our Frontier*, 207.
50. Margaret Mead, "How Summer Camp Changes a Child," *Redbook*, August 1971, 49.
51. Mead, "Summer Camp," 49.
52. George, *My Side*, 76.
53. George, 76.
54. George, 126.
55. George, 166–67.
56. George, 168.
57. George, 173.
58. Mead, "Summer Camp," 175.
59. George, *My Side*.

## 10. JONNY QUEST, MAYA, AND THE PROMISE OF "WORLD BROTHERHOOD"

1. Ken Heyman, personal correspondence with Margaret Mead, March 8, 1961.
2. Edward Steichen, *Family of Man* (New York: Museum of Modern Art, 1955; reissue, 2002).
3. Mead and Heyman, *Family*, 11.
4. Margaret Mead, "Education for Tomorrow's World," *Redbook*, May 1967, 36–38.

5 Margaret Mead, "Patriotism Redefined," *Parents*, September 1962. Note the way this rhetoric of children as "natives" paves the way for the idea of "digital natives" that has shaped American education policy for the past three decades.
6 Margaret Mead, "And Children Shall Lead the Way," *Redbook*, February 1967, 46.
7 Mead, "Knowledgeable Young."
8 "Margaret Mead Answers . . . ," *Redbook*, February 1972, 45–49.
9 Goddard, *Our Children*, iv.
10 Mead, "Education for Tomorrow's World."
11 Katie Day Good, *Bring the World to the Child: Technologies of Global Citizenship in American Education* (Cambridge, MA: MIT Press, 2020), 20.
12 Good, *Bring the World*, 134.
13 Honeck, *Our Frontier*; Benjamin René Jordan, *Modern Manhood and the Boy Scouts of America: Citizenship, Race, and the Environment, 1910–1930* (Chapel Hill: University of North Carolina Press, 2016).
14 Boy Scouts of America, *Citizenship Merit Badge Series* (New Brunswick, NJ: Boy Scouts of America, 1953), 70.
15 Boy Scouts of America, *Citizenship*, 96.
16 Boy Scouts of America, 76.
17 For more on American childhood and the Cold War, see Margaret Peacock, *Innocent Weapons: The Soviet and American Politics of Childhood in the Cold War* (Chapel Hill: University of North Carolina Press, 2014).
18 Mead and Heyman, *Family*, 168.
19 Jim Corkis, "In His Own Words: Doug Wildey on Jonny Quest," *Cartoon Research*, November 1, 2017, accessed October 1, 2023, https://cartoonresearch.com/index.php/in-his-own-words-doug-wildey-on-jonny-quest/.
20 Leslie Fiedler, "Come Back to the Raft Ag'in, Huck Honey!" *Partisan Review*, June 1948, 7.
21 Fiedler, "Come Back," 12.
22 Klein, *Cold War Orientalism*, 24.
23 Klein, 144.
24 Klein, 146.
25 Hadji's persona was modeled on that of Sabu Dastagir, the son of an Indian mahout, who was cast in the role of an elephant driver in Robert Flaherty's 1937 film *Elephant Boy*. Later, Sabu played the Arab boy Abu in Alexander Korda's *The Thief of Bagdad* (1940) and Mowgli in Korda's *The Jungle Book* (1942). After becoming an American citizen in 1944, Sabu joined the air force and was awarded the Distinguished Flying Cross. His career declined afterward as he was unable to secure equivalent roles in Hollywood. He was considered for the role of Birju in Mehboob Khan's 1957 film *Mother India*, which would have marked his Hindu-cinema debut, but he was denied a work permit. He died in Los Angeles in 1963 as the *Jonny Quest* cartoons were being produced. Hadji's Americanization—and gradual dislocation within his own country—paralleled that of the actor who was his archetype.

26 Klein, *Cold War Orientalism*, 146.
27 Manu Bhagavan, ed., *India and the Cold War* (Chapel Hill: University of North Carolina Press, 2019), 4.
28 Ashis Nandy, "Reconstructing Childhood: A Critique of the Ideology of Adulthood," *Alternatives X*, Winter 1984–85, 359–75; see 366.
29 The dismissive use of the term "childish" in a children's program encourages the young viewers to feel superior to, or perhaps to hope to outgrow, the primitive state of these foreign cultures rather than to fully embrace a concept of global brotherhood.
30 "Anubis" aired less than a decade after Egyptian president Gamal Abdel Nassar seized the Suez Canal and the country was invaded by Israel, France, and Great Britain. The United States had lobbied the British Crown against the invasion and ultimately joined with the Soviet Union to send UN peacekeeping forces to the region to force its European allies to withdraw. This international standoff is credited with enhancing Egypt's leadership among the Arab countries, further signaling the end of the British Empire, and setting the stage for how future Cold War conflicts in the region would be handled.
31 Mead and Heyman, *Family*, 98.
32 *Maya* may have been partially inspired by Alexander Mackendrick's 1961 film *Sammy Goes South* (released in a shortened form in the United States as *A Boy Ten Feet Tall*), in which a ten-year-old British boy makes a five-thousand-mile journey from Egypt to South Africa, alone, after his parents are killed in a Port Said bombing during the Suez Crisis.
33 Kidd, *Making American Boys*, 7.

## 11. "DANGER, WILL ROBINSON"

1 Margaret Mead, "Changing Family Styles," unpublished, 1964, Margaret Mead Papers, Library of Congress, 146.
2 Mead, "Children Shall Lead," 50.
3 Alvin Toffler, *Future Shock* (New York: Random House, 1970).
4 Rebecca Onion, *Innocent Experiments: Childhood and the Culture of Popular Science in the United States* (Chapel Hill: University of North Carolina Press, 2016), 42.
5 Writer Jackson Gillis penned a series of episodes centered on Penny and her own challenges as the middle child, as a girl on the threshold of puberty, and as someone who also suffers from a lack of children her own age. Gillis had built his reputation as the creator of boys' stories through his role in developing two serials for Walt Disney's *Mickey Mouse Club*. *Spin and Marty* depicted the bonding among boys attending a Western-themed summer camp; in *Mystery of the Applegate Treasure*, the Hardy Boys find a pirate treasure in their own backyard. Starting with "My Friend, Mr. Nobody," Gillis crafted seven of *Lost in Space*'s best episodes, mostly centering on Penny or in one case, Judy, and asking questions about what it means to become a young woman. Gillis recognized that Penny was often slighted

by the other writers, sometimes getting into trouble and requiring rescue, sometimes simply doing chores in the background but rarely the center of attention.

6   Margaret Mead, "A Redefinition of Education," *NEA Journal*, October 1959, 15.
7   Rhoda Métraux, "A Scientist Is a Man (or Sometimes a Woman)," unpublished, March 17, 1961, Rhoda Métraux Papers, Library of Congress.
8   Rhoda Métraux, "The Image of the Scientist," unpublished lecture presented at the "Northwestern Science Seminar for Public Information Officers," March 21, 1961, Rhoda Métraux Papers, Library of Congress.
9   Métraux, "The Image."
10  Rhoda Métraux, "Children and Space," unpublished draft, October 4, 1957, Rhoda Métraux Papers, Library of Congress.
11  Eugene Blum, "Toys Based on Space Themes," *Anthropology* 271, December 1958, Rhoda Métraux Papers, Library of Congress.
12  Blum, "Toys Based on Space."
13  Métraux, "A Scientist Is a Man."
14  Onion, *Innocent Experiments*, 179.
15  Onion, 120.
16  Onion, 125.
17  Cynthia J. Miller and A. Bowdoin Van Riper, *1950s "Rocketman" TV Series and Their Fans: Cadets, Rangers, and Junior Space Men* (New York: Palgrave Macmillan, 2012).
18  Miller and Van Riper, *1950s "Rocketman,"* 42–43.
19  Henry Jenkins, "Foreword: To Infinity and Beyond," in Cynthia J. Miller and A. Bowdoin Van Riper, *1950s "Rocketman" TV Series and Their Fans: Cadets, Rangers, and Junior Space Men* (New York: Palgrave Macmillan, 2012).
20  In a curious connection to *Lost in Space*, *Man in Space* (1955) was narrated by Dick Tufeld, the voice of Robot.
21  Onion, *Innocent Experiments*, 98–99.
22  Leibman, *Living Room Lectures*, 250.
23  Leibman, 253.
24  Lynn Spigel, "Seducing the Innocent: Children and Television in Postwar America," in *Ruthless Criticism: New Perspectives in U.S. Communication History*, ed. William S. Solomon and Robert W. McChesney (Minneapolis: University of Minnesota Press, 1993).
25  Dreikurs and Soltz, *Children*, 9.
26  Dreikurs and Soltz, 10.
27  Dreikurs and Soltz, 301.
28  Jeff Bond, *The Fantasy Worlds of Irwin Allen* (New York: Creature Features, 2021), 222.
29  Betty Friedan, *The Feminine Mystique* (New York: W. W. Norton, 1963), 60–61.
30  Friedan, *Feminine Mystique*.
31  Spock, *Problems of Parents*, 121.

32 Friedan, *Feminine Mystique*.
33 Spock, *Problems of Parents*, 228.
34 Spock, 229.
35 Spock, 99.
36 Margaret Mead, "Job of the Children's Mother's Husband," *New York Times Magazine*, May 10, 1959, 7, 66–67.
37 Mead, "Job of the Children."

## CODA

1 Margaret Mead, correspondence with Dr. Sey Chassler, April 21, 1971, Margaret Mead Papers, Library of Congress.
2 "A Redbook Dialogue: Dr. Margaret Mead and Dr. Benjamin Spock," *Redbook*, April 1972, 80–81, 138.
3 Margaret Mead, "A New Understanding of Childhood," unpublished manuscript, 1972.
4 Mead, "New Understanding."
5 Benjamin Spock, *Dr. Spock on Parenting: Sensible, Reassuring Advice for Today's Parents* (New York: Gallery Books, 1989), 247–48.
6 T. Berry Brazelton, *Toddlers and Parents: A Declaration of Independence* (New York: Delta, 1974), 29–30.
7 Mead, "Changing Family Styles."
8 "A Redbook Dialogue."
9 "A Redbook Dialogue."
10 "Agnew vs. Spock," *New York Times*, October 3, 1970. https://www.nytimes.com/1970/10/03/archives/agnew-vs-spock.html.
11 Spock, *Dr. Spock on Parenting*, 46.
12 Spock, 92.
13 Benjamin Spock and Mary Morgan, *Spock on Spock: A Memoir of Growing Up with the Century* (New York: Pantheon, 1989), 247–48.
14 James Dobson, *Dare to Discipline* (Carol Stream, IL: Tyndale House, 1977), 15.
15 Dobson, *Dare to Discipline*, 3.
16 Martha Tesema, "Remember That Time Fox News Said Mister Rogers Was 'Evil,'" *Mashable*, June 18, 2018, accessed October 1, 2023, https://mashable.com/video/fox-and-friends-mr-rogers-evil.
17 "Where Did the Term Snowflake come from?" *This Week*, January 26, 2022, accessed October 1, 2023, https://www.theweek.co.uk/news/955539/where-did-the-term-snowflake-come-from.
18 https://www.freerangekids.com.
19 http://www.howtobeagirlpodcast.com.
20 Jacob Gallant and Holly Emery, "Board Upholds Firing of Principal Who Read 'I Need a New Butt,'" *WLBT*, May 12, 2022, accessed October 1, 2023, https://www.wlbt.com/2022/05/12/board-upholds-firing-principal-who-read-i-need-new-butt/.

21 Tyler Kingkade, Ben Goggin, Ben Collins, and Brandy Zadrozny, "How an Urban Myth About Litter Boxes in Schools Became a GOP Talking Point," *NBC News*, October 14, 2022, accessed October 1, 2023, https://www.nbcnews.com/tech/misinformation/urban-myth-litter-boxes-schools-became-gop-talking-point-rcna51439.

# INDEX

Abbott, Bernice, 117
Abrashkin, Ray, 118
*The Addams Family*, 292
Adler, Felix, 55, 58
*The Adventures of Huckleberry Finn* (Twain), 262
*Adventures of Tom Sawyer* (Twain), 135
advertisements, 5, 100
Africa *Texas Style*, 242
Agee, James, 216
Agnew, Spiro, 312–13
Aldrich, Thomas Bailey, 135
*Alfred Hitchcock Presents*, "Bang! You're Dead," 19, 103, 123, 124, 126–27, 233, 282
Allen, Irwin, 283. *See also Lost in Space;* biography, 289
Allison, Clyde, 258
Allison, Mary Emma, 258
*Amahl and the Night Visitors* (opera), 205
Amidi, Amid, 162
"Anger Transference" (Sargent), 87, *88*
*The Animal World* (documentary film), 289
Applegate, Maurice, 77
*Are You My Mother?* (Eastman), 45, 79
Arlitt, Ada Hart, 15, 16
Armstrong, William H., 219
Arsenal Family and Children's Center, 11, 12, 19, 191, 192, 194, 206, 309
art therapy: clay, 2; coloring books, 176; D'Amico and, 173–74; Kramer, E., on, 217–18; of Lindstrom, M. and C., 173–75; Lowenfeld on, 176; Rubin and, 191
*Art Therapy in a Children's Community* (Kramer, E.), 217

Asimov, Isaac, 288
Auerbach, Alice B., 102
Autry, Gene, 119, 166

*Baby and Child Care* (Spock), 1, 10, 26–28, 131, 303–4, 307–9
backyards, 235, 301; adventure play and, 238–39; as childhood's domain, 234; as home base, 236, 239, 244; as home region, 236; Jenkins and, 237–38
bad-boy tropes, 133–34; early books with, 135; fathers and, 144–46; *Peck's Bad Boy and His Pa* and, 136–37; "saintly child" and, 136
Bandung Conference, 266
"Bang! You're Dead" (*Alfred Hitchcock Presents*), 19, 103, 123, *124*, 126–27, 233, 282
*Barnaby* (comic strip), 176–78, *177*
*Bartholomew and the Oobleck* (Seuss), 87
Baruch, Dorothy, 9–10, 189, 304, 307, 312; biography, 42; children's literature, 93, 204–5; on democracy, 76–77; on emotional foods, 82–83; on emotional release, 110, 112; Freud and, 104; *Glass House of Prejudice*, 42–44; on protest of children, 87; on regimentation, 91; Sally, Dick, and Jane books and, 94; Sendak's *Kenny's Window* and, 114; on submission of child, 84; on war, 83; *Your Child Meets the World Outside*, 84
Bateson, Mary Catherine, 33–34, 254–55
*Beany and Cecil*, 202
Belafonte, Harry, 218

353

Bell, W. Kamau, 219
Bell Telephone science series, 288
Benedict, Ruth, 31, 109; books, 44; on "patterns of culture," 157
Berenstain, Stan and Jan, 131–32
Berman, Shelly, 2
Bernstein, Robin, 149, 156
Berry, John, 271
Bhagavan, Manu, 266
*Bicycle Thieves*, 117
*The Big Honey Hunt* (Berenstain, S. and J.), 132
*Birdman*, 261
Bixby, Jerome, 123
Black Arts Movement, 224
*Black Child Care* (Poussaint), 28, 209–14, 222
*Black Culture and Black Consciousness* (Levine), 223
*Black Like Me*, 273
Blackness, 19, 94, 126–27, 133, 149, 207–30
Blair, Mary, 259
*Blaming the Victim* (Ryan), 208
Blazia, Akeba, 187
Boone, Daniel, 247
"Boy Culture" (concept), 136
boys: "boys will be boys" idea about, 2; gangs, 59; as protagonists, 7; in striped shirts, iconography, 7
Boy Scouts, 59, 136; handbook, 249; segregation in, 257–58; World Brotherhood Merit Badge, 258
*Boy's Life* (magazine), 249
*The Boy With the Green Hair* (film), 19, 49, 63, 68–73, 209, 292
Bradbury, Ray, 288
Braun, Wernher von, 288
*The Brave One*, 271
Brazelton, T. Berry, 11; *Toddlers and Parents*, 309
*Bright Roads* (film), 218–19
*Bringing the World to the Child* (Good), 257

Brown, Margaret Wise, 93
Browning, Riccou, 242. See also *Flipper*
Bruegel, Pieter, 132
Buck, Pearl, 42, 263
Buck Buck (game), 220, 223
Bufano, Remo, 201
Bureau of Educational Experiments, 83
Burroughs, Edgar Rice, 275
Burt, Olive W., 66–67
Burton, Douglas, 242
Butler, Daws, 202

Caldecott Medal, 175
Calloway, Cab, 65
Campbell, Eleanor, 94
Campton, Gertrude, 161
Cannon, Robert, 162
Capra, Frank: *Our Mr. Sun* directed by, 288–89; Signal Corps unit, 77, 79
Capshaw, Katharine, 224
*Captain Kangaroo*, 64, 198–201, 200
Carey, Josie, 189
Carnegie Foundation, 224
Carson, Rachel, 245
Cartwright, Angela, 283
*Casper the Friendly Ghost*, 168
*Cat in the Hat* (Seuss), 77, 92, 95–99, 99
Caulfield, Rick, 47
*CBS Children's Film Festival*, 259–60
*CBS Radio Workshop*, 30–31
Ceplair, Larry, 78
Charlie Brown (character), 7, 78, 132, 178–82, 181, 189, 226
Chassler, Sy, 33
Chermer, Norman, 179
*The Child From One to Six* (Arlitt), 15
*Childhood in Contemporary Cultures* (Mead and Wolfenstein), 31, 35–37, 47–48, 157
*Childhood's Domain* (Moore, R.), 238
children: as animals, 5, 17, 54, 100–103, 107–9, 112, 115; as clocks, 54; fictions, 7, 45–46; as Indians, 5, 106–7; as mon-

sters, 107; rights of, 3; as "Wild Things," 4, 5, 17, 114
*Children* (Dreikurs), 14, 293
*Children and Movies* (Mitchell, A.), 239
*Children in Wartime* (Child Study Association of America), 69
Children's Bureau, of United States Department of Labor, 31–32, 178
*The Children's Corner*, 185, 189
*Children's Games* (Bruegel), 132
*Children's Humor* (Wolfenstein), 196–97
Child Study (method), 9, 18, 36, 47–73, 77, 157, 304, 314; emotional life and, 60; imagination and, 57; immigrants and, 56; media consumption and, 61–62, 63; on "normal" child, 41, 56; origins, 55; parents education and, 56, 57; racism and, 40–46; on war, 42, 68–72; women and, 47–48
Child Study Association of America, 55, 58, 61–62, 102, 192, 244; *Children in Wartime*, 69; *Outlines of Child Study*, 56
*The Child Worshippers* (Lear), 123, 125
Christianity, 66–68
*Christian Science Monitor* (magazine), 201
*Christopher John's Fuzzy Blanket* (Haas), 114–15, *115*
Clampett, Bob, 202
*Clarence the Cross-Eyed Lion*, 242
Cobb, Edith, 245; Mead and, 235; on "world making," 237–38
Cold War, 85, 288; brainwashing, 101
*Collier's* (magazine), 132
*Come on People* (Poussaint), 222–23
Comer, James P., 209, 211–14, 221; *Sesame Street* and, 210
Connors, Chuck, 240
Conrad, Joseph, 275
Conreid, Hans, 89, 90, 292, 295
*Controversial Problem of Discipline* (Wolf, K.), 38, 122
Cook, Daniel Thomas, 28

Cooper, James Fenimore, 262
Cosby, Bill, 209. See also *Fat Albert and the Cosby Kids*; biography, 219; Buck Buck game and, 220, 223; dissertation, 220–21; education, 221; Fat Albert character, 220
*Cosby Show*, 210
Counterculture, 312–313
*The Cove* (film), 242, 244
cowboys, 119–20, 233
Cowden, Jack, 242
Cowley, Bill, 134
Cox, Wally, 292
*A Creative Life For Your Children* (pamphlet), 178
*Culture Against Man* (Henry), 125–26

D'Amico, Victor, 173–74
Dana, Richard Henry, 262–63
Dandridge, Dorothy, 218
*Daniel Boone*, 295
*Dare to Discipline* (Dobson), 313
Davis, Clara, 102
*Davy Crockett* (series), 233
DC Comics, 62
*Death in the Family* (Agee), 216
De Huszar, George B., 84–85
Dell Comics, 289
Denning, Michael, 7
*Dennis the Menace*, 8, 19, 128, 131–60, 291, 305; Alice, 141, 146, 148; Americanness and, 157, 159, *159*; "The Big Cleanup," 153; Brady family, 145; characterization, 133; "The Club Initiation," 145; clubs, 145–46; Cowboy Bob, 148–49, 233; "Dennis and the Open House," 154; "Dennis in Gypsyland," 146; "Dennis Is a Genius," 281–82; discipline, 141–42, *143*; fatherhood, 144; George, 144–47; George Wilson, 134, 154–56, 158; Gina, 147, 152; girls, 147; Henry, 145, 281; Jackson, 152–53, 156; Joey, 150–51; "The Junior Astronaut," 158;

*Dennis the Menace (cont.)*
"Junior Pathfinders Ride Again," 147; Margaret, 147–49, 151, 281; Martha, 146; mischief, 134; Miss Elkins, 147; mud, 138–39; nudism, 139–40; origins, 131–32; "The Pioneers," 144; Mrs. Perkins, 281; record, 148–49; television series, 134; Tommy, 141, 146; "The Treasure Chest," 146; "Trouble from Mars," 158; verbal, 138–39; whiteness and, 151–56, 155
DeSantis, Ron, 316
*Design for Death* (film), 80, 90
*Ding Dong School*, 197, 202
Disney, Walt, 64, 132; *Davy Crockett*, 233; *Dumbo*, 165–66, 180; "It's a Small World" attraction and, 259; *The Jungle Book* and, 276; "Man in Space" episode of *Disneyland* and, 289; *Mary Poppins*, 14–18, 47, 95; *Pinocchio*, 198; *Swiss Family Robinson*, 289; *Treasure Island*, 295; *Wonderful World of Disney*, 135; *Zorro*, 289
*Disneyland* (series), 289
Dobson, James, 313
Donaldson, Frederick, 236
*The Donna Reed Show*, 137, 156, 291
Draper, Paul, 186–87
Dreikurs, Rudolf, 15, 307; *Children*, 14, 293; on family councils, 293
Dr. Seuss. *See* Seuss, Dr.
*Dumbo*, 165–66, 180
Dyer, Richard, 152

Eastman, P. D., 161; *Are You My Mother?*, 45, 79; biography, 45, 79; *Gerald McBoing-Boing* and, 162; *Go Dog Go*, 45
Ehrenreich, Barbara, 146
Einstein, Albert, 91
Eisenhower, Dwight, 259
Elias, Norbert, 38–39
Engel, Morris, 103, 116–22. *See also Little Fugitive*; Orkin, Ruth; biography, 117

Englund, Steven, 78
Erikson, Erik, 11, 192, 194, 236, 309; on Blackness, 207–8
Ethical Culture School, 58
eugenics, 6
Evans, Walker, 216

*The Fabulous Fifties*, 2
*Family* (Mead and Heyman), 32, 253–54, 260–61, 270
*Family of Man* (photographic exhibition), 117, 253–54
*The Fantastic Four*, 261
*Fat Albert and the Cosby Kids*, 209, 219, 228; consultants, 222–23; "Creativity," 221; fathers and, 227; "Fish Out of Water," 227; "Four Eyes," 227; guilt, 218; Junkyard Gang, 221, 222; punishment, 227; *Revenge* album, 220; Russell and Bill characters, 227; teachers, 227; "The Tomboy," 227
*Father Knows Best*, 137, 291
fathers, 240–41; advice, 293; bad-boy tropes and, 144–46; *Fat Albert and the Cosby Kids* and, 227; Mead on, 250, 300; play and, 86; Tazewell on God as ideal, 66, 68
Federation for Child Study, 55–56
Feiffer, Jules, 201
*The Feminine Mystique* (Friedan), 296–97
*Fibber McGee and Molly* (radio show), 166–67
Fiedler, Leslie, 133–34, 262–63
*Finding Fred* (podcast), 12, 186
Fisher, Dorothy Canfield, 48; biography, 50; *The Home-Maker*, 9, 19, 50–55, 63, 72, 116; Montessori methods and, 9, 49, 50, 52; *Montessori Mother*, 52, 54; *Mothers and Children*, 51–53; *Our Children*, 58
Fitzhugh, Louise, 8, 149
*The 500 Hats of Bartholomew Cubbins* (Seuss), 76, 77, 86

*5000 Fingers of Dr. T* (film), 73, 77, 85, 89–90, *90*, 97–98
*Five Weeks in a Balloon*, 289
Fleischer Studios, 166
Fletcher, Robert, 224
*The Flintstones*, 261
"Flip" Mark (*The Fabulous Fifties* character), 2
*Flipper*, 19, 233, 240, 243–45, 305; production, 242; theme song, 241
*Flipper's New Adventure*, 242
Florida, Marineland of, 242
*Forbidden Planet*, 294
Forray, June, 295
Forrester, Frank, 288
*The 400 Blows*, 117
*Fox & Friends*, 314
Fraiberg, Selma: *The Magic Years*, 171–74; on "ogre problem," 172–73
Frank, Josette, 9, 48, 120, 307; biography, 61–62; work in comic books, 62
Freberg, Stan, 202
Free-Range Kids movement, 315–16
Freud, Sigmund, 6, 34, 308; Baruch and, 104; Mead and, 306; on phases of sexual development, 139; Spock and, 99, 101, 103, 128, 304
Friedan, Betty, 307; *The Feminine Mystique*, 296–97
Frohn, Adolph, 242
frontier, 247
"Fun Morality" (Wolfenstein), 31, 47, 87, 178

Garland-Thomson, Rosemary, 163–65
Geisel, Theodor. *See* Seuss, Dr.
*Generation of Vipers* (Wylie), 148
*Gentle Giant*, 242
*Gentleman's Agreement*, 273
George, Jean Craighead, 19, 233, 245–51
*Gerald McBoing-Boing* (film), 19, 45, 162, 180, 208, 316
Gernsback, Hugo, 288
Gesell, Arnold, 41, 49, 104, 174, 306; *The Gesell Institute's Child Behavior*, 150–51; Institute of Human Development, 280
*Gilligan's Island*, 292
Ginott, Haim G., 2, 11, 307; anal stage, 139; "freedom to wish," 3, 98; gender, 150–51; *Between Parent and Child*, 1, 10, 147
girls, as protagonists, 7; *Harriet the Spy* and, 8, 149; *Lovers and Lollipops* and, 121–22; *Pippi Longstockings* and, 8, 149–50
*Glass House of Prejudice* (Baruch), 42–44
Goddard, Henry, 77, 256
Goddard, Mark, 289
*God Gave Me Eyes* (Burt and Segner), 66–67, *67*
Goldin, Shari, 210
Goldsholl, Millie, 183–84
Good, Katie Day, 257
*Good Housekeeping* (magazine), 132, 296–97
*The Good Neighbor* (King, Maxwell), 11
*Goodnight Moon* (Brown), 93
*Goofus and Gallant* (comic strip), 122–23
Gordan, Gail, 134
Grant, Julia, 56
Gray, William S., 94
Griffin, Sean, 233, 235, 238
Griswold, Robert L., 86, 145
Grosvenor, Kali, 224
*Growing Up Jim Crow* (Ritterhouse), 26
Gruenberg, Benjamin, 58
Gruenberg, Sidonie Matsner, 9, 48, 55; biography, 58; on gangs compared with clubs, 59; on imagination, 61; on motherhood, 58–59; *Our Children*, 58
Guaraldi, Vince, 182
Gwynne, Edmund, 6

Haas, Dorothy, 114–16, *115*
Haggard, Rider, 275
Haggins, Bambi, 219
Halberstam, Jack, 5, 114, 167–68

*Half Hitch* (comic strip), 132
Halifax, Joan, 224
Hall, G. Stanley, 41, 56, 103, 106
Halpin, Luke, 244
Hammerstein, Oscar, II, 263
*Hand in Hand* (film), 260
Hanna-Barbera, 260. See also *Jonny Quest*; shows, overview, 261
*Hans Christian Anderson* (film), 168–71, *170*
*Harold and the Purple Crayon* (Johnson), 19, 162, 171–72, *172*, 175
*Harriet the Spy* (Fitzhugh), 8, 149
Hayden Planetarium, 288
*Hazel*, 137
Heiferman, Marvin, 97
Heinlein, Robert A., 288
Heller, Marriele, 11. See also Rogers, Fred
Henry, Jules, 134, 144; *Culture Against Man*, 125–26
"here and now," 77, 92–95, 98
*Here and Now Story Book* (Mitchell, L.), 94–95
Hersey, John, 95
Heyman, Ken, 34; *Family*, 32, 253–54, 260–61, 270
Higgins, Scott, 239
*Highlights for Children* (magazine), 122–23
*History of Table Manners* (Elias), 38–39
Hitler, Adolf, 78, 81, 89–91
Hitte, Kathryn: *I'm an Indian Today*, 107, *108*; *What Can You Do Without a Place to Play?*, 224, 225
*The Hobbit*, 95
*A Hole Is to Dig* (Krauss), 109
*The Home-Maker* (Fisher), 9, 19, 50–55, 63, 72, 116
Honeck, Mischa, 249
Hoover, J. Edgar, 159, *159*
*Horn Book* (magazine), 149
*Horton Hatches a Who* (Seuss), 82
*Horton Hears a Who* (Seuss), 74–77, 97
Horwich, Francis, 186; *Ding Dong School*, 197, 202

Houseman, John, 271
*House Party*, 138–39
*Howdy Doody*, 199, 201
*How the Grinch Stole Christmas* (Seuss), 79
"How to Be a Girl" (podcast), 315–16
*Huckleberry Hound*, 261
Hymes, James L., 157, 158

*I Dream of Jeannie*, 292
Iftekhar (actor), 272
Ilg, Francis, 41, 104
"The Image of the Child in Contemporary Films" (Wolfenstein), 116–17, 119
*I'm an Indian Today* (Hitte), 107, *108*
*Imitation of Life*, 127
Indian Guides (YMCA program), 106–7
*I Need a New Butt* (McMillan and Kinnaird), 316
Ingersoll, Ralph, 78–79
*In Henry's Backyard* (Benedict and Weltfish), 44
"inner directed, other directed," 161
*Innocent Experiments* (Onion), 282
*In the Streets* (documentary film), 216, 223, 225
*The Invisible Boy*, 294
Ishizuka, Katie, 75
*It's a Small World*, 259
*It's the Great Pumpkin, Charlie Brown*, 19, 180–83

Jack Armstrong (character), 261, 267
Jackson, Kenneth T., 235
Jacobson, Emilie, 189–91
Jenkins, Henry: autobiography, 5–6, *6*, 23–27, *27*; backyard, 237–38; camp, 246
Jessol, Bernard, 187
*The Jetsons*, 261
*Jimmy the Storyteller* (film), 117, *118*
Johar, I. S., 272
*Johnny Ringo*, 289

INDEX | 359

Johnson, Crockett, 109, 161; *Barnaby*, 176–78, *177*; *Harold and the Purple Crayon*, 19, 162, 171–72, *172*, 175; *A Picture for Harold's Room*, 174
Johnston, Johanna, 30
Jones, Chuck, 79
Jones, Kathleen W., 49, 56
*Jonny Quest*, 19, 234, 305; "Arctic Splashdown," 264; "Calcutta Adventure," 264–65; "The Curse of Anubis," 268; "Double Danger," 265, 268; Dr. Ashida in, 269; Dr. Benton Quest in, 267, 279; Dr. Zin in, 268–69; "The Dreadful Doll," 267; "The Fraudulent Volcano," 267, 269; Hadji in, 261–79, 262; Kareem in, 268; "Monster in the Monastery," 265; origins, 261; Pasha Peddler in, 264–65; permissiveness and, 269–70; "The Pursuit of the Po-Ho," 267–68; Race Bannon in, 267, 269; "Riddle of the Gold," 265, 269; "Shadow of the Condor," 265; "Skull and Double Crossbones," 265; "A Small Matter of Pygmies," 265; "Treasures of the Temple," 270; "Turo the Terrible," 267, 269; "yellow peril" discourse in, 268–69
Jordan, Benjamin René, 257
*Journey Into the Unknown* (Wildey), 261
*The Jungle Book* (Kipling), 276

*Katzenjammer Kids* (comic strip), 134, 136, 137
Kaye, Danny, 168–69, *170*
Keane, Bill, 132
Kearns, Joseph, 134
Keats, Ezra Jack, 175–76
Keeshan, Bob, 186; books chosen and read by, 199; Bunny Rabbit character and, 199; in *Captain Kangaroo*, 64, 198–201; Deitch and, 200–201; in *Howdy Doody* (as Claribell), 199; Lewis and, 202; Mr. Green Jeans character and, 200; Mr. Moose character and, 199; Tom Terrific character and, 200; Zippy the Chimp and, 199–200, *200*
Kennedy, Caroline, 159
*Kenny's Window* (Sendak), 114
Ketcham, Hank, 8, 138, *139*. See also Dennis the Menace; biography, 132; as conservative, 132–33; *Half Hitch*, *132*; *Merchant of Dennis the Menace*, 131, 151–52; misogyny of, 148
Khan, Sajid, 272
Khrushchev, Nikita, 259
Kidd, Kenneth, 114
*Kids Say the Darnedest Things!* (Linkletter), 138–39
Kimball, Ward, 288
King, Martin Luther, 210
King, Maxwell, 12, 188, 192, 194
King Brothers Productions, 271–72
*The King's Stilts* (Seuss), 86, 92
Kinnaird, Ross, 316
Kipling, Rudyard, 275–76
Kismaric, Carole, 97
Klein, Christina, *263*–65
Knight, Eric, 79
Kramer, Edith, 217
Kramer, Peter, 137
Kramer, Stanley, 79, 89
Krauss, Ruth, 116, 161, 171; Benedict and, 110; *A Hole Is to Dig*, 109; Mead and, 110; Sendak and, 109–10, *111*; *A Very Special House*, 109, 110; *111*
Kristen, Marta, 283
*Kukla, Fran and Ollie*, 202, 259

*Ladies' Home Journal* (magazine), 132
*Land of the Giants*, 289
Lane, Howard, 85
Langer, Susanne, 174
Lankford, Ronald D., Jr., 165
Lantz, Walter, 132
*Lassie*, 79, 135, 242–45, 289
*The Last of the Mohicans* (Cooper), 262

Leaf, W. Munro, 79
Lear, Martha Weinman, 41, 103–4; *The Child Worshippers*, 123, 125
*Learning From the Left* (Mickenberg), 77, 161–62
*The Learning Tree* (film), 219
*Leave It To Beaver*, 8, 291, 307; Eddie Haskell character in, 123; production history, 137
Lee, Pinky, 186; *The Pinky Lee Show*, 195–97
Le Guin, Ursula K., 288
Leibman, Nina C., 291
Lerner, Max, 78
*Let Us Now Praise Famous Men* (Agee), 216
Levine, Lawrence, 223
Levitt, Helen, 9; biography, 223; *In the Streets*, 216, 223, 225; *A Way of Seeing*, 223–24
Lewis, Shari, 186; puppets of, 202–3
Ley, Willie, 288
Lindstrom, Miriam and Charles, 173–75
Linkletter, Art, 138–39
Lionni, Leo, 161
Lipsitz, George, 153–54
*Little Fugitive*, 19, 103, 118, 120, 120–22, 217, 233; *Bicycle Thieves* contrasted with, 117; camerawork, 119; *400 Blows* and, 117; neorealism and new wave influences of, 116–17
Little Golden Books, 67
Little League, 136
Little Rascals, 26, 153, 195
*The Littlest Angel* (Tazewell), 19, 49, 63–64, 209
*The Littlest Snowman* (Tazewell), 64
Lively, Johnny, 187
Lockhart, June, 289
Long John Silver (character), 295
*Los Angeles Mirror* (newspaper), 135
Losey, Joseph: *The Boy With the Green Hair*, 19, 49, 63, 68–73, 209, 292; Living Newspaper genre and, 71

*Lost in Space*, 19, 123, 234, 280–301, 305; actors in, 283, 289, 294, 295; Alonzo P. Tucker character in, 295; "The Android Machine," 297; Cartwright on, 283; "The Challenge," 299; "A Change of Space," 280; "The Colonists," 296; Don West character in, 292–95, 297, 299; Dr. Zachary Smith character in, 282, 289, 294–95, 299; "Follow the Leader," 294; "The Girl from the Green Dimension," 292; Harris on, 294; "The Hungry Sea," 292; John Robinson character in, 290–91, 293–94, 297, 299; Judy Robinson character in, 283, 292, 297; Kristen on, 283; Maureen Robinson character in, 280, 291, 297–99; "No Place to Hide," 282; Penny Robinson character in, 283, 292, 296; "The Prisoners in Space," 294; Quanto character in, 299; "The Questing Beast," 295; Robot character in, 282, 289–90, 292, 294; Salmi in, 295; Sir Sagramonte character in, 295; "The Sky Is Falling," 290, 292; "The Sky Pirate," 295; "Space Beauty," 297; "There Were Giants on Earth," 291–92, 293; "Treasure of the Lost Planet," 295; Will Robinson character in, 280–81, 282–83, 290–93, 295–96, 298, 301; "The Wreck of the Robot," 292
*The Lost World* (film), 289
*Lovers and Lollipops* (film), 117, 121–22
Lowenfeld, Viktor, 176
*Lullaby of Christmas* (Tazewell), 64

MacFarland, Margaret, 11, 191–93, 206, 307, 309
Mack, Marlo, 315–16
magazines. *See also* newspapers: back before, 131; *Boy's Life*, 249; *Christian Science Monitor*, 201; *Collier's*, 132; *Good Housekeeping*, 132, 296–97; *Highlights for Children*, 122–23; *Horn Book*, 149; *Ladies' Home Journal*, 132;

*McCall's*, 132; *National Geographic*, 265; *Parents*, 6, 32, 56, 101, 108, 144, 201, 224, 256, 280, 314; *Popular Mechanics*, 242; *Redbook*, 20, 33, 210, 254–55, 281, 303–7, 309–10, 314; *Saturday Evening Post*, 87, 131, 132
*The Magic Years* (Fraiberg), 171–74
Marineland of Florida, 242
Martha, Lynda, 187
Martin, Michelle, 175
*Mary Poppins*, 14–18, 47, 95
Mason, Jerry, 254
Matsick, Anni, 122
Maya, 8, 19, 234, 260; "The Allapor Conspiracy," 275; brownface performance in, 273–75; "Caper of the Golden Roe," 274–75; "Deadly Passage," 277; Jang Bahadur character in, 275, 277–78; "The Khandur Uprising," 275; Lansing character in, 277; "The Legend of Whitney Markham," 278; Maya the elephant in, 272, 278; production, 271; Raji character in, 271–76, 274, 278–79; Ram Singh character in, 270–71; "Roots of India," 278; Terry Bowen character in, 270, 272–74, 274, 276–79; "Tiger Boy," 276–77; "Twilight of the Empire," 277
*McCall's* (magazine), 132
McFarland, Margaret, 191, 192, 206
McLuhan, Marshall, 256
McMillan, Dawn, 316
Mead, Margaret, 6, 18, 20, 23, 30, 301, 305, 307, 317; on American family life, 31–32, 35; Bateson and, 33–34, 254–55; Benedict and, 31, 44; on breast feeding, 311–12; "Changing Family Styles," 310; *Childhood in Contemporary Cultures*, 31, 35–37, 47–48, 157; on children's art, 179; on children's literature, 95; on Child Study, 48; circle (colleagues), 161, 235; Cobb and, 235; Columbia University Seminar on Contemporary Culture and, 31, 235; *A Creative Life For Your Children* pamphlet and, 178; on day care, 310; Family, 32, 253–54, 260–61, 270; on fathers, 250, 300; female researchers and, 47; on Freud, 306; Gesell Institute and, 306; on "gifted child," 280–81; on global village, 256; on grandparents, 198; Krauss and, 110; on latency, 105; Métraux and, 284; "Modern Children's Stories" (project), 36; on neighborhoods, 188; "A New Understanding of Childhood," 304, 306; on outdoor life, 245–46; on play, 181, 183, 236–37, 239; postwar shifts and, 32–33; on public intellectual role, 32–33; on race and racism, 255–56; on recapitulation, 107, 109; scientists and, 284; on segregation, 188–89; Seventh International Congress on Mental Health, 256; on sexuality, 104–5; Spock and, 103–6, 303–5, 311–13, 317; on summer camps, 246, 249–50; on symbol-makers, 35, 317; on traditional compared with contemporary cultures, 31; Wolfenstein and, 31, 39, 178; world brotherhood and, 255–56, 279
Meléndez, José Cuauhtémoc "Bill," 180
Melville, Herman, 262
Métraux, Rhoda, 35; biography, 284; on children's art, 284; Northwestern Science Seminar for Public Information Officers, 286; scientists and, 284–87, 297
Michener, James, 263
Mickenberg, Julia: *Learning From the Left*, 77, 161–62; on "Lyrical Leftists," 161–62
Miller, Cynthia J., 288
*Mister Rogers' Neighborhood?*, 185. *See also* Neighborhood of Make Believe, 186, 204–5; Rogers, Fred; War on Change in, 205; young artists/performers on, 187
Mitchell, Alice Miller, 239

Mitchell, Lucy Sprague: biography, 93; *Here and Now Story Book*, 94–95
*Moby-Dick* (Melville), 262
Model United Nations, 259
Modern Language Association, 257
Molotov, Vyacheslav, 91
momism, 148
Montessori, Maria, 9, 52, 54
*Montessori Mother* (Fisher), 52, 54
Moore, Juanita, 127
Moore, Lilian, 161
Moore, Robin C., 238
moral philosophy, 6
Moskowitz, Golan Y., 114
*Mother India* (film), 272
*Mothers and Children* (Fisher), 51–53
Moyers, Bill, 112
Moynihan, Daniel Patrick, 208, 211
Mumy, Bill, 103, 123–24, *124*, 282
*Munro* (film), 201
*The Munsters*, 292
Muppets, 226
music, 12
Mussolini, Benito, 80, 81
Myers, Garry Cleveland, 122–23
*My Friend Flicka*, 239
*My Little Golden Book About God* (Watson, Jane), 67–68
*My Side of the Mountain* (George), 19, 233, 245–51

Nakamura, Mitsugi, 76
Nandy, Ashis, 266–67
NASA, 158
National Association for Better Radio and Television, 244
National Comics, 62
National Educational Television, 185
*National Geographic* (magazine), 265
*National Velvet*, 239
*The Negro Family* (Moynihan), 208
Nehru, Jawaharlal, 266

Nel, Phillip: on *Harold and the Purple Crayon*, 171; Krauss and, 109; Seuss and, 44–45, 82
Neville, Morgan, 10
New Deal, 75, 78
Newson, John and Elizabeth, 236
newspapers, 131, 227; *Los Angeles Mirror*, 135; *PM*, 77–79, 118
Newton, Robert, 295
"A New Understanding of Childhood" (Mead), 304, 306
Nichols, Nichelle, 283
Norden, Tommy, 244
North, Jay, 134, 144, 270, 272–73
Nunes, M. Da Costa, 157

O'Barry, Richard, 242, 244
Ogata, Amy F., 179
Onion, Rebecca, 282, 284; *Innocent Experiments*, 282
"Only Johnny Knows" (CBS radio episode), 30–31
Orkin, Ruth, 9, 103. *See also* Engel, Morris; biography, 117; *Jimmy the Storyteller*, 117, *118*; *Lovers and Lollipops*, 117, *121*; photography, 117; *Weddings and Babies*, 117
*Our Children* (Fisher and Gruenberg, S.), 58
*Our Children Face War* (Wolf, A.), 68, 83
*Our Children in the Atomic Age* (Goddard, H.), 85, 256
*Our Mr. Sun* (documentary film), 288–89
*Outer Limits*, 282
*The Outlaw Kid* (Wildey), 261
*Outlines of Child Study* (Child Study Association of America), 56

paperback book publishing, 32
*Paper Girls*, 315
*Parents* (magazine), 6, 32, 56, 101, 108, 144, 201, 224, 256, 280, 314
*The Parents' Manual* (Wolf, A.), 64

Parent Teacher Association, 56, 84
Parks, Gordon, 219
*Peanuts*, 162, 225, 227; Charlie Brown in, 7, 78, 132, 178–82, *181*, 189, 226; Great Pumpkin mythology in, 181–82; Linus in, 180–83; Lucy in, 180; origins, 131; products, 179; Sally in, 182; Schroeder in, 178
Peck, George, 136–37
Peck, Gregory, 164
*Peck's Bad Boy and His Pa* (Peck, George), 136–37
pen pals, 257
People2People, 259
permissiveness: adoption and, 263–64; adult power and, 4; Americanness and, 7–8; autocratic parenting compared with, 14; Blackness and, 211–30, 305, 307; bodily functions and, 4; boyhood idealization and, 7–8; breastfeeding and, 16; bullying and, 87; clubs and, 136; conservative backlash and, 305; defined, 1–3, 305–6; democratic parenting and, 14, 76–77, 83–85, 157, 293, 304; demographics and, 23–27; disability and, 162; discipline and, 2, 3, 14, 15, 16, 38, 65, 122; empathy and, 57, 58–61; family councils and, 293; feeding on schedule/on demand and, 3, 9, 16, 34, 213, 304; feminist backlash and, 305; German parenting and, 76, 85; imagination relation to, 8; media consumption and, 61–63; mud and, playing in, 139–40; nudism and, 140; origins of, 23; parody on, 2; periodization of, 6–7; religion relation to, 63–68; repression and, 104; sensuousness and, 100–103; spoiling relation to, 16; toilet training and, 16; transition and, parenting in, 37–40; Understanding Angel character and, 65, 128; whiteness and, 19
*The Permissive Society* (Petigny), 10
Petigny, Alan, 10

Phillips, Mary, 93
Piaget, Jean, 174
*A Picture for Harold's Room* (Johnson), 174
*The Pinky Lee Show*, 195–97
*Pinocchio*, 198
*Pioneers of American Television*, 283
Pippi Longstockings (character), 8, 149–50
*PM* (newspaper), 77–79, 118
*Poems by Kali* (collection), 224
*Poems to Read at an Early Age* (collection), 61–62
*The Popeye Club*, 202
Popular Front, 75; core beliefs, 78; newspaper, 77–79, 118
*Popular Mechanics* (magazine), 242
Poussaint, Alvin F.: *Black Child Care*, 28, 209–14, 222; *Come on People: On the Path from Victims to Victors*, 222–23
*Practical Application of Democracy* (De Huszar), 84–85
Private Snafu (animated shorts), 45, 79
*Problems of Parents* (Spock), 138, 298
*Psychological Care of Infant and Child* (Watson, John), 100–101
puppets, 201–5

*Queer Art of Failure* (Halberstam), 167–68
Quick Gloss Floor Wax, 100–101
*The Quiet One*, 209, 214–19, 228

*The Races of Mankind* (Benedict and Weltfish), 44
*Racial Innocence* (Bernstein), 156
*Raising Children in a Difficult Time* (Spock), 28–29, 301
Rankin-Bass (company), 167
*The Real Diary of a Real Boy* (Shute), 135
recapitulation, 6, 106, 107, 108–9
*Redbook* (magazine), 20, 33, 210, 254–55, 281, 303–7, 309–10, 314
Red Ryder, 207
Reisman, David, 35, 161

Rettig, Tommy, 89
*Revenge of the Creature*, 242
Ribble, Margaret A., 102
Riefenstahl, Leni, 90
*The Rights of Infants* (Ribble), 102
*Rin Tin Tin*, 244
Riper, A. Bowdoin Van, 288
Ritterhouse, Jennifer, 26
*Rocket Ship Galileo* (Heinlein), 288
Rockwell, Norman, 87, 249
*Rocky and Bullwinkle*, 295
Roddenberry, Gene, 283
Rogers, Fred, 9, 133, 185–206; *Amahl and the Night Visitors* opera work of, 205; Arsenal Family and Children's Center and, 12, 191, 194, 206; Black teacher guest and, 185; Blazia and, 187–88; Carey and, 189; in *The Children's Corner*, 185, 189; Child Study, 192; on civic imagination, 13; Daniel Tiger character and, 11, 189, 195, 203; Draper and, 186–87; empathy and, 203–4; Erikson and, 194; on expression, 187–88; *Finding Fred* (podcast), 12, 186; *The Good Neighbor* biography on, 11; Handyman Negri character and, 204–5; Henrietta Pussycat character and, 205; Jacobson and, 189–91; Keehsan and, 198; King, Maxwell, biography of, 12, 188, 192, 194; King Friday character and, 10, 187, 189, 205; Lady Aberlin character and, 187, 204–5; Lady Elaine Fairchilde character and, 205; Lewis and, 202; McFarland and, 191, 192, 206; ministry of, 13; *Mister Rogers* (Canadian broadcast), 185; Mr. McFeely character and, 189; on music education, 12; Neighborhood of Make Believe of, 186, 204–5; on neighborliness, 188–89; Officer Clemmons character and, 185; opera and, 204, 205–6; permissiveness and, 314; on Pittsburgh, 188; puppets of, 201, 203–5; race relations and, 185–86; reconsideration of, 10; Rubin and, 191–92; songs, 188, 194–95; Spock and, 194; talented teens and, 187; television as medium and, 198, 201; Vētra and, 187; on "visits," 188; War on Change and, 205; *Won't You Be My Neighbor?* documentary on, 10, 11, 12, 13; X the Owl character and, 195, 205

Rogers, Roy, 119
Roosevelt, Eleanor, 214–15
Roosevelt, Franklin D., 78
Roosevelt, Theodore, 61
Rose, Jacqueline, 36
Rotundo, E. Anthony, 136–37
Rousseau, Jean-Jacques, 5
Rubin, Judith, 191–92
"The Ruckus" (Seuss), 88
*Rudolph the Red Nosed Reindeer*, 166–67
Russell, Kurt, 299
Ryan, William, 208

Saguisag, Lara, 137, 178
Sally, Dick, and Jane (book series), 9, 94, 97–98, *98*
Salmi, Albert, 295
Sammond, Nicholas, 157
Sandburg, Carl, 253
Sargent, Richard, 87, *88*
*Saturday Evening Post* (magazine), 87, 131, 132
Scarry, Richard, 166
Schulz, Charles, 133–39, 227. See also *Peanuts*; Charlie Brown character of, 7, 78, 132, 178–82, *181*, 189, 226; *It's the Great Pumpkin, Charlie Brown*, 19, 180–83; *Peanuts* origins and, 131
science fiction, 287–88
Scott, Bill, 162
*The Sea Around Us* (documentary film), 289
*Sea Hunt*, 242
*Seduction of the Innocents* (Wertham), 121
"See How They Run" (Vroman), 218

Segner, Ellen, 66–67
segregation: in Boy Scouts, 257–58; Mead on, 188–89
Sendak, Maurice, 9, 116; biography, 109; Jewish roots, 114; Johnson work with, 109; *Kenny's Window*, 114; Kraus and, 109–10, *111*; *A Very Special House* illustrations by, 109, 110, *111*; *Where the Wild Things Are*, 5, 19, 103, 109, 112–13, *113*
Serling, Rod, 123
*Sesame Street*, 209–10, 224, 227, 314; *Street Gang* and, 226
Seuss, Dr. (Theodor Geisel), 9, 73, 124, 305; *Bartholomew and the Oobleck*, 87; biography, 77, 78; *Cat in the Hat*, 77, 92, 95–99, *99*; on children's emotional needs, 82; *Design for Death* (film), 80, 90; disillusionment of, 80; editorial cartoons of, 78, 79–80; *The 500 Hats of Bartholomew Cubbins*, 76, 77, 86; *5000 Fingers of Dr. T* (film) and, 73, 77, 85, 89–90, *90*, 97–98; *Gerald McBoing-Boing* (film) and, 19, 45, 162, 180, 208, 316; *Horton Hatches a Who*, 82; *Horton Hears a Who*, 74–77, 97; *How the Grinch Stole Christmas*, 79; on imagination and "on beyond Zebra," 97; on isolationism, 79; Japan and, 75–76; *The King's Stilts*, 86, 92; Kramer, S., and, 79, 89; La Jolla Museum, 174; persuasion skills, 77, 79; Private Snafu animated shorts and, 45, 79; racism and, 44–45, 75, 81–82; "The Ruckus," 88; *And to Think That I Saw It on Mulberry Street*, 76, 78, 81, 95–96; Utah lectures, 81–95; *Yertle the Turtle*, 77, 88–89, 97
*Shall Our Children, Too, Be Free?* (Lane), 85
*Shane*, 116
*The Shari Lewis Show*, 202
Sherman Brothers, 259
Shute, Henry A., 135

*Silent Spring* (Carson), 245
Skenazy, Lenore, 315
*Skinny and Fatty* (film), 260
Smuts, Alice Boardman, 56, 57
"snowflake" (metaphor), 12, 314
*The Snowy Day* (Keats), 175–76
Society for the Study of Child Nature, 55
"sonic color line," 156
*South Pacific*, 43
space, becoming place, 247
*Space Family Robinson*, 289
*Space Ghost*, 261
space programs: NASA, 158; Sputnik, 158, 286–87; toys, 287
Spigel, Lynn, 147, 292
Spock, Benjamin, 9, 11, 18, 20, 23, 24, 33, 47, 306; on anal phase, 139; as "anti-permissive," 28–29, 40, 303–4; Arsenal Family and Children's Center and, 192; *Baby and Child Care*, 1, 10, 26–28, 131, 303–4, 307–9; Blackness and, 207, 209; on breast feeding, 311–12; conservative critiques and, 312–14; counterculture and, 312–13; on disability, 165; on discipline, 141, 142; feminist critiques and, 48, 296–98, 307–11; on fighting, 299–300; Freud and, 99, 101, 103, 128, 304; gender and, 7, 144–45; on generational conflict, 39–40; isolation, 310; Mead and, 103–6, 303–5, 311–13, 317; on nudism, 139; on overpermissive parents, 40; premises of, 103–9; *Problems of Parents*, 138, 298; *Raising Children in a Difficult Time*, 28–29, 301; on recapitulation, 106; Rogers and, 194; on rudeness, 312–13; on "sissy" choices, 311; verbalism, 138; writing, 27
Sputnik, 158, 286–87
*Star Trek*, 283
Steichen, Edward, 117, 253–54
Steig, William, 161
Stein, Tobert, 33
Steinem, Gloria, 308

Stephens, Ramon, 75
Stockwell, Dean, 69
Stoever, Jennifer Lynn, 156
Stone, Jon, 226
*Story of a Bad Boy* (Aldrich), 135
*Story of Ferdinand* (Leaf), 79
Strand, Paul, 117
*Stranger Things*, 315
*Street Gang* (documentary film), 226
*Stuart Little*, 95
suburbs, 233–340
*Super Friends*, 261
superhero, 119
Swarthmore College, 257, 259
*Swiss Family Robinson*, 289

Tazewell, Charles: background, 64; God as ideal father, 66, 68; *The Littlest Angel*, 19, 49, 63–64, 209; *The Littlest Snowman*, 64; *Lullaby of Christmas*, 64; radio, 64, 164; *The Small One*, 64; Understanding Angel and, 65, 68, 164
Tenniel, John, 95
*Think That I Saw It on Mulberry Street* (Seuss), 76, 78, 81, 95–96
Thom, Douglas, 56
Thoreau, Henry David, 246–47
*The Three Stooges*, 195
Thurer, Shari L., 48
Tillstrom, Burr, 202, 259
*Time for Beany*, 202
*The Time Tunnel*, 289
*Toast of the Town*, 187
*Toddlers and Parents* (Brazelton), 309
Toffler, Alvin, 281
*To Kill a Mockingbird*, 8
*Tom and Jerry*, 261
*Tom Corbett, Space Cadet*, 288
"Tomorrowland" (in *Disneyland* series), 289
*Tootle* (Campton), 161
Tors, Ivan, 242. See also *Flipper*
Toth, Alex, 261

toys, 5, 17, 287
transgender, 316
transitional objects, 180
*Treasure Island* (film), 295
Trik-Trak (toy), 5
*Triumph of the Will* (documentary), 90
Truffaut, Francois, 116–17
Trumbo, Dalton, 271
Trump, Donald, 13
Tuan, Yi-Fu, 247
Turner, Morris: biography, 227; Nipper character of, 227–28; *Wee Pals*, 209, 227–28, 229
Twain, Mark, 135, 262
*Twilight Zone*: "The Big Tall Wish," 126; "It's a Good Life," 19, 103, 123–26, *124*, 282
*Two Years Before the Mast* (Dana), 262–63

"The Ugly Duckling" (in *Hans Christian Anderson*), 168–71, *170*
Understanding Angel (character/role), 66, 72, 128, 168, 240, 305; Tazewell and, 65, 68, 164
UNICEF, 258–59
United Productions of America, 44, 79, 162, 201
United States Children's Bureau, 31–32, 178
United States Signal Corps, 45, 77, 79
University of Utah, 81–83
*Up is Down* (animated short), 183–84
US Information Agency, 259

*VE Day, Times Square* (photography), 117
Verne, Jules, 275
*A Very Special House* (Krauss and Sendak), 109, 110, *111*
Vētra, Vija, 187
*Voyage to the Bottom of the Sea*, 289
Vroman, Mary Elizabeth, 218

Wallace, Carvell, 11, 185
Wanzo, Rebecca, 228

Ward, Montgomery, 166
Watson, Jane Werner, 67–68
Watson, John, 15, 16, 17, 47; behaviorism and, 9, 57; on desired child, 100–101; on parents as blacksmiths, 100; *Psychological Care of Infant and Child*, 100–101
*A Way of Seeing* (Levitt), 223–24
*Weddings and Babies* (film), 117
*Wee Pals* (Turner), 209, 227–28, 229
Welcome House, 263
Welles, Orson, 271
Weltfish, Gene, 44
*We Need to Talk About Cosby* (docuseries), 219
Wertham, Fredric, 62, 121
Westinghouse Science Fair, 290
*What Can You Do Without a Place to Play?* (Hitte), 224, 225
*When I Grow Up*, 116
*Where the Wild Things Are* (Sendak), 5, 19, 103, 109, 112–13, *113*
Whitaker, Johnny, 65
white flight, 133, 153, 155, 215
*Who Is My Friend?*, 189, *190*
Wildey, Doug, 261
*Wild Things* (Halberstam), 5
Williams, Guy, 289
Williams, Raymond, 40; model of cultural change, 8–9; "structure of feeling" and, 9
Wiltwyck School for Boys, 214–18
Winnicott, D. W., 180
Winship, Florence Sarah, 115

Wolf, Anna M. M., 9, 48, 59, 65, 70, 244, 304; *Our Children Face War*, 68, 83; *The Parents' Manual*, 64
Wolf, Katherine M., 38, 122
Wolf, Mark, 204
Wolfenstein, Martha: *Childhood in Contemporary Cultures*, 31, 35–37, 47–48, 157; *Children's Humor*, 196–97; "Fun Morality," 31, 47, 87, 178; "The Image of the Child in Contemporary Films," 116–17, 119; Mead and, 31, 39, 178; on "moron" trope, 196–97
*Wonderful World of Disney*, 135
*Won't You Be My Neighbor?* (documentary film), 10, 11, 12, 13
Woody Woodpecker (character), 132
*World's Worst Mom* (reality show), 315
Wylie, Philip, 139, 148

Yeh, Charlotte, 187
*The Yellow Kid*, 135, 153
*Yertle the Turtle* (Seuss), 77, 88–89, 97
YMCA, 106–7
*Yogi Bear*, 261
Young, Loretta, 65, 164
*Your Child and His Art* (Lowenfeld), 176
*Your Child Meets the World Outside* (Baruch), 84

*Zebra in the Kitchen*, 242
Zelizer, Viviana, 136
Zippy the Chimp (in *Captain Kangaroo*), 199–200, *200*
*Zorro*, 289

ABOUT THE AUTHOR

This is HENRY JENKINS's twenty-first book on various aspects of media and popular culture, including *Textual Poachers: Television Fans and Participatory Culture*, *The Children's Culture Reader*, *Convergence Culture: Where Old and New Media Collide*, *Comics and Stuff*, and *Popular Culture and the Civic Imagination*. A product of the baby boom, Jenkins writes in *Where the Wild Things Were* about popular texts that shaped his own childhood. He is the Provost's Professor of Communication, Journalism, Cinematic Art, Education, and East Asian Languages and Cultures at the University of Southern California.

www.ingramcontent.com/pod-product-compliance
Lightning Source LLC
Chambersburg PA
CBHW051523020426
42333CB00016B/1759